W9-BCG-840

The Great War and the
French People

The Great War and the French People

JEAN-JACQUES BECKER

Translated from the French by ARNOLD POMERANS
With an Introduction by JAY WINTER

ST. MARTIN'S PRESS
New York

English translation © Berg Publishers Ltd 1986
Originally published as Les français dans la grande-guerre
Translated from the French by permission of the publishers,
Editions Robert Laffont, Paris
© Éditions Robert Laffont 1983

First Published in the United States of America in 1986

Printed in Great Britain

ISBN 0–312–34679–4

Library of Congress Cataloging-in-Publication Data

Becker, Jean-Jacques.
The Great War and the French people.

Translation of: Les Français dans la Grande Guerre.
Bibliography: p.
1. World War, 1914–1918—France. 2. France—History—
German occupation, 1914–1918. I. Title.
D548.B3413 1986   940.3'44   86–1749
ISBN 0–312–34679–4

Contents

Tables

Figures

Maps

To my mother

Preface

It is a commonplace that the Great War was a total war in that its shadow fell across the lives of all the inhabitants of the major combatant countries. But the full dimensions of the catastrophe of 1914 to 1918 and its meaning for people in different walks of life have only recently been the subject of scholarly concern. Jean-Jacques Becker is a leader in this field, having already contributed studies of the French labour movement in 1914, the plans for the arrest of French 'subversives' at the outbreak of the war, and the mood of ordinary Frenchmen in the first phase of the conflict.[1]

Becker's command of the vast provincial archives which throw light on wartime public opinion is clear in this general study of French society at war, which first appeared in 1980. Aside from some volumes in the series on the economic and social history of the war, sponsored by the Carnegie Endowment for International Peace and published in the 1920s, there is nothing as comprehensive in either French or English.[2] In this book, Becker has drawn together a vast store of unpublished material to help unravel three central questions concerning the French war effort: Why and how did French society hold out for four years? Why did French workers prefer the national cause to that of the revolution? And

---

1. *1914, la guerre et le mouvement ouvrier français* (en collaboration avec Annie Kriegel) Collection Kiosque, Armand Colin, 1964; *Le Carnet B: Les pouvoirs publics et l'antimilitarisme avant la guerre de 1914*, Klincksieck, 1973; *1914, comment les Français sont entrés dans la guerre* (contribution à l'étude de l'opinion publique printemps-été 1914), Presses de la Fondation nationale des sciences politiques, 1977.
2. For example, Arthur Fontaine, *French Industry During the War*, New Haven: Yale University Press, 1926; and P. Fridenson (ed.), 1914–1918; *L'autre Front*, Paris: Cahiers du Mouvement Social no. 2, Paris, 1977.

1

why were 1914 and 1940 in France diametrically opposed responses to war?

The complex and subtle answers to these questions form the core of this study. His fundamental argument is that, despite increasing doubts and difficulties as the war dragged on, the French people accepted the direction given them by their political, intellectual and religious leaders. This is very far from a claim for the cohesive force of *union sacrée*, or nationalist feeling transcending all other loyalties. Such views did exist, but Becker shows them to have been marginal and to have been eclipsed by a broader body of opinion committed to an essentially pragmatic and temporary alliance to get the German army off French soil. That alliance lasted in part because standards of living were not seriously diminished for most people during the war.

Of greater importance, though, was what Becker calls the 'psychological direction' of mass attitudes. The implicit claim here, made at the time by Lenin among others, is that a different leadership with a different knowledge of war would have presented a very different lead: thus Russia in 1917 and France in 1940.

This reassertion of the 'primacy of the political' is in line with other recent developments in the study of social history.[3] It represents a break both with interpretations of social history as a mere reflection of economic history and with historical arguments about that timeless, ineffable and mysterious entity — the French *mentalité*.

By providing us with a wealth of new information on popular attitudes in wartime France, and by opening a debate on the intellectual and political dimensions of social stability in wartime, Becker has not only made a major contribution to our understanding of this turbulent period, but he has laid down as well a strong challenge to historians of other countries; for the questions he poses in this book have not been answered rigorously with respect to any other combatant country. That work remains to be done.

JAY WINTER
Pembroke College, Cambridge

---

3. See Gareth Stedman Jones, *Languages of Class: Studies in English Working-Class History 1842–1982*, CUP, Cambridge, 1984.

Introduction

When the men of Reparsac, a small village near Cognac, went to war in August 1914 they looked forward to being in Berlin within a month. Their comrades from Saint-Lormel, near Plancoët, in northern Brittany, thought it might take until Christmas. At Thoiry, in Haute-Savoie, near the Swiss border, people expected victory in three months at the most.

One month, three months, five months, the grape harvest or Christmas — no one on either side imagined that the war could last any longer.

Nor was this an absurd assumption. The Germans had good reason to believe in their imminent victory when the war was no more than four weeks old; another fortnight and it was the turn of the French. Both sides had to suffer many disappointments before their hope and their belief in a short war eventually faded.

I have tried to show elsewhere[1] that one of the keys to French behaviour in the summer of 1914 was the widespread conviction that the war would turn out to be an adventure, cruel perhaps, but of short duration, and that, coming as it had done after a long period of peace, this martial interlude would be no more than a brief interruption of the normal course of events.

The French were caught unawares, and with much less enthusiasm than has often been alleged, when they read the order for mobilisation on 1 August 1914, following an international crisis as short as it had been sudden. Nevertheless, most of the men left home in the firm belief that the French government had had no hand in unleashing the conflict and that unprovoked aggression had

1. *1914, comment les Français sont entrés dans la guerre*, Presses de la Fondation des Sciences politiques, 1977.

3

to be resisted.

The leaders of the labour movement, for whom the maintenance of peace had been a major issue, came to share the same conviction and to lend their support to a war that, in any case, they had no power to prevent.

In short, while not abandoning their political or religious differences, nearly all Frenchmen rallied to the cause of national defence, a unity soon afterwards christened the *Union sacrée*.

In the course of the summer, French morale rose and fell according to circumstance: unbounded enthusiasm when Mulhouse was occupied for a short time, pessimism turning to panic when the full extent of the German advances became known, renewed enthusiasm when the Battle of the Marne seemed to be turning the tide. Soon afterwards it became clear that this was not going to happen and euphoria was quickly followed by dejection and anxiety. Though beaten in battle, the Germans had clung on to large slices of territory; though they had retreated, they had not been routed as wishful French correspondents had too hastily given their readers to understand. *Le Matin* put it with unconscious humour: 'The Germans are tired of retreating. They are trying to resist.'[2]

For Germany, too, immediate victory had become unlikely, but defeat was very far away. On both sides, clear-thinking people were beginning to wonder whether the war might not continue much longer than anyone had expected. An intermediate phase thus set in, in which irrational enthusiasm had become unacceptable but in which the idea of a long-drawn-out war had not yet become established.

When autumn came, there were no signs of an end to a conflict that, on 1 January 1915, was to last for nearly another four years; just over forty-six months.

Countless words have been devoted to the soldiers of the Great War, those men whose sacrifices and sufferings are so hard to imagine. By contrast, little has been said about the home front, the 'other front', as it has recently been called.[3] And those who have described the experiences of the civilians have rarely bothered to ask *why it was that they held out*, as if it were as a matter of course. Now the answer to that question is important. For while military discipline could be used to keep the army, however recalcitrant, in line, it could not do the same for civilians. An army cannot survive without the support of the home front, if only because of its supply

2. 15 September 1914.
3. '1914–1918. L'autre-front', in *Cahiers du Mouvement Social*, no. 2, 1977.

of arms, equipment and provisions. Should the home front yield to despair or refuse to go on, then the army would soon follow suit and disintegrate.

How and why, then, did the French of *la belle époque*, those people who were said, somewhat glibly, to be easy-going, fun-loving and without ideals, bear and accept fifty-one months of sorrow and destruction? The aim of this book is to answer that question.

France was not alone in fighting what was soon to be called the Great War and much later the First World War. The question we are trying to answer would lose much of its interest if all belligerents had 'held out' in the same way. This was by no means the case; in fact, just three countries were able to keep their morale in line with their material resources: France, the United Kingdom, and Germany. It hardly needs to be pointed out that the Russian Revolution, by contrast, was inspired not so much by political or social objectives as by the desire to put an end to the war; that a large part of the Italian population never felt genuinely involved in the conflict, which explains certain spectacular defeats; that, starting from 1917, Germany was hindered rather than helped by an Austria–Hungary torn apart by the centrifugal strivings of her constituent peoples. In fact, all the nations that 'held out' enjoyed a comparable standard of material wealth, and had a similar social and even political structure, something that was probably no accident. Can we, however, claim that an analysis of what happened in France must automatically apply to the two other great European nations?

Their situations were not really the same: the French had to 'hold out' in a context that was quite different from that of their major ally and of their enemy. Of the three, France alone saw her territory partly invaded and occupied; France alone saw destruction piled upon destruction on her own soil — though the gradual destruction of the British merchant fleet was no trifling matter, of course. The problem of 'holding out' was posed much more acutely in a country that had been invaded and forced to resort to defensive measures that were sometimes desperate than it was in Germany, whose soldiers fought on enemy soil and whom, to the very end, the operational map seemed to favour.

Another variable, the casualties suffered by the three countries, also differed. It goes without saying that although the full extent of losses was not known during the course of the war, people had some inkling of whether they were great or small. In this connection all estimates show that the British suffered much smaller losses than the two other protagonists.[4] The absolute figures for those *killed in action* were respectively:

> France   898,000
> United Kingdom   485,000
> Germany   1,473,000.

Casualties as a whole (killed in action, missing, fatally wounded, killed in accidents or by disease and so forth) totalled:

> France   1,327,000
> United Kingdom   715,000
> Germany   2,037,000.

Judging by these figures, Germany seems to have suffered by far the most. But these figures are absolute. Expressed in relative terms, things look quite different. Thus, out of 1,000 inhabitants, France mobilised 168 and lost 34; the United Kingdom mobilised 125 and lost 16; Germany mobilised 154 and lost 30. In other words, France was the most severely affected, followed closely by Germany.

The comparison is not, however, quite complete, since France and Germany also differed in demographic respects. Thus Germany enjoyed a vigorous and sustained population growth while France had for long been demographically stagnant. In the decade before the war the birthrate was 31.6 per thousand in Germany and 20.2 per thousand in France, while the mortality rate was slightly higher in France than in Germany.

Under these conditions — with fewer than 40 million inhabitants in France (1911) and almost 65 million in Germany (1911) — any French death had greater demographic impact than that of any German.[5]

Thus the situation in France was quite different from that in either Britain or Germany. Even though the Allied naval blockade forced Germany to introduce much more stringent food rationing than was in force in France or Britain (but, incidentally, much less so than claimed by Allied propaganda), it nevertheless remains a fact that the French were the most sorely tried of the three. It would be instructive to compare the development of French morale with what

---

4. See Jean-Claude Chesnais: *Les Morts violentes en France depuis 1826*, Comparaisons internationales; Institut National d'Etudes Démographiques, 1976, Presses Universitaires de France.
5. During 1916–20 the German birthrate fell to 17.9 per thousand; the French to 13.9 per thousand.

we know of similar developments in Germany (although this type of study is less advanced across the Rhine), but for the moment we shall confine ourselves to France alone and merely try to determine why and how it was that the French managed to hold out for so long.

Is it possible, however, to find an answer to this question? How can we probe the hearts and the souls of so many people belonging to different social categories, coming from such different regions, and subscribing to different religious beliefs?

It is certainly not possible to give a complete or definitive answer. Nevertheless, because the war of 1914 was the first war to involve all the forces of the nation over so long a period, the civil and military leaders were forced to gauge the morale, not only of the combatants, but also of the civilians. Step by step, proceeding by trial and error, the analysis of the nation's morale became a major preoccupation. This does not mean that all the necessary documents are to hand. At the beginning of the war they were few and far between, but from 1916–17 they became quite abundant, although the authorities often focused attention exclusively on those social strata or regions that struck them as being the most turbulent. In practice, this means that we have much better information on the behaviour of workers – and workers in certain regions – than on peasants and the middle classes, so that the historian, slave that he is to his sources, is forced to dwell, at what may be thought excessive length, on those groups about which he is better informed. Moreover, workers were able to express their attitude in more spectacular ways, for instance by strikes, than were the other social groups. In short, though the working class was a minority in France at the time (and an even smaller minority in Russia in 1917), the authorities felt, no doubt with justification, that their importance was out of proportion to their number.

At certain moments the workers probably held the fate of the nation in their hands, as the country could not have survived any prolonged stoppage of the munitions factories. Why then (even if a small fraction of them wavered) did French workers clearly prefer the cause of their country to that of the Revolution? Here we have a question that concerned the future of the whole nation.

One final remark: while it is important to clarify why the attitude of the French differed from that of other European nations during the war, it is equally important to explain the behaviour of the French in terms of their own history. Why were the French so ready to make sacrifices in 1914 when they had been so unprepared for them in the past and would manifest even less of a spirit of sacrifice in the future? The nation has not always given the same response to the challenges of history, but why did it do so in such diametrically opposed ways in 1914 and in 1940?

NOTE Chapter 11, 'Writers and the War', and Chapter 12, 'The Churches and the War', were largely written by Geneviève Colin and Annette Becker respectively. For greater ease of reading we have reduced footnotes to a minimum. For our main sources the reader is referred to the bibliography.

I

AUTUMN 1914

Autumn 1914, the first autumn of the war. Would general depression set in on top of the melancholy of the season? How, after the turbulent events of the summer, would the French react to a different and unknown world, to a world at war?

During the first few weeks it was possible to shelve the political, economic and social problems raised by the conflict. The exaltation of apparent national unity had supplanted everything else. But this state of affairs could not last as the war began to drag on.

During the autumn of 1914, the first and most urgent of these problems was very simple to formulate: the economic survival of a country, millions of whose men had been mobilised, and, in particular, the maintenance of a standard of living to enable their wives and children to 'hold out'.

There was another problem allied to this one. How could the country be helped to 'hold out' on the psychological plane; that is, how could its morale be held steady over an indefinite period?

Other problems were bound to arise as well. Was it conceivable that political and trade-union organisations would continue to lie low until the end of the war? In particular, could the forces which were prepared to stifle their pacifist convictions for a time when faced with 'German aggression' in August 1914, and then with a mortal threat to their country, be expected to continue stifling them indefinitely?

CHAPTER 1

To Live at War

We may take it, without much risk of contradiction, that once the reality of war was accepted (and it was), and once things had settled down without much hope of a speedy victory or fear of a quick defeat (and that is how it began to look at the start of the autumn), the behaviour of the French nation at large reflected the country's ability to survive in the absence of a significant part of its male population.

This aspect of the war was the more urgent as it had not been anticipated. Military problems had been considered, but the fact that war could also bring about economic and social upheavals had been completely ignored, simply because no one had imagined that it could last for more than a few weeks.

Solidarity in the Countryside

In a country that was still very largely rural, the major problem, apart from the war itself, was getting the farm work done.

'The harvest has been gathered in, thanks to mutual aid', wrote the mayor of Colombier to the prefect of his department, Haute-Saône. Was it the same throughout the country?

In August 1914, the historian Charles Petit-Dutaillis, rector of the Académie de Grenoble, suggested to all schoolteachers in his district that they keep notes of the events in which they became involved. On 18 September 1914, Albert Sarraut, minister of education, extended the same invitation to schoolteachers throughout France, asking them to be the 'living echo of public opinion' in their communes and to 'compile an exhaustive catalogue of local history'. As a guide, he suggested a number of specific topics: mobilisation,

13

economic life, village administration and so on. Of that survey, only a few contributions have survived, among them a fair number from the departments of Charente, Côtes-du-Nord, Gard and Haute-Savoie. Most reports from the latter and from the rest of the Dauphiné were compiled during the mobilisation period and there are very few that continue much beyond that point.

From the teachers' (or, as in Haute-Savoie, the priests') records we can build up a picture of the reactions of rural France. The reader will not be surprised to find that agricultural questions held pride of place.

They are mentioned in thirty-two of the sixty-eight communes in Côtes-du-Nord for which we have any records. Complaints were the exception rather than the rule: 'The land. . .has not been worked quite as well as it might have been, and poorer harvests have been reported'; 'The lack of manpower [made itself] felt, and on the larger farms many fields were left fallow'; 'During the first two years, some fields could not be tilled'; 'The first year was hard and the harvest showed the effects'.

In all other communes, by contrast, evaluations were optimistic: 'The crops and the harvest did not suffer'; 'The fields were worked satisfactorily'; 'Agricultural activity was maintained'; 'The harvest was brought in without any serious delays . . .'; 'All the work was done'; 'Sowing went well'.

There were no miracles, of course, for the work had to be done by old people, by children and, above all, by women. 'The most significant factor of local history in every rural commune during the war,' wrote the Sévignac schoolmaster, 'is the almost total absence of agricultural labourers. . . . One cannot but stress the arduous work, even the heroism of the men and women who have stayed behind . . .'.

The same appreciation was voiced almost everywhere: 'Women in large numbers brought in the harvest'; 'Women, old people and children[1] were anxious to finish the harvest and get on with the sowing . . .'; 'The men having left, all who remained behind courageously shouldered the onerous task that had fallen to them. Women, children, old people, all set to work. . .to take the place of the men on the farms and in the fields.' Farmers' wives 'have been wonderful. Choking back their tears, stifling their anxieties, they have buckled down valiantly . . .'; 'The women have replaced the men in the fields'.

---

1. On the debit side, many teachers mentioned a drop in school attendance at the beginning of term.

The picture presented by Côtes-du-Nord was clearly not unique: things were much the same in Haute-Savoie, for example. Thus agricultural topics were mentioned by twenty-seven communes out of the thirty-six for which we have records. Here, too, difficulties were rarely mentioned: At Annecy-le-Vieux, the morale of the population was low 'because the workers were called away at harvest time'. There was 'a danger that the harvest might not be brought in', but in the end solidarity ensured that there was nothing worse than a delay in the threshing. In some other communes 'agricultural work was undertaken with greater difficulty'; some vineyards 'were not worked'; in Lyaud there were 'difficulties', but for the rest 'conditions were almost normal'.

In nearly all the cases mentioned, agricultural life suffered few setbacks, thanks to the women and children. In Les Houches, where, because of the altitude, the hay had not been cut before mobilisation, a united effort by everyone, including visiting tourists, saw to it that the work was done in time.

Most extraordinary of all was the cooperation and mutual support shown in parts of the country renowned for the individualism of their inhabitants. In Côtes-du-Nord, farmers who had stayed behind went to the aid of neighbours who had been called up. In Haute-Savoie, this fact was mentioned quite frequently: 'Thanks to the efforts and devotion of those who have stayed behind, the harvest and threshing were accomplished satisfactorily; Agricultural work proceeded as normal, thanks to the organisation of local hands by the village schoolmaster, who is also the [parish] clerk; [The] work [was] done because everyone cooperated and with thanks to the old people and to the women . . .; all credit to them', wrote the parish priest of Les Gets. The results were surprising: at Morzine 'the 1914 harvest was brought in much more quickly than anyone could have hoped'.

Let us end with two sketches, the first of which comes from the schoolmaster in Lalley, Isère.

After those few feverish days of intense activity, the appearance of our village changed. Out of a population of less than 400 inhabitants, 53 men, the young, the strong, those who shouldered the weight of the work in the fields, had gone. A grim calm, a sense of the void, descended. Haymaking had not yet been finished; the harvest beckoned imperiously, with a south wind drying the corn and turning the oats yellow. And so, people came to each other's aid. There were signs of remarkable dedication: young lads aged 15 to 20, young girls taking off their aprons and putting aside the needlework they had begun, resolutely took up their sickles and lent a hand to the women left alone with their young children. 'There's a war on!' people said. The job was not badly done, and, moreover, without the help of foreign labour which the prefecture had placed at the disposal of those who asked for it.

Very little was left undone that day. Just one more effort and the stacks of sheaves would be in the barns! (13 August).

A second description, by a schoolmaster from Yonne:

Women carried their husbands' scythes, spread the manure, wielded the harrow. Some even did the ploughing, but above all, the old folk had become heads of their families once again, watching over the children, running the farms, ploughing, threshing the corn, herding the sheep, coppicing the wood, trying their hands at being wheelwrights and smiths and sawyers. Never before had they been seen in such numbers. Grey beards, white beards, bald heads, stooped backs, crooked hips, twisted bodies, halting legs, breaking arms — thanks to their experience and resolution — resumed the work from which they had retired.

No one would ever have believed that they could be so strong.

Thus, the appeal by Viviani, the prime minister, on 6 August 1914, to Frenchwomen to take the place of their menfolk in the fields and to bring in the harvest, had been answered by, or rather had probably done nothing more than *reflect*, the instinctive efforts of the rural population.

Those prefects who, as members of the commission in charge of agricultural output, made regular tours of the countryside and watched the harvest being brought in, were equally impressed by the women. As the prefect of Yonne put it: 'How often have I not seen young mothers following the plough, the horse being led by their ten-year-old sons . . .'

In their reports to the government, the prefects stated that in general the agricultural situation was favourable. The prefect of Lot-et-Garonne even thought it excellent, the more so as the good weather had returned: 'Everything leads us to hope that the process of bringing in crops, which has so far been done so calmly and in such perfect order, will continue in the same way in the coming period'.

The prefect of Lot, who had intended to take charge of the organisation of farm work, very quickly realised that there was no need for him to do so: 'I discovered with pleasure that in many communes the people had organised themselves to replace the workers who had gone. Today several mayors assured me that the harvest will be brought in and the next prepared for without the help of strangers'.

All the same he remarked that the work was being slowed down by the refusal of farmers' wives to hire outside labour which would have cost them money at a time when they wanted to economise.

On the debit side, also, some mayors complained to the prefect of Lozère that farm labourers were asking for double or triple the normal daily wage. Again, General Belin (of GHQ Eastern Command) put it to the prefect of Ardennes that able-bodied men were loafing about in the villages when the harvest was waiting to be brought in. However, all these were purely local difficulties; the harvesting and the ploughing were both done in good time.

Still, the work was evidently not done with the old gusto, as may be gathered from this account of the grape harvest in Gard:

> The grape harvest did not suffer. It was brought in more or less as usual. . . . However, it was quite unlike that of previous years: there were no more roars of laughter, no more saucy stories, no more dancing in the shade of the trees to the sound of the clarinet or the oboe: everything was subdued. The talk was about the war, people read out bits from the papers during meal breaks; more than one deep sigh escaped from weary chests, more than one tear lingered in the corner of an eye while thoughts flew to those absent!

However, the realisation that agricultural work could be done despite the absence of their young men lessened the strain on the country people, making the waiting easier.

Separation Allowances

A second factor, the payment of benefits, did a great deal to restore calm.

The law of 5 August 1914 authorised an allowance of 1.25 francs per day, plus an additional 0.50 francs per child below the age of 16 years, to every needy family whose breadwinner had been called up. That sum was not enough to make up the wages lost by a skilled worker — in 1911 the average daily wage of a pit-face worker was 5.70 francs; in 1913 a joiner could earn 0.80 francs an hour in Paris; in 1911 the average daily wage for all workers varied between 3.72 francs (Vendée) and 6.87 francs (Seine-et-Oise); in Paris it was 7.24 francs — but it was a sizeable amount for day labourers and even more so for agricultural labourers, who could in addition count on a number of fringe benefits.

As a schoolmaster from Haute-Savoie put it: 'Never before has the wife of a day labourer, the mother of three children, received 82.50 francs per month, the amount of her allowance. . . . More than one mother of a family, whose husband has been called up, is now able to buy things she has wanted for a long time'. 'Thanks to the allowances [wrote Yves Lequin], rural Savoie has switched to a cash economy. In the old self-sufficiency system used before 1914, cash payment was rare and reserved for important purchases'.

The records kept by the schoolteacher make frequent reference to allowances: in the department of Côtes-du-Nord, the common view was that they were excessive.

One opinion had it that the allowances were far too liberal, with people living much better than before and many women having high hopes of a continuation of the war; another held that 'what with the husbands continuing to be away the women would have had no respite were it not that they are raking in the allowances . . .'. Others stressed that the allowances were granted with 'generosity', with 'too free a hand', that people who were not in need, such as rich farmers' wives, drew allowances for themselves and their children, that 'most people in the commune collect allowances. . .', and that 'many have seen improvements in their situation thanks to the war'.

Some even went so far as to declare that the allowances had 'taught certain women the habits of profligacy, laziness and drunkenness', that they had led them into 'debauchery'. However, not all denied their usefulness. 'Salutary effect', one schoolmaster commented:

> Here in the countryside where people live very simple lives, it should be recognised that the monthly sum drawn from the tax office is generally higher than the earnings of the absent member of the family. However, since the amount of work achieved is considerable, it would be churlish to reproach the beneficiaries of the allowances for this increase in their income.

The allowances were above all thought to have a favourable effect on morale: 'This allowance has helped to keep courage and morale at the highest level, chiefly among small farmers . . .'. Another commented that 'the allowances contribute considerably to the maintenance of morale . . .'. Even if they were excessive, they were thought to have done 'a great deal to maintain the morale of the population'.

The schoolmaster from Uzel used a revealing phrase: the allowances 'have made it possible to continue the war'. In fact, the full effects of the allowances did not make themselves felt during the first weeks of the war, particularly as they were not at first distributed very liberally, as witness the following remark: 'In 1914, the tribunals turned down far too many justified claims and there was some grumbling. Later the authorities proved more generous, sometimes even too much so'. Moreover, we find a number of judgments by courts martial in the autumn of 1914 against soldiers who had deserted at the news that their wives had not received any allowances.

We must therefore qualify some of our recorders' appraisals; however, it is undeniable that from the very beginning the allowances played an important part in the growing acceptance by the inhabitants of Côtes-du-Nord of a war that seemed to be dragging on.

The tone was a little different in Haute-Savoie. Here the stress was laid above all on the abuses of the system: 'Many families are not needy and could do without assistance'; 'The allowances are being handed out regardless of the recipients' financial situation'; the allowances were welcome, but were not indispensable; they were being gradually extended 'to many people who do not really need them'.

A great many informants stressed the abuse of the system: where on the one hand the parish priest of Copponex claimed that few families used their allowances to live an idle and dissolute life, on the other hand, an informant in Annecy-le-Vieux took the opposite view: 'The provision of separation allowances with blind prodigality has. . .encouraged sloth and loose living in many a home . . .'.

The same view was also expressed by many others: 'It is obvious that the soldiers' wives do not always make the best use of their money'; 'Simple women have never before had the kind of clothes they have been wearing since the war started'.

Others decried the 'far too frequent visits to the *patisserie*', 'drunkenness', or stressed affluence: 'Thanks to the far too liberal allowances, some families are much better off than they were before the war'.

However, a fisherman's wife, confiding in the schoolmaster from Sciez, refuted all these criticisms: 'The truth is that we don't own anything and that my husband is defending the property of those who do. They will have to pay for it . . .'.

There were few comments, by contrast, from Haute-Savoie on the positive role played by allowances in keeping up morale, even though the views of the fisherman's wife just quoted did have some bearing on the subject. This aspect was not, however, completely ignored, as witness this commentary: 'At first the tribunals were very strict (and some soldiers wrote to complain about political bias in the allocation of the allowances). . . . Since then the government has realised if the civilians are to "hold out" generosity will have to be shown.'

There are not many references to the allowances in the reports of teachers from Gard, but one of them mentions among the causes of public resilience 'the allowances to needy families' which 'have prevented many complaints or criticisms'.

It would have been surprising if the many reports from Charente[2] had not broached the question of the allowances at some length. There were many more shades of opinion here than in Haute-Savoie or Côtes-du-Nord, but there was a clear preponderance of caustic comments on the allowances: 'Many could have done without them. Some thrifty persons invested the money; others just squandered it'; 'The allowances, which were first demanded for those in need, were soon granted to everybody. . . an infectious example rather than a real need'; the allowances 'enabled [certain people] to spend money on luxuries, on clothes or else inclined them towards idleness'; 'subsidised idleness'; 'the allowances make you weep, people say, because they are poured out to those who can do without them, to women who spend a lot of money on clothes and little time on work, and to others who do nothing at all . . .'. Others not happy with the system included the families of those who had not been called up and who feared an increase in their taxes!

However, these complaints were often accompanied by the commonsense observations that abuses were 'inevitable', that despite them the allowances were 'essential', that the wives left behind worked 'with courage' and 'deserved' special assistance, and that although the allowances may have favoured 'ideas of luxury incompatible with the needs of the present hour, they have led to the almost total eradication of pauperism'.

The same idea was expressed several times over; thus another teacher also remarked that 'in most cases' the allowances had 'the excellent effect of curing pauperism', even if they had led some people to 'indolence' and a large number to indulging in 'the luxury of acquiring a bicycle'.

It was also repeated several times that the allowances were 'used wisely and beneficially', even if 'in a very small number of women, they unfortunately encouraged waste, profligacy, idleness and neglect of the land'.

Beyond all these criticisms, reservations and positive evaluations there was wide agreement about 'the unaccustomed prosperity', the near-affluence of many families and the consequent tranquillity of the people of Charente. The same assessment also came from as far afield as Berneuil in the south of the department: '. . .the allowances

2. Reports are available from 360 out of a total of 424 communes in this department.

have done a great deal of good and are helping to maintain calm' and Benest in the north:[3]

> 166 persons are drawing the daily allowance. Many of them are needy, others could easily have dispensed with it, but as all are doing their duty at the front, the measure is sound. In providing everybody with the necessities of life it has been *the main cause of domestic peace and public calm*. The allowances are therefore a great benefit, a reward that does credit to our democratic government.

The schoolmistress from Bioussac summed it up as follows: 'The results are excellent, because the allowances help the families of soldiers to look forward with greater patience to the end of hostilities. The soldier, for his part, is easier in his mind for he knows that, whatever happens, his family will not go short'.

The impact of the allowances has perhaps been too much neglected by historians of the First World War. As the mayor of Fieux (Lot-et-Garonne) wrote: 'This law [concerning the allowances], despite all its imperfections, may well have prevented popular agitation in the face of a war for which neither the country nor public opinion had been adequately prepared'.

Economic Recovery

The preservation of adequate, and in some cases improved, material circumstances, was an important factor in persuading the rural population to accept the unforeseen extension of the war. But what of the working class?

The income of many rural families did not fall appreciably with the departure of the men; in urban working-class families, by contrast, it was enough for the breadwinner to be called up for the family income to disappear.

A series of factors nevertheless explains why the situation did not become disastrous.

The first factor, of course, was the separation allowance, even though it did not have nearly the same impact as in the countryside — it being not a topping-up of, but a cut in, real income. To see things in perspective, we must, however, remember that at the same time there was also a 'moratorium' (as it was then called) on rents. Since there was one mouth less to feed, the drop in income was

---

3. The village had 1,200 inhabitants. With an average of four persons per family, this meant that about half the population benefited from allowances.

further offset by a drop in living expenses. Compared with the loss in wages, the allowances were none the less very small. Thus Charles Favral declared that '. . .the wives of servicemen. . .could not live on the inadequate family allowance. . .'; Charles Tillon remembered that 'the allowances did not seem enough except for families that could have dispensed with them in any case'.

Other opinions were less clear-cut. In a mining village in the department of Gard, 'the allowances were received with *enthusiasm*. However, many have found them *barely sufficient* while others feel that "the government is doing a lot". A reporter from Beauvais wrote: 'In any case, the population is not badly off from a material point of view. The allowances have even made some people happy'.

In these circumstances, the rapid industrial recovery, which boosted the employment of non-mobilised men and of women, proved a crucial factor in the restoration of tolerable economic conditions. 'Luckily,' Charles Tillon noted, 'the arsenal [in Rennes] and its gunpowder annexe in La Courrouze were constantly short of manpower, and it was here that the wives and daughters of servicemen learnt to make cartridges and to turn shells.'

C. Favral drew a different picture: 'They [the wives] had two options: either to starve to death at home or, like their husbands, to sacrifice their health and life to Capital'. His view may seem oversimplified, but it nevertheless reflected a stark reality: the massive influx of female labour into industry. Thus, while 17,731 women were employed in the metal industry before the war, their numbers had gone up to 104,641 by July 1916 and to 132,012 in January 1918, a rise of 75 per cent. In fact, these figures are for civil establishments alone; if we add the military establishments, then we find that 300,000 women were employed in war production in 1917 and close to 425,000 in September 1918.

Thus, much as with rural families, many urban working-class homes had their income boosted by the work of women.

Let us now try to put a date to the moment when the economic recovery began to make an impact on the French working class.

The need to protect serving workers' families weighed heavily on the leaders of commerce and industry from the beginning of the war: on 11 August, the president of the Paris chamber of commerce appealed to his colleagues 'for each one to use his influence to ensure that companies and factories continue to stay open and that those which have closed reopen and provide work for the greatest possible number of workers'. On 8 September, the socialist, Pierre Renaudel, called for a maximum effort. After giving examples of what could be done, as for instance the production of machine guns at Châtellerault, he concluded: 'Let the government give the orders, let it not lose any time. It ought to act *as if the war is going to continue for a long time.* Let it not be afraid of long-term plans'.

It was in fact on 20 September, as Jean-Noël Jeanneney wrote in his *François de Wendel en République*, that Millerand invited a number of leading industrialists to Bordeaux to tell them that the run on shells had been so unforeseen that within a month no more than 200 rounds for each 75mm field gun would be left. Hence it was essential to launch a huge manufacturing programme without delay. In this connection, G. Hardach has pointed out that the production target of 100,000 shells per day, decided upon in September 1914, was reached in the autumn of 1915; the national arsenals alone were producing 300 field guns per month in August 1915 and 600 in December of the same year; at that time 1,500 rifles and 36 machine guns were also being turned out every day. The production of gunpowder rose from 41 tonnes a day in August 1914 to 255 tonnes in July 1915.

On 16 August Saint-Venant, the secretary-general of the northern section of the General Federation of Labour (CGT), sent a circular to affiliated organisations urging them not to spend all their time and energy on organising aid for needy families but to help in the *organisation of work* as well. A return to work was essential if 'the proletariat is to live from its labour and not from humiliation and begging. . .'. On 20 August he wrote to the president of the Lille chamber of commerce asking for help in the setting up of 'joint committees charged with the supervision and organisation of work for the duration of the war'. On 1 October Parisian stone-cutters called for a full return to work.

Company reports enable us to follow the resumption of business activity. From August the blast furnaces in Denain-Anzin began to supply the needs of the artillery and the engineers; at Saint-Gobain, industrial life, which had been suspended in August, gradually recovered in September: new operations sprang up, among them the manufacture of concentrated sulphuric acid, an important element in the production of gunpowder and explosives. At the beginning of October the blast furnaces in Pompey, damaged by the sudden stoppage of work in August, were repaired and quickly converted to the manufacture of shells; that same month the factories of the Compagnie des Mines, Fonderies et Forges d'Alais — particularly those in Tamaris near Alais and those in Firminy — began to manufacture shells, as well as a selection of spades, pickaxes and other implements.

At Air-Liquide, by contrast, production was still disorganised and at an almost complete standstill in October, and it was only in subsequent months that manufacturing output was stepped up. At Penarroya, production remained sporadic until the end of October. Other companies gave less accurate details of the resumption of operations. The Châtillon–Commentry group quickly concentrated its efforts on the Montluçon and Commentry factories: during the last few months of the financial year 1914 the Martin furnaces produced twice as much steel a day as before the war. At the Penhoët works some operations were suspended, but the building of warships was stepped up and at the same time the production of shells and 75mm shell-cases was begun. This resumption of work allowed the company to end the financial year on a very satisfactory note. The size of the workforce at Tréfileries et Laminoirs du Havre (wire-drawing and rolling mills), which had been reduced by a third by the time of mobilisation, was a few months later twice what it had been before the war, and as a result was raised to an unprecedented level.

Other sources enable us to fill in the details of this picture. The monthly reports by the special commissioner for Nantes stated on *13 September*: 'economic situation relatively good, full production in the big naval construction yards'; *16 October*: 'very little unemployment, naval yards operational'. The special commissioner for Saint-Etienne noted on *6 October*: 'gradual resumption of economic life'; *11 November*: 'life almost back to normal in Saint-Etienne, marked activity in the mines and in the metal industry'. As a sign of the recovery, the Oise chamber of trade and industry resumed its meetings on 18 November.

Public records and schoolteachers' notes from various parts reflect the economic recovery. Thus the teachers at Bellevue, in the commune of Thiers, mentioned that work, having been broken off, was resumed in about October and that in December 1914 many people were astonished at the amount of work available, for 'it appeared that in 1870 the workforce had remained unemployed throughout the hostilities'.

The small industrial town of Saint-Florent-sur-Cher had four factories and 500 workers before the war. All the factories closed upon mobilisation. Gradually, however, work was resumed; the factory producing household goods began to turn out mess tins, water bottles, and, later, bombs for the artillery. Other factories started to manufacture 'appliances for the national defence'. In September, a factory making wheels and trucks for the army was opened. The stone quarries, by contrast, remained idle.

At Toulouse, according to P. Bayoux, economic recovery started in October, first of all in the workshops for the unemployed run by the municipality and the *bourse du travail*[4] (public works and military clothing), and then very quickly with the sudden spread of industries supplying the services. The gunpowder factory, which had employed 100 workers before the war, employed 4,000 in June 1915. It would have a complement of 20,000 in June 1917, and of 30,000 on Armistice Day.

In Charente, a predominantly rural department, the local workshops closed down, but the labour force found work in neighbouring villages; at Barbezieux, the factory making agricultural machinery was able to resume work after a short interval, but within weeks it was converted to the production of spades for the trenches and the finishing of shells. Other factories turned out boots and trousers for the army. At Cognac, all industrial activities which had ceased in August were gradually resumed from October onwards.

In the department of Gard, there were signs that industrial recovery was not as general as other sources suggest. In the mines, operations were barely slowed down by the war. In the metal industry, too, recovery was rapid: in September the factory in Tamaris, near Alais, received an important order for narrow-gauge railway track: 'From then on, life in Tamaris resumed its normal course'. In October the factory received large government orders for steel for the manufacture of shells.

Other industries, however, and textiles in particular, did not fare nearly so well. Factories in Sauveterre received orders for military supplies from firms in Avignon, but at Sauve the industrial output (linen and cotton hosiery, bushels, shoes) was reduced; in Saint-Jean-du-Gard, the mills were all but closed; in Notre-Dame-de-Rouvière, one only of the two mills was reopened on 1 October; in Lasalle, several mills remained closed, and others cut their output; in Massilargues, unemployment in the mills of Anduze and Tornac helped the recruitment of grape-pickers; at Anduze, where four spinning mills, one paper mill, and a hat-maker's workshop had employed 400 workers (mainly female), the closure of these enterprises caused a great deal of hardship. The spinning mills, in particular, did not reopen until March 1915.

At L'Estrechure, thanks to the allowances, there was no economic hardship, but the two silk mills were closed. At Genolhac it was the same, young girls finding work in the vineyards.

4. A labour exchange run by trade unions and also serving as a centre of education, social life and trade-union activity.

We can therefore say that while industrial activity in general began to make a good recovery in October, thanks largely to the war effort, some sectors, and such luxury industries as silk in particular, were much slower to recover or to adapt. But as the prefect of Yonne wrote, 'the industrial activity of the nation recovered under the pressure of necessity a few months after the declaration of war, and there was a gradual return to normal conditions'.

At the end of this survey, it thus appears that the real problem was not, paradoxically, that of unemployment, but the recruitment of the workpeople needed for the country's 'industrial mobilisation'.

Most of the new labour-force was, as we have said, made up of women who now entered occupations to which they were quite unaccustomed — in the naval dockyards at Penhoët the employment of 'numerous women' was the cause of astonishment for some time.

Old and retired workers also played their part: 'Our old workers constitute an important contingent', we read in a report by the Compagnie des Mines, Fonderies et Forges in Alais.

But that would not have been nearly enough: the bulk of the workforce was provided by 'essential workers' exempted from military service and by active servicemen sent back home from the front. Even before the war it had been expected that workers in certain industries would not be called up; railwaymen, for instance, or at least those of them in the operational sector, and to some extent miners as well. The schoolmistress at Chambon-Tarrabias noted that 'a fairly large number of miners who were family men were kept back'. In addition, large numbers of men had to be brought back from the front.

As the schoolmistress at Saint-Martin-de-Valgagues put it: 'Although the list of our dead is very long already, our village has been less hard hit than many others. This is because most of our men were exempted for work in the Nord d'Alais mines, in the foundries at Tamaris and in the chemical factory at Salindres . . .'.

This is what the schoolmaster from Alès-Tamaris had to say about the return of servicemen: 'Following substantial government orders, the majority of the labour force from the Tamaris factory has returned to work. They have been mobilised for the manufacture of steel tubes. With their arrival Tamaris has returned to normal. December 1914: all the workers, or nearly all, have returned to the factory, which is working day and night'.

This reverse flow from the front thus began in early autumn: at Saint-Florent-du-Cher production called for the return of forty mechanics from the front. The same happened at Creusot: metal-workers were sent back from the front and from the depots to the workshops: 'A large number of Creusotins were brought back, and outsiders, too, were allocated to the factories of Schneider & Co., so much so that our town looked as busy as ever. If the workers one met in the street had not been wearing the red armband with grenade, one might have believed everything was back to normal'.

In a report dated 11 November, the police commissioner of Saint-Etienne reported that servicemen had been brought back to speed up the production of shells; he added that it had also been necessary to bring in workers from other regions. On 6 October he had already noted that many 'immigrants' had found work in the local mines and in the metal industry.

By the end of 1915, 500,000 servicemen had been sent back to the factories, and army command concluded that a further drain would stretch combatant strength too far.

This return of the workers did not of course take place without protest, nor without abuses. The police commissioner of Saint-Etienne reported that some leaders of industry took advantage of the new circumstances to bring back relatives who had never worked in the metal industry. Similarly, many workers wrongly described themselves as 'metalworkers' and were brought back to the factory from the front.

At Creusot the families 'favoured' in this way 'tended to make perhaps too frank a show of their delight at a time when others were learning of the death of those who had remained at the front', with the result that there was some jealousy and envy: 'This situation could be very distressing . . .'. At Alès-Tamaris, workers between the ages of twenty and thirty 'were looked upon by the public as not being in the right place at that time'.

This inequality before death was the more deplorable since, all other things being equal, married servicemen were not always brought home first, as a reporter from Saint-Florent-sur-Cher pointed out. Differences in wages also caused complaints: 6 to 11 francs a day for metalworkers, compared to 2.50 francs for railway guards.

Resentment was inevitable as soon as the call-up of some workers was deferred, and differences between town and country threw up some glaringly unfair discrepancies in the sacrifices that had to be made. For our purpose the important fact is not that there were complaints but that, with the distribution of the allowances at the beginning of September, with the recruitment of women workers during the industrial recovery in October, and then with the return of some of the servicemen, the *overall* material situation of the working masses was not so intolerable that extreme poverty could be invoked as an ally in a protest movement against the continuation of the war.

The prefect of police, who, moreover, drew attention to the scale of public assistance — 100,000 meals distributed each day — had this to say about the attitude of the working class in the outlying districts and in the suburban communes at the end of November: 'The population is content'. If this erred somewhat on the optimistic side, there was still a good deal of truth in it.

CHAPTER 2

The Dissemination of News

Though French morale depended on material conditions, other factors were also involved. One of these was the dissemination of news — or so, at least, it was thought at the time.

In the early days of the war, the general staff was convinced that the less that was told to people, the better. This approach had caused difficulties and, since it was in any case not always possible to keep quiet, it seemed preferable to substitute control for complete silence. Censorship thus became one of the main concerns of the authorities in the autumn of 1914.

The Attitude of the Press

From the outbreak of the war, the French press was censored. In principle, censorship bore on military questions only, but no one could tell where these questions began and where they ended in wartime. Moreover, for the sake of national defence, the newspapers were persuaded to censor themselves, thus engaging in a sort of pre-censorship.

The result was a long series of bombastic remarks, although what may seem to be fatuous today may well not have looked like it at the time.

After the war, the magazine *Le Crapouillot* published a collection of the most memorable of these remarks from various papers and journals. Another magazine, *Evolution*, subtitled a 'Monthly Review of Questions of International Peace and the Reconciliation of Nations', founded by the writer, Victor Margueritte, edited by Gouttenoire de Toury and concerned with lengthy denunciations of French responsibility for the war, also published, during the first quarter of 1931, some of the most fatuous comments made at the time. Because of their documentary value, it seems useful to reproduce them here.

WARTIME BOMBAST[1]
(1914–1918)

MOBILISATION, TROOP CONCENTRATION AND INITIAL SKIRMISHES
(2–20 August 1914)

Rue des Martyrs. . .a sergeant, uncertain how to react to the ovations, raised his rifle and kissed it passionately. (*Le Matin*, 7 August 1914)

My wound? It doesn't matter. . . . But make sure you tell them that all Germans are cowards and that the only problem is how to get at them. In the skirmish where I got hit, we had to shout insults at them to make them come out and fight. (*Echo de Paris*, 'Story of a wounded soldier', Franc-Nohain, 15 August 1914)

I think what is happening is a very good thing. . .I've been waiting for it these last forty years. . .France is pulling herself together and it's my opinion she couldn't have done that without being purged by war. . . . (*Petit Parisien*, statement by Monseigneur Baudrillart, 16 August 1914)

Antwerp, by contrast, is believed to be virtually impregnable. (*Le Matin*, 20 August 1914)

MORHANGE, CHARLEROI, THE RETREAT ON THE MARNE
(20 August–15 September 1914)

As far as our slight retreat in Lorraine is concerned, it is of no consequence. Just a minor incident. . . . I would add. . . that the enormous quantity of material we captured from the Germans bears witness to a remarkable weakening on their side. (*Petit Parisien*, Lieutenant-Colonel Rousset, 22 August 1914)

It is impossible for this great battle [of Charleroi] to end in anything but success for us. And even if it should not give us the decisive victory that we still have every right to expect, the enemy will have been winded, crushed, a prisoner of his own losses and supply problems. (*Echo de Paris*, General Cherfils, 29 August 1914)

The wing-beat [of victory] shall carry our armies to the Rhine. . . . That will spell their complete collapse. (*Echo de Paris*, General Cherfils, 15 September 1914)

Play on, then, you blind fools, play the game of your Kaiser and of his vile brood. Play on, but at least while you do so, think about what you

---

1. *Evolution*, January, February, March 1931.

are doing and weep with rage. And may they think of it too, our dear soldiers, and may they double up with laughter, our good lads, as they merrily split your hides, you miserable fools. (*Petit Journal*, Jean Riche-pin, 25 September 1914)

My impression is that the great German army is about to retreat. . .it is only a question of days. . . . The German objective is to beat a retreat on as wide a front as possible. (*Le Matin*, dispatch from the war correspon-dent of *The Times*, 16 October 1914)

Like a wasp trapped in a clear crystal carafe, the vile and brutish [German] army is beating against the walls of its prison. . . . It struggles, damaging itself a little more with every vain attempt. It is wearing itself out. . . . (*Le Matin*, 22 October 1914)

Right at the end of a luncheon given by the general staff, attention was drawn to a few political figures: one of them tried to persuade General Joffre to reveal something of his strategic plans. The victor of the Marne contented himself with a smile, and declared in calm, good-natured tones: 'For the moment, I am eating away at them'. (*Le Journal*, 29 October 1914)

THE FIRST WINTER OF THE WAR
(January–May 1915)

The year 1915 will bring us victory and peace. (*Echo de Paris*, General Cherfils, 2 January 1915)

Nothing better could have happened to us than this new wave in the Boche offensive. (*Echo de Paris*, General Cherfils, 1 May 1915)

THE 1915 OFFENSIVES

They all go into battle as to a fête. (*Petit Parisien*, Lieutenant-Colonel Rousset, 15 May 1915)

A sudden delirium seizes each of the men. At last, we are going to emerge from our torpor! A storm of steel passes over our heads but leaves us unmoved. . . . Magic nights. (*Petit Parisien*, 'Letter from the front', 17 May 1915)

Apart from about five minutes a month, the danger is minimal, even in critical situations. I don't know how I'll be able to do without this sort of life when the war is over. Casualties and death. . . that's the exception. (*Petit Parisien*, 'Letter from a soldier', 22 May 1915)

'Are you happy to go on the offensive?'

'Why, Monsieur, that goes without saying!' (*Petit Parisien*, 30 Septem-ber 1915)

They looked forward to the offensive as to a holiday. They [the soldiers] were so happy! They laughed! They joked! (*Petit Journal*, 'Our Brave Lads. Report by a lieutenant of a colonial infantry regiment', 3 October 1915.)

VERDUN
(February–December 1916)

The very fact that he [the enemy] is not advancing is an outstanding success and raises immense hopes. (*Echo de Paris*, Marcel Hutin, 24 February 1916)

At the gates of Beaumont, our soldiers, who had pretended to retreat, were tremendously amused. (*Journal*, reporting the remarks of an evacuee from Verdun, 28 February 1916)

However, *our losses have been great.* (*Petit Parisien*, 1 March 1916)

The fact is that they [the cellars of Verdun] were relatively comfortable — central heating and electricity, if you please — and that we were not too bored in them. (*Petit Journal*, 1 March 1916)

The troops went through their manoeuvres at Verdun as they might on a field exercise. (*Petit Parisien*, 'Report by an officer', 5 March 1916)

THE ALLIED OFFENSIVES OF 1917

Our heroic defenders will learn with joy that they are about to throw themselves at a foe whom the whole human race considers a noxious breed and the enemy of all civilisation. (*Le Matin*, 2 February 1917)

It has to be clearly said, because it is the truth, that this slight [British] withdrawal was not dictated by the enemy but simply reflected the wishes of the British command. (*Petit Journal*, December 1917)

THE GERMAN OFFENSIVES OF 1918
(March–June)

I am delighted. . .delighted. . .things are going well. (*Le Matin*, remark attributed to Clemenceau, 23 March 1918)

The results of the German attack are insignificant. . .he [the enemy] is reverting to the encircling tactics that are in his blood. I can honestly say we have nothing to worry about. (*Petit Parisien*, Lieutenant-Colonel Rousset, 29 March 1918)

But I would wager that during the Boche drive on Amiens our gunners would much prefer to 'pitch into' the enemy with our splendid 75mm shells which, unlike the vitriol-throwers, do not spread poison but cleanly annihilate entire battalions. (*Petit Journal*, Abbé T. Moreaux, 8 April 1918)

What do a few kilometres matter, or a few wretched cities in flames? (*Journal*, André Tudesq, 13 April 1918)

THE RUSSIAN FRONT
(1914–17)

He [the Cossack] has no trouble in running several Hungarians through at one go, as many as will fit on the shaft of his lance, then he flings the whole skewer away. (*Le Matin*, Halperine-Kaminsky, 5 October 1914)

The 'decisive defeat' at Warsaw with which the Russian armies have this time opened up unlimited prospects to the West must seem disastrous to the Hohenzollern Empire. Let us watch now as hour by hour our allies continue their great thrust towards the Oder, towards Breslau, towards Berlin. (*Petit Parisien*, 26 October 1914)

The [Russian] army is admirably equipped with everything it needs for modern battle. (*Le Matin*, 8 February 1915)

The Russian fleet. Irresistible advance from the Nieman to the Carpathians. (*Le Matin*, headlines, 7 March 1915)

The Russian army at Przemysl is retiring in good order.... The Russian army in Galicia is intact.... Geographical lines mean nothing.... Time is on our side. (*Journal*, Ludovic Naudeau, 17 June 1915)

Warsaw has been taken. The military result is nil.... The result is insignificant.... (*Echo de Paris*, C. Stieron, 10 August 1915)

A new retreat by our allies will, by all accounts, turn out to be a cruel let-down for the German general staff. (*Journal*, Ludovic Naudeau, 21 August 1915)

The distress of our men was moving. They fell to their knees before their officers and implored them: 'Let us fight with stones, with sticks, if need be with our fists.' (*Le Matin*, statement by Madame Motelev, a Russian nurse, 14 May 1916)

Here, too, in Russia the *Union sacrée*...will survive the war. (*Journal*, statement by Protopopov, 1 June 1916)

Russia will fight to the death.... There will be no quitters among the Allies. (*Echo de Paris*, statement by Lloyd George, 30 September 1916)

If there is an upsurge in Russia, it is an upsurge in favour of total war. (*Echo de Paris*, J. Herbette, 11 January 1917)

We know that no one loves the Germans, either in the sovereign's (the Tsar's) or in any other circles that reflect the mood of the country; we know that the army is equipped with thousands of guns and millions of shells... we know that the country...is holding out wonderfully and will hold out indefinitely.... (*Echo de Paris*, J. Herbette, 6 March 1917)

THE RUSSIAN REVOLUTION
(1917–18)

Russia has been liberated.... If her people are in revolt...it is not to shirk the harsh duties of war, but on the contrary to acquit themselves with even more nobility and self-sacrifice.... Long live liberated Russia, which tomorrow will be Russia the liberator. (*Journal*, C. Humbert,

17 March 1917)

'How did the men at the front receive the theories of those few socialists who preached a separate peace?'

'Nobody worried about them, because no one took that poisonous propaganda seriously.' (*Journal*, statement by General Filatier, Paul Erio, 2 May 1917)

Russia will never agree to a separate peace. (*Le Matin*, declaration by Milyukov to the Soviet of Workers and Soldiers, 5 May 1917)

'The Russian situation is improving by the day', says M. Albert Thomas. (*Echo de Paris*, Havas dispatch, 24 June 1917)

[In Russia] incendiary phrases no longer count, Jacobin gestures have just fizzled out. (*Echo de Paris*, Serge de Chessin, 15 August 1917)

You ask me if revolutionary Russia is inclined to lay down her arms and sign a separate peace with the enemy? I reply: Never! (*Petit Journal*, declaration by Rubanovich, 4 November 1917)

As for the political influence of the maximalists, it has been checked. . . . In Russia, we abhor blood. (*Petit Journal*, declaration by Maklakov, 8 November 1917)

The [US] State Department does not believe that Lenin and Trotsky can stay in power for long and is ready for their fall. Those who know Trotsky consider him a lightweight, without personal worth and quite incapable of taking on the job of an organiser. (*Petit Journal*, 27 November 1917)

The Russian loans and the Revolution. The coupons will be paid. (*Echo de Paris*, 10 December 1917)

The reign of Lenin and Trotsky seems to be reaching its end. . . . Lenin no longer dares to leave Smolny. . . . Lenin. . .trembles for his miserable person . . . . Their dream will not be realised . . . . The hours of Lenin and Trotsky's reign are numbered. (*Journal*, Paul Erio, 26 December 1917)

THE DARDANELLES AND SALONIKA
(1915–18)

Nothing can stop us, we shall march onward, our strapping lads will chase out the Turks at bayonet point. (*Le Matin*, statement of a combatant)

ITALY AND THE WAR
(1915–18)

Heal me, heal me quickly! I want to get back to the fight and kill those Austrians; I promised His Majesty the King. (*Petit Parisien*, words attributed to a wounded Italian, Serge Basset, 2 August 1915)

Among other things, we understand that the Italians have withdrawn from the Carnic Alps and the Dolomites, that the enemy has returned to Cortina d'Ampezzo. . .and that he will soon be at Bellune. . . . We need be neither surprised, nor alarmed. (*Petit Journal*, General Berthaud, 8 November 1917)

THE SERBIAN FRONT
(1914–18)

'Belgrade ignores the bombardment.' (*Journal*, headline to a dispatch, 6 August 1914)

The Serbs are retreating in perfect order. . .and this fact is as sickening for the Austro-Germans as was the retreat of the Russians. . . . The Serbs are withdrawing according to a plan drawn up by the Allies, who, when they decide to intervene, will find the Serbian troops ready to resume the offensive. (*Echo de Paris*, translation of an article in the Rumanian paper *Dimineatza*, 21 November 1915)

ROMANIA

It [the entry of Romania into the war] is clearly the beginning of a phase that will rapidly lead us to final victory. (*Le Matin*, E. Théry, 30 August 1916)

The public need not worry themselves too much about the fall-back of the Rumanian troops to the alpine ridge of their northern frontier. (*Echo de Paris*, General Cherfils, 11 October 1916)

The Rumanians are withdrawing. . .but they are sure to have a plan. (*Echo de Paris*, M. Hutin, 27 November 1916)

BULGARIA
(1914–18)

The decision [in favour of the Allies] by King Ferdinand of Bulgaria will be put into effect before the end of the week. (*Journal*, Saint-Brice, 25 March 1915)

Will Bulgaria attack Turkey? (*Petit Parisien*, 25 March 1915)

'Bulgarians to march with the Allies.' (*Petit Parisien*, headline, Serge Basset, 26 March 1915)

She [Bulgaria] leans towards the Triple Entente. (*Petit Parisien*, 31 March 1915)

As can be seen, the Bulgarian government has taken a further step towards cooperation with the Allies, a fact of some importance. (*Petit Parisien*, Claude Anet, 12 April 1915)

'Bulgaria will not under any circumstances attack Rumania.' (*Petit Parisien*, dispatch headline, 22 May 1915)

THE WAR AT SEA
(1914–18)

All the forts [in the Dardanelles] will be blown to smithereens by the shells of the Allied squadron. (*Echo de Paris*, General Cherfils, 2 March 1915)

Let us pay homage [to the sailors] and do not let us feel sorry for them. (*Echo de Paris*, General Bauer, 6 September 1916)

THE WAR IN THE AIR: ZEPPELINS AND AEROPLANES
(1914–18)

The sight of a German airship over Paris is most improbable. (*Petit Parisien*, 20 August 1914)

Rest assured, Parisians, you will not be hearing the hum of [Zeppelin] engines. (*Echo de Paris*, Grandval, 5 January 1915)

They [the Zeppelins] have arrived. They are even less fearsome when seen at close quarters. (*Journal*, Georges Prade, 22 March 1915)

But if the Gothas [German bombers] should appear. . .don't worry. (*Journal*, 29 January 1918)

Oh, if only the Germans could see how little they are affecting the nerves of the Parisians, who have grown used to them! (*Petit Parisien*, 13 April 1918)

POISON GAS
(1915–18)

There is no need to be inordinately alarmed about the deadly effects of poison-gas bombs. Rest assured, they are not as bad as all that. . . . They [the bombs] are quite harmless. . . . If. . . we were to tot up all the victims of poison gas and compare their numbers with all the others, we should not pay them any further attention. (*Le Matin*, André Lefebvre, 27 April 1915)

Our soldiers don't give a b— for poison gases. (*Echo de Paris*, 16 December 1916)

GERMANY, AUSTRIA, THE KAISER
(1914–18)

Following the terrible shortages, Berlin seems to be on the eve of a revolution. (*Le Matin*, statement by a German to the *Daily Citizen*, 14 August 1914)

'Scarcities beginning to bite in Germany. Berlin fears grave disturbances.' (*Le Matin*, headline, 31 August 1914)

'Berlin anxious. Vienna in a panic.' (*Le Matin*, headline, 2 September 1914)

Goethe and Schiller are great poets, but how overrated! (*Echo de Paris*, Camille Saint-Saëns, 19 September 1914)

The burst of shells, the shrapnel. . . . So many jokes. (*Echo de Paris*, Franc-Nohain, 11 November 1914)

Bluff, rubbish and double Dutch — that's how to sum up that famous science from across the Rhine. (*Journal*, Emile Gautier, 27 November 1914)

As far as I am concerned, the German army has been knocked out. (*Journal*, Francis Laur, 6 February, 1915)

'They are eating straw.' (*Petit Parisien*, headline to a dispatch from Amsterdam, 29 February 1915)

Their vegetables are not growing. (*Le Matin*, 26 March 1915)

They are running out of wood. (*Journal*, 2 April 1915)

Boche corpses smell worse than French. (*Le Matin*, statement by 'women from Lorraine', 14 July 1915)

The enemy has lost five million men. (*Petit Parisien*, 27 October 1915)

Reports are contradictory, but everyone knows that Wilhelm II's malignant growth is following its course. It is quite likely that the Kaiser will die in the near future. But it is equally possible that he will linger on for several months. (*Le Matin*, 15 January 1916)

Who lends to the State, gives to the soldier! Who subscribes, fights! Who holds back, deserts. . . . Germany will foot the bill. . . . Germany must be made to pay, to compensate and to reimburse. (*Le Matin*, Louis Barthou, 14 October 1916)

After the defeat . . . Germany will have to pay the Allies sixteen billion a year. (*Le Matin*, De Verneuil, 7 April 1917)

THE GERMAN ARTILLERY

The Germans aim low and poorly; as for their shells, 80 per cent of them do not burst. (*Journal*, 19 August 1914)

Like them, their heavy artillery is nothing but bluff. Their shells have very little effect. . .and all the noise. . .just comes from firing into the blue. (*Le Matin*, 'Letter from the front', 15 September 1914)

Anyway, our troops laugh at machine-guns now . . . . Nobody pays the slightest attention to them. (*Petit Parisien*, L. Montel, 11 October 1914)

The German shells are not nearly as bad as they appear to be. (*Petit Parisien*, 'Letter from a soldier', 19 January 1915)

REFLECTIONS ON THE WAR AND ITS CONSEQUENCES

Germany will have to pay our back rent. (*Journal*, Jacques Dhur, 23 September 1914)

I tell you, this war. . .is reviving the French spirit. (*Journal*, Lucien Hubert, 10 November 1914)

French finances: clarity and candour.

German finances: secrecy and perfidy. (*Le Matin*, 26 April 1915)

Even so, our hero declared that he was much more afraid when he sat his school-leaving certificate than when he dashed to the conquest of Vieil-Armand. (*Petit Journal*, 11 July 1915)

Time and the Germans are working for us. (*Echo de Paris*, René Bazin, 26 November 1915)

There are no more poor in England. (*Echo de Paris*, 28 December 1915)

1916 will see our liberation and victory. (*Le Matin*, Louis Barthou, 1 January 1916)

The present war will have brought us great advantages. (*Le Matin*, André Hesse, 21 March 1916)

And as we apologised for the mud dropping from our boots, she uttered just one cry: 'Oh! that mud, I could kiss it!' (*Le Matin*, words attributed to a woman from a recaptured village, 26 March 1917)

Even if a German offensive should succeed, this would not be a breakthrough (which is a meaningless expression. . .), all it would do would be to create a bulge and would mean no more than a local retreat by our side and the establishment of a German salient. . . . (*Petit Journal*, General Berthaud, 14 January 1918)

COMBATANTS AND CASUALTIES
(1914–18)

Our brave young lads [though injured] are far from beaten. They laugh, joke and beg to be allowed back to the firing line. (*Le Matin*, 19 August 1914)

Not at all, they said to me, we're not all that bothered, the danger is not nearly as great as you think. (*Petit Journal*, 26 October 1914)

The longer the war goes on, the less dreadful I find it. (*Echo de Paris*, 'Letter from the front', 31 October 1914)

Show me the point of your bayonet – let me see if it pricks! (*Journal*, remark by a general, 12 November 1914)

The war, for all its devastating appearances, only *seems* to be destructive. . . . (*Echo de Paris*, General Cherfils, 13 November 1914)

The war is purifying. (Jules Delafosse, 14 November 1914)

All the trenches at R— have central heating. (*Petit Journal*, 27 November 1914)

When it comes to returning to the trenches to relieve comrades who have done their turn, the men almost fight with each other to be first. . . . The temptations of danger are irresistible. (*Le Matin*, 15 November 1914)

Died from wounds: 3.48 per cent. (*Petit Parisien*, speech by Bourgeois at the Musée Social, 18 December 1914)

Our soldiers are becoming spoiled, the parcels will have to be less lavish. (*Petit Parisien*, 14 March 1915)

It's nothing to speak of, I'll be disabled, that's all. (*Le Matin*, remark attributed to a badly wounded soldier, 19 April 1915)

'You know, I'm not married, so I'm going to get engaged.'
'To whom?'
'To victory.' (*Journal*, remark attributed to a combatant, E. Helsey, 20 May 1915)
But at least they [those killed by bayonetting] will have died a beautiful death, in noble battle.... With cold steel, we shall rediscover poetry... epic and chivalrous jousting. (*Echo de Paris*, Hébrard de Villeneuve, 10 July 1915)
We have suffered and have shed a great deal of blood for France. It was needed for expiation. (*Echo de Paris*, R. Bazin, 15 July 1915)
The average mortality in hospitals in the country is less than 2 per cent. (*Echo de Paris*, C. M. Savarit, 19 December 1915)
'A whole month before I can return to fight alongside my comrades, that's a long time.'
'Well, my dear fellow, we shall have to try to cut your convalescence short.' (*Petit Journal*, remark attributed to a wounded lieutenant, 5 May 1916)

This array of quotations, read end to end, makes us laugh, of course. We must nevertheless remember that the whole exercise is rather contrived. Wartime readers did not consider these comments in the same light as we might do. It remains a fact, however, that this *bourrage de crâne* (eyewash), as it was later called, was typical of the period. Even so, not all French journals took the same line, and in particular they had very different views on the *Union sacrée*. On the other hand, their reports of battles and of German and French behaviour were virtually identical, the more so as all of them had to rely on the same scant communiqués.

Whether we look at *L'Humanité*, the organ of the Socialist Party, or at the *Echo de Paris*, the organ of the militarist and Catholic right, we find the same accounts of poor German morale, of high German losses, of German cruelty, of shoddy German equipment and of the fine qualities of France and the French soldier. Thus Alain Lévy's analyses of the content of *Le Midi socialiste*, the Toulouse socialist daily, led him to the following conclusion: 'For several weeks, it resembled its bourgeois brethren. It spared no details when listing the untold crimes of the "Teutonic barbarian" and served up the most fanciful news; the first casualties to come off the trains at Béziers told a *Midi* reporter: "Half the German shells are made of cardboard, they don't even burst!" '

It seems, moreover, that the casualties lent themselves readily to this type of fable (autosuggestion? bragging?). Thus the prefect of Ain claimed that according to most of the wounded travelling to Bourg: 'The German artillery makes more noise than ours and causes less damage. And the German rifle is less deadly. As for our bayonets, they work wonders'. (ANF 7 12937. 20 August)

The prefect of Aisne noted: 'They believe a curious legend very characteristic of the spirit of the French soldier. "Their lead? It isn't even hard, they say it's made of gingerbread!" ' (ANF 7 12937. 15 August)

The same invention can be found in soldiers' letters. Marius Beaup, a schoolmaster from Lalley, quotes one of them: 'These jokers send over shells that look like dirty blue enamel balls; most of them do not burst and cause little damage. . .'.

This kind of *bourrage de crâne* — an expression that is misleading because there was not always a deliberate intention of falsifying the facts — covered many topics in the autumn of 1914. We have noted six of them in particular:

French qualities compounded of panache and a Spartan spirit. This is how Albert de Mun described a bayonet charge in the *Echo de Paris*: 'Bravo, my lads! That's the good old French way. . . . Oh, I can well understand why they look so surprised, why they throw down their arms and why the prisoners have such dejected faces!'

Or again, 'Junius',[2] who had a charwoman say: 'I've lost three sons: it's only today that [I am beginning] to miss them!' Or Gustave Hervé addressing his mother in *La Guerre sociale*: 'Well, let's be quite frank with each other. I wager you would feel ashamed if, at a time when a million French sons are presenting their breasts to the bullet down there, at the frontier, to protect us all, you hadn't at least one of your boys to represent the family'.

German baseness. The base nature of the Germans was high-lighted in an article reproduced by the *Journal des Instituteurs in its Revue des Revues*:

> The *Petit Provincial* protests against those Gretchens whose letters were found on the German prisoners: they wrote asking their fiancés, their brothers or their husbands to be sure to bring them back souvenirs. . . . By souvenirs they meant valuable jewellery, gold watches, rings set with precious stones, fine linen, works of art — objects they can resell.
>
> What a singular education they must have had!
>
> While the gentle French schoolgirl treasures the little wild flowers, or the prettily coloured engravings that remind her of a favourite girl friend,

2. 'Junius' was the collective pseudonym of the leading political journalists on the *Echo*.

all carefully tucked away in the pages of her school books, the Teuton female, coarse and thieving, dreams of showy and expensive Nuremberg knick-knacks, then, being a girl after all, of richly flowing gowns.

A fine mentality created by their schoolmistresses!

German cruelty. Accounts of German cruelty filled the columns of all the papers, for instance the (falsely reported) execution of Alexis Samain, former chairman of the *Souvenir Français* in Metz, or the (real) devastation wrought during the 'march of the barbarians', as A. de Mun called it.

The superiority of French arms and of French field guns in particular. 'According to all the reports that have reached us about the first skirmishes,' Gustave Hervé wrote, 'it appears that he [his brother, an artillery officer] did not exaggerate when he told us that our guns had an overwhelming superiority over those of the Germans.'

More lyrically, A. de Mun exclaimed: 'Let us therefore love and glorify our good old 75; from today it holds the mastery of the battlefield . . .'.

The excellence of French soldiers. 'It is quite obvious that they have more drive, more spirit and more enthusiasm. . . .' (G. Hervé)

On the subject of French and German casualties: 'Much as the beardless, bony faces of the Kaiser's men seem mournful and sad, much as their eyes look empty and lacklustre, reflecting their total absence of will, so is the expression of our soldiers full of vitality, the longing for action and the determination to recover from their wounds'. (Compère-Morel in *L'Humanité*)

The strength of the Russians. The *Radical* carried the following headline on 29 August: 'The Cossacks are coming! A torrent of 400,000 centaurs is flooding the Prussian plains'.

All these contributions were clearly seasoned with patriotic clichés: outside the ministry of war, where a captured Bavarian flag had been hoisted, Franc-Nohain had a 'gallant' policeman tell a little boy: 'Move on, my lad, and grow up quickly, so that you, too, can bring us back one like that . . .'. (*Echo de Paris*)

The examples we have quoted come principally from the *Echo de Paris* and the *Guerre sociale*. These papers were not the sole purveyors of this sort of literature, but the first was certainly a leader in the field, while the second, which — before the war at least — had been the spokesman of socialism with a smattering of anarchism, was, contrary to appearances, one of the few French journals to show some temperance, at least by comparison with the excesses of its rivals.

> Because there happen to be some savages in the German army, in Alsace, in Lorraine and in Belgium [wrote Gustave Hervé on 20 August], because here and there some vile creatures have dishonoured their steel helmet by mowing down women and children, and perhaps finishing off wounded men, are we not being too quick to conclude that Germans everywhere are a race of brutes and assassins?

It is only fair to add that on 17 September *L'Humanité* also published a leading article by Jean Longuet protesting against the exaggeration of German atrocities, and rounding on those who demanded reprisals or at least the harsher treatment of German prisoners; for example Franc-Nohain, who had written this on the subject: 'I have already said that we must not behave like "mugs"; nor must we allow ourselves to be taken for idiots'.

Clearly then, there were differences between the various publications and these very differences, however small, make one wonder whether the *bourrage de crâne* was accepted without question by public opinion at large. Pierre Albert claims in his *L'Histoire générale de la presse* that his studies have led him to the conclusion that 'by 1915 the civilian population was beginning to become less and less credulous'. But before that?

Until the retreat at the end of August, readers of French papers had no particular reason to doubt what they were being told, but after the first defeats, when the seriousness of the losses began to be known, scepticism must surely have begun to creep in. Even so, public opinion, in its desire to be convinced of the justice of the French cause and of the certainty of victory, was ready to accept a great deal that common sense would have made it reject at other times. Even those who tried to be objective had great difficulty in remaining so, lest they hamper the war effort. This was noted by Michel Martin after an analysis of the *Revue historique*, a journal that, because of its detachment and the professional standing of its contributors, ought to have been more objective than most: 'Henri Hauser declared at the end of the war that historical propaganda ought at times to have blushed for itself'.

There are signs, however, that some had begun to mistrust the press very early in the war. To begin with, there were papers which themselves warned their colleagues against exaggeration. Thus, on 25 August, Pierre Renaudel protested in *L'Humanité* against those who claimed that the Russians were a five days' march from Berlin, when they were in fact 450 kilometres away. 'Who is going to believe their story that the Russians are going to advance 90 kilometres a day?'

And then there were the letters of the philosopher Alain to the historian Halévy:

25 November: 'The *Journal de Genève* is eagerly seized over here and officers make cuttings from it; the military reports are admirable and everyone agrees that our journals are ridiculous by comparison . . .'.

[A few days later Alain added] The French papers are impossible to read these days. Officers and gunners read the *Journal de Genève* from cover to cover. . . .

The same view, expressed if anything even more strongly, is found in the letters that Eugène Lemercier[3] wrote to this mother from the front: 'For the past week, I have been reading the newspapers fairly regularly. The ———[4] is a miserable rag. Everything it prints dishonours France and her army. France surely has enough beauty and grandeur to dispense with the kind of methods for which we blame the enemy'.

On 26 November 1914, the historian, Louis Debidour, wrote in a letter to his family:

Something that all of us find *intolerable* is the kind of literature produced by journalists about the trenches, the ingenuity of our men, the general air of enthusiasm, the forced gaiety displayed by the troops, the picturesque layout of the trenches etc. All that is pure invention. The troops are no more than calm and collected; they are resigned to putting a good face on the dreadful misery caused by the cold and the awful weather. That is as it should be. The picture these civilians are labouring so hard to convey in an attempt to give the public a completely false impression of this harsh and unhappy war — finding subjects for fine phrases, describing sham emotions about our toiling in the mud to the point of exhaustion under bullets and shells, describing the dangers, the misery endured in *silence* — this picture is getting on all our nerves. Barrès has a very bad press among us, and as for my old friend Franc-Nohain (Maurice Legrand), who is exactly my age and has never handled a gun or a pick-axe, he fills me with utter disgust.

This view is the more interesting as its author tended to be something of a nationalist.

We must, however, mention a different viewpoint, one expressed

---

3. Painter and composer; reported missing at the front on 6 April 1915.
4. The omission of the paper's title was probably the publisher's decision.

by a schoolteacher from Gard:

> The papers, which were reduced at first to two pages, have resumed their
> normal format and anybody can buy them now. They are most interest-
> ing to read, bearing witness to so many acts of bravery on the part of our
> troops, and provide us with so many noble examples of devotion and
> kindness side by side with instances of thoughtless cruelty and pointless
> acts of barbarism by our enemies that we would not dispense with this
> kind of reading for a single day.
>
> Above all, our papers are a fine tonic: all of them alike are so patriotic
> that their politics matter not, and one may safely take any that comes
> along.
>
> How much does all this make one love a people whom some have
> pleased to depict exclusively from the bad side.

Should we dismiss this naive witness or, on the contrary, consider
that public opinion, in part at least, found in the papers precisely
what it expected to read in them?

It is difficult to come to any definite conclusion; we can, however, quote the view of P. Albert, a student of the history of the
French press. According to him,[5] although 'the civilians found
reassurance in the papers', ultimately 'the press was one of the main
factors in causing a rift between combatants and civilians'. He
emphasises that the troops, unlike many civilians — and we have
been able to read that for ourselves — were filled with animosity,
even contempt, for the journalists, and above all that the press had
forfeited whatever confidence it had enjoyed before the war.

This press, so uniform according to our last witness, was not
uniform enough for the taste of others. Writing in *Evangile et
Liberté*, a pastor, having first praised the discipline of a press 'that
allowed itself to be muzzled without complaint', rounded fiercely
on Clemenceau, the 'only journalist who spends his life subverting
governmental authority. . . [and who] has been working to unsettle
public opinion and to discredit the government . . .'.

After the Moroccan crisis, General Lyautey, too, protested vigorously against the freedom with which *L'Homme libre*, Clemenceau's
paper, and *L'Humanité* were allowed to express their opposition to
the replacement by territorials of the regulars brought back to
France. In a telegram preserved in the army archives, he wrote:

> *L'Homme libre* of 19 and 23 August, and *L'Humanité* of 24 August,
> which have just reached us, protest against the sending to Morocco of

5. *Histoire générale de la Presse*, vol. III, Paris, 1972, pp. 426–427

territorials in terms that can only cause trouble and demoralisation here, at a time when, thanks to these columns, to their active deployment and an élan that nothing has so far impaired, I succeeded against all expectations in sending you 37 battalions. . . .

The vicious and misleading campaign waged by M. Clemenceau during the Taza and Zaiane operations has already had grave effects on discipline and on the authority of the local command, without one official word having been said to put matters right. We had firmly expected that there would be a [political] truce — at least during the war.

It is difficult, even impossible, to exercise my command and to continue with so grave and thankless a mission if a personage in so prominent a position in the state continues to spread disorder and indiscipline here.

I therefore ask the government with all the powers at my command to stop, by virtue of the state of siege, this campaign of subverting the minds of the territorials and to ban the dispatch to Morocco of *L'Humanité* and of *L'Homme libre*, of which I shall henceforth give orders to seize all issues containing similar articles. I implore the government to consider the contribution to the national defence effort Morocco has made and will continue to make to the very end, and not to tolerate any attacks upon it. Let there be unanimity for I need the confidence of everyone here and cannot have my authority questioned.

In fact, no one at any level wanted the press to have too much latitude, the less so as even by their excess of zeal the papers could produce the most untoward results. This was precisely what happened with their accounts of German atrocities: on 6 August, the special commissioner for Bordeaux mentioned the 'distressing effect' of reports of German atrocities. On 30 August, the prefect of Seine-et-Marne was more precise: speaking of panic among those under his jurisdiction, he wrote: 'I believe that the stories of German atrocities which one can read each morning in newspapers from *Le Temps* to *La Guerre sociale* are the root of all the evil. No doubt the papers want to whip up feeling against the Germans, but in reality they spread fear and demoralise the population.'

The minister of war accordingly asked all prefects to instruct editors 'in future to avoid detailed descriptions of acts of cruelty committed by the Germans; repeated accounts of this type might have a deleterious effect on the morale of the population . . .'; an outcome, incidentally, that is nowhere recorded.

Moreover — but this is only a hypothesis — the military might have thought it best not to exaggerate these atrocities, since it was not impossible that the French army could be guilty of the same outrages should the occasion arise. As the historian, H. Contamine, put it:[6]

6. *La Revanche (1871–1914)*, Paris, 1957, p. 19.

Moltke's dictum: 'The first command in every war is to finish it quickly. To that end no means can be too foul', was countered by [the French general] Bonnal with: 'In war everything must be sacrificed to the success of the military operation, and if the demands of the army, when they go beyond what is strictly necessary, are rightly termed odious, all forms of sentimentality, all weaknesses that can undermine the will of the troops and finally their success, are crimes of *lèse-patrie*'.

On 22 August the minister of war sent the commander-in-chief a list of measures to be taken in enemy territory in the event of its occupation. The first step was: 'To take a great number of hostages among the state employees, chiefly schoolteachers and tax officials . . .'.

In the letters sent by a soldier from Cher (69th Regiment, 11th Division) we can read:

> Brin-sur-Seille, 9 August 1914
> Yesterday we crossed the frontier. . . . You have to be careful in enemy country. The day before we caught two Uhlans disguised as reapers and did away with them . . . .

> 11 August
> A group of Hussars came upon a German farm and asked if there were any Germans hidden there. The farmer said no, but no sooner had two Hussars walked in than they fell to the bullets of two Uhlans hidden in a barn. Summary justice. Farm surrounded. Inhabitants caught and taken to the village square, shot on the spot and a few minutes later the farm was up in flames. You must be careful in enemy country — there are too many ambushes — Alsace-Lorraine may be on our side, but there are many real Germans there as well. . . . (AD Cher R 1516.)

And this occurred not in Germany, but in Lorraine!

We must also quote this recollection of a schoolteacher, Joseph Pascal, even though it refers to a later date and happened near the Dardanelles:

> The regiment of our Foreign Legion here is unlikely to uphold the French reputation for magnanimity: our men respect neither white flags, nor raised hands, nor surrender; they take no prisoners but kill them out of hand, they finish off the wounded, in short they do what the Turks will not do to us. And this despite a proclamation by General Gouraud on 2 June: 'You will spare all Turkish soldiers who throw down their arms'.

As the peasant writer, Emile Guillaumin, put it so plainly: 'Our men in Germany behave no better than the Germans do in France. This odious war brings out all the worst instincts of rape and brutality'.

Another initiative of the papers, namely to publish the names of the dead and the wounded, was found to be prejudicial to the nation's morale, particularly as the losses were mounting quickly.

The precise casualty figures could obviously not be determined in the heat of battle but were compiled when the fronts became stabilised, that is in the late autumn of 1914: on 20 November the special section assigned to this task put the French casualties at 581,167 officers and men. While public opinion was not aware of the enormity of these losses, common sense allowed people to make informed guesses, as the following example shows. In La Capelette, a village in Tarn-et-Garonne, a woman noticed that seven or eight men from the community were dead already, whereas in 1870 there had only been two.

It was, moreover, at the beginning of that autumn that notifications of death began to arrive everywhere. The mayor of Fieux in Lot-et-Garonne remembered: 'During September... we received notification of our missing and dead. . . . The first casualty from our commune whom the town hall heard about officially was Gaugean Adrien, aged 28, who was killed on 22 September 1914. . . in the battle of Lesseux (Vosges)'.

At Saint-Bonnet-le-Bourg in Puy-de-Dôme, news of the death of the 'first child of the commune' killed by the enemy was received on 25 September.

At first, the minister of the interior ordered all prefects to prevent any contact between wounded soldiers and civilians in the railway stations, but at least one prefect, of Bouches-du-Rhône, was afraid that the drawbacks would outweigh the advantages if this ban were also applied to the press. Later, the regional papers received orders not to publish lists of killed or wounded soldiers, on the pretext that these lists were not needed, the families concerned having already been notified.

These two examples, the ban on the publication of the names of casualties and the ban on dwelling on German atrocities, show that with the prolongation of hostilities the authorities came to feel that it was no longer enough to hand out as little information as possible, but that there was also an urgent need to direct the flow of information. Above all, it had emerged that the most important issue was no longer the protection of military secrets, but the preservation of the nation's morale. Within a very short period, the official attitude to news in wartime had completely changed, and the new task of the censors was to make sure that the population fell into line.

Public opinion could also be moulded in other ways. Thus, in a circular, Albert Sarraut, the minister of education, told teachers that they had a special mission, namely:

> To recall the 'noble memory' of the dead; to explain to pupils the 'causes of the war', 'the unprovoked aggression', 'France, the eternal champion of progress and of justice. . . .' And this from the first lesson of the day, so that a 'manly attitude' be imprinted for ever on the mind of pupils, the 'citizens of tomorrow'. The master who is able to instil this spirit will have earned the trust of the Republic. . . .

Still, it was obviously in the control of published information, in the authorisation of certain news items and the banning of others that the authorities saw their best hope of moulding public opinion.

The Control of Information

The Archives Militaires and the Bibliothèque de Documentation Internationale Contemporaine contain a vast collection of records of the activities of censors during the war. A brief summary in the file of the press section of the Archives Militaires helps to ease the historian's path. According to this, 'the organisation of press censorship was rudimentary at the time of mobilisation'. However, the principles had been laid down earlier, in the proclamation of the state of siege, and strengthened in the law of 5 August 1914 that banned the publication of all non-official information of a military nature. The implications of a state of siege had been spelled out in the law of 8 August 1849 and brought up to date in October 1913: it entitled the military authorities to 'ban all publications and meetings judged to be of a nature to excite or encourage disorder'. 'Publications', according to the law of 29 July 1881, included 'the press, books and pamphlets, posters, placards and printed papers. The military authorities therefore have the right to ban all newspapers likely to endanger public order and discipline or likely to have a bad influence on the morale of the army or of the population' (Articles 24 and 25).

These articles also set out what information or details could not be published, over and above those specified by the government or army command:

> All information liable to harm our relations with allied countries, neutrals, or relating to political negotiations.
> Attacks on officers; all references to new military formations; repro-

duction of articles from foreign papers.

Obituary notices specifying the place of death.

All references to experiments with, or deployment of, new military machines; all postcards or illustrations depicting field guns or new engines of war or of older models against a background that could reveal their location.

All interviews with generals.

Anything that might be taken for peace propaganda.

All postcards depicting scenes or bearing legends likely to have a bad influence on the morale of the army or the population, postcards depicting new military supplies, munitions and machinery of all kinds.

All headings on official communiqués.

Article 26, moreover, stipulated that any violation could lead to the immediate closure of the publication; Article 28 that these provisions also covered pamphlets or writings of any kind published abroad; Article 31 that offences were to be tried by courts martial.

Once war was declared, all these stipulations had to be translated into practice. At the beginning of hostilities, the minister of war set up a press bureau under his control, but housed in the offices of the military government in the Hôtel des Invalides in Paris. The bureau was to take charge of general censorship and control of the press throughout France, and also to dispense information to journalists. On 4 August all prefects were advised by telegram that no news of a military nature could be published until it had been approved by the press bureau.

On 13 August 1914, the various press associations having formally accepted the need for such controls, the minister of war appointed a 'French Press Commission' made up of delegates from these associations, under the chairmanship of Jean Dupuy, editor of *Le Petit Parisien*.

At the same time a circular was sent to all prefects asking them to prevent the publication not only of falsehoods but also of 'exaggerated commentaries, good or bad, that might weaken the morale of the population'.

According to the summary in the Archives Militaires, censorship 'was still in an embryonic state' when the government left Paris; attempts were made to improve matters in Bordeaux, where part of the press bureau had followed the government while another section had stayed behind in Paris. When the government returned to Paris at the end of November 1914, most censorship problems passed under the control of the prime minister, no doubt as the result of a number of serious complaints.

During the early weeks of the conflict, the censors had run into few problems, the less so as the war was not supposed to last very long and people were prepared to put up with all sorts of short-term inconveniences. As the historian Georges Weil remarked: 'At first everything seemed easy. The spirit of national solidarity could be felt everywhere'. True, there were some clashes, for instance between the Lyon press and General d'Amade, who wanted to ban *Le Progrès*. He accused it of publishing information of military interest, but the prefect was amazed to see that the local censors were stricter than those in Paris who had approved the publication of the same news item. After this incident, relations between the military authorities and the press remained strained in Lyon. The editors declared that they felt disheartened: if one of them was attacked, all the rest would stop publication. Much the same thing happened in Lille.

Gradually, however, the censors stepped up their interference. Figure 1 shows the size and chronological distribution of censorship cuts in *L'Humanité*, *Le Temps*, *Le Figaro*, *La Guerre sociale*, *L'Echo de Paris* and *Le Petit Parisien* in September 1914.

The first of these journals to have been subjected to the censor's measures was *Le Figaro*. On 14 August it appeared with ten-column cm (four-column in) gap at the bottom of page 4, a whole article having been removed. The paper was so mortified that it saw fit to explain the cut to its readers, lest they thought their paper lacking in public spirit:

> Our readers may be surprised to find a rather large blank space at the bottom of our second column on page 4. Here is the explanation.
> That space was originally occupied by a news item. However, as we were going to press we received a telephone call from the ministry of war notifying us that the press bureau had decided it was inopportune to publish this item and asking us to refrain from presenting it to our readers.
> We agreed because it was our duty.
> But let the reader rest assured that we do not treat the publication of war reports lightly or thoughtlessly.
> The censored news item concerned Morocco, and strangely enough it was published in absolutely identical terms in *Le Gaulois* and *L'Eclair* yesterday morning, and in the afternoon edition of *Le Petit Parisien*. Our colleagues would certainly not have published it had it appeared objectionable to them.

The censors' second victim was *L'Humanité*, on 31 August. Two-column cm were blanked out on the first page; they dealt

Fig. 1. *Censorship in Parisian journals, September 1914*

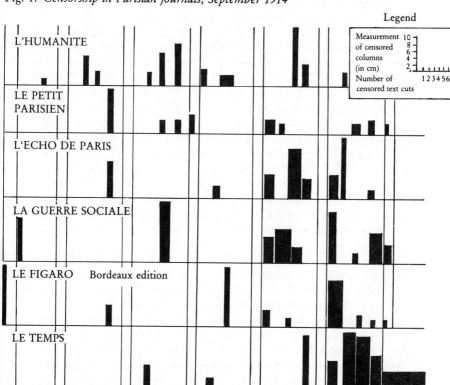

with the flight of a German aeroplane over Paris.

In August, the censors scarcely intervened, partly because they were not properly organised, partly because of the self-discipline of the press and probably partly because of a dearth of news.

Things had changed by September, the censors intervening with increasing frequency during the last two weeks and particularly so during the last ten days of the month, except in the case of *L'Humanité* where most of the cuts came during the second ten days of the month.

Did the political colour of the paper play any part? We find that *Le Figaro* was left relatively untouched, and that *La Guerre sociale* was hardly interfered with until 20 September, much like the *Echo de Paris* and *Le Temps*. But after that date, while *L'Humanité* was left in peace, *L'Echo de Paris*, *La Guerre sociale* and above all *Le Temps* were ordered to make increasingly frequent cuts. These cuts were not significant in themselves; what we need to establish if possible is whether their extent and nature was the same for all these papers.

L'Humanité was ordered to make cuts in twelve issues; most cuts were short and, except in one case, amounted to just one per issue. *La Guerre sociale* had to make cuts in nine issues, but there were several cuts per issue, and many were fairly long. *Le Figaro* also made cuts in nine issues, of which two occurred in the Bordeaux edition. The seven censored issues of the Paris edition contained a single cut each, but six out of the seven cuts were to short articles. *Le Petit Parisien*, too, had nine of its issues censored; most carried just one blank space, and a very short one at that. In *Le Temps*, eight issues were affected; the cuts were very long and numerous, with a record of ten cuts on 30 September. *L'Echo de Paris*, finally, had eight issues cut but most of the cuts were very short.

Here, too, it is difficult to draw any conclusions. There was a certain similarity between the cuts in *Le Figaro*, *L'Humanité*, *Echo de Paris* and *Le Petit Parisien*: they concerned, as far as we can tell from the context — censored articles for that period have not been preserved — news and facts.

There was also an apparent similarity between the cuts in *Le Temps* and those in *La Guerre sociale*. But, on closer examination, this proves not to have been the case. The largest number of cuts in *Le Temps* concerned news of a diplomatic nature, while those in *La Guerre sociale* concerned commentaries that might have had awkward political repercussions: thus on 22 September, *La Guerre sociale* was ordered to cut an article by Gustave Hervé appealing to the socialist ministers Guesde and Sembat to intervene on behalf of those Carnet B[7] prisoners who had not yet been released.

The nature of the cuts seemed indeed to vary with the character of the paper. Thus a daily such as *Le Temps* was censored because it had a much larger network of international correspondents than the other papers and hence received a particularly large number of diplomatic news items that the censors found unacceptable. *La Guerre sociale*, for its part, suffered for the polemical ardour of its editor, and the censors' intervention here was more of a political nature. A paper like *Le Petit Parisien*, which confined itself to major news, was less vulnerable.

These conclusions are by no means definitive, but one can already see that the censors were leaning increasingly towards political

---

7. A police list of 2,501 'most dangerous revolutionaries' in France, who were to be arrested the moment mobilisation was ordered: see J.-J. Becker, *Le Carnet B*.

interference.

One thing, however, is perfectly clear: the weight of censorship was growing apace, reaching out not only to this or that unsigned or subsidiary but also to the great names in French journalism and to the leader writers. On 17 September the 'Bulletin du Jour' in *Le Temps* fell foul of the censors; on 23 September it was almost an entire article by 'Junius' in *L'Echo de Paris*; on 24 September, it was the turn of Albert de Mun and on 26 September of General Cherfils, the military correspondent of *L'Echo de Paris*. *Le Petit Parisien* of 28 September had to make two cuts in an article by Lieutenant-Colonel Rousset, the military correspondent of that paper. Of an article by Daniel Renoult in *L'Humanité* of 14 September, nothing remained but the writer's initials; on 17 September there was a cut in an article by Jean Longuet, oddly enough a quotation from an article published in *Le Matin*. Gustave Hervé's article in *La Guerre sociale* of 2 October was reduced to his signature; the same thing happened again next day. Dismayed, he began his next article, which was finally allowed to appear, with: 'Is it worth my trouble to write at all?'

This spectacular tightening of the censor's hold on the French press was not the result of a relaxation of discipline on the part of French journalists, but followed in the wake of new ministerial instructions. On 19 September Millerand, the minister of war, had sent a circular to all regional commanders reiterating and clarifying his earlier instructions: restriction of special editions, no larger editions than before the war, no shouting out of papers on the public highway (news-vendors had to be 'no more than walking news-stands'), no sensational headlines, all headlines limited to two columns. Now these guidelines greatly extended the censor's prerogatives: it was reasonable that the press should be forbidden to 'publish anything that could give any indication of the movement of French troops'; it was understandable that a ban should be placed on 'false and excessively optimistic or pessimistic news' — 'the news published by the press in the south-east concerning the disembarkation of 250,000 Russians in France is a typical example — a ministerial circular stipulated; or that there should be a ban on 'stories of German atrocities which threaten to terrify the population, and to cause a most deplorable exodus'. But it was quite different to ban 'leading articles carrying violent attacks on the government or on the army high command', or 'articles encouraging the termination or suspension of hostilities'.

The minister of war thus set up a blatant and quite arbitrary form of political censorship.

Three days later, regional commanders were given a new directive. Millerand's colleagues had apparently objected to political censorship being placed in the hands of the military, so that a slight modification seemed called for:

> Bordeaux, 22 September 1914
> The French Cabinet believes that a distinction should be made between political censorship and military censorship of the press, and has delegated the task of scrutinising articles on the subject of internal affairs to representatives of the Minister of Interior.
> The circular I addressed to you on 19 September will therefore be modified. The general principles of censorship will remain the same, but the prefectorial authorities will now relieve you of the duty of curbing violent attacks on the government and of stopping potentially harmful press polemics . . .

Political censorship may have been transferred from the military to the prefectorial authorities, but it remained in force nevertheless.

In the circumstances, the increase in the censors' activities at the end of September shown in Fig. 2.1.1 was only to be expected, as was their increasing secrecy. The historian Camille Bloch, examining just thirteen dailies, counted forty-two articles devoted to the problems of censorship from 26 August to 1 December 1914. Some writers were in favour of the new measures, including Maurras, who, in an article in *L'Action française*, advanced reasons for accepting censorship even of political articles. Curiously, *La Guerre sociale*, too, though not overtly in favour of censorship, did at least publish a warning against excessive attacks on the government: 'Do not let us abdicate our right of criticism. But do not let us go too far, sowing unrest or bitterness in the minds of the people'. Admittedly these lines came from the pen of André Lichtenberger and not from that of Gustave Hervé, who did not spare his irony:

> Censorship is the institution that underpinned the greatness of our former kings and that still underpins the greatness of Russia.
> The censors do their job very well.
> What upheavals there would be. . .if we were allowed to tell the people how organised or. . .unorganised our health service is.
> All glory to the censors!
> May their scissors be blessed!
> They alone have intelligence, probity and patriotism enough to know what should be said. . . .
> The censors were very kind yesterday. They did not mutilate my article.

On 27 September, Hervé returned to the fray:

For some days now, there has been a growing misunderstanding between those wonderful patriots who wield the scissors of Anastasius at the press censorship office and the no less wonderful patriots who do the redoubtable work of journalists. . . .

With the perversity natural to journalists at all times, we persuade ourselves that censorship has been introduced for the sole purpose of preventing us from thoughtlessly divulging military secrets.

And after listing all the cuts suffered by *La Guerre sociale* without having so much as broached the subject of military secrets, Hervé continued:

The government would do well to tell us once and for all where the censors' rights begin and where they end, the more so since from now on we have two censorships, one military, the other civilian.

Let us hope that in order to reconcile these two we do not end up by restoring religious censorship!

And Hervé was not alone. In the *Echo de Paris*, Franc-Nohan argued:

The need for military censorship — even if it is not at all clear how the political criteria of the censors and their concern not to embarrass the High Command can differ appreciably from the same concern and the same patriotism that animate (to mention none except our own correspondents) General Cherfils or my friend Marcel Hutin — is one thing, but political censorship is quite a different matter! Where exactly do military questions end and purely political questions begin?

Alfred Capus of the Académie Française, writing in *Le Figaro*, attacked the kind of suspect and turbid censorship that 'might make one think the Republic was trying to threaten one of the very liberties on which it was founded', and recalled the name of the paper for which he wrote: 'Providing one does not mention the authorities, the government, politics, registered companies, banks, the wounded, German atrocities, or the postal services one may print anything freely with the blessings of two or three censors'.

However, the most determined enemy of censorship was Georges Clemenceau: 'Every man *endowed with good sense* will realise that censorship can only be applied to matters of military importance', he proclaimed. The result: *L'Homme libre* was suspended soon afterwards because Clemenceau refused to cut certain passages from an article. *L'Humanité* protested, but with enough restraint not to be censored in turn:

It is well known that we have never professed any great sympathy for M. Clemenceau, who, when he himself was in charge, did not always spare free men ['hommes libres'] and sometimes even muzzled them, but on the compelling principle of the liberty of the press and the right to write which ought to be fully respected by any republican regime, we deplore both[8] the repressive measures directed against this journalist.

Clemenceau himself did not become discouraged and continued his campaign against the censors. He described their *psychology* in an article entitled 'History without Morals': 'Whoever mentions a fault harms the national defence. . . . A fault that goes unmentioned does not count because no one can know about it. There might be people who suffer from it, but the public must be kept in ignorance of it . . . '.[9]

In November he devoted another five articles to the censors.

It is regrettable that we have no way of determining whether opposition to censorship, that is, ultimately, to the dictates of the military and civil authorities, remained confined to journalists or whether it was shared by their readers. In particular, we cannot tell how many readers shared the fears of the radical columnist, A. Moméja: 'The political future looks gloomy. Military censorship sets to work with stupid brutality. . . . The censors are naturally praised to the skies by the conservative press which they handle with consideration, while they proceed ruthlessly against the republican journals . . .'.

This observation may well have reflected a widespread opinion, but, in the event, it was false: with some exceptions, the conservative papers never showed great enthusiasm for censorship which, at least during that period, did not in fact treat it with particular consideration. Thus Franc-Nohain, writing in *L'Echo de Paris*, waxed indignant about a form of censorship that tried to protect 'politicians' responsible for the very shortcomings the military authorities were trying to repair!

The symmetrical character of these reactions is easily explained: to the left, the censors were the minions of 'clerical' generals; to the right, they were the tools of 'radical' prefects!

In reality the aim of censorship was not merely to prevent the propagation of news harmful to the army, nor was it to attack or support clericals or republicans, but, as the historian Georges Weill

8. The suspension of *L'Homme libre* was followed immediately by the suspension of *L'Homme enchaîné*, which Clemenceau had started in its place.
9. *L'Homme libre*, 23 October. For a time *L'Homme libre* reappeared in Paris at the same time as *L'Homme enchaîné* appeared in the provinces.

has stressed, to persuade the press to 'propagate ideas and sentiments likely to contribute to final victory'. And he added that this was the more essential as compulsory military service made no social distinctions, families of all classes having men at the front. Hence it was necessary to mould the *whole* of public opinion. This meant taking control of all information, which could not be reconciled with the idea of freedom of expression, however well-meaning.

How was this attempt to direct public opinion managed in practice? It is impossible to tell by looking at the papers themselves; in fact, most cuts were a consequence of the papers' own misinterpretations of official instructions. When they rigidly adhered to these instructions, at least in the view of the censors, the papers were left alone. For all that, the censors did make their mark, busily banning the publication and commentaries on this, and actively encouraging the propagation of that, press dispatch. Hence it is by a study of the dispatches that we can determine what attitudes the censors wanted to impose on public opinion. Lists of dispatches stopped or authorised exist from October onwards.[10]

In addition, a list of specific directives issued from 30 November to 16 December 1914, for example, makes the attitude of the censors even more patently obvious: their chief objective was the 'calming' of public opinion, that is, anaesthetising it by cutting all disturbing news and authorising the publication of all items that reflected any weakness, however slight, on the part of the enemy. Let us look at these directives first.

The following news items were authorised for publication: Germany is short of manpower because she is *vainly* trying to recruit Italian workers, all able-bodied Germans having been mobilised; the Central Powers have grave supply problems; there are shortages in Vienna, Trieste and also in cities in the occupied territories: in Malines, Antwerp and Louvain; shortages are also severe in Hungary; Fiume and other Austrian cities have asked the Italian government to save them from famine; grain has had to be rationed in Germany because of severe supply difficulties; Austria is in financial difficulties, her loan was undersubscribed; her sanitary conditions also leave much to be desired: cholera is spreading; Austrian soldiers suffering from frostbite in the Carpathians have had their legs amputated; the bad weather is having a bad effect on the health of the Germans. According to the Agence Fournier, confirmed by the Agence Havas, the Kaiser himself is in poor health; he has had a

10. Bibliothèque de Documentation Internationale Contemporaine, F 270 Res. Tac.

severe bout of influenza, and he is also about to have an
operation. . . . The situation in Hungary is particularly bad: discontent in growing; in Turkey the fleet is in open revolt, the women
are demonstrating against the war and the nation is opposed to
participation in the conflict. The German Chancellor, Bethmann-
Hollweg, has just missed being killed by a bomb; in Berlin there is a
rumour that a foreign airman has flown over the Krupp factories,
and even that bombs were dropped.

In this last case, however, the censors also authorised publication
of the formal German denial. Paradoxically, while the censors
passed news that German soldiers of the *Landwehr* sent to the front
were restless, they stopped a telegram to the effect that the *Land-
sturm* had refused to go to the front. Were they afraid that this news
item might set a bad example?

All dispatches confirming that the war had been engineered by
the Germans were of course passed, and so were those reporting
that the German socialists had been voting war credits and that
Liebknecht had been expelled from his party.

Also passed without question were eulogies of the French army
and its commander-in-chief, especially when they came from
abroad, and all expressions of British confidence in the Russian ally.

By contrast, when a French general, General Besset, committed
suicide at Versailles, the news was censored. The death of this
officer could not be made known except 'without reference to
suicide or to the circumstances preceding the retirement of General
Besset and his death'.

News *stopped* by the censors fell into various categories — apart
from those we cannot interpret. For instance, we cannot tell why,
on 30 November, a cable received by *Information* giving the number of prisoners taken by the Russians was censored.

All bad news was stopped, for instance, reports that the British
pits were beginning to close for lack of miners, that German
submarines were carrying out successful raids, that the Bulgarian
government was not allowing the transit of French arms destined
for Russia. Also stopped were critical comments, for instance by the
military correspondent of *The Times*, who argued that the current
situation was a result of mistakes in the planning and conduct of the
war; and distressing news items such as the report that amputations
were being performed in certain northern railway stations under
deplorable conditions.

Another forbidden category included news items likely to
weaken resolve at the front: there could be no references to favourable treatment of French prisoners in Germany, perhaps for fear

that some French soldiers might allow themselves to be captured too easily. No references to peace efforts were allowed either: a speech by President Wilson was censored because he declared himself the champion of world peace.

Nor could there by any mention of French politicians whose actions might encourage peace hopes, for instance of Caillaux. Thus news of his arrival in Brazil was stopped, and so were reports of his interviews with the minister of finance and later with the president.

Excessive optimism was also proscribed: the return of the government to Paris could not be presented in such a way as to encourage the view that the tide was about to turn.

Finally, no critical comments about France's allies could be published. Thus when Guesde, although a minister, spoke to an Italian journalist about relations between French socialism and *Russian imperialism*, his comments were censored.

A single list, covering a short period and chiefly concerned with news of foreign origin, does not, of course, allow us to give a clear definition of the censors' attitude. It is nevertheless possible to deduce the frame of mind the censors tried to foster in the French public, who needed to be encouraged to believe in German responsibility for the war, and to think that there was no alternative to the continuation of the war; equally, they had to be convinced that the Central Powers were in such difficulties that there were legitimate grounds to hope for an Allied victory, albeit there could not exist the slightest suggestion that this victory might be imminent.

From the list of news items passed and barred by the censors, we gain the impression that they preferred to encourage an atmosphere of resigned acceptance of a conflict that must inevitably continue for some considerable time, rather than to whip up public opinion, which might have been dangerous, since an excess of enthusiasm, unless followed by positive achievements, could have provoked an excess of despair.

The nature of the conflict rapidly led the censors to a preoccupation not only with French public opinion, but also with attempts to influence public opinion in neutral countries. As Georges Weill has remarked: 'There was a very strange psychological phenomenon: each of the warring nations persuaded itself that its government had neglected propaganda, whereas the enemy, on the contrary, had been most effective.' Thus the French 'spoke with secret dread of the Germans' infernal ingenuity', while the Germans believed that the fury aroused among neutrals about the cruelties committed in

Belgium was the result of a well-orchestrated propaganda campaign.

On 6 August, *L'Humanité* used the headline: 'Europe united against German aggression', and even at the beginning of September Pastor Monod could preach: 'Except for a few people momentarily exploited by a lying press, all the nations of the world have their eyes fixed on our country, eyes burning with the most ardent sympathy... World opinion is on our side ...'.

A few days later, however, this ardent sympathy appeared to be no longer quite so evident, since in two successive issues of *L'Humanité*, first Edouard Vaillant and then Pierre Renaudel had to explain the need for a world-wide propaganda campaign to offset that of the Germans, and to prove that Germany bore sole responsibility for the war.

Foreign opinion was in fact far from unanimous in its support of France, the less so as, whatever the sympathy, it was felt that French chances of victory were doubtful. French diplomats abroad testified to a variety of opinions: 'The state of mind of the people in and around Basle is deeply hostile to us, as is that of many officers of German-Swiss contingents stationed in that region', the French representative in Switzerland wrote; his report was confirmed by the special commissioner in Pontarlier: 'The general attitude of the population of German Switzerland is pro-German'.

Romain Rolland remarked on the same phenomenon in his *Journal* on 16 August: 'The whole of French Switzerland is in a rage against the Germans... On the other hand, the lower-middle class in Switzerland is pro-German'. A few days later he wrote: 'The rift between French Switzerland and German Switzerland is becoming more pronounced. In the latter, pro-German demonstrations are increasing in number'.

However, on 21 August the French military attaché wrote: 'Public opinion about us in German Switzerland seems to be calming down'.

The Spanish press, too, was lukewarm: though it published a great deal of news of French origin, it did so with 'some scepticism'. The French military attaché reported the view of a Spanish journalist that 'all the neutral countries have an interest in seeing that none of the belligerents wins an outright victory, lest the small powers be dominated by it'.

A similar response was elicited by an article in the *Diario Universal* which claimed that the French government had put pressure on Spain to abandon its neutrality and espouse the French cause. A confidential note from Hendaye to the ministry of foreign affairs on 25 August put it as follows: 'It seems that Spanish public opinion is not prepared to go further than the benevolent neutrality towards us she has practised until now, and that the transformation of that neutrality into an alliance would provoke serious opposition . . . '.

In Sweden things were worse: 'The general tone of the Swedish press is one of confidence in the final victory of Germany, thanks to her superiority in numbers, organisation and an invincible will to vanquish that surmounts all obstacles'.

This attitude was reinforced by the French defeats: 'Those Swedish papers which have remained sympathetic to us are shaken by the rapid advance of the Germans, and are astonished that, with the forces they believe us to have, we were unable to put up more resistance . . . '.

The French representative in Sweden also noted that the Swedish press offset French protests against the arson and murders committed by the German troops with 'stories of crimes of which the Germans accuse the *franc–tireurs* and French and Belgian civilians; they [the Swedish press] are clearly indifferent to evils they have not suffered themselves and give their readers to understand that both sides exaggerate . . .'.

American public opinion, on the other hand, was more satisfactory; the French ambassador in Washington cabled: 'Despite the efforts and the communiqués of the German Embassy. . . American public opinion is clearly and warmly in our favour, and conspicuously so'.

Thus, contrary to what people seemed to believe in France, at least during the first few days of the war, world public opinion was not uniformly in favour of the *Entente*. This was not a matter without significance, because the French belief in the justice of their cause, in being the victims of aggression, was greatly strengthened by the idea that the whole world — apart from the Central Powers — sided with them. Had French public opinion realised that this was not the case, its faith could well have been shaken. Hence the demand by French papers that the authorities do their utmost to counter the effects of German propaganda. The French government, which had never expected this challenge, was hard pressed to meet it effectively.

Banning the importation of foreign newspapers into France might have led people to believe that this step was intended to suppress bad news. The authorities accordingly hesitated to do so. Thus, on 29 August, when *La Stampa* headlined an Anglo-French defeat at Saint-Quentin, the prefect of the department of Alpes-Maritimes contented himself with seizing the issue at the border, and so did not have to ban it. He dealt with other Italian papers in the same way.

The second method was to exert pressure on foreign journals and so prevent the publication of 'false news'. Following an official telegram from Paris on 13 August, *La Tribune de Genève* explained that it would carry no further dispatches from the German Wolf Agency without express mention of its source, and that it would always be happy to give prominence to any Havas dispatches it received. The paper went on to explain: 'Had the Agence Havas been allowed to flood us a little more, and flooding there has been, then the Wolf Agency would not doubt have flooded us a little less'.

In the case of the *Tribune de Genève*, therefore, the French policy of keeping quiet during the early period of the war worked against the desired effect.

The third method was to exert discreet diplomatic pressure on foreign governments: thus the prefect of Alpes-Maritimes intervened with the Italian consul-general in Nice to good effect. . . at least for the time being. On 26 August, the prefect complained again about the Italian paper *Secolo*, which had dwelt at length on the German victories in Lorraine but had reduced the battles in Upper Alsace to 'incidents of war', but this time he felt that it was up to the ministry of foreign affairs to intervene directly with the Italian authorities. Similarly, the French ambassador to Sweden, indignant about the 'odious comments' of certain papers which published French bulletins under the heading: 'How the French lull public opinion', intervened 'energetically' with the Swedish minister of foreign affairs, asking him, 'despite the freedom of the press, to call on those papers to display the impartiality demanded of them by the neutrality of their country'.

The last method, finally, was to *buy* foreign newspapers. But this was not easy, as the French ambassador to Sweden discovered:

Three Stockholm papers are openly pro-German. . . . The radical or socialist papers tend to be on our side, but without believing in a French victory either. A subsidy could only be paid to a second-class paper, whose already indifferent influence would be reduced to nil once it was suspected of having been 'bought'. [The ambassador concluded with some sagacity that the best propaganda would be] a decisive victory.

He was, of course, quite right, the more so as the number of readers of the Swedish press in France must have been few and far between.

Attempts to influence thought through the control of information and of public opinion were bound to be rudimentary during the first few months of the war, but the authorities soon came to think that such control was a matter of primary importance. In time, therefore, any gaps through which news influencing French public opinion adversely might have passed were effectively sealed.

By and large, as *L'Histoire générale de la presse* concludes, the ends seem to have justified the means. So much so that, for example, French censorship must take the credit for making sure the German general staff were kept unappraised of the gravity of the crisis of French army morale in the spring of 1917.

To the question: how could so excitable and so volatile a nation show so much constancy during so protracted a war, our analysis of the censors' procedure bring the first glimmer of an answer: there is no doubt that by leaving it in ignorance of the gravity of certain military defeats, of diplomatic failures and of the horrors of the war, censorship went a long way towards helping the French civilian front to stand firm.

CHAPTER 3

Political Movements and Trade Unions: Revival or Lethargy?

When the authorities began to mould public opinion, the political movements and the trade unions might have been expected to act as a counterweight, guarding or re-creating free thought in the country, the more so as, having all but called a halt to their former activities during the first month of the war, they realised that unless they staged a comeback, they would simply disappear. This applied especially to such organisations as the Socialist Party and the Confédération Générale du Travail (CGT, General Federation of Labour) on the left and Action Française on the right.

Action Française

Action Française seemed particularly slow to recover its momentum. Thus, in April 1915, the Préfecture (Paris police headquarters) reported that 'the reactionary opposition which has been dormant since the beginning of hostilities, and which apparently wished to eschew militant action during the war, has perceptibly changed its attitude during the past two months'. It was therefore not until the beginning of 1915 that groups of the Action Française, which had been crippled by the call-up of successive classes, were reorganised, that its scattered militants came together again and, moreover, engaged in activities that the authorities considered to be 'a flagrant violation of the patriotic self-restraint advocated and displayed by the leaders of the movement'. It was at this stage that Henri Vaugeois, 'commercial traveller in royalist propaganda', visited the west, the centre and the south of France, and that royalist propaganda began to be disseminated among the troops, particularly among the wounded.

Government informers considered that the revival of Action Française was connected with the belief that the end of hostilities would lead to a *violent reaction* in favour of the radical right. However, it still took an organisation as lively as Action Française six months to relaunch itself. It had felt no need to do so earlier, because the war reflected its own aspirations: it was enough to let events take their course for the movement to flourish.

The attitude of socialists and the trade unions was bound to be different, since, when all was said and done, the war was a setback to their aspirations. They needed time to recover: as the Russian socialist Martov wrote to his compatriot Axelrod on 19 August 1914:[1] 'Little by little one becomes used to living in an atmosphere of world-wide catastrophe, but I felt completely disorientated during the first few days . . .'.

The Socialist Party

Anyone examining the Prefecture records of meetings held in Paris[2] might be persuaded that all socialist meetings had been called off, at least until 28 August. The reality was different: the 'Social Life' column of *L'Humanité*, which published daily announcements of meetings, shows that various party branches and their committees, together with young socialist groups, met throughout August and at the rate of several meetings a day. Thus there were four meetings on the 12th, five on the 13th, six on the 14th, nine on the 15th, twenty on the 16th, eight on the 17th. . . . In September the meetings continued: *L'Humanité* announced five meetings on the 10th, six on the 12th, eighteen on the 13th, seven on the 16th. . . .

With the help of these announcements in *L'Humanité* it is possible to draw up a summary of meetings held by various branches of the Socialist Party, or at least of their committees in the department of Seine, during October, November and December 1914 (Table 1).

To judge by appearances, at least, socialist activity never flagged.

1. Quoted by Francis Conte, *Christian Rakovski 1873–1941*.
2. APP B A 748.

Table 1. Socialist Party branch meetings, Seine, October–December 1914

Week ending	Number of meetings
October 10	53
17	43
24	45
31	37
November 7	52
14	51
21	46
28	47
December 5	43
12	48

The average was 44.5 meetings per week in October, 49 in November and 45.5. in December.

This conclusion was confirmed by the Renseignements Généraux (branch of the ministry of the interior which collected political, economic and social information): they stressed that some branches of the Seine federation, 'considered among the most important', were meeting at 'fairly frequent intervals', or that 'very many if not very large' meetings were being organised by branches of the United Socialist Party in Paris and the suburbs. In general, however, the number of people attending these meetings does not appear to have been very great.

On 3 September, a meeting of the liaison committee of the Young Socialists in Seine was attended by 60 young men and 3 young women, which was a fairly good attendance, but a branch meeting of the Socialist Party held the same day in the XIth arrondissement was attended by about a dozen militants only; a branch meeting in the XIXth arrondissement was attended by some 20 persons, including 7 or 8 women. At the time politics was, indeed, considered a male prerogative, but in its announcements column L'Humanité stressed the presence of the wives of serving soldiers.

On 2 October, 15 young people attended a meeting of the Young Socialists, 32 men and 9 women went to a branch meeting in the XXth arrondissement; 6 were at Vanves, 15 at Lilas, 9, including 3 women, in the XIth arrondissement, a dozen at Perreux, 8 in the XIXth arrondissement. By contrast, no fewer than 120 people attended a party meeting in the XXth arrondissement on 16 October, while attendance that day was very poor at meetings in the XIIth and XIIIth arrondissements and at Pré-Saint-Gervais. . . .

These figures are too scanty to allow reliable conclusions; we may nevertheless take it that socialist meetings did not attract a very large number of militants. And however large the number of socialists away at the front, there were certainly many more left behind than continued to attend meetings. On 30 December 1914, only 300 militants renewed their party membership in Paris and the department of the Seine (in 1914 the Seine federation had counted 9,516 members).

The objectives of these meetings were generally fairly non-political, the sole items on the agenda being aid for soldiers' families, unemployment, correspondence, rents: in a word solidarity and the wish to ameliorate economic hardships caused by the war. In fact, it was often announced that 'no politics' would be discussed at these meetings.

Thus the meetings held on 28 August were expressly called 'to foster solidarity and mutual aid'. Those held on 3 September in the XIth arrondissement were in aid of the unemployed, and at Aubervilliers for the purpose of organising a soup kitchen. On 13 September, the socialist section of the XVIIth arrondissement held a 'grand family matinée', the proceeds of which were intended for the 'alleviation of war suffering'.

Politics was not, however, completely ignored: on 3 September, the Young Socialists decided not only to organise a 'farewell punch' in honour of the class of 1915 but also to republish the *Voix de jeunes* in order to 'reply to attacks by reactionaries'; on 12 September, it was announced that Frédéric Brunet, the deputy for the XVIIth arrondissement, would be reviewing recent events; on 2 October, Pierre Dumas, a trade unionist, chaired a party meeting in the XXth arrondissement and informed the audience that he had joined an action committee 'formed several days before mobilisation by members of the CGT and the PS [Socialist Party] for the express purpose of stemming the tide of reaction'. 'The Nationalists are beginning to hold up their heads', he said, 'and reactionaries in the XXth arrondissement are already resuming their propaganda campaign and distributing pamphlets advising the working class to "pray for our soldiers". Earlier, in August, addressing the same branch in the XXth arrondissement, the Parisian socialist leader, Paul Fribourg, explained that France had not wanted this war, that she was not waging it against the German people, but against an emperor 'whose removal we desire for the good of all mankind'.

As far as it is possible to tell, socialist activity in the provinces was even less pronounced. The presence of a number of members of parliament in Bordeaux made it possible to hold a large meeting of the socialist branch of that city on 19 September. The deputies explained why socialist ministers had joined the government: they had remained representatives of the working class, but their participation in government activities was needed to prevent the 'capitalist bourgeoisie, which has not renounced the pursuit of its own interests', from taking advantage of the situation. Elsewhere, there were scarcely any signs of activity, except in Brest where the local branch held two meetings, the first in August and the second in November.

In the Parisian region, Socialist Party groups continued to function, at least formally so. The members met regularly, and, as Amédée Dunois wrote in *L'Humanité* in connection with a branch meeting of the Socialist Party in Bordeaux, '. . . although deprived of the youngest elements, it did not think it necessary to adjourn until after the war'. And adjournment was widely considered a possible alternative, because most people still believed that the war would be short enough to justify the suspension of political agitation.

However, this activity was the work of a very small number of militants and, in any case, was more of a humanitarian than of a political character. There are some indications nevertheless that a few socialist leaders felt the need to explain themselves, from which it is only fair to deduce that rank-and-file members had been voicing reservations.

There was, it seems, a wide divergence between the wish of the activists to maintain political activity and the reality of political life. Thus when A. Dunois wrote, once again in connection with a meeting of the Bordeaux branch, that 'meetings like yesterday's attest that the socialist idea has fully preserved its vigour', he was being disingenuous.

Is the explanation perhaps to be found in disillusionment with a party that had not fulfilled its mission? There are no data or documents to bear out this interpretation. What does appear to have happened, however, is that once war had been declared, many socialists saw no further reason for political activity. Besides, the leaders of the party never tried to give the movement a fresh impetus. They had been forced to reorganise very quickly after the depletion of their ranks by death and mobilisation. At *L'Humanité* Jean Jaurès had been replaced by a management committee led by Pierre Renaudel, the paper's business manager. In the same way as *L'Humanité* did not stop publication, so the leading party officials met at fairly regular intervals, but mainly for the purpose of examining such problems as the payment of rents, the evacuation of children and the repatriation of members from the provinces. The socialist group in parliament also met regularly, at least in committee, but the minutes of these meetings do not reflect a flourish of political activity. Thus, at the permanent committee of the group meeting on 10 September under the chairmanship of Henri Sellier, a councillor from Puteaux, Vaillant spoke about milk distribution, Sellier about the possibility of bringing in large stocks of foodstuffs to replenish supplies, Pierre Laval and Weber, both deputies from the department of the Seine, proposed to intervene with the director of civil affairs in the military government and Jean Longuet quoted two articles from the *Daily Citizen*. At the next meeting of the same group two days later under the chairmanship of Mayeras, the deputy from Alfortville, Vaillant, was concerned about refrigeration, Gaston Lévy about the price of meat, Merrheim, the trade-union leader present by special invitation, about methods of work allocation and finally Laval and Marcel Cahin about the deferment of bakery workers.

All these questions were, of course, of some importance, but they were unlikely to boost the spirit of party workers.

In fact, if one looks at all the documents compiled by the Socialist Party during that period, one finds that not a single political declaration was issued by the CAP (Permanent Administrative Committee), by the socialist group in parliament or by the editors of *L'Humanité* between 27 August, when the party published a manifesto, and 25 December when socialist ministers joined the government and released a further statement.

One has the feeling that if the engine of the Socialist Party was indeed still 'ticking over', the vehicle itself was running in neutral.

The Confédération Générale du Travail (CGT: General Federation of Labour)

More so than even the political parties, the trade unions, made up chiefly of active members who were generally of the right age to be called up, were drained of their lifeblood by the outbreak of war. Moreover, one cannot avoid the impression that during the early period of the war, the leaders of the CGT were resigned to suspending all activities during what was expected to be a war of short duration. 'The central committee', a report stated, 'closed its accounts on 4 August. Membership fees will no longer be paid.' What with most active members away in the army, trade-union life was bound to go into hibernation.

The Préfecture put it as follows on 31 October: 'The vitality of the unions has suffered a considerable decline; however, some have managed to maintain a degree of activity, among them the building workers' union, even though, for lack of funds, it has been forced to cut down on the number of officials.' For the rest, the union had been urging members to demand a full return to work and had drawn their attention to the possible difficulties they might have to face in that area as well as to possible attempts by employers to cut wages. It had asked all members in work to send in their membership dues.

At a meeting of the Association of Trade Unions in the department of the Seine, held on 3 August, the secretary, Bled, placed the union premises at the disposal of the chief health inspector of the Paris market. He then turned his attention to the organisation of 'communist soup kitchens', which opened on 17 August and began to distribute 6,000 meals every day.

Before the war, the association had comprised 200 affiliated unions, including 50 with a very small membership even in peace time. Their existence now became precarious, and some of them survived only thanks to older activists. Others, on the contrary, continued to be active, among them the stonemasons, the bricklayers, the metalworkers, the engineers, the clothing workers, the leather workers and the shoemakers.

Only the union of *terrassiers* (representing labourers on building sites, excavations; navvies) gave the authorities some cause for concern. During the last two weeks in August large numbers of men were needed to throw up defence works round Paris: many of these men were sent by the union of *terrassiers* and were paid the going trade-union rate, namely, 0.90 francs per hour. However, we are told, they were remarkable for 'an excess of apathy resulting in an output very much below normal'.

The military engineers then turned to the 'free' labour exchanges (as distinct from the *bourses du travail*) and to the town halls, which supplied workers whose wage was from 0.60 to 0.65 francs, and who, although not navvies by trade, had the great advantage of being disciplined and hardworking. Their employment led to a conflict with the unionised labour they had ousted on some sites. At Voisins-le-Bretonneux and at Guyancourt the two groups of 'yellow and red' clashed violently, and Hubert, the secretary of the union of *terrassiers*, protested in *La Bataille syndicaliste* against the employment of 'yellow' workers. Officers were injured and legal proceedings were taken against Hubert. He was defended by Pierre Laval, found guilty and sentenced to one month in prison.

Apart from these unions, about a hundred or so others also held meetings to discuss unemployment, mutual aid, the distribution of soup and meal coupons and cash aid.

Before the war, the Associated Committee of Young Trade Unionists had been considered a particularly revolutionary organisation, but following the conscription of most of its active members it was all but disbanded. As for the CGT daily, *La Bataille syndicaliste*, its print run had fallen by more than half, from 46,000 to 20,000 copies, of which about 30 per cent remained unsold. In the circumstances, the paper, which had found it hard to survive even before the war, was threatened with closure.[3] *La Voix du Peuple*, the CGT weekly, and the bulletin of the Seine Association of Trade Unions both ceased publication.

All in all, in the judgment of the government officials appointed to watch over it, 'the trade-union movement has experienced a period of complete stagnation since mobilisation'. The organisation was 'skeletal'. That opinion was no doubt exaggerated. There may not have been very much trade-union activity, since circumstances did not permit it, but the unions did not decamp, and the clashes between the military authorities and the unionised navvies showed that the old dynamism had not vanished altogether.

We know very little about trade-union activity in the provinces: the *bourse du travail* in Bordeaux, in which the Renseignements Généraux took a special interest when the government moved to that city, barely made its presence felt.

Though signs of trade-union activity elsewhere were very sparse, there are some indications that it was never totally suspended.

On 21 August, the police commissioner of Montceau-les-Mines reported to the prefect of his department that the miners' union was protesting against the extension of the working day to eleven hours from 19 August. The socialist mayor and deputy, Bouveri, remarked that the miners could not be expected to work such long hours unless they were properly fed, which was impossible because the military authorities had requisitioned all available supplies.

At the same time, the Loire miners' union in Saint-Etienne also protested against the extra hours the companies wanted to introduce and insisted on compliance with the eight-hour law.

In December, there were fresh protests by miners in Montceau-les-Mines: while they agreed to continue their efforts 'in the interests of the war effort', they felt that the new demands were excessive

---

3. Renamed *La Bataille* on 3 November 1915, the journal managed to survive until 31 December 1920.

and injurious to their health. The local police inspector listed a number of complaints against the young miners. According to him, these were the result of *the secret influence* of the miners' union which insisted, despite the war, on *making a show of strength*. The inspector did not, however, believe that they posed a serious threat, because 'most miners at Montceau-les-Mines are on deferment and hence under military orders. They cannot fail to realise what untoward repercussions they could suffer from following the directives of a workers' movement that has no justified claims'.

The overall impression, therefore, is that, like the Socialist Party, the trade unions suffered a greater drop in activity at leadership level than they did among the rank and file. That was also the impression of the government observers: after having mentioned the activities of several unions, they concluded that 'the main organs — the Association of Trade Unions in the department of the Seine, and the CGT — do not evince a great deal of activity'. Thus, though they did not mention this particular example, by 18 December the central committee of the Trade Unions Association in the department of the Seine had met just twice since mobilisation.

This does not mean, of course, that the leadership of the CGT had ceased to exist but, shaken by events and torn by contrary currents, it no longer took an interest in anything except the running of internal affairs, thus making it tempting to reduce the history of the CGT during that period to the growing antagonism from September onwards between Jouhaux, its general secretary, and Merrheim, secretary of the Federation of Metalworkers. Historians of the CGT disagree about the moment the conflict started, a moment that is of some importance for determining the date of the birth of organised opposition to the war. Annie Kriegel believes that in September 'Merrheim and Jouhaux still did not think of each other. . .as being in opposite camps', and that whatever differences they had were 'occasional, tactical and concerned with detail'. The Russian historian Dalin, however, believes that this interpretation is not supported by an examination of Merrheim's personal archives, 'kept in the Institute of Marxism–Leninism and not consulted before', and that from September Jouhaux and Merrheim looked upon each other as adversaries.

The affair was summed up by Merrheim himself in a letter to Pierre Monatte dated 29 September 1914.

During the very first days of September, Jouhaux had agreed to become a 'delegate to the Nation', 'in a personal capacity'. These delegates or commissioners to the Nation had no clearly defined task, but Jouhaux's appointment meant that on the morning of 3 September he left Paris for Bordeaux accompanied by Griffuelhes. Learning of this by chance, Merrheim flew into a violent rage and demanded that instead of leaving, Jouhaux summon the federal committee. The ensuing meeting was stormy, but despite the opposition of Merrheim supported by Lenoir, another secretary of the metalworkers' union, Jouhaux left for Bordeaux all the same accompanied by several CGT leaders. In his absence, Merrheim became acting secretary of the CGT.

At Bordeaux, Jouhaux's attempts to demonstrate that the job of commissioner to the Nation was not without substance, and also to organise a series of meetings throughout France, came to nothing, but not before Merrheim had issued a series of sharp protests. Having come to Paris to justify himself before a federal committee meeting on 27 September, Jouhaux, under violent attack, tendered his resignation and went back to Bordeaux, but returned to Paris a few days later to resume his post at the head of the CGT.

The crux of the dispute was that, while Jouhaux saw himself as some kind of revolutionary 'missionary',[4] his adversaries saw him as nothing but a 'class collaborator'. Merrheim, like the other union leaders, had accepted the war, but not the idea that the CGT should be turned into a government institution. His position was, moreover, strengthened by the scant respect the government showed for Jouhaux's good offices.

The leaders of the CGT in Bordeaux gained the impression, as one of them put it, that they had been 'taken for a ride' by the minister of the interior, and felt the more incensed about it as their collaboration with the government was likely to be held against them by the working class after the war. It did not take Jouhaux long to realise that he and those who had accompanied him to Bordeaux had compromised themselves for nothing, which rendered their situation awkward to say the least, and even a little ridiculous.

Hence, though there were strong differences between the leaders of the CGT, it is difficult to tell whether they felt these differences to be insurmountable. It seems unlikely that old comrades should, within days, have reached a point of no return, although Merrheim's 'we'll know what to do after the war' may have reflected a wish to settle accounts within a period which, at the time, still meant a few weeks.

4. B. Georges and D. Tintant: *Léon Jouhaux, cinquante ans du syndicalisme.*

It is also difficult to determine what effects these polemics had on
the rank and file. It does not appear that they caused many ripples.
Despite the criticisms of some militant building workers, 'the
policies of the CGT and the Association of Trade Unions have the
approval of their members . . .'. That at least was the view of the
Préfecture.

In fact, the trade-union leaders themselves were more concerned
about their lack of activity than about their differences of opinion.
Merrheim wrote that 'the administrative life of the CGT is non-
existent for the time being, and it is essential to give it a most
energetic impetus without delay if the death of the CGT is to be
averted'.

The Committees of Action

The period under review nevertheless saw an initiative of socialist
and trade-union organisations which, though it did not have
marked repercussions at the time, was a completely new departure.

Relations between the CGT and the Socialist Party had been very
tenuous, owing either to indifference or to hostility, mainly on the
part of the CGT. During the last days of July 1914, however, the
trade unions, incapable of devising their own strategy for saving the
peace, had been forced to approach the Socialist Party, and as a
result their ties were renewed in September.

On 9 September 1914, the federal executive of the CGT appointed a delegation which was to contact the Socialist Party for the
purpose of setting up a joint 'committee of action'. In fact, though
the first meeting took place that day, the CGT federal executive had
taken the decision as early as 3 September. Their approach was well
received by the socialists, at least by the deputies and the representatives of the Seine federation, who, according to a communiqué
published the next day in *L'Humanité* and *La Bataille syndicaliste*,
thanked the trade union delegates warmly for their move and
assured them that it 'agreed' with their own feelings. From the
outset the socialists outnumbered the trade unionists on the committee by eleven to seven.

Officially the aim of the committees of action was 'to tighten the
links between active members and their organisations, so that all can
play the most useful role in the present circumstances, and to
cooperate with the authorities in all areas affecting the life of the
working-class population (supplies, unemployment, soup kitchens,
allowances, etc.) and in the field of national defence'.

In the event, the committee largely focused attention on problems concerning the day-to-day life of Parisians. On 10 September it was split up into eight sub-committees:

(1) Allowances and benefits (secretary: Cachin)
(2) Rent (secretary: Vaillant)
(3) Work and unemployment (secretary: Merrheim)
(4) Information on wounded soldiers (secretary: Lévy)
(5 & 6) Prisoners and clothing, gifts to soldiers (secretary: Poisson)
(7) Ambulances, aid to refugees (secretary: Broemer)
(8) Provisions (secretary: Roldes).

The most important of these committees was that of work and unemployment, run by the two secretaries of the metalworkers' union, Merrheim and Lenoir. It included many socialists, among them Pierre Renaudel, Pierre Laval and Jean Longuet. The sub-committee intervened constantly and vigorously with the minister of war, protesting particularly against the cut in wages imposed on the navvies employed at the fortified camp in Paris, and on metal- and clothing-workers supplying the army.

The authorities were not opposed to the committee of action, which they believed confined itself largely to rendering what help it could to the civil administration and military authorities.

The committee of action itself – as its very name indicates – had originally had much wider ambitions. This is how Merrheim put it in a letter dated 28 September 1914:

> Since at the time there were reasons to fear an imminent siege of Paris by the Germans and the rise of a reactionary movement, the committee was given a mandate to contact the PSU [United Socialist Party] for the purpose of setting up a committee of action that would help to frustrate possible reactionary moves. This committee is concerned with the examination of a variety of problems.

The political implications of the creation of the committee of action did not escape the observers from the Renseignements Généraux: 'In reality its founders seem to have aimed at pursuing Jaurès's project of forging a union of socialists and trade unionists on the political as well as on the economic plane.'

The prefect of police, having noted the effectiveness of the committee of action and the 'prestige' it enjoyed in the eyes of the population, 'of which the Socialist Party and the CGT would certainly be able to take advantage after the cessation of hostilities', also stressed that 'certain activists even believe that the committee of action will survive the war and will prepare the way for the union of socialism and trade unionism advocated by Jaurès'.

The creation of the committee of action and its brief existence have been ignored by most historians. However, as Annie Kriegel remarked, it was 'a serious violation of the Charter of Amiens',[5] a complete disruption of the established relationship between the political and industrial wings of the French working class. Suddenly a situation had been created which Jaurès had tried so hard to bring about before the war. A posthumous triumph for the socialist leader, the committee of action thus heralded major changes in the structure of the French workers' movement.

Faced with their inability to affect the course of events, and with the erosion of their power by the war, socialists and trade unionists alike realised the importance of making a common stand. Their very impotence in the present forced them, more or less consciously, to open new paths into the future.

The continuation of the war and a series of new circumstances led to the collapse of the embryonic action, but it is important to remember that beneath the lethargy of the workers' movement a new balance of forces was beginning to emerge.

Did the political forces and the trade unions experience a revival or were they in a state of lethargy? With some qualification, we have to plump for the second option. Faced with a conformist and muzzled press, the political organisations did not dare to voice an unorthodox point of view. The trade unions behaved in much the same way, the more so as the leadership of the CGT had been put out of joint by the continuation of the war. The tactical differences between them nevertheless show that some of them felt the movement had gone too far along the road of national consensus. Is it therefore here that we must look for the seeds of organised resistance to the war?

5. The *Charte d'Amiens* laid down the complete independence of the trade unions from political parties and stressed the essentially revolutionary nature of the trade unions.

CHAPTER 4

The Anti-War Current

The first months of the First World War have often been scrutinised by historians of the labour movement in an attempt to detect the birth of a war-resistance movement and to record the evidence for it. Undoubtedly the beginning was slow. Even the most fervent revolutionaries seemed very unsure about what to think and what to do. Lenin argued early on, in October, that the *imperialist* war must be transformed into *civil* war; but another 'internationalist', Christian Rakovsky, 'admitted frankly that because of the complexity of the problem, he had been unable to tell in 1914 what form the opposition [to the war] should have taken'. Rakovsky also admitted that, at the beginning of the war, the fact that the great majority of French and German socialists had seen fit to vote for war credits had not struck him as being a 'radical departure from the old socialist tactics'; he agreed implicitly that he would have done the same in their place.

The Labour Movement

A report published at the end of the war by the Renseignements Généraux made an appraisal of anti-war activity during the war.[1] Strongly biased as it was against all forms of pacifism, it exaggerated the importance of the pacifist movement in an attempt to shake up the politicians and to force them to a more vigorous reaction. The preamble clearly reflects this attitude:

1. AN F 7 13372, *Rapport sur la propagande pacifiste de 1914 à 1918.*

Former agitators who had stayed behind were waiting for the soldiers to grow weary or the people's misery to become insupportable and, having been unable to prevent the war, they were all the more determined to impose a premature peace by engaging in agitation among the people, regardless of the consequences. Their agitation before the war was called anti-militarism and internationalism: it is now called *pacifism*.

There is not a minute to lose [the preamble concluded] if we are to avoid insurmountable difficulties within a very short time.

It is not surprising that with this attitude the authors of the report included practically anything that seemed to support their thesis, so much so that the first part (there were six others), entitled: 'Pacifism among the working class', ran to 125 typewritten pages!

However, as they were unable to mention more than a few tangible facts during the first months of the war, the gist of their argument was that the 'agitators', frightened at first, particularly by Carnet B, had taken courage again as soon as they realised that they would be left at liberty.

A resolution adopted at a meeting of the federal committee of the CGT on 29 November 1914, was the first to be blamed on 'pacifism': though they refused to send delegates to the socialist conference in Copenhagen, the federal committee decided 'timidly', by *21 votes to 20*, 'that all peace efforts should be warmly welcomed'.

More remarkable was a manifesto entitled *Pourquoi je démissionne du comité confédéral* [Why I am resigning from the federal committee] by 'the anarchist Monatte', one of the committee's 'most prominent members', which gave as his grounds the belief that the leaders of the CGT were too half-hearted and had betrayed their principles. From that moment, the report continued, the committee consisted of two factions, 'those who, without renouncing their revolutionary principles, believed that nothing must be done to impede the arduous work of government, and those, led by Merrheim and Bourderon, who intended to take advantage of any circumstances that might favour the advent of social revolution'.

In the thirty-four pages devoted to the anarchists, the report includes a manifesto by Sébastien Faure, 'Pour la Paix' ('For Peace') dated December 1914, as its first piece of tangible evidence.

The pacifism of the socialists was dealt with in 150 pages; the socialists included 'men who have the temerity to trample the *Union sacrée* underfoot and to foment for motives of future domination the most dangerous dissension in a country under arms . . .'. As early as November 1914, the socialist group in Oyonnax had sent a letter to all groups in the federation in the department of Ain, calling for an extraordinary meeting of the national executive of the party. Members of the same group also posted anti-war stickers on the walls of Oyonnax.

On 13 December, Lafitte, of the Vincennes branch and a member of the staff of *L'Humanité*, published a circular in which he declared: 'If the Germans leave French territory, peace with them [should] be signed immediately.'

The report mentioned no activity by the members of the teachers' union (thirty-one pages of the report) before February 1915. On 14 January the federal committee of that union was resuscitated under the promptings of its treasurer, Loriot, and of the assistant secretary, Hélène Brion: its first step was to take up the case of Julia Bertrand, a teacher from Vosges, who had been dismissed on 11 October 1914, 'for spreading unpatriotic ideas on the duty of individuals in wartime'.

Another report was devoted to Russian revolutionaries;[2] it alleged that in November, 1914: 'Despite the war and the state of siege in Paris, a form of propaganda that is not merely anti-tsarist but anti-militarist and patently pro-German is being disseminated by Russian émigrés and refugees in Paris'. This campaign was blamed on Victor Chernov, 'a member of the Russian Socialist Revolutionary Party', and on 'his two lieutenants, Martov and Lunacharsky, two well-known social democrats'.[3] At meetings held on Sundays at 76 rue Mouffetard, they called for 'heroic acts', but 'against the war and those who had caused it'.

Though the anti-war movement was small in the autumn of 1914, though its traces are almost indiscernible, it existed all the same. But when did it begin and what was its impact on public opinion?

The turning-point appears to have come in November 1914, though this statement needs to be qualified. As we saw, anti-war ripples appeared within the CGT as early as September; in fact, Pierre Monatte contended that opposition to the war began to be voiced as soon as part of the federal committee moved to Bordeaux, but it was only towards the end of November that he became convinced that the differences between him and the majority of the CGT leadership demanded a public stand.

2. AN F 7 13074. M 12/5 U.
3. The Russian labour movement was deeply divided on the question of the war, but Chernov, one of the leaders of the Socialist Revolutionary Party, was an 'internationalist', and so was Martov, who was not in fact one of his 'lieutenants' but a leading Menshevik. Lunacharsky, for his part, was the future Bolshevik commissar for education.

Raymond Lefebvre, for his part, had this to say six years later at the Socialist Congress in Strasbourg, in February 1920: 'We did not for a single second accept the *Union sacrée*, nor agree to collaboration, on 4 August.' There is no reason to doubt him, even if no such view was put on record at the time, and even if his statement tells us nothing at all about whom he was referring to by that 'we'!

Similarly, the National Federation of Workers in the Food Industry let it be known, but only as late as 22 June 1915, that it was among 'those who had maintained, from the first days of the war, that organised and class-conscious proletarians must not collaborate with the ruling class in the abominable evil they had been unable to prevent'. The federation went on to declare that it did not blame the CGT for not calling a general strike, 'because it was not in any real position to do so', but that it did blame it for not having remained true to its ideals.

As early as 24 November 1914, by contrast, the prefect of the department of Ain drew attention to an anti-war campaign waged by the socialist group in Oyonnax and to the posting of stickers in the town: 'The Church wanted war. . . . Clericalism means war; socialism and free thought means peace! Down with the Church! Down with the war!'

Again, from December onwards, two provincial socialist dailies, *Le Midi socialiste* and *Le Populaire du Centre*, began to take a different line from that of *L'Humanité*. Thus, on 17 December *Le Midi socialiste* awarded a 'certificate of savagery' to the military reporter of *La Libre Parole*, and on 26 December another contributor denounced those who extolled war for war's sake:

> Long Live War! War reinvigorates nations, strengthens governments, toughens races, gives to all the flame of life! Long live wars; they restore men's powers and strength!
>
> What matter that commerce is paralysed, industry halted, regions are devastated, towns annihilated, provinces ruined? What matter the villages to be rebuilt, the vast sums to be paid in pensions, the enormous debts, the restructuring of economic life, the disabled to be cared for?
>
> What matter orphans without protectors, mothers without sons, women without husbands, young girls without fiancés!
>
> What matter sadness, suffering, ruin and death! Long Live War! .

Were the Renseignements Généraux right to claim that the first protests by the teachers' union were not made before January 1915? In fact, a distinction must be made between that union – of which it is true to say it was almost inert until June 1915, as the authors of the *Histoire de la fédération de l'enseignement* ('History of the

Teachers' Federation') allege, going even further than the Renseignements Généraux – and their journal, *L'Ecole émancipée*. When
the latter reappeared on 3 October 1914, at the beginning of the new
school year, the leading article, written by Marie Guillot, was
clearly pacifist in tone and was, moreover, cut by the censors: 'Why
should we, Frenchmen, Germans, Russians, Austrians, people who
ask only for peace and for work, butcher one another?' Though not
all the articles were of the same tenor, the authorities kept a very
close watch on the journal after that. In the issue of 17 October an
article by J. Maillan, a schoolteacher from the Basses-Alpes, was cut
by half. On 24 October, *L'Ecole émancipée* was suspended by order
of the press office in the 15th Region, the journal's place of publication being Marseille. The charges included the 'publication of
articles likely to exert blatantly internationalist ideas on the minds
of schoolteachers'. *L'Ecole émancipée* was soon afterwards replaced
by *L'Ecole*, which showed greater prudence. Nevertheless, once the
war was over, *L'Ecole émancipée* could pride itself on having kept
aflame 'a small light in our federation in the middle of that terrible
night into which everything around us was plunged, because *for
more than one year* our organ was *the only publication in France* not
to bow to that hideous monster, war. . . '
     On this subject, police intelligence was therefore incomplete:
L'Ecole émancipée had become a focus of anti-war sentiment well
before November.
     Thus it was during the last quarter of 1914, towards November —
in some cases a little later and in others a little earlier — that the first
grains of opposition to war appeared, without, however, combining
to take definite shape. But why just at that moment, it may be
asked? 'Once the first numbness had gone, the workers' movement
recovered its courage', wrote Annie Kriegel. But was that the only
possible explanation?
     In one of the first lines of a manifesto drawn up by Marie
Mayoux, an 'internationalist' teacher, it says:

> We did speak out in August 1914, because we, like all of us who
> responded to the call of our country, accepted the cruel necessity of a
> rapid and effective defence against the invader; we did not speak up later,
> despite the sorrow in our hearts at the sad Calvary Europe ascended that
> winter, because our sympathies for all the victims of the countless
> slaughters went first and foremost to heroic Belgium, to our ravaged
> France.

In other words, when one's country is in danger of being crushed,
one may not speak out. When the situation has changed, one may.

Not surprisingly, the beginning of open opposition coincided with the end of the so-called war of movement. After the failure of the great German offensives, and also of the French counter-offensive, the war became static. The threat to France was no longer mortal, or immediate, and so fewer concessions had to be made for the sake of the nation.

The historian may think it important to determine the precise beginnings of the movement, however weak, but was public opinion even aware of its existence?

Pierre Monatte's letter of resignation, in fact a manifesto, was printed, and addressed 'to militant officials of the trade-union movement'. Now, we are told by Jean Maitron, co-publisher with Colette Chambelland of Monatte's letters, that 'when we look at the replies Monatte received — and we know that he tried to keep them all — we find that the number of those who responded to his appeal was rather small'.

Among the total of twenty-seven letters, eighteen expressed frank agreement. But most of these letters were individual replies, binding on their authors only. These included several anarchist personalities and writers such as Sébastien Faure, Francis Jourdain and Mauricius, intellectuals such as Henri Guilbeaux, the future associate of Romain Rolland, two other writers and a doctor known as an anarchist. Apart from the replies of two leaders of the teachers' union, Marie Guillot and Lafosse from Marseille, there were seven letters from militant members of the labour movement, of whom a few were in leading positions: Leguern, secretary of the Association of Trade Unions in the department of Côtes-du-Nord, who was quick to add: 'I am writing to you in my personal capacity'; a trade unionist from Nancy, who seemed, in fact, to speak in the name of a group: 'We here have been. . .disturbed for some time about what has been happening in Paris'; and Francis Million, secretary of the Association of Trade Unions in the department of the Rhône. His was in fact the only reply to commit an organisation of any importance: 'The Rhône Association of Trade Unions has decided to adhere resolutely to its point of view: now, as before the war, it expresses its horror at the barbarous killings and declares itself in favour of peace at all times and under all circumstances.' The Rhône Association not only distributed Monatte's letter but soon afterwards took a vigorous public stand. On 13 January 1915, it ended a very long declaration with the following passage:

> The Association of Trade Unions in the department of the Rhône, placing the broad interests of humanity above all secondary considera-

tions, unreservedly attests to the never-dying principle of working-class internationalism and declares its support of any honest attempt to bring about an equitable and definitive peace as soon as possible.

Make war on war! Long live the Workers' International!

The writers of several letters implied that their feelings were shared by others. Thus Marie Guillot wrote: 'When I read what *L'Humanité* tries to make its readers swallow — but believe me, not all of them can stomach it. . .', or Dr Mignon: 'You have written what many people think.' However, most of Monatte's correspondents tended to complain about their isolation:

'We are a small minority who refuse to let ourselves be drowned in the flood of eloquence which this, the most stupid of wars, has unleashed', wrote Francis Jourdain; '. . .reduced as we now are to the role of isolated individuals . . . ', wrote a subscriber to *La Vie ouvrière*.

At the time, the people round *La Vie ouvrière* formed the most important anti-war group. Leon Trotsky became its chief inspiration on his arrival in Paris on 20 November 1914, supported by Alphonse Merrheim, Alfred Rosmer and the poet Marcel Martinet, but even he caused very few reverberations.

On the socialist, as distinct from the trade-union, side there were few signs of resistance to the party's official line on the war. True, some socialists did think it wrong to put excessive blame on the German socialists. This was the view Pierre Dormoy, a councillor from Paris, expressed at a meeting attended by several members of the Seine executive on 2 September. Dormoy also thought that when they came back, 'those who are in the army' would ask 'those who are in power' to give an account of themselves. Another Seine militant, Sadrin, saw nothing wrong in the fact that yesterday's revolutionaries and anti-militarists should be fighting in defence of justice and liberty, but warned against attempts to take advantage of their temporary patriotism after the war. There was not just an external enemy, but also an internal one who would 'attempt to stifle the revolutionary movement', he declared on 31 January 1915, at a commemoration for Louise Michel at the Levallois cemetery.

However, the expression of anything but unqualified support for the war was exceptional. Any suggestion of a premature peace, before German militarism had been routed, was rejected out of hand; a Parisian socialist pilloried all such proposals as intrigues by financial groups, by time-serving capitalists.

This explains why Laffitte's circular was so badly received: it was more or less dismissed as a German ploy. Mayéras asked branch secretaries to ignore it, while Edouard Vaillant remarked with obvious pleasure on the unfavourable reception it had received and saw it as part and parcel of a campaign launched outside the country. The central committee of the Socialist Party accorded the same hostile reception to Sébastien Faure's *Vers la paix* (*Towards Peace*), a pamphlet he had sent to all members of the committee in January. Dubreuilh, the general secretary of the party, replied with a circular to all federations asking them to ignore such 'scurrilous' pamphlets no matter what their source. The party also showed its irritation at the attitude of the branch in the Vth arrondissement, where there was a concentration of Russian social democrats. This arrondissement was, in fact, the only one where anti-war propaganda was having an undeniable effect, and where 'anti-patriotic' theories were 'paraded before large audiences'. 'These meetings are very well attended.' 'On 1 November more than 500 persons, including several soldiers in uniform, wildly applauded Chernov and Martov.' The note concluded: 'It was not long before this type of propaganda began to bear fruit: Russian refugees who had contributed several thousand volunteers in August 1914 had become overtly hostile to the idea of volunteering by November, and applauded orators who spoke of desertion and of reaching an understanding with the German socialists'.

That these Russians, forced out of their country, and certainly not very happy to find themselves in the same camp as tsarist Russia, should have reverted to a more logical attitude than the one they had adopted in August, is, of course, not very surprising.

Another indication of the response to the first signs of war resistance is the number of subscribers to *L'Ecole émancipée*, and later to *L'Ecole*: 1,600 during the first year of the war. This was certainly not a very large figure when one considers the total number of French schoolteachers, the less so as there is nothing to prove that all subscribers were 'internationalists'. We can therefore reject out of hand the possible existence of marked anti-war feeling in the teaching profession.

In any case, in France as a whole, as distinct from the labour movement, war resistance enjoyed negligible support during the autumn of 1914.

We must now examine the precise grounds on which French war resistance was based. Apart from Julia Bertrand, who, if we are to believe her account, was arrested *without reason* on 21 August and discharged on 11 October without having been questioned, her case therefore throwing no light on the reasons for her opposition to the war — officially she was dismissed from her job for having expressed highly unpatriotic views on what people ought to do in case of war — our main source is Monatte's *Pourquoi je démissionne du comité fédéral* ('Why I am resigning from the federal committee').

According to Monatte the CGT had betrayed its mission in two respects:

1 Abandoning trade-union independence by agreeing to collaborate with the government.

2 Refusing to accept the duty of the working class 'to intercede promptly if war should break out'.

Pierre Monatte was referring to the refusal of the federal committee of the CGT to welcome the peace efforts of Scandinavian socialists and to wish the Copenhagen conference every success.

For Monatte the masses may have failed, but their leaders had shown a deplorable lack of faith.

Monatte's paper marked the greatest height to which the war-resistance movement rose in the autumn of 1914. It was remarkable — for its moderation. It challenged the policy of the CGT, and questioned the CGT's explanations of the causes of the war, but it did not deny that Germany bore the main responsibility. In any case, there was no suggestion of *defeatism* or of anything resembling it. Monatte simply refused to accept the war as a war of liberation and demanded a peace 'based on the international solidarity of the working class and the liberty of all peoples'.

A handful of supporters, a few rare tokens of opposition, a moderate platform – that is all the anti-war movement amounted to in the autumn of 1914.

Romain Rolland Enters the Fray

That was not the whole story, however, because there was also Romain Rolland.

His intervention was, in fact, different, because it was apolitical in character. Yet, mistakenly, what posterity remembers above all about the beginnings of a French opposition to the war are the writings of Romain Rolland and the reactions they provoked.

When – to his great surprise – war broke out, Romain Rolland was in Switzerland, involved more with sentimental concerns than with the international situation. Exempted from military service, he stayed on in Switzerland. Then, in early October, he settled in Geneva to devote himself to work that appealed to him for 'its more human than national character', namely the prisoner-of-war agency founded by the International Red Cross.

By remaining in Switzerland from the outbreak of hostilities, even if his health entitled him to do so, Romain Rolland had cut himself off from the war. However, it would be wrong to conclude that he did so unambiguously. According to René Cheval, he hesitated during the first few weeks about the part he ought to play, 'perhaps because the significance of the war was not fully clear to him'. His first writings show that the French cause seemed just to him, or at least superior to the German; his objections were not to France, but to the German war machine and its methods; it was German intellectuals he put in the dock. His *Journal* reflects the same spirit. Moreover, when he learned of the death of Péguy he extolled his virtues in the *Journal de Genève*: 'My dear comrade Péguy has died as he has lived: fighting for right and for faith'.

His famous collection of articles entitled *Au-dessus de la mêlée* (*Above the Battle*) begins with the 'Open Letter to Gerhart Hauptmann',[4] written on 29 August 1914, and published in the *Journal de Genève* on 2 September 1914. 'I am not . . . one of those Frenchmen who treat all Germans as barbarians', he declared. But the letter was, above all, a protest against German methods of war and in particular against the destruction of Louvain. He exclaimed, with irony, a few days later: 'Gerhart Hauptmann has annexed me to Germany as if I were a simple Belgian', and, with indignation: 'He tramples justice underfoot.'

René Cheval's comments on Romain Rolland are not unlike our own conclusions about the French anti-war movement as a whole:

> Why has it never been pointed out that it was only *after the battle of the Marne*, when the most immediate threat was removed, when France was out of danger, that he permitted himself to voice . . . general ideas about the war that he had preferred to keep to himself since the beginning of August? . . . The time to philosophise is not as the enemy is attacking your house. In brief, Romain Rolland waited to rise 'above the battle' until it became clear that the battle would not turn out to the disadvantage of France.

To appreciate the justice of that remark one has to remember that the title essay of Rolland's *Au-dessus de la mêlee* was not published in the *Journal de Genève* until 22 and 23 September, that is, at a time when there was no longer any doubt about the outcome of the battle. It was, moreover, in his own *Journal* under the date of 22 September that Romain Rolland saluted this victory 'all along the line. . . . It seems as if a weight has been lifted from our hearts . . . '.

Thus it was only when the most pressing danger was past that Rolland, unlike so many of his compatriots, refused 'to come to

---

4. Then the leading German playwright.

terms with the war'. Yet it has been round the article 'Au-dessus de la mêlée' and the polemics it caused that the 'historical' personality of Romain Rolland has been constructed.

'[The] modern reader, even if aware of the climate in which this piece saw the light of day', wrote Annie Kriegel, 'remains astounded by the virulence of the reactions it aroused.'

What in fact did Romain Rolland say? After having rendered homage to 'the wonderful French youth' — 'Oh, my friends . . . no matter what your destiny, you have stood on the peaks of life and have carried your country with you' — he enlarged upon how great a misfortune the war spelled for Europe, how it highlighted the failings of socialism and of Christianity, how, though the three emperors were the main culprits, every nation had to bear some responsibility for imperialism, 'that expression of arrogance and domination', and how, finally, even though war had already been declared, the [intellectual] élite should not commit the crime of 'compromising the integrity of its ideas'.

Two aspects, in particular, shocked his French contemporaries: first of all that a Frenchman could pretend to remain above the fray, that is, attempt to be even-handed towards the antagonists, but, worse still, perhaps, that he should have championed the cause of European civilisation. The idea of Europe was quite foreign to most of his readers and Romain Rolland seemed to be challenging the French conviction that *France* was defending civilisation from the barbarians. He, by contrast, blamed the would-be French 'guardians of civilisation' for having invited the aid of 'Cossacks, Turks, Japanese, Singhalese, Sudanese, Senegalese, Moroccans, Egyptians, Sikhs, Sepoys, barbarians from the pole and from the equator'. It reminded him, he wrote, of 'the Roman Empire at the time of the tetrarchy calling upon the hordes throughout the world to tear each other to pieces'.

This theme was very close to Romain Rolland's heart, because he repeated it in almost identical, though rather more vigorous, terms in his *Journal*: 'I also find it criminal to appeal for help in this war to barbarians throughout the world. . . . The aspect of a great European nation being held at bay by these savage hordes is something I cannot contemplate without revulsion.'

Romain Rolland's remarks would no doubt stamp him a 'racist' today, something that was far from his mind.[5] In any case, cham-

5. In a note written for the printed collection of his articles (p. 62), Romain Rolland

pions of the Entente noted that all the 'barbarians' mentioned, with
the exception of the Turks, who had not yet shown their hand, were
on their side, and that Germany was the implicit beneficiary of his
denunciation.

What reactions did Romain Rolland's article provoke among the
public?

At first, very little. During the greater part of October, Romain
Rolland's *Journal* made no reference to the matter. This is easily
explained: the *Journal de Genève* did not have a wide readership in
France and Romain Rolland's views were not taken up by the
French press. Not that the article was completely ignored. Gyp
referred to it – and with unrestrained violence – in her *Journal d'un
cochon de pessimiste* ('Diary of a pig of a pessimist') dated
27 September: she called it the kind of 'disgusting' article 'one might
expect from someone of Monsieur's moral fibre and known phys-
ique'. Rolland had 'dull and drawn eyes', was a 'total degenerate',
had shown 'frightening cowardice . . .'! But then this lady novelist
made no attempt to hide her extreme right-wing sympathies.

Taking the opposite view, Jean Longuet and Pierre Renaudel
went to Switzerland on 22 October to ask Romain Rolland to write
for *L'Humanité*.

However, the 'Rolland affair' did not really start in earnest until
Alphonse Aulard, the historian of the French Revolution, published
an article in *Le Matin* on 23 October. Though its tone was not
particularly virulent, Romain Rolland himself considered it *perfidious*: 'Monsieur R. Rolland. . .appears to have left us to live and
write in Switzerland. He has now given us his feelings about the war
in the *Journal de Genéve*. . . . It makes strange reading . . .'. Aulard
went on to mention Romain Rolland's 'German friends', and his
'delicate' soul whose 'queasiness is sure to have delighted Berlin-
ers' (a reference to Rolland's condemnation of the use of non-
European troops). He reproached him for alleging that, in defending Königsberg, the Germans were defending the heritage of Kant.
'If Kant were alive today, he would blush to be a Prussian.'

An article in muted tones, but perhaps all the more deadly for
that; Romain Rolland believed at all events that it was this article
which 'unleashed the campaign' against him. This was also the view
of Henri Guilbeaux, who wrote in the *Bataille syndicaliste* of
13 November 1914: 'It was enough for M. Aulard to quote a brief and

---

pleaded that his remarks must not be mistaken for contempt for the races of Asia
and Africa, but as a simple condemnation of the 'shortsighted policy of bringing
Africa and Asia into the struggles of Europe'.

incomplete extract from your noble appeal, for that pack of baying hounds we had thought fast asleep to set up their furious yelping'.

But these 'baying hounds' were journalists of both left and right, as Romain Rolland pointed out, correctly so because in this campaign the demarcation was not between left and right, but between left and extreme right.

On 28 October *Le Radical* compared Romain Rolland and Anatole France:

> While the second begged to be allowed to fight, the first is toasting German *Kultur*, the Crown Prince's *Sehnsucht* and the Kaiser's *Gemütlichkeit*. From the heights of the Alps he is eternally grateful to the Kaiser's thinkers. His boring work, *made in Germany*, was trying to implant German qualities on our soil. Anatole France is in the direct line of pure French tradition. . . .

The leading organ of French radicalism, *La Dépêche* (of Toulouse), to which Jaurès had been a contributor, was not to be outdone, and wrote on 27 October: 'While our armies are challenging the barbarians . . . on the soil of our fatherland, there is one Frenchman who bemoans the suffering of 'his German friends'. He is Monsieur R. Rolland, novelist, musicologist and professor at the Sorbonne'. The paper returned to the charge on 12 November with a long, bitter-sweet article on *Inter arma caritas*, the organisation which Romain Rolland helped in caring for prisoners of war as a sign of his impartiality: 'But why the devil does M'sieur R. Rolland forget that it was Germany who first unleashed systematic terror on the people she dreams of enslaving?'

One of the most virulent articles was written by Henry Bérenger, a radical senator from Guadeloupe, in a small left-wing journal, *L'Action*: 'You have done wisely, sir, to put a barrier between your prose and your country', or again: 'We have no time to waste on the ravings of an academic Germanophile . . .'.

As for the press of the centre and the right, it showed little benevolence, of course, the less so as its hostility, at any rate that of the nationalist wing, was a logical continuation of its pre-war attitude to Romain Rolland. Such contributors to *L'Action française* as Henri Massis and René Johannet had long been sniping at him and at the German sympathies with which they credited him.

Le Temps published its opinion fairly late: on 17 December it compared Rolland's attitude unfavourably to Bergson's: 'Even a good patriot can refuse to adopt unilateralist views.' However, one might not take R. Rolland for a Frenchman when one reads 'his very singular articles'. 'He ignores the most blatant facts. . .'. When he pretended to put French and German intellectuals on a par 'his comparisons [were] nothing but duplicity and iniquity'. *Le Temps* thus showed sorrow rather than anger, in keeping with its customary style.

The right-wing journals, by contrast, were full of rancour, *La Liberté* castigating 'that apologist of Germanic *Kultur*', and *La Croix* objecting to his 'intellectual cacophony'. The great Catholic journal alleged, moreover, that Rolland was no Frenchman — he was said to have taught at the Sorbonne 'as a foreigner' — and warmly applauded Alphonse Aulard for stigmatising 'the way a pillar of impudence poses as a pillar of civilisation'.

L'Action française did not attach excessive importance to the behaviour of a man of whom no good could be expected. Moreover, on 9 September Marcel Pujo mocked Romain Rolland's reply to Hauptmann in which the rest of the press had found nothing exceptionable: 'Puerile games! Touching lamentations, but how infantile . . .'.

Rolland's *Au-dessus de la mêlée* did not take *L'Action française* by surprise. Deep down, its author was not part of French literature: 'If he had some sense [of race] Monsieur R. Rolland. . .would not allow himself to oppose the defence of his country'.

Attacked as he was from the right, from the centre and from the left, did Romain Rolland have no friends left at all? He was never able to count on more than the support of *La Bataille syndicaliste*, and also of certain provincial socialist papers. *Le Midi socialiste* took up his defence in an article on 15 November, waxing indignant about the 'cartloads of mud' flung at him as they had been at Zola and Jaurès before him. 'Your hour has come. . .but rest assured, Romain Rolland, those who love you, you and your work, will be your unfailing bodyguards.'

On balance, *L'Humanité*, too, may be said to have come down on Romain Rolland's side. Over the signature of Amédée Dunois, it proclaimed on 26 October:

> A French intellectual has spoken out eloquently against imperialism.
> Truly, for almost three months nothing has been written more perfectly noble than these pages full of sorrow, of love and of hope, pages worthy of a Quinet or a Mechelet, or, better still, worthy of 'eternal France'! No one else, unless I am mistaken, has risen 'above the battle' with so much passionate exaltation. . . .

But the article was not very long and was tucked away discreetly at the bottom of the first page. Moreover, while its author regretted that, for an unspecified reason, he had been unable to quote from

Rolland's articles in the *Journal de Genève* when they appeared, he chose a brief extract that was unlikely to shock French readers. We may therefore take it that it was only the savage article by Aulard that had forced *L'Humanité* to speak up. A few days later, however, Amédée Dunois extolled Romain Rolland in *L'Humanité* as 'our Barrès — the Barrès of the revolutionary tradition and of European humanism'.

La Bataille syndicaliste trumpeted its support much more loudly, although it, too, did so belatedly. Across two columns, prominently displayed, the CGT daily published an open letter to Romain Rolland by the young writer, Henri Guilbeaux: 'In the name of all your friends and in the face of all the attacks upon you, I affirm my affection and unwavering admiration for you'.

Though Amédée Dunois and Henri Guilbeaux (who had moved to Switzerland in 1915 and become a neighbour of Rolland's) were not Rolland's only champions, it seems that the number of journalists who supported him was very small.[6] This is easily understood: at a time when serious papers of such opposite views as *Le Radical* and *La Liberté* explained solemnly to their readers that Beethoven was not a German but a Belgian, it was unlikely that they would show appreciation for someone extolling the virtues of fairness and objectivity!

One of the leading regional papers, *La Petite Gironde*, reflected the prevailing spirit by splashing the word 'Hatred' across three columns on its front page: 'Today there is such a thing for the French as the beauty, the dignity, the nobility of hatred. Which one of us, before August, would have written such a phrase without a shudder or without a blush? And nevertheless it is true. . . . After the war? We shall see . . .'.

The article went on to explain that Romain Rolland was only able to escape this hatred, which was so essential, because the noise of battle was muffled before it reached him on the 'mountain peak in the neutral country where he lives'. In the face of so much incomprehension, Romain Rolland began to feel that the French press *must* have been incited against him, the more so as he received a host

6. Romain Rolland himself drew up a list of them in the introduction to his *Au-dessus de la mêlée*: 'It is my pleasant duty to thank those courageous friends who have defended me, for a year, in the Parisian press: at the end of October 1914, Amédée Dunois in *L'Humanité* and Henri Guilbeaux in *La Bataille syndicaliste*; in the same paper, Fernand Després; George Pioch in *Les Hommes de Jour*, J.-M. Renaitour in *Le Bonnet Rouge*; Rouanet in *L'Humanité*; Jacques Mesnil in *Le Mercure de France* and Gaston Thiesson in *La Guerre sociale*. To these faithful comrades I express my affectionate gratitude. R.R., October 1915'.

of basely insulting letters. In his *Journal* for 4 and 5 November, he wrote: 'The campaign against me continues to rage'.

It is not surprising that he was deeply disturbed by the violence of attacks that must have seemed grossly unjust to him, but we must not exaggerate the space the French papers devoted to him at the time. That they were — with some exceptions — hostile to him is certain. But it was probably mistaken to speak of a 'campaign'. Important papers, such as *L'Echo de Paris*, kept their counsel. Most other papers did not devote more than one article to Romain Rolland, generally between 23 October, the date when Aulard's attack was published, and the end of the month; as for *Le Temps*, it waited until 17 December. It must also be stressed that few French papers accorded either a great deal of space or much prominence to the story, and that the historian must therefore be particularly careful not to jump to conclusions.

Thus the article in *L'Action française* ran to half a column in an unobtrusive position on the second page and was signed 'Interim'; the venomous attack in *La Croix* occupied a mere 5 cms at the bottom of the fourth column on the second page; in *La Liberté* of 19 November, Romain Rolland was not mentioned except in a short general news item on the second page. *Le Radical* attacked him on the front page, but in an article at the bottom of the third column. *La Dépêche* (Toulouse) devoted an editorial to him, but only in the regular daily events column and without drawing any particular attention to the matter.

At the time, other polemics took greater pride of place. Thus *L'Action française* was busily launching several broadsides a week against Gustave Hervé as, for example, when it wrote with no more kindness than it had shown to Romain Rolland: 'What is so striking about G. Hervé is his prodigious weakness of judgment'.

All in all, therefore, it would seem that for most papers Romain Rolland's article was the kind of aberration one mentions, denounces and castigates but to which one does not attach very great importance.

But did Romain Rolland's views perhaps make a wider impact on French public opinion than they did on the press at that time? Let us note first of all that any influence he may have had was bound to be indirect, since very few people in France were in a position to read the article. He said so himself: 'It was not until June 1915 that 'Au-dessus de la melée', my main article which caused such a storm. . .could be published (almost) in its entirety, thanks to the malicious zeal of an inept pamphleteer to whom I am indebted for causing my words to reach the public of France for the first time'.

Before that date, Alfred Rosmer and his friends, anxious to read the article at first hand, 'had been forced to have it copied out on a typewriter or even by hand'. This method clearly did not allow the article to reach more than a small circle, the circle of those from whom Romain Rolland received warm support and whom he mentioned in his *Journal*: Louis Gillet, Marcel Martinet, *et al.* but, as he also said: 'Very few have responded to my appeal, nowhere less so than in my own country. My efforts have met with more insults than understanding . . .'.

In July 1915, Rolland admitted defeat. René Chaval believes that his stand probably evoked a greater response than he thought. This is probably true of the war as a whole but not for the time when the article was published — the records, at least, do not support this view. The case of Romain Rolland therefore does not alter the general conclusions to be drawn about the French anti-war movement.

Once the immediate danger was past, when public opinion at large became accustomed to the idea of a war of long duration, some of them began to swim against the current, to wonder whether the war could really be justified. But they were very few and far between and, as Rolland's champion, Alfred Rosmer, has put it: 'A census of our forces could have been completed very quickly'.

CHAPTER 5

Adaptation

Only a small number of Frenchmen came to oppose the war. Others adapted themselves to the unforeseen situation. But in what state of mind?

The feelings of the French, caught as they were between the anxieties of a war that seemed to go on and on and the needs or habits of daily life, must have been in considerable conflict.

We live here peacefully under a lovely sky [Jules Moméja, who kept a diary throughout the war, wrote on 26 September at Moissac]. The grapes are pouring into the market; you might think these were times of utter delight, of idyllic happiness; it seems incredible that over there, in the north-east, the guns keep rumbling away and death is reaping a harvest of millions. The contrast is too great; our contentment is too complete to continue for long . . .

Other witnesses spoke of a return to normal life and of learning to adapt. André Lottier, a schoolmaster from the department of Yonne, noted on 18 September:

It has been raining for days now.

No more chats under the chestnut trees or in the shade of the church. The wet and the wind have put an end to our open-air gatherings, have dispersed the regulars. The season is moving on and fine days are becoming rarer as September draws to a close. And twelve days from now I shall be back at school. I shall hardly ever be present at the morning chats where everyone gives his views, at the open discussions — echoes of public feeling — which I have become so used to listening to and noting down.

[In Saint-Florent, a small town in Cher] the people were sad at first, but they have gradually become used to the new state of affairs, despite news every day of the death of one of the town's children: 'What can we do?' people say. 'We just have to grin and bear it.'

94

In some cases it was no longer even a question of adaptation, but, as the Bordeaux police commissioner put it bluntly a few months later: 'Everywhere, the same indifference towards the war.'

Worse still, in October, when a thousand men of the 6th African Foot Artillery came to take delivery of guns at Creusot, we are told that 'more than one Creusot woman forgot her most elementary duty' while they were there, so much so that when the gunners delayed their departure 'some fanatics dropped all restraint and accused our guests of not wanting to get back to the front and of debauching the women of Creusot . . .'.

The dead, too, began to be treated with indifference. A Beauvais journalist drew attention to this new development on 18 February 1915:

> Funeral of a soldier. . .died at Félix-Faure hospital from war wounds. A horse, a poor man's hearse, completely plain, a flag on the coffin. Behind, two gentlemen from the *Souvenir français*. The priests walk briskly to the cemetery, in a hurry.
>
> At the funerals of the first soldiers who died for their country, the hearses were draped with a dozen flags and scores of people, deeply moved and thoughtful, followed behind.
>
> People grow weary of everything.

This change in attitude also struck Jules Moméja:

> [At the beginning of the war] there were long days of anxious waiting, of fear, despondency, brief joy; impressions followed one another in rapid succession; there was no respite. . . . For almost a month now, the attitude has been different. The everlasting battles. . .the monotony of the daily communiqués, have reduced us to a kind of dazed and abstracted passivity . . .; we are imperceptibly resuming our old habits; we hardly ever speak of that frightful eruption of all the forces of evil. . . .

Clearly the attitude was no longer what it had been at the beginning of August, or what it would be, fleetingly, at the time of the victory on the Marne. True, the prefect of Yonne and some other observers claimed that morale remained high, even though there was an obvious dip in September (Fig. 5.1), but others felt this was taking a rosy view. As Moméja put it on 14 October:

> The wave of pessimism continues to spread. . . . The length of the struggle has become exasperating; people are indignant. . .give vent to their anger. . .a wild nihilism rumbles away in their hearts. They are beginning to appreciate the full meaning of all the ruins and all the

Fig. 2. *The morale of the population of Yonne, August to December 1914, according to G. Letainturier, prefect of the department.*

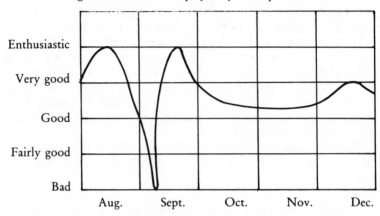

Military and political events, 1914

9 August: News of the capture of Mulhouse — *19 August: Advance continues. Recapture of Mulhouse* — *22 August*: Anglo-French troops withdraw — *27 August*: Our lines hold from the Somme to the Vosges.

2 September: Government leaves Paris — *From 2 to 6*: Arrival of refugees. Retreat of French army — *7 September*: German offensive halted — *From 8 to 14*: Enemy continues to be driven back. Victory of the Marne. General Joffre's Order of the Day — *From 14 to 31*: Russian advance in Galicia and East Prussia. French advance on the Aisne.

October. War at sea — Russian victories in Galicia — Setback in East Prussia — Belgian Government in Le Havre — Battle of the Yser — Armies immobilised in the trenches — German retreat in Poland.

November. Turkish attack — The battle of the Yser continues to our advantage — In East Prussia, the Germans go over to the defensive — Russian victories in Galicia — Winter campaign seems inevitable.

December. Return of French Government to Paris — Return of Serbians to Belgrade — Russian operations continue with marked success — Russians cross the German frontier — Allied offensive in Belgium; floodings — Italians land at Vallona.

---

misery, whose toll. . .keeps rising, rising. Childishly, they blame it on the politicians who were unable to avoid this catastrophe. . .and even more on the generals. . .they are beginning to ask themselves what the Russians are doing. . . . Black pessimism reigns on all sides. . . .

At the beginning of December, he even noted mutterings of revolution: 'Expressions of public exasperation heard this morning: if the war goes on, people will rebel, there will be a revolution. . . .

There are a lot of people who would like a revolution to punish the deputies for having done absolutely nothing to prevent the war. . . '. (9 December)

Similar remarks at Saint-Florent-sur-Cher: 'One often hears whispers that there will be a revolution after the war, but no one says for what, or who is going to make it'.

These testimonies are too few and far between, too fragmentary and too contradictory to help with arriving at a reliable assessment of public opinion during that period; at most it may be said that it was being buffeted by contrary winds. Can the teachers' records tell us anything more?

The French people, in the towns no less than in the country, had learned to live with the idea of a long war, that much seems certain. But did they do so with resignation or did they retain some of the patriotic fervour that had filled them during the first days of August? Many teachers in Charente completed a column headed 'Signs of patriotism'. The phrase was vague and the teachers interpreted it in various ways. Some thought they were expected to enter patriotic *deeds*, in the strict sense of the word; others felt that they should record expressions of, and changes in, patriotic feelings, which is obviously more helpful to us since country people, in particular, are not — except on rare occasions — given to dramatic demonstrations.

Nevertheless the opinions were formulated in so many different ways that they are not easily reduced to a few major categories.

Among a total of ninety-three expressions recording popular patriotism, we were able to distinguish forty-eight different types, that is, no expression was, as a rule, repeated more than once or twice. It nevertheless proved possible to divide these expressions into five categories:

• The *first category* covers expressions without clear significance. Thus the absence of signs of patriotism was mentioned on nine occassions, but the contexts make it clear that the phrase referred to public demonstrations only, as the following example shows: 'In 1914, 1915 and 1916 there were no signs'. Now this is no clear indication of popular attitudes as the absence of any outward sign could easily have gone hand in hand with generous contributions to the various soldiers' charities.

In one case at least, the formulation nevertheless had a pejorative character, since the teacher wrote: 'It was not given to me to witness any sign of patriotism. On the contrary, the peasants often protested against the requisitions. . . . To what must one attribute this attitude? To sheer cupidity . . . '.

In this first category we have also included remarks on the absence of noisy demonstrations (once), on the fact that the population never came out to demonstrate (once) and also that it was not very demonstrative (once).

• The *second category* comprises expressions of a popular patriotism. Let us note first of all that there was no longer any patriotic fervour except in one commune and there only 'when. . .the tide of the war is in our favour'. By contrast, a whole series of expressions, each used once, reflected good morale: a 'sound patriotic attitude', the population is always 'very patriotic', 'evinces patriotism', 'thrills with patriotism', is 'deeply attached to the country', 'prepared to make any sacrifices', 'resolved to go on to the end'.

Another set of expressions reflects the existence of an equally healthy state of morale, albeit a tone lower. They refer to the 'goodwill' of everyone, the 'equanimity' of the population, the 'courage' to wait for the outcome of military operations, their 'valiant' bearing in the face of weariness and sorrow, a 'patriotism without boisterousness', a 'patriotism without exuberance', a patriotism marked by 'silence'.

Closely related were 'calm', mentioned nine times, and 'resignation', mentioned three times and not in a pejorative sense: 'Since the beginning of hostilities, the people of Baignes-Sainte Radegonde have always shown admirable calm and resignation'.

'Calm' was sometimes coupled with 'dignity': patriotism is expressed through a 'calm and a dignified attitude'.

• In the *third category* we have placed actions reflecting a patriotic attitude.

Some of these actions implied the patriotism of the teacher concerned rather than that of the people, for example at Barbezieux, where the headmaster had the local scouts swear an oath on the flag at a ceremony attended by a large crowd, gave numerous lectures on the war and delivered a long speech on the occasion of the death of an assistant teacher at the front. However, a whole series of expressions bore witness to patriotic actions, not just on special occasions, but 'steadfastly'.

The action that most impressed the teachers was public generosity, and contributions to collections and to loans were, indeed, excellent indicators of the deeper feelings of the population. Now this was by far the most frequently noted sign of patriotism: it was mentioned nineteen times, even though, in some cases, the generosity of the majority was said to contrast sharply with 'the selfishness of a number of citizens'.

Other, comparable, expressions of collective patriotism were the generous reception accorded to wounded soldiers (twice), the linen and money collected for their benefit (once), generosity to war victims (once), the warm welcome of refugees (twice), later the warm welcome of soldiers on leave (mentioned once). Another sign of patriotism, according to some teachers, was a positive attitude to work (five times), the desire to hold out and to produce (once). Finally, interest in the outcome of the military operations was also put down as a sign of patriotism (once).

The last two categories, in which we have combined expressions reflecting a patriotic attitude with patriotic actions or what were taken for such, covered the great majority of the expressions recorded here.

• We were, however, able to distinguish two further categories, *a fourth* reflecting a decline in patriotism, and *a fifth* reflecting a lack of patriotism.

A decline in patriotic fervour appeared in six recorded opinions from six different communes. The teachers were rather vague about the moment when this decline set in, except in one case: the schoolmaster from Esse wrote: 'At the beginning of the war patriotic fervour was great; *at the end of three months*, it abated'. Elsewhere it was merely noted that, because of the monotony of the war of positions, the fervour gradually died down, 'not to reveal itself again except from time to time . . . '; that with the prolongation of hostilities the 'original fervour has made way for a calmer patriotism'; that people 'no longer read the papers except for form's sake; that they were 'no longer interested in the communiqués . . . '; and that the ardour of 'some people [who had] shown their generosity' at the beginning, had 'quickly cooled down'.

Six communes also figure in a final category: in one of them the atmosphere was one of 'covert pessimism', due more, in fact, to fear of defeat than to a conscious lack of patriotism; in four other cases the term 'indifference' was used though it is not always clear in what sense: thus 'indifference' did not stop people from giving to collections in one case; in another case the informant's 'character' was said to be rather 'cold and indifferent'; in a third case it was only 'some people' who lived a 'life of indifference and selfishness'. Finally, just one schoolmaster deplored the fact that, in his commune, there were too many people who seemed 'indifferent to the triumph of France'.

The results of the enquiry can be summed up as follows:

1. Expressions without particular significance   12
2. Expressions reflecting a patriotic attitude   33

3. Actions implying a patriotic attitude   36
4. Expressions showing a decline in patriotism   6
5. Expressions showing a lack of patriotism   6
                                          Total 93

If we may take it that patriotism does not necessarily express itself conspicuously, that there can be 'a deeper patriotism, which does not make a display of itself', as one teacher put it, then our list does indeed give us a fairly reliable indication of the attitude of the people of Charente during the autumn of 1914.

The majority view could be described as follows: 'The patriotic spirit of the population is excellent; though it is not exuberant, it is sincere'; or: 'The patriotism of the population is more in the nature of acceptance and of obeying the law than one of enthusiastic demonstrations which are often more showy than sincere'.

There were also two minorities, the first exemplified by this opinion: 'In general, the population is of a cool temperament and not very high-minded. Too selfish and too ignorant of the meaning of *la Patrie*, they rarely display signs of patriotism. . . . Every patriot suffers from living among such people . . . '. As for the second minority, their view was summed up as follows: 'As events took their course, people responded, invariably thrilling to victories, but gradually reverting to their ordinary preoccupations, accepting the continuation of hostilities with a sort of resignation, but nevertheless with confidence . . . '.

Patriotism was therefore still the rule and lack of interest the exception, with a whole spectrum of attitudes between these two.

From September to October, the original fever of excitement began to wane, but it was not until 1915 that people began to take the war more or less for granted. Thus when the first soldiers returned from the front on leave, their arrival was an event but, as the war continued, 'curiosity was quickly replaced with indifference. Some went, others came, nobody seemed to pay much attention, apart from relatives and next-door neighbours. People still talk about the war, of course, but their day-to-day concerns have gradually gained the upper hand . . . '. Or: 'It has to be said, for it is nothing but the truth, that the dominant attitude among the people of Nanclars after two years of war, is one of adaptation . . . '.

Can these conclusions be applied without qualification to the rest of France? Was Charente, a rural department with traditionally moderate opinions, and far from the firing-line, representative of French public opinion as a whole?

While we have no means of answering this question, we do have a number of indications.

Some of them come from the department of Gard. Here, we are told by one witness that the bereavement which had unsparingly afflicted so many families after the battle of the Marne had become a source of 'moral despondency'. However, the schoolmaster from Saint-Jean-de-Valériscle: 'Good morale all round; the speed with which they [the people] have contributed so generously to the various appeals bears striking witness to this fact'. And the schoolmaster from Sommière wrote on 8 May 1915: 'The morale of the public has been admirable'.

A note made by a schoolmaster from Puy-de-Dôme between 2 August 1914 and 4 August 1915 concludes: '[The population] has proved, up to now and despite the cruel bereavement that has stricken so many families, to be admirably calm'.

At the end of his account of the first year of the war, the mayor of Fieux wrote: '2 August 1915! One year of the war has passed. Weariness is *beginning* to take hold. The hostilities are dragging on'.

These sporadic reports in no way invalidate the impression gained from our analysis of public opinion in Charente. With more subtlety than any statistical curve could reflect, this impression bears out that of the prefect of Yonne (see Fig. 2 above).

The original fervour had clearly declined, but, assured of satisfactory economic conditions, the French people were certainly not prepared to rebel against the war.

Public opinion had lost its illusions; it now faced the war calmly, gravely and resignedly: the French had become accustomed to living in a topsy-turvy world, and one in which they had to go on living. Soon the first signs of weariness would appear in the face of a conflict that was continuing longer than anyone could have imagined. But people were gradually becoming used to the idea that this was no brief interlude: the postwar period was fading further and further into the future.

'Settling Down to the War . . . '

A reporter from Beauvais noted on 18 October 1914: 'The Paris papers are resuming their feature articles. Clearly everything is going well'.

Apparently casual, this comment hides the bitterness of an observer who saw signs all around him that people had become used to the new circumstances or, as he put it: 'People are settling down to the war as they might settle in to a new home'.

In August 1914, people still believed that they were living in a world they knew. By the autumn of 1914, they had begun to feel that they had moved into a new world, quite different from the one they had always inhabited. Resolute or disenchanted, resigned or outraged, people had taken their first steps into the unknown.

The war of 1914 is usually divided into two phases, the so-called war of movement, and trench warfare. It is not always appreciated that, over and above describing specifically military events, this distinction covers the no less important problem of the behaviour of the population faced with a war of unpredictable duration.

The first day of August is a key date in contemporary history because the French people, like all the other belligerents in Europe, accepted a conflict they had not wished for, but the autumn of 1914 is perhaps equally important because it was then that they accepted the prolongation of their trial.

Why did they do it? One might simply retort that once their country had joined battle there was no alternative, and this is certainly, to a large extent, true. It does not, however, alter the fact that they could have gone about it in quite different ways. In particular, was it inevitable that socialists and trade unionists should continue 'to lie low' while their country seemed in deadly peril, to such an extent that they would not even raise the question of whether the particular form of participation in the national defence effort they had chosen was fully justified? Was it inevitable that in France, a country in which revolutionary forces were not unimportant, the opposition to the war should have been so feeble?

Was it inevitable that the authorities should have been able to introduce, and very quickly at that, a system of thought-control intended to avoid the threat of defeatism and also the danger of patriotic over-exuberance?

Was it, finally, inevitable — when no special economic and social provisions had been made — that a country whose efficiency was not of the highest standard should have been able to manage a creditable system of family allowances and effect large-scale industrial mobilisation, thus avoiding unacceptable social hardships and supplying the army with the equipment it needed?

After all the hullabaloo of the summer of 1914, it might seem as if France had lapsed into autumn dreariness. In fact, however, crucial decisions were being taken at that time, decisions that would help the French to settle down to a long war, to what might be called the 'routine' of war.

I I

THE BANALITY OF WAR

It goes without saying that some people came to terms with life in wartime without even being aware of the war's existence. It would, however, be quite wrong to suppose that most French people did not know what was happening. True, there was some lack of perception in August 1914, but by the autumn there were some limited signs of greater insight.

P. Bouyoux has described the attitude of the inhabitants of Toulouse in November and December: 'The war is going to last for a long time, there's no doubt about that. Popular opinion is now resigned to the fact that the war is a natural calamity which one can do nothing about and that one just has to live with'. But what is the meaning of 'a long time'? A few months, a year or several years?

One incident allows us to be more specific. At the end of 1915, François de Wendel opposed the application by his competitor Schneider to open a blast furnace in Normandy on the grounds that the furnace could not start production before the autumn of 1917, by which time the war would be over. Wendel was convinced that his rival was misleading the authorities into thinking that his furnace would help the war effort, when all he wanted was financial support from the state. Later, Wendel admitted that he had been wrong: 'We thought, on 1 January 1916', he explained in 1919, 'that the war would be over by the end of 1917 at the latest. . ., and we were wrong, as I hasten to admit . . .'.

This mistaken belief was in fact widespread: it took the French people a long time to realise that they were in for a very long war; meanwhile they buckled down to a series of successive campaigns of uncertain duration, each taken for the 'final push'. The Archbishop of Paris, Cardinal Amette, expressed this view at a solemn commemoration service for the French war dead on 12 November 1915: 'As for those of us who are in the rear, we must show ourselves worthy of them [the dead] by our indomitable patience and perseverance. Until then? As He said to the dead of the Apocalypse, so God tells us now: "A little while and you will see the light of victory shine out".'

It is difficult to grasp the French people's state of mind during the war unless we remember that no one dreamed the conflict might last for several years. The generations that followed, having had the experience of two world wars, realise that the duration of a war depends on the resources committed to its conduct: the greater the resources, the longer the war. The French, like other Europeans, believed the very opposite in 1914. Adapting themselves to the idea of a long war was therefore a gradual process for them.

Two accounts, both by intellectuals, one a professor and the other a lawyer, and both direct witnesses because they served at or near the front, may help us to follow this process.

The first is taken from a collection of letters to his family written by Louis Debidour, a senior history master and a Territorial for more than forty years, who fought at the front until his death in Champagne, in September 1915:

> *21 September 1914* (the author was still in a depot in Chartres): Today, through the courage and sacrifice of our comrades [at the battle of the Marne], the situation has been totally reversed and the enemy has begun to beat a retreat that will sweep him back well beyond the Rhine.

. . .

> *24 September*: Louis Debidour asks his wife to be patient a little longer; she will be able to return home very soon, 'once the enemy is out of France'.

. . .

> *8 October* (the author was now fighting in Picardy): 'We must take it that this [the campaign] is going to go on for some time yet'.

. . .

> *15 October*: 'Everyone is hoping for the end [of the war], but to get there, we know we must press on to the finish, and that will take a long time'.

. . .

> *27 October*: 'It feels to me as if it's dragging on and on. . . . It is going to last a long time and the prospect of a winter campaign troubles all of us'.

. . .

> *2 November* (a new captain has arrived): '. . . he has a very pessimistic nature. . . he believes firmly in final victory, but he thinks the war will go on for another 10 to 12 months at least. . . . I hope to have returned home long before then'.

. . .

30 November: 'If things go on like this all through December, there are many who believe that fortune will smile on us and that we shall see the end! Let us hope they are not mistaken! I myself think it will take longer, but I don't worry about it, and all I regret is that it will mean being away from you even longer'.

. . .

15 December: 'Many people think that the end is very near. To tell the truth, I don't. I believe, like you [his father, a historian and expert on international relations], that it will be many long months yet'.

. . .

18 December: '[This year] is ending on a very sad note, sadder than I could ever have imagined. May the year which is soon to begin bring us the joy of an eventual reunion'.

. . .

31 December: 'You will have come to appreciate the terrible nature of this war, and I must tell you, I find it impossible to say how it will end'.

. . .

10 January 1915: 'Everyone is planning to take out a [hunting] licence during the [1915] holidays' [game had multiplied so much].

. . .

24 January (in reply to a 'rather sad and despondent' letter from his father about the duration of the war): 'We shan't see the end of it until the summer, until the next holidays. But my firm conviction is still: we shall win'.

. . .

2 February: 'It's six months now since the war started! Let's hope it won't go on for another six!'

. . .

20 February: 'Here we are, my sixth month in the field is about to start, and my seventh since I left you. Truly, it has been a long time'.

. . .

27 April: 'The war seems to be going on for ever: no one can see a solution and that gets on all our nerves'.

. . .

16 June: 'One can't help feeling rather weary about a campaign that has lasted so long and that seems to be endless. [This feeling] is rife everywhere, coupled with a determination not to stop before victory'.

. . .

25 June: 'We must resign ourselves to the fact that this war will go on and on'.

. . .

26 June: 'It will be a long, a very long time yet. Just between ourselves, I think it will be next spring'.

. . .

30 July: 'You speak of the duration: I am afraid it will be a very long time still, and unless something quite unforeseen happens, I expect a winter campaign. We have received encouraging messages about October, but I am quite unconvinced by them'.

On 20 August 1915, in one of his last letters before the attack in which he died, Louis Debidour wrote that he hoped to be at home on the same date the following year, for his mother's birthday.

Our second series of extracts is taken from letters sent to his wife by André Kahn, a Jewish lawyer from Lorraine who became a stretcher-bearer, a medical orderly, and later acted as advocate at courts martial. He served at the front or in its immediate proximity from 1914 to 1918.[1]

14 September 1914: 'If things go on like this, there is hope that within a month people will be talking of peace and we shall be making ready to meet again . . .'.

. . .

1 October: 'Here we are, two months of war. And when will it end?'

. . .

15 October: 'I believe, indeed I am sure now, that this war will not be over by All Saints' Day as I had hoped. There is no doubt it will last until the spring.'

1. *Journal de guerre d'un Juif patriote* [1914–1918]; Paris, 1978.

. . .

1 November: 'It will be with us for a long time yet. I've become used to the idea. I am patient. I am stewing in a state of mindlessness'.

. . .

8 November: 'Here we are in the middle of a terrible battle, from which France will emerge victorious before long'.

. . .

19 November: 'It will still take months and months and who knows how many lives to humble arrogant Germany'.

. . .

6 December: 'Despite your confidence in a speedy end to the war, I still believe that it will be a very long time yet, as well as a very painful one. I am turning into a pessimist. We are losing our nerve . . .'.

. . .

11 December: 'It's now the 133rd day of the war and we still see no sign of the shining hour of its end!'

. . .

22 February 1915: 'My view of the war? It will be a long one. It won't take a hundred years, or even seven, but it will go on until November at least'.

. . .

5 March: 'You say I'm mad because I think the war will last another seven months at least. It is almost impossible for it to end to our advantage before that'.

. . .

12 March: 'A rumour has reached me from the General Staff: they have the impression down there that the war will end with victory in July'.

. . .

15 March: 'Like you, I believe in victory, but not before the end of the summer'.

. . .

17 March: 'The last engagements in Champagne and Argonne and the advance of the British Army on Lille prove it all. . . . Take heart, without a doubt we shall be spending the end of the summer together'.

. . .

25 March: 'Yesterday Major Kieffer set out his reasons for thinking that the war will not last for more than four to six months'.

. . .

11 April: 'Morale is high. . . By next winter I am sure the trenches will be no more than curious mementoes of the war'.

. . .

22 September: 'Everyone is full of confidence. I believe that this time "we shall have them" ' [he was referring to the Champagne offensive].

. . .

14 November: 'The first snow of 1915! Shall we still be facing the same conditions when the first snow falls in 1916? I am afraid I am beginning to think so'.

. . .

19 February 1916: 'The British papers are probably right about the duration of the war. I believe that we shall all be back at home next winter, victorious and at peace'.

. . .

11 May: 'I am sure the war will be over soon. The Boche is in a bad way. . . . He will no doubt sue for peace sooner than we think'.

. . .

2 July: 'I feel more and more confident about victory and the end of the war before the end of the year'.

. . .

3 February 1917: 'Monsieur Simon, although he is the mayor of Nancy, is an idiot to think that the war will go on until 1918. I am convinced that we will be back home bv next winter'.

. . .

26 September: 'I am twenty-nine today. How sad to think that, having already lost three years of a good, happy and fruitful life, I may be robbed of another two or three years of joy, work and happiness'.

. . .

7 May 1918: He believes that he will make sergeant in five or six months' time.

. . .

13 June: 'With American help, next year [1919] ought to ensure our superiority, bring us victory. . .'.

. . .

4 August (after the victorious start of the French counter-offensive): 'This is marvellous. . . . Can we now take it that the war will be over this year? Certainly not. . . . We must 'hold on' with patience and strength, until the spring of 1919. Then . . . the final battle may be fought. . . . The war will last another year at least'.

. . .

14 August: 'The war will not, alas, finish this year. . . . You are still going to have to write lots of letters to me'.

. . .

7 September: 'In a year's time, Wilhelm, faced with ruin, will beg for peace. . .'.

And so, until late in 1917, the expression 'a long war' simply meant a further extension by several months, from autumn to spring, from winter to summer. The change came in 1917, when the phrase began to mean 'a war without a foreseeable end', so much so that by the summer of 1918 few people felt the final curtain was about to come down. Such then was the mental attitude of *ordinary* French people to what had become an *ordinary* event.

But how did the French adapt themselves to the idea of a long war, how did they react? In an attempt to answer this question we have chosen a number of examples with different time scales and from different geographical and social sources: the peasants of Côtes-du-Nord throughout the war, the peasants of Charente in 1915 and 1916, Paris at the end of 1915, Le Creusot and the surrounding area from 1915 to 1918. Our choice has obviously not been an entirely free one, but was dictated by the availability of source material. We have nevertheless deliberately tried to concentrate on rural France, which at the time of the census of 1911 contributed the majority of the country's total population — almost 56 per cent. It is almost inconceivable that France would have borne so long an effort had it not been able to count on the support and resolve of the peasantry, which, moreover, accounted for an appreciable percentage of the armed forces, and of the infantry in particular. Thus 45 per cent of the men called up were peasants, and so were more than 500,000 of the 1,300,000 dead.

Yet if there was a silent or apparently silent majority in France at the time, it was indeed her rural population. References to it are few and far between in writings on the war or in extant administrative records. Can we, for instance, take the blunt opinion of a police inspector in Noirétable in the Loire, expressed on 31 August 1918, as a correct view of the French peasantry as a whole? 'Agricultural workers seem to ignore the war. They don't talk about it any more, cupidity having apparently supplanted everything else'.

CHAPTER 6

Côtes-Du-Nord during the War

> All did their duty bravely; by their conduct, their
> endurance, their tenacity, their love of their country, their
> sacrifice, our dead have contributed to the victorious end of
> the Great War.

With the above words the schoolmaster from Chatelaudren closed his account of wartime life in his commune.

It was not until the end of the war that the chief education officer of the department of Côtes-du-Nord asked all teachers under his jurisdiction to hand in the notes they had compiled following the ministerial circular of 23 September 1914. The schoolteachers of sixty-eight communes complied,[1] but few of their contributions were in the form of day-by-day entries. Most had preferred to use their notes for filling in a questionnaire they had all been sent. That document with its clear-cut headings — economic life, government assistance, children, hospitals — had been designed for a conflict lasting several weeks, not for a war of four years. In particular, it ignored the passage of time, making no allowances for changes in attitude. Moreover, most replies looked like summaries edited after the event rather than spontaneous reactions.

Some teachers were very brief, either because they felt they had little to say, or else because they were naturally laconic. Others wrote profusely and composed whole memoirs. Thus the schoolmaster from the village of Pordic handed in a sixty-page foolscap notebook on 20 September 1919, while a colleague from elsewhere contented himself with two sides of a single sheet. Some adopted the

---

1. Documents in the Archives Départementales des Côtes-du-Nord — Series T, *Notices communales sur la guerre, 1914–1918.*

bare style of official documents, others let themselves go in elevated patriotic pathos. After copying out the list of local war dead, one of them wrote: 'Oh, ye dead, rise up, to you the victory! Dear fallen comrades, be sure that your death has not been in vain. . . . And you who have returned, take up your labour again. France expects our effort to continue. We shall not be fouind wanting'.

These phrases strike us as ridiculously grandiloquent today, but who can fail to be moved when, in the list of sixty-eight dead from her town, beautifully compiled in her own handwriting by the schoolmistress from Trebry, we find in the eighteenth place the name of her husband, killed on 9 May 1915; or again, when G. Le Roux, headmaster of the boys' school in Ploubazlanec, asks leave, at the end of his report, 'to render pious homage to the memory of [my] son, in training as a teacher, decorated with the Croix de Guerre, who fell on the field of honour at Mont-Haut (Champagne) on 31 May 1917'?

According to the schoolteachers' reports, the people in Côtes-du-Nord fell into three distinct groups, each with a characteristic attitude.

The first, quite rare, showed near-indifference:

'Here [in the commune of Rouillac], far from the bloody fray, people live a normal, quiet and peaceful life. News of the war is awaited without impatience and received without emotion'.

'The inhabitants of Plourivo are very hard to move; nothing seems to matter to them. . . . Nothing . . . shakes them out of their old ways.

If it did not happen that from time to time a family is struck by bereavement, the people round here would be unaware that there was any fighting'.

It ought to be said that, in this village of seafaring people, the men were often away from home even in peacetime so that war made little difference to the daily round of the womenfolk, except perhaps that they were rather better off.

The most widespread attitude was one of calm confidence: 'The inhabitants of this commune have never for a single instant ceased to be equal to the situation'; they were of firm resolve, patently calm, full of energy, showed courage in misfortune, had complete faith in final victory, and their unflagging patriotism was said to do them great honour; they were never discouraged and never expressed the least doubt in victory.

A third attitude, less untroubled, was also fairly well represented.

It took the form of anxiety and despondency and apparently began to surface in 1916. After the shocks of the summer of 1914, no major event, at least on the French front, disturbed the calm of the population for almost two years. Then came the battle of Verdun. That night, a crowd waited with 'anguish' at Paimpol for the arrival of the last train bringing news from the battlefield. In the Ile de Bréhat, the inhabitants snatched up newspapers with bated breath as fast as they arrived. Here — as we can see — confidence in the press had not yet been eroded; some of our witnesses even claimed that the press had played a major role in maintaining morale, because, they said, French papers were 'written on a very high patriotic note'. And at Pordic, for instance, the average joint circulation of dailies and periodicals had more than doubled from about 500 copies before the war to 1,060. In a village of some 900 families, this meant that the papers — in this case, almost exclusively *L'Ouest-Eclair* and *La Croix* — were very widely read.

In 1917, anxiety and disquiet began to give way to spells of despondency. The schoolmaster from Plouguenast allows us to follow the development of the state of morale of his fellow citizens from close quarters.

Taking advantage of the Christmas holiday and that of New Year's Day 1917 to visit the parents of all his pupils, he found that most of them were despondent and disillusioned. He redoubled his efforts to instil fresh courage wherever he went, but all that people wanted was 'to see the back of this accursed war'. In April 1917, when the United States joined in, the response was not nearly as joyful as he had expected — on the contrary, some people only saw it as a sign that the war might drag on even longer. Fortunately, he tells us, the morale of the soldiers home on leave was very high, and he hoped that their confidence might prove contagious. The sudden end of the Chemin-des-Dames offensive, where men from his commune were sorely tested, produced great disillusionment. Nevertheless, by August 1917 the men on leave had recovered their good humour and confidence. If only the Russians held out, they said, everything would be over before the Americans turned up. Unfortunately the Russians did not hold out, and the soldiers home on leave became extremely agitated. They were afraid of a tremendous German offensive before winter, and they were reported to be 'in a terrible humour and often take three extra days of leave or more. Their wives and the old people are also badly affected'. Christmas and New Year's Day 1918 were very sad: 'One does not dare ask questions any more'. In April 1918, the soldiers on leave seemed increasingly disheartened: 'It is high time that a successful offensive came to restore the courage of our brave *poilus*,' our reporter declared. Everything changed finally in August. Faces became serene once again: 'Now one can speak to people about the war without being exposed to looks full of hate and harsh words'. From this we can see that the end of 1917 and the beginning of 1918 were a time of especial strain. However, what was true of Plouguenast was not necessarily true of the whole department of Côtes-du-Nord. Our schoolmaster, for one, did not think it so, for he added: 'How much better the morale in the countryside round Tréguier!' However, again by contrast, in the Ile de Bréhat the inhabitants who had greeted news of the American declaration of war with enthusiasm were heard, in December 1917, to utter defeatist remarks that tended to 'lower morale'. Elsewhere the events of May to August 1917 did not seem to affect the people of the commune, but by March 1918 many of them felt despondent: 'We at home are gloomy and our morale is very low. That of the soldiers at the front is not very high either. One has the impression that the army is becoming undisciplined and does not want to fight any longer. Broken glass from the railway carriages is scattered along the line'.

Interactions between the front and the rear were frequent and complex: at times the soldiers on leave raised the morale of the civilians, at others they failed to inspire conviction and their disorderly behaviour was widely condemned, as, for instance, when 'they make it a point of honour to be rude, and even coarse sometimes, smashing the windows of railway carriages, respecting neither regulations nor their own officers. One saw saddening examples of indiscipline at the railway station [of Quintin] after the failure of the Champagne offensive.' 'Nauseating spectacles.'

But on other occasions, the letters that soldiers wrote home were full of confidence in victory, and the resolve they showed as they rejoined their units strengthened that of their families.

The effect of casualties on the morale of the home front was, curiously enough, not altogether predictable. Certain deaths did make a deep impression, especially when soldiers who had died at a hospital behind the lines could be brought back to their native soil for burial amid great ceremonial. At Saint-Lormel, the first of such burials was held in June 1915. There was a huge crowd, and the entire commune attended, filled with emotion and reverence. Bugle calls and drum rolls accompanied the cortège: 'All eyes were filled with tears. His old mother followed the hearse, her aching heart broken. But her eyes were dry and she held her head high. She seemed to say: "I have given my son to France. What more can I do?" '

But, in the nature of things, the death of so many conscripts took on an almost abstract character, particularly during the long period when no leave was granted — while it still looked as if the war would be over very quickly, there seemed to be no need for it — and separations became inordinately long. Some comments on deaths at the front strike us as being oddly dry at times and we may be slightly taken aback to read: 'In short, there was nothing to regret save the death and disappearance of a rather large number of soldiers, but that was inevitable, because there is no battle without victims, and a war so fierce and so protracted is bound to cause heavy losses in all units engaged in it'; or again: 'The list of those who "died for their country" grows longer, but the countryside is bustling with activity'.

Why this apparent callousness? Certainly not because these villages were spared. Thus there were 89 deaths out of 1,900 inhabitants in Yvignac; 53 dead and 5 missing out of 1,185 inhabitants in Tremeur; 120 dead out of 2,778 inhabitants in Sévignac, to choose a few random examples. Among conscripts — and an appreciable percentage of them were not sent to the front — we find that 21 per cent were killed from Saint-Gouéno, 31 per cent from Saint-Bihy, 21 per cent from Rouillac, 20.5 per cent from Meslin, 20 per cent from Maroué, 16 per cent from Broons. In one village, four brothers were killed, and the headmaster of the school in Uzel counted among the dead three of the five assistant teachers who had served under him during the previous fifteen years. If we bear in mind that, over France as a whole, the proportion of dead among conscripts was between 16 and 17 per cent, we find that the figures for Brittany were among the highest.

It would seem that the effects of this slaughter on French morale were softened by the fact that the losses did not come all at once, but were spread over the war years as a whole. However, as Table 6.1 shows, the heaviest losses occurred during the first two years.

Table 2. *Number of war-dead per year in selected towns and villages*

	Broons	St-Julien	St-Méloir	Trefumel	Trebry
1914	13	3	3	5	11
1915	23	7	3	3	22
1916	15	4	2	5	11
1917	13	5	1	1	4
1918	23	5	0	3	2

The explanation is simple. At the time, the tactics and strategy employed, coupled with the inexperience of the combatants, resulted in veritable massacres. The moment when morale began to flag, however, did not coincide with the peak of the slaughter. Furthermore, death was accepted as a fate few combatants could escape, which explains why there was so much resignation in the face of the carnage.

The most widespread attitude, as we saw, was one of confidence. But is there any method for deciding whether that confidence did indeed go hand-in-hand with intense patriotic fervour? There is one barometer, one yardstick, which may lead us towards an answer: the response of the public to the war charities, the collections, the appeals for gold, the appeals for refugee aid. . . . Yet applying this yardstick in the Côtes-du-Nord does not produce the impression of any great burst of enthusiasm. It is true that in the main the population was poor, and this may explain why there were few communes where teachers could congratulate themselves on the generosity of their fellow citizens. In a number of places, such as the Ile de Bréhat, the collections produced better results, and at La Harmoye the combined zeal of the teacher and the priest-in-charge resulted in an extraordinarily high response to the war loan campaign. But what about the rest of the department? In one place, people mistrusted the war loans and refused 'with regret' to support war charities; in another, the reaction was chilly, some contending that to subscribe to loans would only help to prolong the war. In a third, little eagerness was shown for the loans, and still less for the collections. One teacher complained: 'What rare displays of generosity there are strike no spark and thus do not set an example to be followed by others . . .'.

It should be emphasised — and naturally the teachers did so — that while state schools often fulfilled the function of being centres for the organisation of collections and loans, they were not immune to the general atmosphere, and their pupils' fervour gradually weakened as well. As one teacher put it, 'the school took part [in war charities] with ever-diminishing enthusiasm'; in the end he did not believe that he had had more than a 'relative success'.

When refugees were mentioned, it was rarely to commend any generosity being shown towards them. The selfishness of the 'countryman' was stigmatised; he was 'too greedy' and 'almost deaf to the misfortunes of others'.

What are we therefore to make of a fairly widely shared confidence in the outcome of the war which had no base in any pronounced patriotic fervour? In other words, what was it that made these people 'hold out'?

A teacher from Pordic, a large village close to Saint-Brieuc, asked himself this very question. He adduced four reasons. At the outset, the essential response was a feeling of righteous outrage in the face of aggression; later the prevailing mood was that defeat would turn France into a second-class nation that would never recover. A third, if subsidiary, reason was the very important role played by the newspapers. The fourth reason was the maintenance of acceptable economic conditions.

The standard of life in this essentially agricultural region was dependent upon the prosperity of agriculture; here the moratorium on rents and the problem of feeding the family made much smaller impacts than they did in the towns. In general, tenant farmers were able to pay their rent, though when they did not, small landlords often became hard-pressed. Fresh food supplies did pose many problems in rural areas, as a few examples show: thus in August 1918, at Plouha, people had to queue for an hour to obtain 'a chunk of hard bread, black, and indigestible, not even fit for the beasts'. There was a bread shortage at the same time at Paimpol. 'People queue outside the bakers for hours on end.' At Ploubazlanec, bread was scarce in June 1918, and at times customers had to queue for half a day outside the baker's door, but potatoes never ran short. Some items such as sugar, paraffin or chocolate could be difficult to obtain at times, but most agreed that supplies of essential foodstuffs were almost normal. As one witness put it, no single product was ever totally unobtainable.

What problems there were therefore had to do with the situation on the land. Mobilisation had come at a time when work in the fields was in full swing. As we saw in Chapter 1, thanks to the combined efforts of those left behind, the harvest was brought in. But could this *tour de force* be repeated? Could agricultural output be kept up when most young men had left for the war? The answer, at least in Côtes-du-Nord, was in the affirmative. In a few communes the land was left fallow, but these were very much the exception. There was also just one place, Rouillac, where it was reported that the harvest had suffered. Elsewhere only the large estates were not fully cultivated. But even these negative findings show that there were no serious problems: some fields were worked less intensively but very few were left uncultivated.

The most widespread opinion was that the former level of agricultural activity had been maintained. 'The land has not suffered from the absence of the men. . .' ; '*the fields have been tilled thanks to the women; there are no untilled fields; not a square metre of land has remained uncultivated; good harvests; the crops did not suffer. . . .'*

How can this be explained? The first factor, of course, as we have already said, was the determination of those who stayed behind, but then a second factor, the rise in prices, added a powerful incentive. This was particularly evident in the few communes where the yield had at first declined: thus at Pludual, 'the good price levels revived production and deliveries', but afterwards; at Trédaniel, too, field-work had suffered during the first two years, but later, by virtue of the high prices, there was a new vigour, and 'nearly all the abandoned fields were worked again'.

Oddly enough, agricultural effort, far from running out of steam, had a tendency to redouble. At Yvignac the first year was hard and the harvest reflected this fact. But then, when people became used to the new conditions, no fields were left fallow: during the last three years of the war the land produced as much as it had ever done.

To many Frenchmen, the rise in prices was probably more surprising than the war itself. War seemed in some ways part of human nature, the rise in prices was not. This may explain why the forms filled in by the teachers in Côtes-du-Nord refer to the matter at such length.

To start with, what was the extent of the price rises, and what the sequence of events? Chronological information is scarce, but it would seem that 1916 marked a turning point. At that time, in the Ile de Bréhat, for instance, prices had already risen, but were still relatively moderate. By the end of 1916, however, they had not only risen noticeably but were not to fall back again. At Broons, too, there were few price rises before the end of 1916. Table 3, showing prices at Saint-Connec, a small village on the borders of Morbihan, is revealing.

At Saint-Méloir-des-Bois, a kilo of butter fetched 4 francs in the winter of 1916, and 14 francs in 1918–19.

Unfortunately indications of the intermediate stages are few and far between; all we are given is the overall increase between 1914 and 1919. Two examples are shown in Tables 4 and 5, below.

Many witnesses contented themselves with even more general estimates: prices had doubled, or even tripled. For another, the prices of potatoes, strawberries and chickens had risen *tenfold*; yet another claimed that prices were four or five times what they had been, or even six or seven times. It was not only the cost of food that had gone up, however, but also the prices of textiles, shoes and firewood.

The attitude to the price increases was not the same for buyers

Table 3. *Price rises at Saint-Connec, near Morbihan (in francs)*

	Prewar	End of 1916	End of 1918
Butter (per kg)	2.20	3.50	12
Eggs (per doz.)	0.80	2.20	5.50
Roast coffee (per kg)	5.60	7	10
Beef (per kg)	1.50	3	6
Veal (per kg)	1.60	3	6
Pickled pork (per kg)	1.50	4	9

and sellers. Teachers, whose salaries failed to keep pace with the rises, or barely did so, felt very bitter and did not disguise that fact. According to them, prices had become 'excessive' or 'exorbitant'. The farmers were 'stuffed with gold', they were making 'fabulous' profits, their produce was fetching 'unlooked-for' prices. Farmers themselves were complacent about the increases, and so were the shopkeepers, who were also thought to be taking advantage of the situation.

'Business is doing nicely', said the farmers.

We have already mentioned in Chapter 1 how, from the beginning of the war, separation allowances enabled most families to keep their heads above water, and how, in the autumn, when the war had gone on longer than most people had anticipated, these allowances helped to boost the morale of the home front.

Payment of the allowances continued; generously, according to some commentators. Early injustices were put right, and allocations were awarded with increasing liberality. In fact, at least in this department, nearly every family with a man at the front seemed to be getting them, regardless of its actual needs.

When we remember that work on the farms was continuing and the farmers were getting excellent prices for their produce, the claim that the farmers were growing rich on the war may be seen to have some justification. Thus, the schoolmaster from Saint-Etienne-du-Gué de l'Isle claimed that the 'allowances and the price rises have helped to enrich the farmers'. 'Most farmers have grown rich; they are buying their farms, but one must remember that they have contributed to the salvation of our country with their labour and the sacrifice of their children.'

Another teacher concurred: the farmers' work was hard and wearisome, but 'their efforts have been rewarded with prosperity'. The upsurge in material well-being was evident in the purchases of farms, farm machinery and the bicycles in almost every home, as

Table 4. *Overall increase in food prices, Hénansal (in francs)*

	Prewar	1919
Wheat	22.24	75
Potatoes (per 100 kg)	3.5	35
Butter (per pound)	25–30 sous	100 sous
Young pigs (each)	4–8	180–200
Cider (per cask)	20–30	200–220
Chickens (each)	1.50–2	13–15
Eggs (per doz.)	1	4.50–5
Bacon (per kg)	0.75–2	4.50–5.50

well as in the way the women were turned out. In one commune, only two farmers' wives had not taken over the running of their farms from their husbands, and these two regretted their failure bitterly. One said that when their men returned, they, unlike their 'luckier' comrades, were not going to discover 'piles of thousand-franc notes tucked away in a cupboard'. In that commune, as elsewhere, the courage of the women was highly praised, but it was acknowledged that most of them had 'taken advantage of the situation and amassed tidy sums of money'. Some people claimed that farmers' incomes had quadrupled or 'even more', which bolstered their courage. 'They have nice little nest eggs.' 'They prove it by vying with each other in buying houses, fields and farms.'

Many people believed, indeed, that this new affluence was well merited, the more so as it was sometimes said to be relatively modest, but others saw it as unhealthy. For though the new affluence had helped to keep up morale in the countryside, it was a selfish morale reflected in the general reluctance to contribute to war charities. 'Their indifference is striking.' This criticism is also reflected in a sketch of the congregation leaving mass at Saint-Lormel in April 1918:

> The sight is no longer what it was in 1914. Less simplicity in dress, more preoccupation with fashion and its excesses. Just as in town, one can see shortened skirts, knee-high boots, hats copied from the latest fashion magazine. The traditional headdress is no longer worn except by very old women. Every young girl has a bicycle.
> In the countryside, money abounds and young countrywomen make sure that everyone knows it.

Does that mean that there were no more poor people? The

Table 5. *Overall increases in food prices, La Harmoye (in francs)*

	Prewar	1919
Bullocks	800	2,500
Cows	200	900
Pigs (per kg live weight)	1.50	5
Calves (per kg live weight)	1.30	4.20
Eggs (per doz.)	0.90	7
Butter (per kg)	2.50	15
Bacon (per kg)	1.50	8

records often make this claim, while not holding that everyone had become rich. To use an expression of the time, 'pauperism' had disappeared. Few or no families were in want, said one reporter; most of the poor had received relief. There were no truly indigent families left in the commune, no needy people during the war. The schoolmaster of Yvignac was not alone in thinking that while there was certainly adversity, there was, on the whole, little financial hardship.

Day labourers, however, were a special case. They had work, as a rule, but according to several reports their wages did not keep up with the rising cost of living, although others reported that some farmers were having to dispense with domestic servants because their wages had become too high.

Other victims of the rise in prices were state employees, whose cost-of-living allowances were inadequate. Some teachers deplored the fact that the government, 'by affording extravagant protection to agriculture, had helped to raise the cost of living'.

It would be wrong to conclude that all tenant farmers had made a fortune, or that all of them were able to buy their own farms. It remains a fact, however, and all our sources agree on this point, that at least in the Côtes-du-Nord, tolerable economic conditions encouraged the people to 'hold out', despite the length of the conflict — to hold out not only behind the lines, but also at the front, where the troops had been freed of worry about the financial situations of their families.

By successive strokes of the pen, our reporters have thus drawn a homogeneous picture of the attitude of the rural population in this part of Brittany. The anguish caused by the continuation of the war was sometimes hard to bear, particularly when news from the front was bad and when the final outcome seemed uncertain. At times people hated the war. But acceptable economic conditions, as all the witnesses assert, helped them to 'suffer' without rebelling, and 'fostered courage'. We should not deduce from this, somewhat simplistically, that selfish people accepted the fearsome sacrifices of the soldiers unmoved, because they helped them to attain affluence. Nor are we entitled to conclude that, without acceptable economic conditions, these people would have 'caved in'. We do not know. All we can say is that their refusal to accept defeat and their confidence in final victory were certainly helped by prosperity.

And what about the *Union sacrée*? Well, curiously enough, people did not refer to it very often, if at all. We have only one reference to it from one commune: 'The *Union sacrée* lives among all the inhabitants of Maroué'. What are we to make of this? It was probably a political reflex rather than one which came from the heart. People did not mention the *Union sacrée* because it was not very important in their daily lives. They supported the war because they belonged to a country, and not because political forces had decided for the time being to shelve their differences.

CHAPTER 7

Charente in 1915–16

Charente, a predominantly agricultural department, provides us with another good example of rural attitudes during the war. It is also the department for which we have the greatest number of communal records compiled by local teachers.[1] There is thus a large amount of information, which is, however, confined in the main to the first two years of the war. Less frequently the records cover the beginning of 1917, and very exceptionally they continue into 1918. This was the result of the zeal of the chief education officer, who began to collect the records at the beginning of 1917, at which point most of the teachers stopped keeping them. But the result was not altogether bad: the authenticity of these documents is all the greater in that they were not compiled after the war but soon after the events themselves. Their contents have not therefore been distorted by hindsight (see Table 7.1).

The teachers' accounts of conditions on the land in Charente during 1915 and 1916 do not create the same euphoric impression as those compiled in Côtes-du-Nord. In a few cases, conditions were said to have been 'normal', 'quite good', 'almost normal'. 'Not too many difficulties', said one; 'agricultural work proceeds smoothly enough', said another. But these opinions were far from general. The main problem was the straightforward one of lack of hands, which made itself felt with particular force in a wine-growing region. At the beginning, in 1914, the problem was dealt with by mutual aid. Mutual aid continued, of course, but as one teacher put it, this was bound to decrease, particularly as the labour force continued to shrink. In 1915, for instance, and again in 1916, new classes were called up, which meant so many fewer labourers.

1. AD Charente J 76–95.

Table 6. *Local school contributions to the National Defence Fund,*
commune of Merpins (in francs)

Charitable works			Amounts received	Charitable works	Amounts received
Linen for the	in kind	1050	1,213	School inspectorate	
wounded	in cash	163		workroom	20
Clothing for refugees			250	Prisoners of war	30
Christmas for soldiers			15	Nuts for soldiers	30
Knitted	in kind	254	254	Wine for soldiers	300
articles	in cash	—		Blanket collection	620
National Aid Day			92	Adopted sons of the war	80
'75' Day			103	French reception	80
Serbian Soldiers' Day			55	Cotton rags	7
French Soldiers' Day			64	Collections in aid of refugees	200
Belgian Soldiers' Day			64	Contributions to State	
War Orphans' Day			153	School Orphans	3
War Victims' Day			118	Contributions by the Staff	
Subscription to the League				to the Amicale (2%; Francs	
of the Children				for Belgians, etc)	
of France			118	Contributions to the Cognac	
Ambulance vehicles			76	military hospitals. Monthly	
Sandbags			128	contributions by the	
			2,521	schoolmaster	560
					4,341

Total sum collected (staff) 2,814 + (pupils) 1,447 = 4,341 francs
Total amount of gold collection — capital subscribed to 2 loans, 9,500 francs (by
the schoolmaster)

On the other hand, the older peasants of the 1888 and 1889 classes,
that is, men aged between 47 and 48 in 1916, were sent back home,
but not enough of them. Wages, too, exacerbated the problem: the
shortage of hands had evidently increased the cost of labour. In one
commune, domestics who had been paid 250 francs for six months
received 400 francs at the beginning of 1916, while labourers were
paid 2.50 to 3.00 francs a day, plus their keep. Agriculture, which
had suffered little during the first year of the war, 'suffers a great
deal now'. The number of uncultivated fields increased, in one
commune by at least a quarter, and the harvest of 1916 was judged
to be two-thirds of a good normal harvest, the yield having dropped
even further for lack of fertiliser.

The schoolmaster from Mazerolles summed up the situation as
follows:

During the first year everything went more or less well: mobilisation had left us with enough men, and the harvesting and ploughing were done everywhere in time. But by the second year there were already some properties without farmers, and at the beginning of the third year, there were four abandoned properties in this commune. This is obviously disappointing, but if we recall that the younger classes, the last of the reservists, the auxiliaries declared unfit for active service, etc., had been called up by this time, so that the only hands left were old men, the situation may be said to be as good as human effort could hope to make it, the more so as agricultural machinery cannot be used in our hilly country. On those farms which have not been abandoned all the fields have been ploughed and sown: but they have not been dressed properly. The women and children have done the best they could. Those men who have not been called up never grudged their help. It is also true to say that agricultural exemptions, granted largely to the auxiliaries and as a last resort to reservists at the front, proved invaluable: soldiers on leave did the ploughing and the reaping, work impossible for women. Agricultural labourers are very scarce, and the cost of manpower reflects this fact: up to 8 and 10 francs per day for reaping. Complete hostility towards the use of German prisoners of war.

Weather conditions assumed a new importance during the war. In normal times, farmers would greet bad weather without joy, but now, having had to make exceptional efforts and having to stand by as their efforts were reduced to nothing, they were plunged into despair, so much so that some of them gave up the struggle.

It goes without saying that agricultural conditions vary from one department to the next and from one region to another, and have always done so. Even so, the difference in tone between Charente and Côtes-du-Nord is remarkable. One explanation is that teachers in Côtes-du-Nord, unlike those in Charente, set down their overall impression at the end of the war, by which time price rises had apparently helped to make the peasants considerably better off. Although by 1916 inflation had begun to make itself felt, it still had a long way to go: it was not until 1916 and 1917 that the gradual increase in prices suddenly made way for the explosion exemplified in Table 7.2, compiled in 1920 for the commune of Métairies.

The schoolmaster from the commune of Blanzac gives a good account of this process. He begins by describing the despondency of some of the people in 1915, and then shows how, by redoubling their efforts in response to the increases in prices and the high returns, 'gentry' were able to 'watch their profits go up considerably'. It is possible that had our records on agricultural conditions in Charente been compiled in 1918 and not in 1916, the picture would have been the same as that for Côtes-du-Nord: a satisfied farming population, at least so far as finances were concerned.

Table 7. *The cost of living: price changes in basic commodities (in francs)*[a]

	1914	1915	1916	1917	1918	1919	1920
Bread per ½ kg)	0.15	0.15	0.20	0.25	0.25	0.30	0.50
Meat:							
beef, veal, mutton (good cuts)	1.25	1.25	1.50	2	4	5	5
Wine (per 100 litres)	20	60	80	100	110	125	125
Sugar (per ½ kg)	0.80	0.80	0.90	0.95	1.15	1.25	1.25
Cheese (Gruyère, Roquefort) (per ½ kg)	1.50	1.50	5	6	7	7	7
Butter (per ½ kg)	1.60	1.75	—	—	—	8	8
Eggs (per dozen)	1	1.20	3	5	6	8	6
Milk (per litre)	0.10	0.10	0.15	0.30	0.40	0.60	0.75
Coffee (per ½ kg)	5	3	3.50	4	4.50	5	5
Dried beans (standard)	0.25	0.25	0.40	0.60	0.75	1.50	1.50
Split peas (per ½ kg)	0.50	—	—	—	3	3.25	3.25
Lentils (per ½ kg)	0.40	—	—	—	—	2.90	2.90
Chickens (per ½ kg)	1.25	1.50	2	3	4	4.50	4.50
Paraffin (per litre)	0.40	0.55	0.65	1	1.10	0.90	0.80
Petrol (per litre)	0.30	0.80	1	1.40	1.50	1.40	1.40
Coal (per tonne)	55	60	70	115	130	110	140
Charcoal (per 10 kg)	7	10	25	30	40	35	35
A suit	70	200	250	300	325	400	400
A pair of shoes (men's)	20	35	40	45	50	80	80
Chalk (per box)	0.75	—	—	—	1.75	2	2
Steel nibs (per box)	1.30	3	3.75	4	5.50	7	7
School books	1	1.25	1.50	1.75	2	2	2
Potatoes	0.05	0.05	0.10	0.30	0.40	0.25	0.25
An ordinary workhorse	800	—	—	—	—	3,000 to 4,000	—
A milch cow	200	—	—	—	—	1,500 to 1,800	—
A pair of working oxen	1,200	—	—	—	—	6,000 to 7,000	—
A fat pig	120	—	—	—	—	800	—
A sucking pig	30	—	—	—	—	150	—

15 February 1920

[a] Departmental Archives, Charente J 86

In 1916, the time of riches had not yet arrived, but there was no longer any poverty. Opinions are unanimous on this point: 'The war did not cause people material impoverishment'; the war 'did not make a pauper of a single inhabitant of this commune'. Unlike Côtes-du-Nord, the region was not poor. The schoolmaster discovered that in certain communes 'pauperism had hardly ever been known', and that the few vestiges of it which remained were now tending to disappear. The situation of many families had improved. If people were still badly off, it was their own fault, one report said, for there was no shortage of work.

In fact, however, some casual labourers did find it difficult to obtain work, not for lack of vacancies, but because of the very high wages that all hands now fetched. As for local government officials, they had to face inflation with salaries that scarcely altered.

Fresh supplies caused few serious problems. There were temporary shortages of such items as paraffin, sugar or cod, and in 1917 pasta, tinned food, rice, soap and oils became scarcer. In places, the call-up of a grocer and the closing of his shop may have caused some difficulty, but on the whole this would be more of an inconvenience than a real hardship. Provisions were as plentiful as before the war, one of our witnesses said in July 1916, another adding: 'We lack for nothing'. Even later, when there was bread rationing, this could not have been called stringent, at least in practice, and except for rare periods the quality of bread remained acceptable.

One sentence sums up conditions of life in Charente during these first two years of war: 'Those families whom the war did not put into mourning were truly well off'. But there were deaths, and here as elsewhere their number mounted with regularity. Some communes were spared 'as if by a miracle', for instance, Angeduc, which had not a single death to mourn in August 1916, but then its total population had been no more than 156 inhabitants in 1911. Charente regiments, it would seem, suffered fewer casualties in 1914 than those from other regions: thus at Mansle there were 'only' (!) four dead in 1914, but thirteen in 1915; at Bouchage, no dead in 1914, but four in 1915 and four in 1916; at Birac, one dead in 1914, five in 1915 and three in 1916; at Bessé, no dead in 1914, three in 1915 . . . Exceptions to this rule were few; thus Ansac, a small village with 921 inhabitants, lost eight dead in 1914 as against three in 1915 and three in 1916. Though there are no complete statistics, it would seem that Charente was asked to make fewer sacrifices generally than Côtes-du-Nord, but it paid its tribute none the less. From the end of 1916, almost 14 per cent of all conscripts from Bonneuil were killed, almost 13 per cent of those from Boisbreteau, almost 17 per cent of those from the very small commune of Brettes (380 inhabitants) and more than 23 per cent of those from Bors-de-Baignes (193 inhabitants).

Did this slaughter alter the mood of calm and confidence prevailing in the autumn of 1914? Apparently not: 'The prolongation of the war and the many bereavements have failed to shake the morale of the population.' That claim was repeated several times: 'few complaints from the stricken families'; 'the deaths of the sons of the commune are accepted with stoic resignation'; 'the demise of family members is borne with courage and resignation'. A schoolmaster-cum-parish clerk to whom the mayor entrusted the task of notifying villagers of casualties in their family stressed that 'though I invariably heard expressions of deep sorrow, I never heard anyone raise his voice against *la Patrie*' and he considered this to be a supreme manifestation of patriotism.

In 1915 and 1916, confidence remained the rule. People adapted themselves 'with extraordinary flexibility' to being at war, and this was reflected in 'dogged effort' in an unshakeable faith in a favourable outcome'. The word 'confidence' keeps recurring in the reports: 'firm' confidence in the final result, 'unshakeable' confidence, 'ever-growing' confidence.

This attitude was not expressed in spectacular ways, except at critical moments: 'Then one could detect a recurrence of the old fluctuation between anxiety and a joyous, patriotic pride . . .'. Another teacher wrote that the 'feverish' atmosphere of the beginning had died down, but not through lack of interest, since the population kept giving proof of national solidarity and patriotism whenever the occasion demanded. In any case, these were traditionally reserved people, more given to composure and dignity than to displays of apprehension. Their patriotism was expressed in their regular contributions to the collections and war charities. Many schoolteachers dwelt on this generosity: 'good response to collections'; 'magnificent spirit of solidarity when it comes to war charities'; 'no appeal falls on deaf ears'; 'everyone makes an offering, even those who are not very well off.'

We are rarely told what it was that helped the people of Charente to keep their confidence, but it is clear that as far as they were concerned, and though they felt no need to put it into words, no other attitude was possible. As one schoolmaster put it, there was no salvation save victory.

This also explains the lack of reference to the *Union sacrée*. In Charente, as in Côtes-du-Nord, this concept, which looms so large in the ideological analyses of the war, had little practical value. It was not that it played no part in daily life, but that it did so without pretension, people accepting the evident need for unity in the cause of national defence. Everybody was agreed on it, so there was no need to refer to it. This is what the schoolmaster from Ars meant when he wrote: 'The *Union sacrée* is at work here as it is in the entire region.' But he was one of the few who even thought it necessary to put it into words. One phrase epitomises the attitude of the rural population of Charente: 'It held out.'

Yet these records were being compiled at the end of 1916 and the beginning of 1917, that is, after two years of war. Were there really no signs of deterioration?

They existed, but they were neither pronounced nor ubiquitous. In fact, although there were rumours of widespread pessimism, many places in Charente shrugged them off, with the result that public confidence actually grew, especially once the United States entered the war. But elsewhere, though 'morale was good on the whole' in 1917, 'one can feel weariness creep into all family conversations and even into the children's homework'. The war contributions were the first to suffer from the decline in patriotic fervour. For some time, we are told, 'generosity seems to have been decreasing', collectors and sellers of flags were increasingly sent away empty-handed and grew tired of their task. Apart from local government officials, no one gave anything, noted the schoolmaster from Benest. Many felt that they had given enough.

This was inevitable after more than two years of a war without an end in sight. By the end of 1916 and the beginning of 1917, the enthusiasm of August 1914 had decreased appreciably. On the whole, morale was still good; it was probably no longer proof against every ordeal, but the rural areas had no experience of the despair that at times held the towns in its grip.

Unhappily, we do not know what followed in the next few years, and whether the people of Charente maintained the resolute but circumspect attitude they had adopted by the end of the two first years of war.

In 1916, however, there was no doubt. The records from Charente tell much the same story as those from Côtes-du-Nord: the rural population, with slight differences attributable to regional temperament, showed no signs of rejecting the attitude adopted in 1914. Rural France had settled down stolidly to the war.

CHAPTER 8

Paris 1915

In Paris, the prefect of police compiled regular reports on morale in the capital for submission to the minister of the interior. A file in the Archives Nationales[1] contains his reports for August, September, November and December 1915. Each report consists of some twenty-five typewritten pages and is divided into a general commentary and notes on each of the twenty arrondissements.

The preamble to the August report can serve as a summary of the prefect's general conclusions: 'The new survey conducted in all Parisian arrondissements shows that morale has altered very little since it was examined by us last June [unfortunately this file has not been traced] when economic problems took precedence over questions of morale raised by developments at the various fronts'.

The people of Paris were indeed primarily concerned with the high cost of living. This was true not only in August, but also in September, in November and in December, and it applied to all the arrondissements. In August there were complaints about prices in all twenty arrondissements, in September in eighteen, in November in nineteen and in December in fourteen. This suggests that dissatisfaction was highest in August and November, that it slackened in September, and particularly in December. Even so, no other subject is mentioned so often and so insistently. This was the main concern. A table of complaints made during these four months in each arrondissement (Table 8.1) gives us some idea of the strength of these protests. The terms used, which are nearly always the same — complaints, protests, remonstrations, against the excessively high prices — reflect a mood of deep dissatisfaction.

Food prices were not, however, the only cause for anxiety: there

1. AN F 7 12936.

Table 8. *The attitude of Parisians to price rises, August–December 1915 (by arrondissement)*

	August	September	November	December
Ist	Remonstrations	No improvement	Violent protests	—
IInd	Complaints	More complaints	Astonishment	—
IIIrd	Protests	Apprehension	General grievances	—
IVth	Situation improved	Fewer complaints	Complaints	Main worry
Vth	Complaints	Main worry	Protests	Especially acrimonious remonstrations
VIth	Protests	Fewer objections	More frequent protests	Protests
VIIth	Complaints	More complaints	Protests	Few remonstrations
VIIIth	More anxiety about coal	—	Complaints by the 'well-to-do'	Still very bitter complaints
IXth	Complaints	—	Worries	Complaints
Xth	Complaints	Complaints	Vigorous protests	Big worry
XIth	Anxiety	Complaints and anxiety	Vehement protests	Fierce resentment
XIIth	Protests	Protests	Increasingly bitter objections	Complaints
XIIIth	Protests	Worry and disquiet	Increasingly bitter protests	Less acrimonous complaints
XIVth	Protests	Complaints	Real anxiety	Usual remonstrations
XVth	Protests	Not many objections	Tension	Tension
XVIth	Protests	—	—	—
XVIIth	More frequent protests	Continuing bitter complaints	Vehement protests	—
XVIIIth	Complaints and tension	Less frequent complaints	Calm	Indignation
XIXth	Vehement protests	Worries	Protests	Increasingly intense annoyance
XXth	Protests	Complaints	Vigorous complaints	—

was also the supply of coal and its price. Curiously enough, it was in the heat of August that this problem reached its peak: it is mentioned in six arrondissements, as against just four in November and two in December. In September it cropped up in two arrondissements, but only as the declaration that anxiety had abated. This paradoxical attitude is most understandable; having run short of coal in August, Parisians were panic-stricken at the prospect of spending the winter in the same situation. The restoration of more normal supplies helped to soothe these anxieties.

The question of rents, too, caused concern, though marginally so, for it was not mentioned in August, but was raised in September in two arrondissements, in two others in November, and in yet another in December. In September, the prefect of police brought it to the special attention of the minister, on the grounds that the situation might deteriorate:

> The most irksome problem, and one that looks as if it will daily become more serious, is that of rents. The antagonism between landlords and lodging-house keepers on the one hand and tenants on the other is becoming increasingly obvious. A good many of the landlords appear to be ready to insist when dealing with their tenants — who, relying on the moratorium, have not paid their rents since the outbreak of war — on all the rights which the existing laws confer upon them. The tenants for their part are organising resistance, and in several arrondissements defence groups have already been set up under the aegis of socialist organisations and party officials. And there are grounds for thinking that this resistance has been encouraged by soldiers on leave, who in some areas have declared that on their return, they expect to be completely absolved from the payment of all rents incurred in their absence.

The rent question was complex: in the general expectation that the war would soon be over, the government had been able to pass the moratorium on rents in August 1914. But, as the war continued, the moratorium, valued by tenants, was increasingly resented by landlords, some of whom found themselves deprived of a livelihood. Moreover, if tenants had been called up, so had landlords, and the moratorium, a law made for the occasion, was applied indiscriminately — it would have been very difficult to establish a distinction between those who were able and those who were unable to pay. To avoid long-term problems, the government had decreed that the moratorium must be renewed from one rent day to the next, and the tenants therefore awaited each rent day in fear that the moratorium might end. Moreover, landlords used every possible means to exert pressure on tenants to pay, leading to the worries and conflict evident at the end of 1915, which the prefect feared might end in even more serious trouble.

Wage problems were rarely mentioned in 1915, and then only in connection with women outworkers. In August, for instance, women in the XVIIIth arrondissement complained that they were being paid no more than 0.15 francs for making a pair of underpants instead of the 0.35 francs fixed by the supplies office; in November, women in the XIth arrondissement complained that the wages agreed for the making of military apparel were inadequate; in December, there were complaints in the IIIrd arrondissement about the derisory wages offered to women. Similarly, there were just a few complaints about inadequate separation allowances or their method of distribution. However, in the XIVth arrondissement, the wives of conscripted small shopkeepers complained that they were being paid no allowances at all; in the XIth arrondissement, there were complaints that the allowances did not keep up with the cost of meat and wine in particular; in November allowances were thought to be increasingly inadequate in the XIXth arrondissement.

All in all, therefore, what worried people most was the rise in food prices; relatively few complaints were made about unemployment, and in many arrondissements people even congratulated themselves on 'the recovery of business'. As the prefect noted in December: '[It] is most helpful in diverting attention from the anxieties of the moment'. The observers at the prefecture emphasised that cinemas almost everywhere were full, that patriotic films were particularly appreciated, and that the 'upswing in attendance at entertainments seemed to be connected with economic recovery and with the presence in the district of a large number of essential workers brought back from the front and employed in munitions factories'. The district referred to was the XIIIth arrondissement, a working-class area.

Parisians proved to be most sensitive to what they saw as inequalities of sacrifice. Two groups were particular butts of their anger; 'shirkers' and 'foreigners'. Not a month went by without complaints against 'shirkers' being recorded.

In August 1915, the claim among the many small shopkeepers in the IInd arrondissement was that 'it is always the same people who are sent to the front and the same privileged lot who are kept back in the depots'; in the XIXth arrondissement it was thought that there were far too many young men still in the offices of the Orléans Railway Company and that their work ought to be handed over to the daughters and wives of servicemen. One category of 'shirkers' provoked especially bitter comments: that of workers brought back from the front to work in munitions factories, the more so as — a remark made in the XVIIIth arrondissement — 'these servicemen eating and sleeping at home sometimes put on a bit of a sneering attitude, which antagonises the conscripts' wives . . .'. In the Xth arrondissement, in November 1915 the wives or parents of serving soldiers 'frequently discussed the scandal of men fraudulently invalided out'.

Even more than the 'shirkers', it was the 'foreigners' who provoked a chorus of protest. People claimed that the government
tolerated far too many foreigners, at least in some districts of Paris.
In the Carreau du Temple, there were protests against the presence of young Russians or Poles who continued to ply their trades,
making, their rivals claimed, much higher profits than they had
before the war. In the IVth arrondissement, Russian and Polish
foreigners of an age to bear arms were accused of 'having a sneering
and even arrogant attitude'. Some people wanted them to be forced
to serve in the army or else to pay a special tax.

While some reports merely speak of foreigners, others are more
precise and refer to Russian and Polish 'Israelites'. This was a very
delicate subject. Concentrated particularly in the IIIrd, IVth and XIth
arrondissements, they were indeed disliked by the rest of the
population. Moreover, many were young but had not been called
up and were continuing in their trade or business. Feelings towards
them were thus a mixture of envy — most young Frenchmen of
their age having left — and resentment: they were thought to be
unfair competitors and also to be undercutting the going wage-rate
in the tailoring trade. It must be stressed, however, that in the heady
days following the declaration of war, many of these foreigners had
enlisted or had hoped to be able to do so in order to repay a debt to
the country that had given them shelter. But they had been treated
with some reserve, at first because the authorities did not even know
what to do with the mass of Frenchmen who had been conscripted
— the Territorials were sent back home for a time — and later
because the nationalist press objected to foreigners joining what was
primarily a national cause. As a result, the zeal of these Russian Jews
no doubt abated, the more so since fighting for France meant
fighting for Russia, from which country they had had to flee for fear
of their lives.

But Parisians — that is, the French among them — were so
convinced that their country was right, and so ignorant of what
other people thought, that they took it for granted that all foreigners must be desperate to flock to the colours. This explains their
suspicious attitude: foreigners could never do enough. In this
respect, Belgian refugees did not have a good press either. They
were found to be defeatist, quick to pass demoralising remarks and
hard to please; some were accused of not wanting to pay their rent,
even though they earned 10 francs a day, on the grounds that
without them 'the Prussians would have occupied Paris'. Similar
strictures were applied in general to all refugees: they refused to do
the work they were offered; they preferred to laze about. . . .

There was something strange, even paradoxical, about another aspect of the Parisians' attitude: economic worries seemed almost to overshadow interest in the progress of the war. Military operations, especially on the French front, never succeeded in capturing the attention of Parisians, although in September there was some surprise at the apparent inaction of the troops. This gave rise to a variety of speculations: for some, it showed a French inability to take the offensive; for others, it was proof of the commander-in-chief's determination not to make fresh sacrifices for negligible returns. It is, of course, a pity that no reports exist for October 1915, for these would doubtless have referred to the popular reaction to the offensive in Champagne at the end of September.

While Parisians wasted few words on operations in France, they did remark on developments in the Balkans and the east, that is, on the end of the Dardanelles expedition, on the Serbian situation and on the landings in Salonika. The mothers and wives of the conscripts dreaded that their men would be sent to these particular theatres of war, and especially to Serbia. On this subject, anxiety and pessimism were, if not the rule, at least reported on several occasions.

Thus, we see that, in a country at war, the inhabitants of her capital were deeply dissatisfied with economic conditions while at the same time seeming to show almost no interest in what was happening at the front. This is how the November report for the IXth arrondissement put it: 'The inhabitants. . .are much more concerned about the high cost of living than they are with the progress of military operations'.

Did Parisians then believe that ultimately the war was none of their concern? By no means. The general impression gained by the prefect's investigation was rather one of *confidence* in a favourable outcome. There were numerous signs that this was indeed the case.

In August, the Ist arrondissement faced a possible winter campaign quietly and confidently. In the XIth arrondissement, people seemed clearly unconcerned about the prolongation of the war, and in the XVth arrondissement they seemed in no way affected by it. In the Xth arrondissement there were no signs of despondency. Only in the XXth arrondissement did some people express doubts in the chances of ever driving the Germans out.

Confidence was maintained in December; indeed, the report on the VIIIth arrondissement spoke of unshakeable confidence.

One infallible sign was the success of the National Defence Loan. Parisians responded much more readily than the bankers had expected; indeed, they were even keener to subscribe than they had been to buy National Defence Bonds and Stock.

Were there no shadowy areas at all? No signs of diminishing confidence? Were all social classes of one mind?

In the XIIth arrondissement, in December, women were heard to complain about the war, but a few minutes later they joined others in applauding a patriotic film.

Similarly, in the XIXth arrondissement, 'the continuation of the war, the winter campaign, the Serbian expedition, are all beginning to cause some apprehension among parts of the population. Although posters enjoining the public to be discreet have helped to make the grumblers change their tune, some women were overheard while gossiping to call for the return of their husbands, or for the end of the war'. In the XIVth arrondissement, too, some women 'are showing signs of weariness'.

In August there were growing signs of disquiet among the working class — and to a lesser extent among the middle classes — at the prospect of another winter campaign.

It should be stressed that the police reporters did not ignore the existence of an anti-war movement; they even quoted remarks by women to the effect that they would welcome a revolution if the price rises continued. But they concluded that the population at large remained deaf to those few who wanted immediate peace at any price, and that most inhabitants had retained their usual calm and dignity even though there was no prospect of an economic improvement. So much for the conclusion of the monthly report for August; in December the picture was still much the same:

> No doubt, following the new measures relaxing the rigorous terms of the state of siege, some troublesome elements are trying with increasing audacity to spread demoralising doubts by word of mouth and in writing and they have also been calling for peace. But their theories do not seem to have attracted many disciples. On the contrary, the people of Paris continue to give proof positive of their confidence in the success of our arms and in the future of our country by subscribing massively to the National Defence Loan.

One is entitled to wonder about the real nature of a confidence that failed to be broken down by the resounding successes of the Central Powers on the Russian front and in the Balkans.

The September reports stress the beneficial role of soldiers on leave. Their arrival in the IVth arrondissement was said to have made a good impression. Round the Gare du Nord and the Gare de l'Est, these soldiers were heard to say that they were certain of victory, even though many infantrymen, in particular, were afraid of the new winter campaign. There was no sign of weariness among the many servicemen who passed through Montparnasse station. Soldiers on leave visiting cafés in the XVth arrondissement expressed their determination to fight on until victory, even though they had faith that it would come soon (in January, some thought!). The report from the XVIIth arrondissement stressed the fact that soldiers back on leave showed great confidence in an Allied victory, and in many cases helped to revive the morale of their relatives and friends.

There is, of course, no telling what the real feelings of these soldiers on leave might have been, if, as Henri Barbusse put it in *Le Feu*, they suffered from a split personality and hence dissimulated their suffering when they were back home, pretending instead to a degree of belligerence and confidence that they did not really feel. But comments on their good influence on those at home are too numerous and too general to be ignored.

It nevertheless seems unlikely that their good example was the sole explanation for the excellent state of Parisian morale during this phase of the war. A deeper analysis leads to a complementary interpretation. There was the appearance and there was the reality, and discontent about economic conditions was part of the former. Not that Parisians accepted the hardships of the war without demur. They were indeed discontented, and most were agreed on what the authorities should be doing to improve matters. But, and this is the reality, their grumbling did not mean that they had changed the attitude they had adopted in August 1914 — at least, not yet. The French had accepted the war; and they continued to accept it, basically on the same grounds. In August 1914, they had believed there would be a rapid victory. Despite all the successes of the Central Powers and all the failures of the Allies, they continued to believe in that victory, simply because they thought France was in the right. This reasoning was not based on an objective analysis of the real relationship of forces, but on a firm moral conviction. We can sense — naturally, it was not put in these terms — that underneath it all lay the very tough fabric of a nation. That was true in 1914 and was still true in December 1915, after seventeen months of a war that no one had imagined could last for even twelve.

Why did the French hold out? It is too early to answer the question. But the outlines of a reply have begun to emerge. The attitude of Parisians at the end of 1915 was expressed on two distinct levels: the material and the moral, or rather, the contingent and the fundamental. The contingent level comprised the many difficulties of everyday life in wartime, which explains why it loomed so large, but the fundamental level was one of confidence, and in 1915 the first level did not interfere with the second, or not very much so. And since — apart from catastrophes or brilliant military successes on a scale which had not occurred on the French front for a year — confidence did not draw its strength from the course of military events, the people of Paris paid these scant attention.

CHAPTER 9

Le Creusot During the War

It is possible to gain a general idea of the development of local attitudes in Le Creusot, a town of small dimensions (35,000 inhabitants in 1911) but of considerable industrial importance, by referring to the daily record kept by the town clerk, and also to his annual reports based on these records which are spiced with local detail and personal impressions.[1] By virtue of his position, he was well placed to observe local events. A good Catholic and a great admirer of the Schneiders, industrial overlords of Le Creusot, he expressed himself in a somewhat high-flown and moralising, fiercely patriotic style, and was greatly exercised about the morale of the town. As his notes were not meant for publication, it may be taken that he did not hide any of his anxieties and that his view of the behaviour of the people of Le Creusot was entirely candid. Moreover, being at the pulse of the French war industry, Le Creusot made an excellent point of observation. Finally, since it was small enough to be within easy reach of the countryside, Le Creusot was also an indicator of relations between town and country.

It must be remembered that from 1915 onwards (see p. 27 above) a large proportion of the men from Le Creusot had been brought back from the front as army reservists, this being indicated by the red and later black armbands which they had to wear. Their ranks had been swelled by workers from all parts of France,

1. The first report, dated 10 July 1915, runs to twenty-six typewritten pages and covers the first year of the war; the second, dated 3 November 1916, runs to forty-five pages and covers the period 1 July 1915 to 1 July 1916; the third, dated 15 July 1917, is twenty-two pages long and covers the period July 1916 to July 1917; and the fourth, dated 15 December 1918, has ten pages and covers the end of the war. These documents are kept in the departmental archives of Saône-et-Loire (series R).

especially from the north and from Paris and its surroundings, and also by many foreigners, first the Algerian navvies, then Serbian metalworkers, later still the Chinese and the Portuguese, then Austrian prisoners of war — most of them Croats, Czechs and Slovenes — and German prisoners of war.

In December 1916 there were 550 Chinese, 270 Algerians, 122 Spaniards, 300 Austro-Hungarian and 570 German prisoners; on 29 March 1918, a list mentions 2,770 foreigners in Le Creusot, including 1,700 Chinese, 240 Algerians, 120 Portuguese, 300 Spaniards, 95 Serbs, 250 Greeks, 50 Poles and 15 others. This list excluded prisoners of war.

As women, too, increasingly entered industry, especially during the second half of 1915, the work force became radically transformed. The resulting diversity and the new cosmopolitanism were not without repercussions. First of all, relations between French workers and foreigners became increasingly strained. Foreigners were accused of stealing the jobs of Frenchmen and hence of being responsible for sending them back to the front. The same accusation, incidentally, was also levelled at female workers. The diarist also recorded a remark from the most 'unintelligent' sector of female opinion in Le Creusot: 'Our men are being driven out of the factories by Chinamen, who should rightly be sent to the front and our husbands allowed to stay in the workshops.' No wonder that there were violent clashes. On 23 September 1916, for instance, Chinese workers who had been set upon without justification summoned some of their compatriots for help. A café in which the attackers took refuge was sacked, but one Chinese was killed by a customer with a revolver. The Chinese then seized a hostage, whom they threatened to put to death and whom the police had a difficult time in setting free. This incident was the worst, but it was indicative of the prevailing tensions. As one Chinese put it: 'We love French, but French no good'.

Again, there were sharp differences between the attitudes of Parisian and local workers respectively to their employers.

The Schneider group was the kind of paternalistic concern in which the employers watch over their staff 'from the cradle to the grave'. The system combined considerable social services with very low wages and a docile work force: the Le Creusot worker felt tied to his boss, to his factory. The new arrivals, by contrast, known as 'Parisians' even if they were not from the capital, recognised no personal allegiance to the Schneider family, and the town clerk was scandalised when he heard two of them say, 'We don't give a damn for the boss . . .'!

During the period 1915 to 1916, the great majority of workers in Le Creusot proved to be staunchly patriotic, vying with one another on the production lines. The great majority, but not all. 'There were far too many,' contended the town clerk, 'who, forgetting the war, were only interested in having a good time. A worker who had recently returned from the front was heard to remark: "A Zeppelin ought to come over here and remind this lot we are at war".'

Women whose husbands were away at the front attended dances in the suburbs of Le Creusot, and the men drank immoderately, so much so that in 1916 many bars had to be closed or put out of bounds to soldiers — that is, to army reservists — after having served or sold absinthe in particular outside authorised hours. 'The gendarmes needed to organise proper round-ups of drunken reservists on pay days.'

There was a general decline in patriotism: 'Le Creusot does not suffer from the war; it tends to forget about it a little, for it is a fact that habit blunts feelings, no matter how keen, and it is also true that danger to which one is not personally exposed can only half move one, and then only for an instant. Even worthy citizens — and they were by far the greatest number — had lost their early 'semi-religious serenity'.

In short, the people of Le Creusot, at least until the end of 1916, bore the war all the better because, when all was said and done, they suffered so little from it: people seemed quite unaware of its frightful consequences.

Things changed in the spring of 1917, after a winter campaign that had been accepted 'patriotically', but only because people had felt certain that it would all be over by the spring. For the first time, they 'no longer dared to put a date to the end of the Great War'. To the town clerk, this was a fact of the utmost importance, because, having lost sight of the end point, people found it increasingly difficult to 'hold out'. In the event, he tells us, it was not the morale of the workers which flagged, but that of the peasants in the surrounding countryside. They ought to be spoken to, the clerk felt, told to get a grip on themselves. They did not understand why, after three years of war, the government should feel unable to accept German peace offers, why it refused to grant French socialists passports to attend the Stockholm conference; they did not accept inequality in the face of death — that factory workers, unlike farm workers, should be allowed to stay at home, be paid, and even go on strike. Townspeople, by contrast, grew indifferent to the war, put on showy clothes, and bought in stocks of meat to last three days so as to get round the ban on sales on certain days. The prefect, the town clerk felt, ought to ban the dances: all you ever saw at them were singing drunkards.

Clemenceau's accession to power revived confidence, but this time it was the workers who wavered first. The implementation of the Mourier law, which provided for the mobilisation of reservists of the 1912, 1911 and 1910 classes, was badly received. The metal-workers' union convened meeting after meeting, and on Sunday night, 12 May 1918, some workers even called a strike. For our chronicler, these men were no more than a 'turbulent minority', very few in number. Nevertheless the authorities took them very seriously: gendarmes drawn from all the departmental brigades were quickly drafted in to Le Creusot. In the event, the strike never materialised; on the contrary, many workers wrote to Colonel Roux, the town commander, to protest vigorously against those who had cast doubt on their patriotism. The mayor had this protest posted up and the press extolled the good example of the workers of Le Creusot. Moreover, according to our witness, it was not local workers who had been involved in the first place, but men from outside who were much more reluctant to serve at the front. After this short-lived disturbance, the call-up of other classes produced no further 'lapses'.

That the morale of the population, at Le Creusot no less than elsewhere, should have reflected changes in the military situation was neither odd nor surprising, but the town clerk thought his observations could be fitted into a theory: during the first two years of the war, the approach of winter had led some people to grumble and to give way to despondency, while each spring brought them fresh comfort by encouraging the hope that decisive operations were about to be launched. It was a phenomenon that occurred simultaneously at the front and at home, although it was difficult to say where it originated. In any case, it was a theory which explained the crisis in the spring of 1917, when the failure of the most recent offensive destroyed any hope that the war would soon be over – 'the shipwreck of all hopes, all illusions', our witness called it, the entry of the United States into the war notwithstanding.

And what effect did economic factors have on the morale of the population? At Le Creusot·most people received normal wages, except, of course, in families whose breadwinners were still at the front. As a precaution, the municipality decided to add their own separation allowance to that paid by the state to those families whose breadwinners were still fighting, thus making doubly sure that disparities between the two groups did not become too great.

The cost would have been enormous had the number entitled to this allowance not been very small. However, the wives of conscripted shopkeepers and farmers also tried to get more money out of the municipality, and the farming community became loath to accept the official rate (fixed on 16 October 1915) of 30 francs per quintal (100 kg) for grain. Peasants, as our reporter from Le Creusot put it, 'grant no one the right to force them to sell grain for 30 francs when there is a shortage and they could sell it for 35 francs'.

The same problem arose with the butchers. The price of beef went up rapidly: second-quality meat rose from 1.60-1.80 francs per kilo (the price in October 1914) to 2.20-2.40 francs, an increase only partly justified by the price of animals on the hoof. Nevertheless the butchers insisted that, because wages had gone up, it was perfectly reasonable for meat to be dearer, with the inevitable result that there were somewhat heated exchanges between the wives of butchers at the front and the wives of reservists employed as factory workers. To settle the matter, the municipality, after a fruitless attempt to control the butchers, decided to fix the price of cheaper cuts, a compromise supposed to satisfy everybody. In practice, butchers' wives and the butchers themselves were anything but happy and decided to stop beef slaughter altogether. Dr Rebillard, the mayor of Le Creusot, retorted by opening a cooperative butchery in March 1916.

'War does not destroy the passions,' wrote the chronicler of Le Creusot, 'and selfishness remains the mainspring of many human actions.' On the whole, however, the differences in the incomes of the various social strata did not become too acute a problem, though the old antagonism between producers and consumers had grown even more pronounced. By and large, the workers made 'good money', the peasants were able to sell at the prices they wanted, hoarding their gains in order to buy up land, and the money helped everyone to forget that there was a war on.

By contrast, food supplies, and the supply of bread in particular, caused grave anxiety: there was one crisis in the spring of 1915, and another in the spring of 1916. The peasants, who felt they were not being paid enough for their wheat, preferred to feed it to their cattle and poultry, thus causing shortages. This was a very serious matter for the municipality. On 5, 6 and 7 June 1915, when the bakers ran short of flour, tension quickly mounted and women began to ransack the bakeries to make sure there really was no bread. 'Some even shouted: "If there's no bread, there'll be a revolution!" The days of 6 and 7 June seemed long ones to the municipality.' In March 1917, Le Creusot avoided a fresh bread crisis by asking the ministry of supply to step in. In 1918, again, the introduction of bread cards, leading to rationing, aroused bitter protests which the mayor managed to silence by appealing to everyone's sense of civic responsibility.

There were other supply problems. At various times there were shortages of potatoes, of milk, of sugar. . . . On the whole, however, apart from a few scares, the population suffered hardly at all. Moreover, the proximity of the Schneider works ensured that they would never run out of coal. The municipality nevertheless had to spend a good deal of time and energy on coping with food-supply difficulties.

Hence there can be no doubt that economic problems provoked the strongest and most immediate reactions. Acting almost by instinct, the local authorities tried to contain them to the best of their ability, aware that their success or failure in this field would have direct effects on the morale of those for whom they were responsible.

But were these people, so quick to show their irritation, nevertheless prepared to support the war effort? Gold collections, subscriptions to the four National Defence Loans, participation in the flag days, for the soldiers, for the Serbs — the mayor of Le Creusot would exhort his fellow citizens in stirring terms to give generously to them all. In November 1915, when the first National Defence Loan was launched, he put up a poster phrased as follows:

Ever since the first appeal by our Country, the people of Creusot have offered up their strength and their lives, and have bravely done their duty on the battlefield. They have handed in their gold when gold was needed. Today. . . they are flocking in large numbers to subscribe to our country's new appeal, ready without reservation to entrust all their savings, all their nest eggs, be they large or small, to France.

At no time has Le Creusot ever been cowardly or false, and Le Creusot will not be so today – patriotic above all, Le Creusot will entrust to the State all the savings it has put aside. Once again Le Creusot will do its duty.

The results were so encouraging that the mayor was able to declare: 'An examination of the overall response to the National Defence Loan gives us the most justifiable cause for pride. . . . By your gesture, my dear fellow citizens, you have shown your invincible faith in our Army, in our Country . . .'.

Despite the apparent need for so much prompting, we are entitled to consider the contribution of the people of Le Creusot to various war charities as a fair measure of their patriotic fervour.

The gold collection of July 1915 brought in the equivalent of 1,291,585 francs, an 'undreamt-of' figure, the mayor declared. More revealing still were the successive contributions to the National Defence Loans as well as on flag days.

The four National Defence Loans were launched in November 1915, October 1916, November–December 1917 and November 1918. This is how the people of Le Creusot subscribed to them:

November 1915	478,140 fr.
October 1916	363,590 fr.
November 1917	248,022 fr.
December 1917	248,022 fr.
November 1918	600,920 fr.

Flag days produced the results given in Table 9. The considerable differences between the first and second group of contributions are easily explained: the former were loans and the latter outright donations. The Saône-et-Loire Day was a rather special case — it was in aid of departmental war charities and all the forces of the department in general and of Le Creusot in particular were therefore mobilised in its support: local societies vied with one another in topping the list and the factory works committee alone contributed 4,000 francs.

The next flag day, by contrast, in aid of war victims, probably followed on too soon and suffered from the competition. Moreover, its organisation was said to be 'mediocre'.

It should also be noted that there were five major subscriptions in 1915 alone, in addition to the National Defence Loan, so that public generosity may well have been strained.

On the whole, however, the people of Le Creusot made very considerable financial sacrifices in 1915 and 1916: clear proof of their patriotism, even though the economic recovery made it relatively easy for them to contribute in 1915. The good response to war loans and other subscriptions encouraged the launching of many more, with diminishing returns from 1916 onwards. For though Le Creusot continued to 'donate' proportionally more than the rest of the department, the town clerk remarked with some sadness:

The task of the fund-raisers, the collectors, of all those who have to seek contributions from others, is proving an increasingly ungrateful one. Being at war has come to be accepted as almost normal; compassion has been stifled. The person who is always importuning others by playing on

Table 9. *Flag days, with amounts collected (in francs)*

Date	Name	Purpose	Amount collected
1914			
20–25 Dec.	Belgian Day		2,085.00
1915			
14 Feb.	'75' Day	For front-line soldiers	7,826.80
23 May	French Day	For occupied departments	9,065.60
27 June	Orphans' Day		6,151.20
1 August	Saône-et-Loire Day	Departmental war charities	40,604.85
26 Sept.	War Victims' Day		3,002.00
1916			
16 Jan.	French Soldiers' Day		5,599.95
2 July	Serbian Soldiers' Day		8,669.00
5 Nov.	National Orphans' Day		5,953.95
1917			
4 March	Tubercular Ex-Soldiers' Day		4,128.70
27 May	Local 'Social Duty' Day		2,690.85

heartstrings that bled in 1914 but have long since healed over, often has a cool reception. And this irksome individual, this collector who persists in feeling and thinking, in his turn shies away under repeated rebuffs and affronts.

And he noted in connection with the poor results of the Third National Defence Loan: 'The victory so ardently desired has not yet dawned and cold calculation keeps closed the hand that duty would have opened'.

What are we to make of this situation? It was not simply the result of a decline in the people of Le Creusot's ability to contribute — the Defence Loan of November 1918 would turn out to be a 'triumph' — but also of a growing doubt regarding the need to participate actively in the national effort. In other words, the high patriotic tone that had characterised the two first years of the war was being modified. But to the extent that this modification was not associated with anti-war, let alone defeatist, agitation, it must have been a sign of 'adaptation' to the long war. This war without a foreseeable outcome had become so 'routine', so much part of the daily round that people felt there was no need for them to do more than attend to their everyday chores. The dominant mood of the people of Le Creusot from 1917 onwards was not one of revolution, or even of revolt, but one of slightly weary habituation.

Do the four cases we have examined — Côtes-du-Nord, Charente, Paris and Le Creusot — have any common features? In all four there was a clear lack of exalted patriotism but also of defeatist sentiments, which does not mean that traces of either are not to be found. No less clear was the importance of economic factors, be it in the form of the advantages to be derived from the war or of the inconveniences people had to suffer. Nevertheless, perhaps because the inconveniences were rarely insupportable, the economic problems there were did not provoke major reversals of public opinion or changes in behaviour. Indeed, the choices and views adopted in the autumn of 1914 remained largely unchanged, at least in 1915 and 1916. Showing little concern with the detailed course of a conflict that seemed to them interminable, the French people remained resolutely confident about its outcome.

The Côtes-du-Nord throughout the war, Charente in 1916, Paris in 1915, Le Creusot, peasants and workers, rural and urban France – these four examples have enabled us to build up a picture of French adaptation to a long war. In the France of the time, two groups had a particularly marked influence on the behaviour of their fellow citizens: teachers and the clergy. It will therefore be helpful to take a closer look at the attitudes of these two groups, and also at those of the writers, a group whose influence was less fully appreciated at the time, though it was far from negligible. How did teachers, priests and writers respond to the long war? What effect did they have on French attitudes? The following three chapters will be devoted to these questions.

CHAPTER 10

Teachers and the War

Teachers were not only observers of the war, they were also actors in it: at the front, of course — 30,000 of them were called up — but also behind the lines, the more so as a teaching post was often combined with that of town or village clerk. Many teachers also exerted a considerable influence over their former pupils. Did they take an active part in building French morale during the war, or were they, on the contrary, the bearers of an anti-war message?

The few studies devoted to them have mostly been written from the viewpoint of working-class history. Before the war, a number of teachers did, in fact, combine to form unions that were progressive in spirit, affiliating with the CGT and appearing to share its anti-militaristic ideas. This affiliation had even created a scandal and the government had ordered the dissolution of these unions. But how did these bodies, which had never been dissolved except in theory, behave once the war had started? In particular, did they have an appreciable influence over the majority of the teaching profession?

We are better informed on the first question than on the second, thanks to the Sûreté, which, in 1918, published a long report on anti-war activities between 1914 and 1918.[1] One section, thirty-one typewritten pages long, was devoted to unionised teachers.

According to this document, in 1918 the National Federation of Teachers' Unions numbered at least 2,500 members, divided into 40 branches, indicating representation in 40 departments. It should however be remembered that there were at the time more than 120,000 teachers in France. Unionised teachers were therefore in a minority and far less typical than when, years later, teachers' unions had grown powerful. Is it nevertheless possible to gauge their

1. AN F 7 13372.

150

impact?

The Sûreté report lists the names of thirty-two teachers who played an active role in the French trade-union movement during the war, including ten who waged a sustained campaign. From the list of delegates to the only congress the National Federation of Teachers' Unions was able to hold during the war (on 14 and 15 July 1916), we see that the forty-nine delegates came from twenty-five departments. Their geographical origins are important: not a single department north of a line from Cherbourg to Besançon, except for Seine, sent delegates, as if war-resistance, watered down though it was, held no attraction for teachers in regions close or fairly close to the combat zone. The departments that did send delegates formed two blocks: one in the west, from Ille-et-Vilaine to Charente; the second in the south-east, from Saône-et-Loire to Alpes-Maritimes, the two blocks separated by the Massif Central and the Basin of Aquitaine which were not represented. Moreover — and there is corroboration of this surmise — the anti-war stance of some teachers in western France seemed no more than a continuation of the bitter struggle they had had to wage for secular education in regions that were both conservative and clericalist.

Be that as it may, even at this small congress opinions were far from unanimous. There were two motions, one by Louis Bouët, a teacher from Maine-et-Loire, in support of the socialist and anti-war, if not revolutionary, theses advanced at the Zimmerwald and Kienthal conferences, and another by Rebois, a teacher from Aveyron, stating that France had been unjustly attacked and must therefore be defended.

On the whole, anti-war sentiments were apparently not shared by more than a small proportion of even the unionised teachers. As one study[2] put it: 'Always a minority in their union. . . [the unionised teachers] became a tiny minority following the departure [to the front] of numerous activists'.

Even so, as this author points out, the teachers, accustomed as they were to a degree of isolation and dispersion, found it easier, despite their small numbers, to be more effective than others would have been in their difficult circumstances. In any case, the Renseignements Généraux considered them to be an 'impressive minority'.

We must therefore take a closer look at how they operated. Everyone is agreed that virtually no action was taken by them until January 1915 (if we except an attempt to republish their paper,

2. Joel Tronquoy, 'Le Combat pacifiste, des instituteurs syndicalistes pendant la guerre 1914–1918', master's thesis, Paris, 1977.

L'École émancipée, which was soon brought to a halt by the censors (see Chapter 4). There were several reasons for this: the call-up and death of prominent militants, among them André Chalopin, secretary of the Seine union, killed on 30 October 1914; the wait-and-see policy of those militant teachers who had stayed behind; and the legitimate fear that all attempts to criticise would be stopped by the censors.

According to the Renseignements Généraux, it was in January 1915 that the federal committee, led by Hélène Brion, the assistant secretary, and Loriot, the treasurer, decided to revive union activity. In February, the committee refused to associate itself with the 'patriotic' reply of the Federation of Teachers' Associations to a manifesto from their German counterpart, and in May and June Hélène Brion issued anti-war declarations. But the message they contained could not have been very apparent at the time, since some teachers argued that the secretaries of the federal committee were 'inactive' and called a special meeting of revolutionary teachers at Tours on 13 June 1915. The instigator was Marie Mayoux, a teacher from Dignac in Charente, who had written a *Manifesto of Unionised Teachers* calling for an end to the bloodshed and demanding that the government work for peace and propose an armistice to the other belligerents.

This manifesto aroused many conflicting reactions; to some it was not sufficiently committed to anti-militarism because some of its phrases had a 'patriotic' ring; others, and particularly the leaders of the federal committee, thought it went too far: peace, in the given circumstances, could only seal 'the triumph of force and brutality over right and justice', in other words a German victory.

Five thousand copies of the manifesto were nevertheless distributed, half of them by a teacher in Marseille. The manifesto was, moreover, endorsed by three teachers' unions (Charente, Bouches-du-Rhône, Cher) and by militants in ten departments.

Soon afterwards the federation was to move further into the anti-war camp. At a congress held in Paris on 14 August 1915 and attended by some thirty delegates, the leadership was outvoted after a whole day's debate on a motion by the anti-war group calling for 'the immediate organisation of working-class action in the belligerent countries for the purpose of restoring peace'. Hélène Brion bowed to the majority and agreed to cooperate in applying all the congress decisions in favour of anti-war propaganda. On the next day, 15 August, at the federal conference of the CGT, the teachers' federation sided with the anti-war minority led by Alphonse Merrheim, secretary of the metalworkers' union.

Little more than a year was needed, therefore, for the teachers to begin to display official opposition to the war. Thereafter the teachers' federation did not change its attitude again and remained on the outer fringe of the trade-union movement. In 1916 its delegates, including Marie Mayoux, hoped to participate in the Kienthal anti-war conference, but were unable to obtain passports.

In 1917, Hélène Brion distributed two pamphlets, *The War without End* and *To Members of the Congress*; while François and Marie Mayoux published and distributed a booklet called *Trade-Union Teachers and the War*.

Despite attempts by the police to stop it, a congress was held in August in the Paris apartment of a school teacher, Henriette Izambart.

Several teachers were especially noted for militant anti-war activities: in 1916 two were largely responsible for organising an anti-war majority in the departmental trade-union association in Bouches-du-Rhône; a peace petition drafted by another in November 1916 was signed by 74 people in the Dordogne. A month later a similar petition was signed in Limoges, on the initiative of a schoolmistress. In December 1917, a fund in support of anti-war propaganda was started in the teachers' training college in Angers.

The palm for perseverance must certainly go to the union branch in Finistère. which on 10 November, 1918 resolved steadfastly to continue its campaign for peace!

Though confined to a minority, the anti-war activities of the teachers' unions did not go unnoticed by the authorities. From 1917, prosecutions and convictions cascaded onto the heads of leading militants, or on some of them at least. On 25 October 1917, Marie Mayoux and her husband were sent to prison for six months and fined 100 francs each. At the end of December, on appeal, their sentence was increased to two years and a fine of 1,000 francs, and their dismissal became inevitable. On 17 November 1917, the secretary of the federation, Hélène Brion, was arrested. Her trial was given great prominence in the press, and in March 1918 she received a three months' suspended sentence. Also subjected to house searches, fines or convictions were Lucie Colliard, a teacher from Savoie; Suzanne Dufour, a teacher from Joigny, Piederrière, a schoolmaster and town clerk from Ille-et-Vilaine; Lamy, a teacher from Vaucluse.

By the middle of 1915 a number of teachers had thus taken a stubborn and positive stand against the war. But how far did they carry their fight? Outwardly, at least, not to the point of defeatism.

Louis Bouët, one of the leading militants of the time, a contributor to a historical appreciation,[3] wrote: 'Let us digress for a moment to consider this idea [defeatism], one we have unanimously rejected. The Mayouxes did not accept it, nor did H. Brion. The federal committee...has denounced it....'.

Now, rejecting defeatism also meant rejecting revolution. As Bouët put it again: 'Admittedly, the idea of revolution was never ruled out of our propaganda, but in order to gain any credibility with the masses in a country at war, a sixth of whose territory had been invaded, we were forced to call, not for peace, but for peace without annexations or reparations...'.

Despite its moderation, this stand placed the teachers at the extreme left of the trade-union movement, where in the end they found themselves in isolation. Even so, some critics blamed their restraint for the failure of the anti-war struggle. Unlike Lenin, the teachers had failed to clear the way for revolution.

In fact, this argument was purely 'ideological', the teachers concerned realising full well that, had they gone any further, they would have found themselves even more isolated.

In any case, so little did they look like winning the mass of teachers over to the anti-war cause that they were almost completely ignored by most departmental authorities. As a police report put it in connection with a motion passed by a meeting of unionised teachers: 'It proves [their] ill will, but they are few enough and realise that their efforts do not have great significance'.

Most teachers would have agreed with the observer. 'It gives me profound satisfaction to be able to say that all these decorated heroes...are my former pupils', wrote the teacher from Ansac in Charente in 1916.

The teacher from Aigre, in the same department, commented:

Former pupils now in the army have shown a degree of heroism of which the school can be proud, and it is a great comfort for a schoolmaster to observe the wonderful spirit and valour of the generation he has helped to mould. The many letters his former pupils have addressed to him from the front all bear witness to the same patriotic fervour.

Another teacher recalled that at adult classes, which continued to be held regularly, people discussed the significance of the war and recited patriotic texts. In one commune, the teacher congratulated himself on the fact that while the collections organised by the mayor

3. François Bernard, Louis Bouët, Maurice Dommanget, Gilbert Serret, *Le Syndicalisme dans l'enseignement* ('Trade-Unionism in the Teaching Profession'), 3 vols.

had a poor response, those run by the school produced 'very good results'.

It would be possible to quote similar views many times over, and it is most likely that what influence the teachers had on public opinion was used to boost morale rather than to encourage opposition to the war. Nevertheless, since history is often made by active minorities, historians have tended to pay inordinate attention to the small group of radical teachers, the more so as no comprehensive work on teachers in France during the First World War has been published to date. However, one recent monograph on the role of teachers in wartime Doubs tends to corroborate our conclusion.[4]

Because of its relative closeness to the front, this department may seem unrepresentative of life behind the lines. However, military operations had never been very marked in the eastern part of the country and, once the front was consolidated, the department of Doubs was rarely under direct threat from the Germans.

It must, however, be remembered — and this was not peculiar to Doubs — that the composition of the teaching profession had been profoundly changed by the war. Of a total of 1,383 male and female teachers in Doubs, 315 were called up, 258 as combatants and 57 in non-combatant services. There were 102 killed, two-thirds of them between the ages of 18 and 26. In the nature of things, it was the younger members of the profession who were mobilised first, and the first to be killed in large numbers: in other words, those who were least likely to remember 1870 and who were hence most exposed to the recent wave of militant trade unionism. There are no means of gauging the actual impact of that wave, but we may take it that it was not without significance.

All that is known about the psychology of combatant teachers from Doubs comes from letters published in the *Bulletin départemental de l'enseignement primaire du Doubs* ('Departmental Bulletin on Primary Education in Doubs') and we need not expect to find subversive opinions expressed there. Even so, the letters from soldiers at the front selected for publication in the bulletin might well have reflected their writers' true attitudes. Thus, in 1915, one of them stressed the importance which soldiers at the front attached to opinion at home, using somewhat grandiloquent phrases: 'The thought that our parents, our friends, our fellow citizens are keeping watch over us, sustaining us with their good wishes, is a potent source of comfort for us . . .,' wrote one of these teacher-soldiers in

---

4. Yves Racine, *'Les Instituteurs et l'école publique dans le département du Doubs pendant la guerre 1914–1918'*, thesis, Besançon, 1977.

1915.

Others, though few in number, began to voice contempt for 'all this eyewash'. Thus, in the spring of 1916, one of the letters quoted in the *Bulletin départemental* expressed astonishment, indeed waxed indignant, that the 'popular press' should continue to proclaim Germany's financial and economic ruin, starvation, and lack of fighting men, when the soldiers themselves could see that they were up against a redoubtable adversary.

And though, as we have said, there is little accurate information on their true opinions, we may take it that there was some substance in the report of the chief education officer to the regional council, stressing that all serving teachers 'are doing their duty' and showing 'magnificent spirit and endurance'.

We know a great deal, by contrast, about the ideological pressures to which teachers were exposed. In 1915, the *Bulletin départemental* published a circular letter signed by Albert Sarraut, the minister of education: 'If there is one teacher in whose existence I cannot believe for even an instant, it is a French teacher who ignores the war and continues with the same lessons and the same routine and at these critical times uses the same old phrases to address his pupils'.

The *Bulletin départemental* opened its columns to politicians, to men of letters and to university teachers, the historian Ernest Lavisse contributing on six occasions. In January 1915, addressing himself especially 'to the teachers of France', he argued that the role of those of them who were not fighting was as important as that of their colleagues in the trenches. They should collect examples of heroic acts and hold them up to 'our little ones, so that they learn to admire France'.

Lavisse's advice varied with the circumstances: in 1915 he told teachers to make a study of German liability; in 1916, he explained what oppressive conditions would be imposed if Germany won the war. In general, teachers were enjoined to breathe spirit into any who might be downhearted.

In 1916, the sociologist Emile Durkheim told readers of the *Bulletin départemental* that the military forces involved were such that neither side was likely to suffer a crushing defeat and that what victory there might be would go to those capable of holding out longest.

A favourite medium for driving their duty home to teachers was the annual 'educational conference'. In April 1915, the chief education officer advised teachers to reflect on the following three themes: 'How can we best explain to our pupils for what cause their fathers or elder brothers are fighting; how can we explain to their families that a precipitate peace would be disastrous for the future of all civilised countries; and finally, how can the School best pay tribute to those who have died for their Country?'

Teachers were enjoined to present their subjects in a patriotic light: in reading classes, for instance, they must seek out appropriate passages from the writings of Déroulède, Erckmann-Chatrian, Victor Hugo.

The teaching of history ought to aim at 'creating patriotic feelings and explaining the real meaning of current events' with particular reference to great French patriots, from Vercingétorix to Barra. Geography lessons would allow the pinpointing of military operations. Moral instruction and civics were particularly suited to showing 'how much we owe to our Country, and how devoted to it we should be'.

It is, of course, impossible to say to what extent these injunctions were followed, but it is recorded that thirty schools in the Pontarlier district devoted all lessons on 26 March 1915 to the celebration of 'Serbian Day'. This is how Yves Racine has described it in his thesis:

> In handicrafts class, the children made small Serbian flags and coloured them in. In arithmetic, these flags were pinned to the blackboard in rows of ten which helped the pupils to count by tens. . . . In numeration, the pupils were asked to write and read out the numbers expressing the surface areas of European countries. These exercises helped the children to express the area of France and its population as a multiple of that of Serbia. Some thoughts were written up on the blackboard about our faithful allies: 'I am learning to love Serbia, I am learning to remember her history and her long struggle. I write "Long Live Serbia" which is defending her independence and freedom. I want to help the little Serbians, I am making my small offering.' . . . Prints were handed round and examined. . . .

That day, the teachers also addressed the adults, organising public meetings in support of Serbia in twenty-six communes.

Subjects for examination provide another indication of the new educational approach. Thus pupil teachers were expected to cover the following subjects: 'The role of reading and recitation in patriotic education. Mention some of the excerpts you have chosen. Mention some of the feelings you have tried to foster in your pupils' hearts and explain how you have set about it. Were you fully successful? What did you discover? What have you decided to do about it?'

In the entrance examination for the teachers' training college, in the lower and higher examinations for secondary education certificates (*brevet simple* and *brevet supérieur*) and probably also in the examination for the *certificat d'études* (taken at the end of an elementary course of studies), 'patriotic' themes held pride of place. 'What feelings would you have on learning that the United States had entered the war on our side against Germany?' prospective teachers were asked at a scholarship examination in 1917. In 1916, the essay subject was: 'The Wolf and the Lamb applied to the current war, with special reference to the way in which our enemies provoked it'.

In 1915, candidates for the École Normale were asked to write a dissertation on the following subject: 'A soldier granted leave. A letter from the front announces his probable arrival. He is awaited in vain for several days. Describe the sentiments felt. He finally arrives. Describe the joy of the whole family'.

These examples could be multiplied. Nevertheless, from 1916 onwards the teaching of 'patriotic' subjects began to decline, because, as the primary-school inspector in Ornans remarked, the war was not a subject 'one keeps trotting out year after year'.

Teachers also exerted their influence on adult classes by heeding the ministerial instructions of 1914: 'When lecturing to older people, adolescents and women from their commune or district, teachers will extol our country, and will read out passages inspired by glorious episodes in our past and present history'.

However, if adult classes and public meetings addressed by teachers did indeed make a contribution to the war effort, then it must be said that their impact was much smaller than it had been before the war, not least because there were fewer teachers, because so many of them were overwhelmed with administrative tasks, and because their potential audience, in the absence of servicemen, had little spare time to devote to this type of activity.

The teachers in Doubs were also expected to be active promoters of war charities. On 17 July 1915, the minister of education called on them to participate actively in the gold collection: 'This drive will produce its full effect if our teachers explain its importance to the people'. In the event they did so extremely well, earning the congratulations of the prefect.

In promoting loans and flag days, teachers were expected to play a double role: to exert pressure on the parents indirectly through the children, and directly in their capacity as town clerks. When the 1915 national loan was launched, the *Bulletin départemental* put forward a six-point plan to help teachers encourage subscribers. They were also invited to read out a speech by Alexandre Ribot, minister of finance: 'The public will have read it as it has been

posted up everywhere, but reading the poster by oneself in the
street is necessarily superficial and provokes few emotions. It must
be read with feeling, in an atmosphere of patriotic communion and
with a fervour that will stress its principal points'.

To make certain that these instructions were being followed, in
January 1916 the education officer asked every teacher for a concise
report.

In 1917, when potential subscribers to the national loan were
showing some reluctance, teachers were invited to redouble their
pressure. To that end they were provided with posters, calendars, a
system of good marks and other propaganda devices.

Two charities enjoyed the special attention of teachers in Doubs,
Parcels for Soldiers and the charity supporting orphans in state
schools. The former charity was set up in 1914. It not only collected
gifts in kind and money to buy what was required by the soldiers,
but also organised, under the supervision of women teachers, knit-
ting and sewing by pupils for soldiers' needs; a part of the adult
classes for women was also devoted to this work. As a result, at a
meeting of the regional council held in September 1915, the education officer was able to acknowledge having received 1,737 knitted
jerseys, 4,403 Balaclava helmets, 881 blankets, 3,568 shirts and
numerous other articles in impressive quantities.

Not unexpectedly, teachers devoted themselves with particular
fervour to the orphans adopted by state schools. To obtain the
necessary funds, they organised raffles and charity sales, and even
reclaimed fallow fields, selling the produce for the benefit of their
charity. The primary school inspector in Ornans was able to write
in 1918: 'People talk about it constantly; there is no better lesson in
solidarity'. In 1917, the teachers were asked by this inspector for
explicit replies to the question: 'What have you done for the
departmental orphans' charity?'

Though this charity continued to enjoy very good support
throughout the war, teachers found that their efforts to sponsor
collections proved an increasingly thankless task: people had begun
to grow tired of constant soliciting. Moreover, the education officer
felt that some teachers had gone too far in their enthusiasm, and,
while advising them to continue the good work, he also urged them
'to use greater restraint in their repeated appeals to the generosity of
parents through their children' (September 1917).

In the department of Doubs, the services of the teachers were in
great demand and — it would seem — the teachers complied
enthusiastically. There are no signs, either, that any of them actively
opposed the war. No teacher in Doubs, according to Yves Racine,

questioned the policy of the government, and when, as occasionally happened, an enquiry was held into the actions of a teacher, none was ever found to have acted unpatriotically. This does not mean, of course, that all traces of the traditional conflicts, especially between the advocates of secular and of clerical education respectively, had vanished in Doubs, but when these conflicts were brought to the attention of the authorities, they generally found them to be of slight importance: a priest who kept his children at catechism too long, a teacher who forbade his pupils to wear Sacred Heart badges in class. One case, however, did create quite a stir: a family asked to subscribe to Parcels for Soldiers let it be known that it reserved 'its contributions for purely Catholic charities'. The schoolmistress concerned penned a scathing retort: 'Don't call yourselves Catholics, let alone pure Catholics, because your actions prove the contrary and force me to tell you that you have more than one trait in common with the Germans. You are deceitful and arrogant like them. . . . Yours with contempt'.

The chief education officer tried to smooth things over, but the deputy mayor of Frasne added fuel to the flame by posting a notice in which he vigorously supported the schoolmistress's stand. His message concluded with the following words: 'There should, at this moment, be one France only, the France concerned with its rights and duties, its dignity and its freedom, the one and indivisible France. For those unworthy citizens who have forgotten this, I have nothing but contempt, and I call upon you to join me'.

Was Doubs typical of the whole of France? Probably not. Other teachers and departments may not have put the same effort into supporting the sacrifice and patriotism of fellow citizens. Nevertheless there is a series of indications — and we have already encountered several — that the attitude of teachers in this department was a very widely held one.

A small minority which opposed the war in varying measure confronted a very large majority which, without on the whole loving war, believed it to be their duty to give it their support. On balance, teachers therefore played a very important role in holding the nation together, especially in rural areas, even though their fervour may well have abated during the later years of the war.

CHAPTER 11

Writers and the War

Like schoolteachers, writers and intellectuals in general were expected to make their contribution to the war.[1] Bearing in mind its duration and its character — the First World War was a blueprint for total war — it was only natural that it should have involved a psychological dimension, and that the belligerent countries, and in our case France, should have tried to 'mobilise' writers as well. It needs to be stressed, moreover, that censorship was applied as much to books as it was to the press, and that short of being able to force writers to do as it wished, the government could at least try to prevent them from expressing awkward views. Writers were expected to look upon themselves as 'moulders of public opinion', that is, to encourage a fervent pro-war attitude. One writer who complied willingly was Paul Bourget, who put the matter bluntly in the *Revue hebdomadaire* of March 1917: 'The writers' task has been to foster support for the war in the country'; and he added: 'How better can writers serve their country than in creating superior works of art?'

Writers accomplished this task not only in their books, but more particularly in the newspapers and magazines to which they contributed, so much so that it is often difficult to tell where journalism ends and literature begins. This was by no means unusual: writers have always contributed to papers and journals. Nevertheless, the wide dissemination and immediate effect of the writers' message in wartime needs to be emphasised.

Not surprisingly, it was two writers, both members of the Académie Française, both nationalist politicians and both contributors to *L'Echo de Paris*, Maurice Barrès and Albert de Mun,

1. This chapter was contributed by Geneviève Colin.

161

who headed this patriotic crusade. And on Albert de Mun's death on 6 October 1914, Barrès became sole figurehead. In later years, his activities during the war were severely condemned. Romain Rolland called him the 'nightingale of carnage' and wrote in his *Journal*: 'He flourishes on fresh graves; his art is in full flower. But however beautiful the flower may be, I can see the stem rising from the bowels of the charnel-house . . .'.

Much later still, Jean Guéhenno called him the 'national undertaker', applying to Barrès, as to other journalists of his ilk, the advertising slogan of American undertakers: 'You die, we do the rest'. But how did Maurice Barrès himself see his mission? Aged 52 in 1914, he could have considered enlisting but, deciding that his pen was his best weapon, he set himself the task of writing an article almost every day, 269 in 1915 alone. He also published *Autour de Jeanne d'Arc* in 1916 and *Les Diverses Familles spirituelles de la France* in 1917. If we add the many war charities which he sponsored, the work he did as a parliamentarian, especially on health service matters, he emerges as a man of immense energy, so much so, in fact, that he himself later wondered whether he had not 'lost much time' as well as 'much love' in pursuit of this 'inferior calling' to which he felt compelled to devote himself.

The basic idea advanced in all his writings was that war was a regenerative force, a source of vitality, and, in the given situation, a struggle between two philosophies, the French and the Germanic. France's fight was the fight of humanity against German barbarism and the victor was bound to impose his philosophy on the vanquished. 'After the war,' wrote Barrès in 1915, 'it will be up to the French spirit to teach the German spirit. . .common sense and a sounder view of its destiny.'

However, as Michel Baumont has shown,[2] Barrès's attitude changed as the war went on.

At first, convinced like everyone else that it would all be over soon, he insisted that three spiritual concerns would help France to gain the upper hand in this decisive encounter: the need for unity behind the civil and military authorities, the deployment of all her moral forces, and recognition that the early setbacks must be laid at the door of the prewar government. Barrès's tone changed when the war continued beyond the winter of 1914–15 and his early optimism could no longer be sustained. He realised that moral force alone was not now enough to carry the day, and called for more men and

2. 'Un témoignage sur la guerre de 1914–1918: chronique de la Grande Guerre de Maurice Barrès', *Information historique*, 1973, no. 1.

greater resources. In 1917, haunted by the spectre of defeat, he called for greater energy in pursuit of the war and poured calumnies on Caillaux and Malvy.

For four years, moreover, he made a point of challenging all those whom he called 'wet blankets, sniggerers and defeatists'. 'In time of war individuals, families, the entire nation must have. . . a sense of exaltation and be filled with high ideals and fervour; whoever fails to keep his flame alive in himself and in others does not work for the good of the country.' He extolled courage, the sacrifices of the soldiers, and denounced the barbarism of the enemy.

Barrès's reputation as a purveyor-in-chief of 'eyewash' is probably unjust. At most it applies to the contents of his 'Chroniques de guerre' column during the early months of the war.

In fact, in this first phase, Barrès saw fit to speak of 'blessed wounds', and to commend French youth for shedding its blood so 'cheerfully'. The 75mm guns were 'valiant and delightful comrades' and there was 'something elegant and agreeable about the communication trenches'. The full flavour is reflected in this conversation on the subject of 'facial injuries', reported in one of his articles:

> 'I have just been given news about a young soldier who's been wounded' [he told a cab driver].
> 'Is it bad?'
> 'A wounded arm and a bullet in the jaw. But he'll get over it.'
> 'He'll still be disfigured, poor fellow.'
> 'Disfigured! A wound full in the face, received in war! Oh no, he will be able to tell the story as long as he lives and the whole world will admire him.'

And Barrès added: 'Among the most splendid wounds, we must mention those of the son of the president of the French Bar, Chenu, who received a gash across the eyes and the nose while in action; and, again, young Forain. . .on whose chin a bullet has sketched a scar, finer than any of his father's masterpieces'. A few days later, Barrès began an article with: 'Cheerfulness reigns in the trenches! You can tell this in the newspapers and in the letters from your sons, husbands and brothers'.

Later, and especially in 1918, Barrès often seemed filled with the kind of pessimism he himself would have pilloried as defeatism in others. In particular, we know from his *Cahiers* that he began progressively to have doubts about the task he had set himself. If at the beginning he had taken a mystical view of the deaths of soldiers, as the war continued he increasingly came to feel that the loss of the growing legions of the dead, far from regenerating France, was likely to sap its very substance.[3]

Though Barrès's thought was more subtle than it is generally believed to have been, he had always denied the morality of telling the whole truth at all times. Thus, during the Dreyfus affair, he had attacked those 'wretches who want to teach our children the absolute truth' when what they needed to be taught was 'the French truth', that is, a truth much more useful to the nation. Good was good and evil was evil only in terms of the country's needs.

In these circumstances we can see how he should have become the spokesman of a dual approach: vigorous nationalism in politics and systematic optimism in all reports about the war, both used for the express purpose of boosting French morale. The same approach was also used by, among others, Henri Lavedan, playwright, novelist and member of the Académie Française, who throughout the war wrote a weekly column in *L'Illustration*, the *Paris-Match* of its day, where he joined forces with such other writers as Pierre Loti and Paul Bourget. Referring to the smiling faces of French soldiers in an illustration, he did not shy away from writing: 'Go to it, you cheery fellows, you jaunty lads, you splendid chaps, you daredevils! Go to it, dance, laugh and sing!'

The following extract from one of his articles, chosen at random, is a fair specimen of this type of war 'literature'. The better to extol the qualities of the French soldier, Henri Lavedan first of all praised his 'patience under arms', 'which means staying stock still [it was 1915] when all he wants is to rush forward; and keeping sheathed a bayonet which is crying out to be fixed to the end of his rifle'. And then, the French soldier

> sets 'an example of good humour, seriousness of purpose, sacrifice and staunch devotion, of infinite hope, and courage in all its forms. . . . And he is also unsparing in his most virile and terrible energy, in his gentleness of spirit and sweetness of soul. . .and tenderness of character, in his exceptional, expert and scrupulous way of going about things. And before the immensity of this overflowing beauty, we stand transfixed with admiration [and] respect. . .and with impotence, because most of the examples before us are so noble and so superior that we cannot hope to emulate them!'

Similar views were espoused by Charles Maurras and especially by Léon Daudet, two contributors to *L'Action française*, who specialised in denunciations of defeatists and traitors of every type, true or supposed. Then there was Gustave Hervé, who was, however, more of a journalist than a writer. This former anti-militarist,

3. Michel Baumont, 'Maurice Barrès et les morts de la guerre', *Information historique*, no. 1, 1969.

who had been quite ready to call for insurrection against the war, had not only changed sides but also the name of his paper: *La Guerre sociale* became *La Victoire* on 1 January 1916. Hervé was now an all-out supporter of war to the bitter end, a war he idealised and increasingly used as the subject of his writing.

A special place, finally, must be accorded to André Suarès. A friend of Romain Rolland before 1914, the war caused him to emerge from the solitude to which he had grown accustomed so as to participate in what he, too, considered to be a mission: the struggle against the barbarians in defence of 'beauty, life, and our threatened land'. To that end he wrote numerous articles for the weekly *L'Opinion*, and in 1916 published a patriotic book entitled *Ceux de Verdun*.

A second group of writers was very close to the first in inspiration, but differed in that these novelists, poets and playwrights did not, like the former group, pursue a patriotic mission shot through with politics. Among this second group we may mention René Benjamin, whose novel *Gaspard*, published in 1915, was the first of a dozen or so successful war books. Gaspard, typically Parisian, a jovial snail merchant from the rue de la Gaîté who is a bit of a grumbler, describes a kind of 'war in kid gloves', much less ghastly than people behind the lines had been led to believe, a war in which relations between officers and men were exemplary, in which military hospitals were idyllic havens of rest and in which patriotic phrases dropped quite naturally from the combatants' lips. This view of the war was also shared by such poets as Lucie Delarue-Mardrus:

> Aussitôt une sainte transe
> S'empare en même temps de tous,
> Un seul cri dit: Vive la France!
> L'Alsace et la Lorraine à nous![4]

But then this poet wrote her 'Ballade du mobilisé' ('The Conscript's Ballad') on 16 August 1914. It was in more sombre times, in 1915, that Fernand Gregh delivered his 'war heroes' ' funeral oration:

> Et que perd-il? Un peu de notre sort vulgaire,

4. No sooner had a sacred trance/Seized all of us at once,/Than one long cry of *Vive la France*!/Alsace-Lorraine are ours!

C'est en vivant qu'il perdait le plus![5]

François Porché, who at the beginning of 1916 had contributed 'The Halt on the Marne', a poem running to 800 lines, to *Le Figaro*, staged a play in the Théâtre Gémier in 1917 under the title of *Les Butors et la Finette* ('The Louts and the Artful Lady'):

> L'uniforme des ennemis
> Se confond avec la poussière,
> Avec le sol cru des âpres terrains:
> Ce gris convient sans doute à leur ruse grossiere,
> A leur triste orgueil, à leurs dieux chagrins,
> Mais nos héros à nous gardent dans leur colère
> Les soucis des amants,
> Ce sont des Chevaliers et des Princes charmants
> Pour qui vaincre ou mourir sont des moyens de plaire.
> Je rêve pour toi d'une étoffe claire
> Comme la ligne du coteau
>
> . . . .
>
> Sois désormais sacré, symbole de ma force
> Drap d'azur, enveloppe, écorce
> De mes rameaux vivants![6]

This second group of writers, like the first, must be classified among the purveyors of 'eyewash' as defined by Michael Baumont: 'optimistic lies about military operations; childish denigration of the enemy; an idyllic presentation of life in the trenches', to which we might add 'exaltation of an army permanently frozen in a fixed heroic gesture'.

As Charles Delvert, a professor of history and a captain during the war, wrote about a woman journalist on the *Echo de Paris* in his *L'Histoire d'une compagnie* ('The History of a Company'): 'How does she picture us combatants? Does she really believe we spend our time brandishing great swords with heroic gestures and yelling

---

5. What does he lose? A little of our common fate,/It is in living that he loses most!
6. The uniform of our foes/Merges with the dust, with the bare earth of a bitter land:/The grey is fitting to their uncouth wiles,/Their sorry pride, their woeful gods./But with their wrath our heroes shield/A lover's care,/They are the Knights and Princes Charming/For whom victory or death are means of pleasing./I dream of you in a shining robe/Like the slope of a hill. . . ./Be henceforth sacred, symbol of my strength/Heavenly cloth, earthly shroud, bark/For my living branches!

'*Vive la France!*' at the tops of our voices? When will these ladies and gentlemen in civilian life spare us their fantasies?'

The only difference between members of the first and the second group was that the second did not pretend to a personal mission when writing about the war. But they nevertheless shared in the exaltation of France's 'mission', and as late as April 1916, a lecturer, Auguste Dorchain, could still entitle a chatty article 'Poets and the Mission of France' in the *Annales politiques et littéraires*.

A third group of writers had some affinity with the second, with which it shared a lack of fixed political views. This was largely made up of combatants who tried to be honest about their experiences and to describe the realities of war. Georges Duhamel, a physician and a man of letters with an established reputation, volunteered for service and spent forty-eight months in the army as a medical officer. His experiences at Verdun inspired two of his novels, *La Vie des martyrs* in 1917 (translated into English as *The New Book of Martyrs* in 1919) and, in 1918, *Civilisation 1914–1917* (translated into English as *Civilisation* in 1919). He rounded on all those who tried to present a conventional picture of the war: 'One doesn't cheat about Verdun, it was sheer hell'. To him, war meant suffering and death. His portrait of Verdun after the battle — the sudden waves of wounded men putting up with the deplorable, wretched sanitary conditions, having in the end to face death alone — has been called a novel 'haunted by the truth'. As Romain Rolland wrote in his *Journal*: '[*Civilisation* is] the most perfect work the war has inspired in France, together with *La Vie des martyrs*. . . . In no other work has the naked truth and poignant emotion been expressed with so much admirable restraint and dispassionate precision.

Roland Dorgelès, who in December 1914 published a rather unrealistic article on the war in *L'Intransigeant*, went on to fight as a corporal in the 39th Infantry Regiment, and in 1917 joined forces with Régis Gignoux to write a satirical novel, *La Machine à finir la guerre*. It depicted trench warfare with great realism, also to be found in his later *Les Croix de bois* (1919; English translation: *Wooden Crosses*, 1921).

Other writers also reported their experiences truthfully. André Maurois, liaison officer and interpreter to the British army, did so in *Les Silences du colonel Bramble*, published in June 1918 (English translation, 1919), and so did Maurice Genevoix, a young student from the École Normale, who served as a second-lieutenant in the 16th Infantry Regiment, was wounded in April 1915 and discharged. He then wrote *Sous Verdun* (1916; English translation, '*Neath Verdun*, 1916), *Nuits de guerre* (1917), *Au seuil des gui-*

tounes (1918), all of which were combined much later into *Ceux de 1914*. Maurice Genevoix has been called the 'most gifted witness' to the atrocity of the war, because of the accuracy and authenticity with which he re-created the special atmosphere of the ferocity of battle.

Although these writers had no political objectives — except that Dorgelès' *La Machine à finir la guerre* contained a vigorous attack on capitalists who refused to use the 'machine to end the war' because war had helped them to amass fortunes — their work was an implicit or explicit condemnation of war and of its absurdity, and was therefore the very opposite of 'heroic' literature.

In the writings of Georges Duhamel there is no hatred of the Germans; on the contrary, he depicts a kind of unity in misfortune as, for instance, in the meeting of the doctor with the wounded stranger. Duhamel refused to justify massacres, and denounced war as such: 'A man I knew for his energy and resolve, said between his teeth: "No, no! Anything but war!"' For Roland Dorgelès, war spelled defeat, no matter whether it was won or lost. As for Maurice Genevoix, he showed what the morale of combatants was after five days under attack: 'The whole world is dancing a sort of demented and grotesque farce. None of it makes any sense . . .; may all those about to be killed escape their death sentences in the end'.

Some, though not all, of these writers can be said to have leaned towards pacifism, but all condemned the war and its horrors. Anatole France's preface to Pierre Chaîne's *Les mémoires d'un rat* (1917), followed in 1918 by the *Commentaires de Ferdinand, ancien rat des tranchées*, set the tone:

> Ferdinand does not love the war and finds no beauty in its carnage, no charm in its wounds, however great. We must excuse him: he lacks the aesthetics of the home front; he hasn't read enough newspapers, he cannot tell what is beautiful. And anyway, he has seen so many soldiers cut to pieces that he has lost the taste for it. What do you expect? One grows tired of everything.

A fourth, not very large, group of writers had some affinity with the first in that they, too, had political objectives. Instead of war and nationalism, however, these writers, whose leaders were Romain Rolland and Henri Barbusse, preached peace and internationalism. This may be something of an over-simplification: the reality was much more complex. Barbusse, in particular, stood somewhere between the last two groups, the 'realists' and the declared pacifists. Before the war he had been a journalist and had published three books, including *Pleureuses*, a collection of Symbolist poetry, and

L'Enfer (English translation: *The Inferno*, 1908), a novel nominated for the Prix Goncourt. In 1917 Barbusse was 41, had a lung condition and could at most have been expected to do non-combatant duty. But in a letter to the editor of *L'Humanité*, written on 9 August 1914, he announced that he hoped to be counted 'among those anti-militarist socialists who join up voluntarily'. Detailed to the 231st Infantry Regiment in December 1914, he fought for a year in Artois, in Argonne, and in Soissonnais, before becoming a stretcher-bearer and eventually being discharged.

In an article written for *Les Nations* in June 1917 and entitled 'Why Are You Fighting?', Barbusse explained his reasons for joining up. The war was directed at imperialism and German militarism. He had joined it more as a human being than as a Frenchman; he had been fighting 'for justice and for the liberation of men and for that alone'. The greatest obstacles in the path of progress were nationalism and imperialism in the heart of Europe, but Germany did not have a monopoly in that: 'French nationalism is no better than pan-Germanism and all the other pans. We must fight German militarism, not to substitute our own, or to destroy Germany, but to smash militarism'. *A posteriori* explanations are always a little suspect, but it seems fair to say that Barbusse, like nearly all French socialists and trade unionists, had espoused the cause of national defence, even though some of his motives differed from those of the majority of Frenchmen. Moreover, the letters he wrote to his wife up to 19 June 1915 contain no political comment: they are descriptions of his daily life and of his surroundings. From that date onwards, however, his letters give the impression that he no longer saw any purpose to the war, that its motives had proved to be 'vague, without relevance to the [combatant's] innermost feelings and in conflict with our human destiny'. On 14 April 1916 he wrote that the blame had to be shared between France and Germany:

> When they told us it was Germany who attacked first, they were right. But when they added that we ourselves were some sort of plaster saints who had honoured and practised peace and that at no time — oh, dear Lord, no! — had we harboured the slightest thought of revenge or of military victory, that at no time had we shown the slightest sign of hostility and affront towards Germany, they were really stretching it a bit far, as they say. The present crisis is the logical and fatal outcome of national vanities and each side must take its share of responsibility.

It was at this point that Barbusse conceived the idea of writing a book to denounce the war. He was worried about the future, and foresaw another clash in ten or twenty years' time unless nations were to hold out the hand of friendship to one another. For this war to be the last, it had to be shown up in all its horror. That was the genesis of *Le Feu, journal d'une escouade*, published in instalments in *L'Oeuvre* from 3 August 1916 and in book form (English translation: *Under Fire*, 1917) on 15 December of the same year. In it, Barbusse, using his own experiences, followed the life and death of a group of soldiers 'through the various phases and vicissitudes in the field'. The uncompromising realism of the book earned him the title of the 'Zola of the trenches'. He depicted war in all its horror, all its inhumanity, and with all its sordid and sometimes hideous aspects: 'This war means dreadful, superhuman exhaustion, water up to your belly, and mud, and grime and unspeakable filth. It means rotting faces and flesh in tatters, and corpses that no longer even look like bodies floating on the surface of the voracious earth'. We are here far from the heroism of a Barrès, from glittering bayonets and clarion calls.

However, Henri Barbusse was not the only writer to describe the war realistically, and his uniqueness emerges most clearly in the closing chapter of *Le Feu*. In a kind of apocalypse, the nationality of the combatants evaporates — German or French, it has ceased to matter. There is fraternisation in death. 'Victory in this war is no achievement.' A commonwealth of nations is man's only hope. 'The future is in the hands of slaves and it is easy to see that the old world will be changed by the alliance to be forged one day among those whose numbers and whose misery are without end.'

With his last chapter, Barbusse creates a militant polemic and, moreover, one that, unlike the writings of the other realists, carried an explicit rather than implicit anti-war message. And it went even a stage further in its call for world revolution.

More than Barbusse, however, it was Romain Rolland who may be said to have presided over this political current. Paradoxically, he can be likened to Barrès in the other camp, because, like Barrès, Rolland was neither a participant in, nor a direct witness of, the war. He was in Switzerland when war broke out and he remained there. The reader will remember how his article 'Au-dessus de la mêlée' earned him the somewhat unjustified hostility of many papers, even while he was still voicing support for his country; that he neither glossed over German responsibility for the war nor questioned the justice of the Allied cause. But, thinking himself misunderstood, and abandoned by some of his friends who were enthusiastic in their support for the war, he grew increasingly weary and disillusioned. As he wrote in his *Journal* on 20 December 1914: 'I am beginning to lose interest in the downfall of people who want war and even seem to take pleasure in it.' He was to remain silent until the end of 1916, but in the interval his views gradually altered. At the beginning of 1915, he began to believe that the Allies, too, bore some responsibility for the war. The idea of a 'just war' seemed less and less tenable, and, considering that Belgium had been sacrificed by the great powers, France and Britain, he felt that he had been excessively indulgent towards his own country's faults. As Marcelle Kempf, an authority on Rolland, put it, 'gradually, Romain Rolland's sentimental and idealistic revolt came to be underpinned with political, social and economic arguments'. A turning point had been reached. In the words of René Cheval, another student of Rolland's intellectual development: 'He had come to see that if he was to emerge from the impasse he had reached in the middle of 1915, if he was not to remain immured in silence, he could follow but one path, the path of revolution'.

In November 1916 Rolland published an article entitled 'Aux peuples assassinés' in *Demain*, a review that had recently been founded in Geneva by Henri Guilbeaux. It was a bitter denunciation of all wars, no matter of what kind, but above all a pressing invitation to all nations to break with the existing social order: 'As it continues, every war. . .turns out to be a war for business, a war "for money"', he wrote. In 'La Route en lacets qui monte' ('The Winding Road Uphill'), published at almost the same time, Rolland openly professed his internationalism. Even the union of all the nations of Europe was no longer enough. And as the war dragged on, Rolland's attitude became more and more political: he was no longer satisfied with general statements on the morality of international relations, but had begun to search out the concrete conditions under which all mankind could live together in peace.

Thus, from nationalist and chauvinist to international pacifist, from Barrès to Rolland, the spectrum of attitudes displayed by French writers was wide indeed. Few if any of them were defeatists, however, although it is true that the censors would quickly have clamped down on defeatist writings, and for that matter on overtly pacifist texts as well. Only Romain Rolland, because he was in Switzerland, had the chance to put across his anti-war message, and though the campaign against him in the autumn of 1914 was fairly subdued, he later became the constant butt of increasingly violent attacks by the nationalists. On 24 April 1915, having retired wounded from the front, Henri Massis published an article in *L'Opinion* in which he said, *inter alia*: 'Romain Rolland speaks. . .

while France fights'. He expanded this idea with virulence in a pamphlet published in July 1915 and entitled *Romain Rolland contre la France*. In this, Massis accused Rolland of having fled to Switzerland to escape the realities of war, of being a coward, of having resigned from life, of being riddled with pride and irrationality, all of which explained why he had retreated to his ivory tower. 'Romain Rolland, whose heart is universal,' he wrote, 'loves all the world, no doubt because he cannot love his father or his fatherland.'

According to R. Cheval, Massis 'thus gave the signal to the pack to fling itself upon the quarry'. And, in fact, the attacks on Romain Rolland grew, many coming from former pacifists and some from such old admirers as P. H. Loyson, who wrote *Au-dessus ou au coeur de la mêlée* (Above or at the Heart of the Mêlée) and Charles-Albert, who wrote *Au-dessous de la mêlée* ('Beneath the Mêlée'). At the prompting of his opponents, he received letters addressed to 'Herr Professeur Rolland, author of Jean-Allboche' (a pun on Rolland's famous novel *Jean-Christophe*). When he was awarded the Nobel prize for literature in 1916, his detractors claimed that it was not a token of merit but a sign of Swedish Germanophilia! These attacks, it should be stressed, were aimed at Romain Rolland despite the fact that he had written practically nothing since the autumn of 1914. When he took up his pen again and became fêted as a kind of figurehead and rallying point for the anti-war movement, the attacks against him were of course redoubled. But ultimately, despite the claims of his detractors and even though he might be looked upon as a supporter of French defeatism, his own message was never defeatist — indeed, he repudiated defeatism formally — but was on quite a different plane, one that transcended Franco-German confrontation. Again, while some of his friends were revolutionaries, he himself remained somewhat reserved. 'My internationalism. . .is one of love and not of hatred.' And though he saluted the Russian Revolution in February 1917, he feared the consequences of the October Revolution: 'I would not rejoice if France made peace at the expense of the Russians [he wrote to Henri Guilbeaux]. 'Do not ask me to rejoice when Russia makes peace at the expense of the French . . .'.

Neither was Barbusse spared. Maurras kept up an incessant denunciation of him in *L'Action française* from March to August 1917. In a letter to his wife dated 17 August, Barbusse referred to an 'article by the ignoble E. Lavisse in *Le Temps*'. And without seeking to exaggerate the importance of such tirades, we might draw attention to the following question, posed from the pulpit by the senior schools' chaplain in Lyon: 'If a court martial orders a poor soldier who refuses to sacrifice his blood for his country put up against the wall and shot, what kind of punishment do you deserve, Monsieur Barbusse?'

At a lecture in Chicago, a French officer described *Le Feu* as German propaganda and the squad depicted in it by Barbusse as a 'gang of ruffians and internationalist riffraff'!

Barbusse's reply in *La Flamme* on 6 July 1918 was interesting. He began by insisting on the absolute veracity of his account, and then added: 'The soldiers do their duty and do so to the end for nobler reasons than fear of the miseries of war, of suffering and of death. . . . [Not one of the soldiers who have written to me] has given me to understand that the truth is likely to weaken his resolve to go on . . .'.

We may argue about the effects that a book like Barbusse's had on young men about to be called up — soldiers themselves did not need to be told the truth — but it is hardly likely to have boosted the nation's morale. Nor can it be assumed that people wish to hear disagreeable truths. Nevertheless, like Rolland, Barbusse was accused of holding views which he himself strongly disavowed.

As far as the quality of the arguments was concerned, the balance was fairly equal: on the one side the 'bitter enders' declared roundly that the fight must continue until victory while, on the other, their anti-war opponents contented themselves with calling for peace without specifying, or indeed knowing, the means by which this could be achieved. But what was the *quantitative* effect, that is to say, what influence did the two camps exert? An unequivocal answer is, of course, very difficult to give since it is impossible to make an accurate assessment of the influence of any literary work or newspaper article on public opinion at the time it was published.

What we can say is that, from the autumn of 1914, regardless of their political or patriotic feelings, soldiers came to despise *heroic literature*. But what of the influence of the various schools of writers on civilians? It is self-evident that works that attained fame after the war can have made little impact at the time of publication, the less so as they were brought out in such small editions. This was, for instance, the case with the work of Guillaume Apollinaire, unclassifiable despite his notorious: 'God! How nice the war is . . .'. His *Calligrammes*, which contained his war poems, was not published in its entirety until April 1918, and even then in a very small edition.[7]

Let us note finally that the influence of either side can only be

7. Claude Debon-Tournadre, *Guillaume Apollinaire de 1914 à 1918*, Paris, 1978.

assessed against the changing backcloth of time.

In 1915, and during most of 1916, the pro-war camp, 'the literature of the home front', took pride of place. *L'Echo de Paris*, for which Barrès wrote, was, with its circulation of 500,000, by far the most important of the political papers. *L'Action française* saw its circulation increase. René Benjamin's novel, *Gaspard*, appeared in the bookshops in November 1915 and won the Prix Goncourt, and 150,000 copies of it were printed. One literary critic, Jean-Ernest Charles, hailed the work as being 'by way of a masterpiece of truth, feeling and spirit'.

On the other side there was very little: 'Au-dessus de la mêlée', Rolland's essay, was not published in its almost complete form until the spring of 1915, and then only as part of Henri Massis's campaign of denigration: paradoxically, Romain Rolland's work thus first became widely known through the unintentional publicity it received from his adversaries. The book form of *Au-dessus de la mêlée* was not released until November 1915, but it proved so successful then that within a year it had run to sixty-three editions. Even so, Romain Rolland's influence remained confined to a relatively small circle. Some trade-union delegates, meeting at the *bourse du travail* during a CGT conference held on 15 August 1915, sent him a message of support, endorsed in a covering letter from Merrheim: '[The delegates] wish to assure you that your words have met a profound response among those workers who have remained true to their convictions and to the ideal of human fraternity'.

However, the CGT conference refused by 81 votes to 30 to ratify this message. By contrast, Romain Rolland's ideas elicited a continuing strong response in the journal of the teachers' union — nearly every issue carried the name of Rolland, to the extent where Maurras felt free to denounce him in *L'Action française* as the mouthpiece of state schoolteachers. We have already seen, however, that unionised teachers were no more than a very small minority in the teaching profession.

A number of intellectuals, too, voiced their support for Romain Rolland, among them the poet Marcel Martinet, Georges Pioch, Henri Guilbeaux — who even glorified him as 'our Goethe' — and Roger Martin du Gard, who sent Romain Rolland this mesage on 25 August 1915: 'The first breath of fresh air, I can even say the only one for a year, if I except some letters from one or two friends, has once again come to me from you'.

But these were lone voices; for the rest, it is almost certain that Rolland's influence was chiefly confined to a marginal group of socialists, trade unionists and anarchists who had increasingly grown to reject the *Union sacrée*. As for the majority of Frenchmen, particularly until 1916, very few of them had even heard of his ideas. From the end of 1916 onwards, a series of pointers indicated that heroic literature no longer enjoyed an exclusive influence over French morale. The first sign was the appearance and success of journals that broke with the conformism of the early days, chief among them being *L'Oeuvre*, which came out in September 1915, and *Le Canard enchaîné*, which appeared in July 1916.

Le Canard enchaîné invited its readers to take part in a referendum to elect the 'big white chief of the tribe of eyewashers', from which Gustave Hervé, closely followed by Maurice Barrès, emerged the victor on 20 June 1917.

L'Oeuvre, for its part, published Barbusse's *Le Feu* in serial form. Then, as a result of the interest it aroused, a number of provincial papers did likewise. When the work eventually appeared as a book, it was an immediate bestseller. Thus, on 7 February 1917, Barbusse recorded that the two leading bookshops in Chartres had sold their last copies and asked for more. By July 1918, 200,000 copies had been sold, which was quite exceptional. The author received a large number of letters, among them one from a soldier of the 90th Infantry Regiment who thanked him for having had the courage to 'speak up on his behalf' in front of the 'spectators behind the lines'. Barbusse noted: 'What letters!. . .*Le Feu* is catching on everywhere, the conflagration has caught'. Many papers saluted the book for the quality of its testimony, in particular *Le Radical*, *Le Populaire*, *La Dépêche de Toulouse*, (Gustave Hervé's) *La Victoire* and *Le Pays*, most of them publications of the left. Numerous writers also applauded Barbusse, among them Anatole France, Pierre-Jean Jouve, Victor and Paul Margueritte, Edmond Rostand, Maurice Maeterlinck, Paul Reboux and Paul Adam.

When the 1916 Prix Goncourt went to *Le Feu*, it succeeded *Gaspard* in the honours list, and the interest of the public in the new laureate was exactly proportional to the lack of interest it now showed in the old.

It is astonishing that *Le Feu* should have passed the censors and that it should have been awarded the Prix Goncourt. Romain Rolland remarked: 'Utterly amazed that so outspoken a work could appear in Paris, without the least cut'. To him, the book was important documentary evidence concerning the French soldier in trench warfare. 'These proletarians under arms [would] clearly be seen as the harbingers of the social revolution, of the union of nations done to death.'

Must it then be taken that there was at this point a reversal of

French public opinion, that heroic literature had been swept away, its influence dissipated?

The answer is complex. Literature fared much as did the papers: it had an undeniable influence over public opinion but, even more so, it reflected the aspirations of the people. This suggests that at the end of two years of conflict, soldiers and a section of civilians had grown tired of the heroic approach and thus ensured the success of realist literature. There had been too many dead, too many maimed, too much destruction, and also too much contact between the front and the rear for people to accept war as some sort of epic poem. Moreover, it needs to be stressed that while most of the 'heroic' writers in the first group had not been combatants, those in the second group had.

Did the retreat of heroic before realist literature — a retreat that was undeniable, for the former, having reigned supreme for so long, no longer did so after 1916 — reflect a parallel rejection of the view that Germany had to be beaten, or at least prevented from beating France? This is most unlikely. There is, indeed, much evidence to indicate that, while realist accounts of battle had become acceptable, the implicit or explicit conclusions (namely, doubts over the necessity of continuing the war, let alone of adopting revolutionary solutions) had not. Barbusse's *Le Feu* is a case in point: much as the first twenty-three chapters were appreciated, so the last chapter, radically different and essentially a denunciation of war, was dismissed as 'literature'. Similarly, as we have seen, Romain Rolland's message went largely unheard.

Nevertheless we are entitled to wonder whether, by showing war for what it was, these authors did not willy-willy undermine French morale and weaken the resolve to win. To take just one example, there are clear signs that, immediately after the publication of *Le Feu*, French morale reached a new low. It would, however, be rash to assume a causal connection; it is far more probable that the popularity of *Le Feu* was attributable to the fact that the country had begun to question the need for continuing the infernal and interminable slaughter. By the same token, the revelation of the full horrors of war persuaded many people that, after so much sacrifice, it would now be wrong to admit defeat.

Moreover, while 'optimistic' literature had been forced to beat a retreat, its 'patriotic' message had not been forgotten. In 1917 the circulation of *L'Action française* rose to 156,000 copies; never before had the influence of the paper been so great. In 1917 and 1918 the denunciations of defeatism by the leader writers of the monarchist dailies still struck their targets with deadly effect. Léon

Daudet could still proclaim proudly that he had been a 'purveyor of eyewash': in an article in *L'Action française* dedicated to Barrès in August 1918, he declared: 'Yes, my dear Barrés,...the two of us, each according to his disposition, have not hesitated to 'purvey eyewash' by declaring that the Boche was not invincible, that, sooner or later, he would collapse and that his inevitable collapse was essential for civilisation'.

There is every reason to believe that a very large majority of French people, who had no sympathy for *L'Action française*, shared these feelings to the end.

CHAPTER 12

The Churches and the War

Was it only coincidence that, with war hardly having been declared, a religious vocabulary should have sprung to the lips of the Republic: Union *sacrée*, patriotic *faith*. . .?[1] Clearly it was felt that French steadfastness in wartime would depend to some extent on the attitude of the Churches, and on that of the Catholic Church in particular.

In fact, all Churches vied with one another in patriotic ardour, even though the Catholic hierarchy, when calling for national unity and cooperation with the government of the Republic, might have felt some reservations as they remembered the persecutions to which they believed their Church had been subjected during the recent past. This may explain why some Catholics contended that the sufferings brought by the war were a much-needed expiation for France. As Guillaume Apollinaire put it in his *Letter to Lou* on 14 July 1915: 'Many Catholics are terrible people: they believe that atheistic France has not yet been chastised enough to justify a quick victory'.

'I suffer, yes I suffer, but so be it! I offer up my life in expiation of my sins and those of France', wrote a corporal in 1915 in *La Semaine religieuse de Nice*. In some cases, the idea of a war justified by the sins of France made way for the corollary: no victory without true expiation. 'What can we expect God to do for a nation that offends Him and persists in its error? Whence cometh Salvation?' asked the Archbishop of Lyon, Cardinal Senin, in *La Semaine religieuse de Clermont-Ferrand* on 21 November 1914.

More generously, however, Catholic theologians, invoking a tradition that went back to the Middle Ages and the Schoolmen,

1. This chapter was contributed by Annette Becker.

contented themselves with defining the concept of the 'just war', as Charles Ducasse did in 1916 in a book entitled *Le Nouveau Testament, la Guerre et le Chrétien* ('The New Testament, the War and the Christian').

Nevertheless, it seems that most Catholics saw no need to search for such justifications and that they broadly agreed with Barrès's Pauline dictum: 'We have ceased dividing ourselves into Catholics, Protestants, Socialists and Jews. Suddenly something more basic has emerged, something all of us share: we are Frenchmen'. According to André Latreille: 'Catholicism is the backbone of French patriotism'. And, indeed, attempts by the clergy and their flock to underpin patriotism knew no bounds. Thus, when Monseigneur Marbeau presided over a memorial service in Saint-Denis for those who had fallen in 1915, he proclaimed:

> And what is the song of those who have died in battle? It is the 'Marseillaise'. It is to the strains of the 'Marseillaise' that they knock at the door of this basilica. Open it for them, admit them to immortality. . . . Our religion is based on traditions. France was born in the baptistry of Rheims, out of the union of battle. We cannot separate God and country: it is religion which has upheld the patriotism of our soldiers and it is with the help of God that we shall vanquish.

According to the chaplain of a Marseille *lycée*, frequent attendance at communion was 'a patriotic duty to the Church and to France'. Public prayer meetings were held, because, as *La Croix* wrote: 'In this hour, patriotism makes it incumbent on every citizen to contribute everything he can for our country's defence and for victory. Now, prayer is a large part of that contribution'.

That the authorities should have persistently refused to associate themselves with these prayer meetings, and even with those invoking Joan of Arc, caused the organisers both sorrow and indignation. Joan of Arc was also the subject of innumerable sermons and devotional prints. St Denis and St Geneviève were also called upon. The cult of the Sacred Heart, 'one of the hallmarks of nineteenth-century spirituality',[2] became infused with nationalist sentiment.

A Catholic Committee for Propaganda Abroad, founded by the future Cardinal Baudrillart, set itself the task of aligning Catholic opinion in other countries against Germany. Protestants and Jews, moreover, did not lag far behind and founded similar propaganda committees. French Protestants, in particular, tried to prove that

2. Jean-Marie Mayeur, 'Le Catholicisme français et la Première Guerre mondiale', *Francia*, 1974, vol. II.

they had nothing in common with their German co-religionists.[3] In 1917, André Spire wrote *Les Juifs et la Guerre*, a book in which he explained that anti-Semitism was essentially a German phenomenon and that all Jews must therefore side with France. An appeal from 'French Israelites to neutral Israelites' declared: 'The French Revolution freed the Jews in the West, the victory of the Allies will free the Jews in the rest of Europe . . .'.

Nor did the churches spare any effort in their support of war charities, subscriptions and loans. In *De l'or pour la Patrie* ('Gold for the Country'), a tract published by the Christian schools, we read: 'Each piece of gold handed in for the National Defence is one tear less shed by mothers. What will we not do for our country, especially when that country is called France? Give your gold joyously; God loves a joyous gift'.

The bishops, too, enjoined Catholics to give generously. 'Let us demonstrate our patriotism and our Catholicism; let us take our gold and subscribe to the National Defence Loan', Monseigneur Belmont, Bishop of Clermont, proclaimed. 'What service our bishops and priests are rendering! Without their help the loan would have little chance of success!' declared Alexander Ribot, minister of finance from August 1914 to March 1917.

The patriotic exertions of the Catholic Church were the more intense as French Catholics felt the war to be an occasion for reuniting the nation and restoring the Church to its rightful place, from which it had been displaced as the result of anti-clerical struggles.

This objective seemed perfectly legitimate to the Church, which had not concealed its intention of pursuing it from the moment war was declared. In August 1914, in an article entitled 'Pour le Christ et pour la France' ('For Christ and for France'), *La Semaine religieuse de Paris* declared: 'In becoming completely French once again, the soul of the nation will discover that it is Catholic. The transformation will take place in individuals: the political effects will follow'.

In September, Canon Poulin proclaimed in the church of Sacré-Coeur that it was essential to be able to point with pride to the attitude of Catholics on the day of victory, and Catholic papers urged the authorities to associate themselves with religious ceremonies. 'What place in history could you not occupy', Pierre l'Ermite, one of the staff editors of *La Croix*, enjoined Poincaré, 'if you were to grasp this wish of an entire people! Not only will you

3. Daniel Robert, 'Les Protestants français et la guerre de 1914–1918', *Francia*, 1974, vol. II.

have witnessed the return of Alsace and Lorraine, you will also have reconciled the France of yesterday with the France of tomorrow'. The Bishop of Auch rubbed it in. He reminded his priests: 'You are priest-soldiers and not merely soldier-priests. What I mean is that God enlisted you before your country did'. The Church often pursued its political objectives so blatantly that it earned stiff reprimands, and not only from journals on the left. In September 1914, *Le Temps* set about 'politicians of the faith', and sparked off a lively debate with *La Croix*.

The *Renseignements généraux* followed this aspect of Catholic activity very closely,[4] and on several occasions drew the attention of the authorities to it: They reported in 1916:

> Those Catholics who propose to win over public opinion for the purpose of changing the country's internal policies are preparing the ground on which they hope to build after the war. As the objectives and real aspirations of the Catholic world gradually become clearer, we discover that they reflect an impatient hope to see the war bring to the hierarchy and religious institutions of the Church official recognition by the Republic.

And in 1917 they reported that 'all the major orders are preparing to make great play of the services rendered to the national defence effort by their mobilised members. . . . Members of religious orders appear avid for medals and rank, obviously following instructions from their superiors whose ulterior motive seems undeniable'.

No one denied the patriotic fervour of the Church, even if the mass distribution of devotional medals to soldiers and the wounded irritated some and certainly provoked among many a hostile reaction to what they considered undue pressure on impressionable minds. We are, in any case, entitled to ask whether, in pursuing objectives not uniquely 'patriotic', above all in the eyes of those who did not believe that the temporal and spiritual spheres were necessarily connected, the Church in fact jeopardised its influence and hence weakened its role in sustaining French morale.

This question is the more justified as the Church was forced, throughout the war, to combine its attempt to capture souls with efforts to refute the charges of its detractors.

Catholics referred to these accusations as an 'infamous rumour', but they had two distinct aspects. The Church was accused, first, of being responsible in part for the war, and secondly, of hoping for the defeat of France — this last being based on the attitude of the

4. ANF 7 13213.

papacy.

One can understand how the first rumour came about. From the idea of an expiatory war, those who were hostile to the Church — and they were many in a country where the fight for secularism had been so fierce — found it easy enough to come to the conclusion that the priests had wanted the war in order to chastise France, a chastisement which would be even more fitting if France were beaten. This assumption about Catholic motives is well documented. In Brittany, for example, the chairman of a regional tribunal reported that the headmistress of a private Catholic school had come to him in tears, claiming that people were saying she had made her pupils pray for the Kaiser and for the Kaiser's victory.

> This was obviously false [our witness declared]. But the source of the 'calumny' was easy to discover: the headmistress in fact admitted that she had said, like so many of the priests she came into contact with, that the war was France's punishment. From that remark it was only a short step to crediting her with the belief that the defeat of France would be an even fitter punishment, that the Kaiser was the instrument of God and that Catholics should pray for the Kaiser's victory.

While it is difficult to tell what precise impact the 'infamous rumour' had, we known that it was ubiquitous. Monseigneur Raymond, Bishop of Mans, did not, for one, think it could be ignored: 'Our priests are accused of being friends of Germany, of praying for a German victory, of sending money to Prussia'.

As for the Vicomte de Lestrange, a Catholic nobleman with a leaning towards the ultra-nationalistic views of Charles Maurras, he felt compelled to collect evidence of Catholic patriotism, because, as he observed: 'Catholics must have great patience, for even in wartime they have to put up with the perfidious attacks of those whose slogan is: "Clericalism is our real enemy"'.

The 'infamous rumour' itself had no other foundation than thoughtless remarks by some Catholics who, moreover, found it difficult to appreciate their anti-patriotic implications. Things were quite different in the second case, which had to do with the attitude of the papacy.

The issue was really quite straightforward: on purely doctrinal grounds, the papacy could not approve of the war, and on political grounds it could not support one side against the other, because there were Catholics on both. As Benedict XV said to a consistory court in 1915:

> The Roman pontiff being on the one hand the vicar of Jesus Christ, who

died for all men and for each one of us, and being on the other hand
father of all Catholics, must extend the same feeling of charity to all
combatants. In each belligerent camp there are many sons whose salvation demands his solicitude to the same degree. . . . If he acted otherwise, not only would he be failing to hasten peace, but he would also be
holding religion up to obloquy and hatred, thus exposing the tranquillity
and internal concord of the Church to serious risk.

The Holy See could not therefore be anything but neutral,
working for the restoration of peace, or at least calling for peace.
During the early days of the war, Pius X, followed by Benedict XV,
his successor, never deviated from this path, a stand many Frenchmen found incomprehensible. Believing that right was on their side
and that they had been the victims of aggression, they could not
understand how anyone could place the two warring sides on a par.
Romain Rolland, albeit that he made it perfectly clear that he sided
with France, had been taken to task simply for wishing to remain
'above the battle'. But the Holy See was much worse. Benedict XV
never ceased calling for a return to peace in his letters, his prayers,
his messages addressed to governments, to the Catholic hierarchy,
to the entire world. Since from the beginning to the end of the war
the 'map of war' favoured the Central Powers, a mere return to
peace would inevitably have been to their advantage: so could a
victorious Germany, if she accepted a compromise peace, really be
expected to return Alsace–Lorraine to France?

Benedict XV was therefore accused of being pro-German. In
1915, Clemenceau mocked him with: 'It would be a Boche's peace,
O Pontiff of the Holy Empire!' Moreover, Austria–Hungary was
said to have the ear of the Vatican, if only because, unlike France,
she had diplomatic relations with the Holy See. It was all enough
to make Monseigneur Duchesne, Rector of the French School
in Rome, sigh: 'I wish Clemenceau were pope, for he would
soon realise that encyclicals are not as easy to write as articles for
L'Homme enchaîné'.

From the beginning of the war, the French Catholic hierarchy was
torn between duty to their country and obedience to the pope. Thus
Cardinal Emette, Archbishop of Paris, had, in one breath, to declare
his faith in a pope who proclaimed 'I bless peace' while adding on his
own authority: 'Our country calls her children to arms. . . .Let us pray
that our arms may vanquish, as they have so often in the past'.
Monseigneur Duchesne endorsed this stand when he declared, not
without humour: 'We can do nothing about the fact that a large
number of Frenchmen are not Catholics, and we are not answerable
for the fact that Catholicism involves the presence of a pope'.

For some time this difficult balancing act did not cause too many problems, but feelings ran high on 22 June 1915, when Louis Latapie published an interview with the pope in *La Liberté*, a paper reputed to be sympathetic to the Church. Asked about the sinking of the *Lusitania*, Benedict XV had allegedly replied: 'I know of no more heinous crime, I have the broken heart of a bereaved father. But do you think that the blockade which is throttling two empires, which condemns millions of innocent people to starvation, reflects any more decent human feelings?'

The French press reacted virulently: 'So there is no difference between aggressor and victim?' asked *L' Humanité*. Public opinion too was taken aback. As Louis Debidour wrote from the front: 'The pope has made a most serious blunder with his pro-German declaration. His Jesuitical arguments, his evasions, have aroused violent fury in Italy and have been very badly received in all the Allied countries. The Holy See will end up having to pick up the pieces. So much the worse for it'.

The reader may think that these were isolated reactions inspired by malevolence or anti-clericalism. However, a letter addressed to the pope by the Archbishop of Paris shows that they were not:

Most Holy Father,

I believe I am doing my duty and performing an act of filial devotion to the Holy See when I convey to you respectfully and in all sincerity the impression produced in France by the publication of an interview that Your Holiness recently granted to the editor of the journal *La Liberté*.

Among Catholics, clergy and faithful, this impression is unanimous, and it is one of profound pain. Reports are reaching me from all sides, from bishops, priests, deputies and leading politicians, Christian journalists as well as a host of ordinary people. All are distressed and say they feel despondent, while our enemies have the base and insidious satisfaction of being able to find ammunition in their fight to prevent France from drawing closer to the Holy See again and to hinder the return to religion of our armed forces. . . .

May Your Holiness forgive me for repeating things that I have found painful to hear; I do so, once again, because I am very profoundly devoted to the Holy Father, because I suffer when I see him misunderstood, and because I believe I am rendering him a service when I convey to him what is in the mind of our people.

Though *L'Osservatore Romano*, the mouthpiece of the Vatican, published a partial repudiation of the interview, quoting several errors, French public opinion remained convinced — and rightly so — that the position of the Holy See was not one of unqualified support for France.

On 1 August 1917, Benedict XV launched an 'appeal for peace to the heads of the belligerent nations' in which he reaffirmed his desire for peace and put forward ideas for attaining it, among them the freedom of the seas and the waiving of reparations. However, he made no reference to Alsace–Lorraine. A few years ago the historian Pierre Renouvin published a study of French episcopal reactions to this papal note.[5] In most dioceses, the reactions were mixed, if not critical. They reflected 'two imperious and contradictory preoccupations of the French episcopate', namely, not to deviate from the general line adopted by the French government and not to fail in obedience to the Holy See — a difficult tightrope act indeed.

The letters intercepted by the postal censorship boards are a good barometer of French public opinion, Catholic and otherwise. From 15 August to 15 September, to take just one period as an example, the board sitting in Bordeaux listed twenty-one letters referring to the pontifical note.

Two of these letters approved the pontifical initiative and deplored the hostile reactions of the press:

> The papal note on peace that was sent to all the belligerents, though worthy of all our respect, has caused a real furore in the French press. If it were better understood it would be assessed more fairly. The Supreme Pontiff could not say everything he felt, it was simply an exordium. In due course, he will say everything that has to be said. *We must have confidence in him.* In France, the sectarian government will not disarm.

> If only people would heed the Pope's appeal now. *He has been given a very chilly reception* by both sides (except in Austria) but nevertheless it seems to me that it is a *good thing* and that his words of peace must have made a deep impression on many people and will gradually lead to the concord we so much desire. It will not be long now.

All the other correspondents believed that the affair had political undertones, and that Austria was behind the pope's intervention. 'I wonder if the Holy See might not have launched this note as a sort of bridge across which Austria can advance,' wrote one. Others

5. 'L'Episcopat français devant l'offre de paix du Saint-Siège', in *Mélanges G. Jacquemyns* (Brussels).

argued that, even if there had been no direct intervention by Austria, the pope's own pro-German feelings needed no prompting:

> There's this pope, meddling, wanting to make these peace proposals. Ah, if the dear Lord of the French could only make him sit up and listen! But there it is, people are quite sure that he's being urged on by those damned Boche and Austrians. We shall see. . . .

> I have just read the pope's letter on peace. What a cheek! It's really made me angry: it's nothing but Boche & Co., and he'd do much better not to say anything at all.

> You may have heard that our Holy Father the Pope has taken it upon himself to make peace proposals. In fact these proposals do nothing but repeat what the Germans have been proposing for a long time. There is no doubt *that our Holy Father is the mouthpiece of Wilhelm* II. It just proves that the Boche is at the end of his tether and that he is ready to try anything. But it won't work any better this time than it did on previous occasions.

> What do you think of the pope's proposal? A German cardinal could not have bettered it. People will laugh, no one will take it seriously, his intervention was very clumsy. Many Catholics in the Allied countries will see him as nothing but a Boche in disguise, something people have been murmuring for a long time. He doesn't mention the causes of the war, says not a word about German misdeeds in Belgium and France. Does none of this mean anything to him? If he hasn't got enough wit to judge things, he had best keep his own counsel.

Good Catholics, too, were truly indignant:

> Benedict XV seems to understand nothing about politics and diplomacy. What a Holy Blunderer! He would do better to stay lying low and say nothing as he did about Boche crimes, than talk such nonsense. I respect him as the spiritual head of the Church, but not as a peacemaker. He can be sure that people in our so generous and so pious country will remember it later during the collection for him [i.e. Peter's pence].

Some were not so much furious as disappointed at the maladroitness of an intervention that retarded rather than advanced the cause of peace:

> I had great hopes when I read that the pope had spoken, but the next day the tenor of his document proved disappointing. It will be a long time yet before we hear news of a peace and no one can seriously want us to lay down our arms at this stage. It would have been far better had we done so

three years ago. But to lose the fruit that is about to fall ripe into our lap after so much effort – that would be stupid.

As another correspondent put it:

What will be the effect of the pope's letter, of Wilson's reply, and of those by the Central Powers? Nothing. Nevertheless the day will come when it all has to end, even without victory and without defeat, for lack of time, lack of money, lack of provisions, lack of something. We have already had the Seven Years War, the Thirty Years War, the Hundred Years War, but not yet the Everlasting War.

The least one can say is that the pope's desire to remain neutral was not understood in France, by Catholics any more than by non-believers.

Was papal neutrality likely to undermine the influence of Catholics on French opinion and hence their patriotic message? A former Radical deputy, Charles Beauquier, said in 1915: 'The indecisive and far too cautious behaviour of the pope, God's representative on earth, in refusing to anathematise the German hordes, sullied as they are by every possible crime. . .does not seem to be of a kind likely to bind believers fast in their faith'.

Though Charles Beauquier, who was 82 and had retired from political life in 1914, may not have been a reliable witness — his entire career had been founded on anti-clericalism and he was president of the National Association of Freethinkers — he nevertheless asked a very important question: did the religious faith of the French grow stronger during the war, did it flag or did it change in any other way?

Religious attitudes in France in 1915, after one year of war, are well known thanks to two enquiries which were conducted almost simultaneously, one by the Catholic Committee for Propaganda Abroad, the other by a literary magazine, *La Grande Revue*.

The questionnaire of the Catholic committee, sent to all French bishops and parish priests in September 1915, was called: 'Enquiry into Catholic France under arms and on the home front'. It consisted of six questions:

1. Did mobilisation elicit a significant religious response in your diocese? Did you notice an increase in the number of confessions and communions and greater attendance at either ordinary or special church ceremonies?
2. Has the religious response been maintained, increased or weakened during the months following?
3. Has there been a real and lasting reconciliation between the civil,

political and municipal authorities and the representatives of religious authority? Have the uncaring sections of the population displayed any more sympathy for the clergy and for religion? Has there been any backsliding?

4. To what extent has the religious response led to greater attendances at retreats and at Lenten sermons, and above all to greater observance of Easter duties?

5. Has the Catholic contribution to the organisation and running of war charities been marked in any particular way? Has there been cooperation in this field between those who were until recently divided by politics or party dissension?

6. Can you give an approximate estimate of the influence of the various Catholic charitable activities on the religious response elicited by the war?

In short, this questionnaire was intended to establish whether or not the war had led to a revival — both quantitative and qualitative — of the Catholic faith in France, and also whether it had helped to reintegrate Catholics in French society.

It is a matter for regret that the findings of the inquiry were never published, and the only reference we can trace is in a work written by J. Bruguerette in 1918, *Le Prêtre français et la Société contemporaine*, based on the result of the inquiry in the diocese of Clermont-Ferrand.

As far as quantity is concerned there is no doubt: the onset of war brought an unquestionable 'return to the altars'. *Le Moniteur du Puy-de-Dôme* published an example on 23 November 1914 which could easily be repeated many times over: 'There was a great crowd at the cathedral. . .today, and there was hardly room in the church for all those who wanted to render homage at this ceremony to our glorious heroes'.

The curé of Orcival recorded 3,950 communions from August to December 1912, 4,115 during the same period in 1913 and 14,480 in the same months in 1914. The number of communions thus more than tripled at the beginning of the war. That proportion was repeated in nearly all the parishes in Puy-de-Dôme for which we have records. The increase in attendance at mass was comparable, and, as the curé of Aigueperse put it: 'There were a great many people in church whom we had not seen for a long time'.

As far as the quality of the faith was concerned, the impression is less clear. One full account came from the parish priest of Job, near Ambert:

There was a religious revival the moment mobilisation was announced, at least as far as prayers were concerned. There was more fervent praying in families, for the diocese, for France and for our soldiers. . . . People prayed more fervently and more frequently in church; particularly when there were services connected with the war, the parishioners would attend more often than usual. However, when it came to living the true Christian life, to the strict observance of the commandments of God and of the Church, the religious revival was not nearly so noticeable.

Then there was the enquiry by *La Grande Revue*, which simply asked: 'Is France experiencing a religious renaissance?' Broader than the first enquiry, it was divided into two parts:

1. Was there a religious revival in France before the war? (Among the bourgeoisie; the masses; the young?)
2. Has there been a religious revival during the war? (In the war zone, or in the rear; among the combatants, be they in the army or in hospital; or among non-combatants, particularly women, families, etc.?)

It was clearly stated that readers should in their replies distinguish between a revival of religious practices, of religious faith and of submission to the authority of the Church.

The replies, which were received between the end of April and August 1915, help us to form a very clear picture of the character of the religious revival, even though they were more in the nature of personal reflections than the product of a systematic survey.

Many correspondents doubted that the revival of religious practices reflected an especially deep religious faith. Some saw it, above all, as a search for protection, something that came very close to superstition. This was the view of Albert Mathiez, the famous historian of the French Revolution: 'It is largely fear of death which explains the sudden resurgence of observance'. Mathiez was no friend of the Catholic Church, but his opinion was in no way different from that of the curé of Saint-Dier d'Auvergne, according to whom the women 'are not entirely disinterested. They feel they must pray for the return of their husband or fiancé. But I doubt if, once the danger is over, these communicants of 1915 will retain their faith'.

Others were openly sarcastic: 'For those who are usually indifferent, religion acts as a lightning conductor at times of great shocks'. More profoundly, a canon serving in the medical corps mused:

Religious revival, yes, certainly; it is indisputable in its range and spontaneity. . .you have only to announce the approach of misfortune to turn minds towards Him who governs mankind, and to make God present to a host of anxious souls eager for hope. . . . Does that mean that they submit to the authority of the Church? Yes, in a sense. But the

Church does not claim to wield any authority beyond dogma and morality. And dogmas are hardly the issue at the moment.

It is a pity that we have no comparative investigation of the 'religious revival' during the postwar period, but the few indications there are tend to show beyond doubt that the religious upsurge was a purely temporary phenomenon.

In 1916, the president of the Union of Catholic Associations of Heads of Families in Puy-de-Dôme spoke of a 'decline in religious life': 'If many of those who returned to the faith at the front failed to persevere in the rear, in the hospitals and in the depots, it was because their response had been to a shock as fleeting as it was real. . . . Here lies the main obstacle to a religious revival in this country.'

At a conference in March 1917 devoted to France's religious revival, a Catholic leader complained: 'This wonderful movement is slowing down; the long duration of the war had led to dejection among those of the faithful whose upsurge of religious fervour was impetuous, and they have lapsed again into indifference'.

A young sergeant planning to become a Protestant minister kept a diary which was published after his death at the front under the title *Impressions de guerre d'un soldat chrétien*. 'Sunday morning', he noted on 25 October 1914. 'Many of my men have gone to mass. At times like these large numbers of people remember that they have a faith and no longer scoff at religious observances.' But on 26 August 1915 he wrote: 'Today is Sunday! Nothing, absolutely nothing makes this day different in any way from any other day in the trenches . . .'.

Must we then take it that the religious revival was a purely superficial response? Was it, in fact, religious at all? To a schoolmaster from Cantal it seemed to be rather a sign of the solidarity of war. 'In rural areas, the church alone holds collective rites for the dead, so much so that people with no religious affiliation are obliged to participate in church services if they wish to pay their last respects to those who have died for their country'.

Of the two objectives of the Church — working towards the strengthening of patriotism and working towards the strengthening of religious faith — the second was not attained, at least not in any substantial way. Indeed, the Church's wish to harness patriotic fervour to the good of the faith rebounded on her. Moreover, it was clear to one and all that the faithful had no more of a monopoly on patriotism than did unbelievers, Catholics no more than Protestants or Jews, priests no more than teachers. The 'religious war', though undeniably muted, had not entirely died down. As Monseigneur Baudrillart put it in his *Journal*: 'At least, many of our politicians are happy to use us to subscribe to the Loan, and are not displeased that some of the people do not thank us for it and hold the priests responsible for the long duration of the war'.

And it was Denys Cochin, one of the leading Catholic politicians, who gave this reason for resigning from the government on 2 August 1917: 'I would accept everything in the name of the *Union sacrée* if it still existed. . . . It exists no more and my presence merely provides a radical–socialist ministry with a false façade'.

By contrast the Church undoubtedly attained its first objective: neither the 'infamous rumour', however distasteful, nor the pope's ambiguous attitude, seemed to have appreciably weakened the appeal of the Church's patriotic message. Was Catholicism then 'the backbone of French patriotism'? It certainly helped to ensure that patriotism did not disintegrate when put to the test.

III

THE CRISIS OF 1917

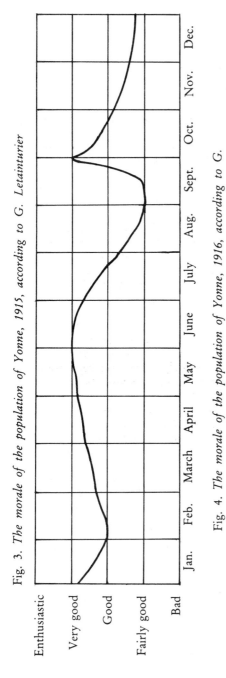

Fig. 3. *The morale of the population of Yonne, 1915, according to G. Letainturier*

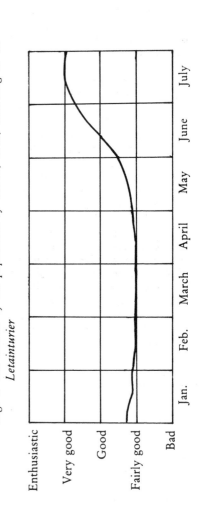

Fig. 4. *The morale of the population of Yonne, 1916, according to G. Letainturier*

By the end of 1916, the French people had gradually grown used to the war; still not believing that it would last for very much longer, they found that each new phase brought with it the hope that this would be the last. They were like the mountaineer who, at every peak, discovers another rising beyond.

The curve (Figs. 3 and 4) prepared by the prefect of Yonne to depict the state of morale in his department during 1915 and 1916 (for 1914, see p. 96), shows that, despite crests and throughs following the fortunes of war in France and elsewhere, morale neither rose above 'very good' nor dropped below 'fairly good'. Were there nevertheless indicators of what was about to happen?

Part of the answer is to be found by making a comparison of two reports submitted by the sub-prefect at Bressiure in Deux-Sèvres to the prefect of his department on 21 February 1916 and 1 December 1916[1] respectively.

In February, the sub-prefect declared that morale left nothing to be desired, this despite heavy losses at the front (some small communes had counted forty dead by then). Careful farmers had made money and soldiers' wives had been helped by the separation allowances. It was essential to keep up all such payments lest 'the interests we serve be gravely imperilled'.

In December of the same year, the sub-prefect adopted an altogether different tone: morale, he believed, had deteriorated, largely because of the bad example set by soldiers on leave, who had previously helped to raise the morale of their families. He felt that, if this trend continued, then leave and the free exchange of letters ought to be stopped. During a tour, he had heard that people were being advised not to subscribe to the current loan 'so as not to prolong the war', and that soldiers on leave were trying to persuade farmers not to sow any late crops, thus hoping to force the government to sign a peace.

Conversations overheard in trains, the sub-prefect added, made it clear to everybody that 'the *weariness* of our soldiers has reached an altogether unexpected level'.

The sub-prefect believed that government control needed to be tightened and freedom of speech curtailed, even though it was

1. AD Deux-Sèvres 4 M 6/29.

difficult to press charges as witnesses to subversive utterances usually proved shy of coming forward.

While we know from other documents that the attitudes reported by the sub-prefect were fairly atypical of France as a whole, they nevertheless did arise and reflect a considerable drop in morale in at least one region of France during 1916.

Does that mean that the national consensus born in August 1914 and named the *Union sacrée* was about to break down?

CHAPTER 13

The Slow Emergence of an Opposition

The Department of Haute-Vienne

One of the first departments in which the Socialist Party voiced reservations about the continuation of the conflict was that of Haute-Vienne, where socialist influence had been very strong before the war. Thus, at the 1914 elections, the socialists had obtained 61.4 per cent of all the votes cast and 4 deputies out of 5; the municipal council of Limoges was in their control.

A meeting of delegates of the Haute-Vienne socialist federation held in Limoges on 9 May 1915 adopted a report for submission on 15 May to the Central Committee of the Socialist Party, to the socialist group in parliament as well as to other departmental federations.[1]

This fairly detailed document — it ran to six typewritten pages — did not contest the fact that the war had interfered with the life of the party, causing a marked drop in its activities. Now, though the departmental federations might have shown greater initiative, the main blame had to be put on the Central Committee, which had failed to give the lead one might have expected from it, and which had not bothered to consult 'socialist France'. The leadership was, in fact, accused of having cut itself off from its rank and file. It would never have done so had 'some of its attitudes been slightly different'.

The delegates went on to observe that, as the war was continued and as deaths and devastation mounted, they had 'come, in the interests of socialism, of the working class, and of our country, to hope for the end of the war'.

1. ANF 7 13023.

197

On what terms? Not 'at any price', not 'whatever the cost', not by abandoning Belgium and the invaded territories: 'Like everyone else, we are concerned for our independence and our national dignity'. However, socialists must seize every opportunity to bring about a peace. In particular, it was wrong to refuse the invitation of several socialist parties in neutral countries to attend a meeting of the International Socialist Bureau; it was wrong to ignore the resolutions of the 1907 Stuttgart Congress that, in case of war, socialists should 'intercede so as to bring hostilities to a speedy conclusion', and of the 1912 Basle Congress that, *come what may*, the International Socialist Bureau must maintain contacts and communications between the various socialist parties.

It was a matter of regret, declared the militants from Haute-Vienne, that some socialists should use such expressions as 'to the very end' because they were ambiguous and dangerous in as much as they implied that no peace was possible until the German Empire had been defeated and every nation liberated.

In short, the delegates were advising the leaders of the Socialist Party to moderate their pro-war stance, to pay greater attention to peace proposals, to lend an ear to all sections of the party, to protest against excessive censorship aimed at stifling the expression of socialist thought, to counter reactionary provocations, and finally to urge parliament to meet in permanent session for the purpose of drafting whatever legislation was needed for the nation's recovery.

This document was signed by the executive committee of the Haute-Vienne socialist federation, which comprised, among others, Léon Bétoulle, parliamentary deputy for, and mayor of, Limoges, and the deputies Adrien Pressemane and Sabinus Vallière.

At first sight, the attitude adopted by the Haute-Vienne socialists does not appear excessively bold, but it must be remembered that their document was issued a mere nine months after the outbreak of war, in the midst of a wave of almost undiluted 'patriotic' conformism. Moreover, because it was signed by three deputies, the declaration seemed provocative enough for the prime minister, René Viviani, to ask the prefect of the department what he thought of it. The prefect, however, minimised its importance; and Léon Bétoulle, one of the signatories, declared that the document 'did not have the importance some people have attached to it' and that it ought to have been kept secret. The local socialist paper, *Le Populaire du Centre*, had not in fact thought it worth a mention, and according to the prefect the declaration had been completely ignored by local opinion.

The national leaders of the Socialist Party did, for their part, take the trouble to reply, and at some length — on sixteen typewritten sheets. They criticised the delegates not only for going over the head of the executive committee, but also, and above all, for being fundamentally mistaken. They pointed out, in particular, that no meeting of the Socialist International could be held before the responsibilities of the various national sections had been agreed upon and the necessary authorisation obtained. As far as the central committee was concerned, it rejected any meeting with German socialists. A premature peace could provide no more than a temporary respite, which was worse than the continuation of the war. What was needed was a peace to put an end to all wars, a just peace that could only be established in a democratic Europe, one rid of Prussian militarism. To that end, the need for a 'painful', 'perhaps long', struggle had to be accepted.

There was thus a marked difference between the views of Haute-Vienne socialists and their national leaders, whose reply, moreover, bore the signatures of all the greatest names in French socialism: Guesde, Renaudel, Sembat, Vaillaint.

Even so, the appeal from Haute-Vienne did not fall entirely on deaf ears, for the prefect of Gironde mentioned that it had been welcomed by socialist militants in his department.

The delegates from Haute-Vienne did not allow things to rest there, but their determination to carry things further led to a split in their ranks. The mayor of Limoges, Deputy Léon Bétoulle, was opposed to all forms of agitation, while the other deputy, Pressemane, and the editor of *Le Populaire du Centre*, Paul Faure, were much less cautious.

In 1916, prior to the election of a new national executive of the Socialist Party, the leaders of the Haute-Vienne socialist federation sent all other federations a series of pacifist tracts, which in fact consisted mostly of extracts from *Le Populaire du Centre*. These tracts, dated March 1916, had one main theme: relations between socialist parties throughout Europe had to be restored for the sake of finding a way to peace; the leaders of the Socialist Party were, however, refusing to hold talks with German socialists until Germany had been beaten, claiming that they shared their country's responsibility for the war. The Haute-Vienne federation summed up its position as follows: 'Continuation of the war in order to secure the independence of our country and to allow the spirit of the nation to develop freely within guaranteed frontiers? Yes, but only on condition that every other solution has been tried first'.

Thus, almost two years after the beginning of the war, anti-war ideas had made very little progress among socialists: not even the most progressive socialists were ready to go beyond calling for the resumption of contacts between socialists in various countries. Moreover, the debate, between militants if not the leaders, on the differences between the majority and minority views in the party was largely ignored by the public. In May 1916, for instance, only four papers took it up: the socialist, *Le Populaire du Centre*, and *Le Droit du peuple* of Grenoble, Sébastien Faure's anarchist *Ce qu'il faut dire* and a new review published in Limoges, also called *Le Populaire*. All four had very small circulations.

Within the Socialist Party, however, the views of the Haute-Vienne federation did not go unheard: at a meeting of the national executive in April 1916, Pressemane's motion received 960 votes, compared with a vote for Renaudel's motion, representing the party leadership, of 1,987. This result encouraged the Haute-Vienne leaders to persevere. During the departmental congress held in Limoges in June 1916 they continued to maintain their stand: socialists must stop collaborating with the government and work instead for a return to the 'principles of the Workers' International'. They expressed their solidarity with the three socialist deputies, Brizon, Blanc and Raffin-Dugens, reviled for their participation in the Kienthal conference attended by a small number of pacifist or revolutionary socialists. It is most important, however, to stress that their solidarity was extended to the men themselves and not to their ideas, because at the same time they expressed the *strongest reservations* about the resolutions adopted at that conference. It may be seen that the anti-war sentiment of socialists in Haute-Vienne was confined within very narrow limits.

Nevertheless these socialists associated themselves with the protest by those in Haute-Marne against the agenda of a national executive meeting on 6 August 1916 — which was devoted entirely to the price of sugar! Haute-Marne insisted that international action against the continuation of the war must be added to the agenda, since the Socialist Party 'cannot, without being untrue to itself, eschew the sole question that preoccupies the proletariat of France and of Europe: the continuation of the war'. The socialists of Haute-Vienne said much the same, but in even more moderate terms!

This was, therefore, the position after two years of war. A minority of organised socialists, among whom the Haute-Vienne federation stood out because it spoke up first, hoped to effect moderate changes in party policy, without, however, jeopardising the national defence effort.

In order to gauge their true influence, we should have to determine how far it extended beyond the ranks of the Socialist Party. According to the prefect of Haute-Vienne in June 1915, their anti-war propaganda boded ill for the country, and Limoges was, in fact, to witness two incidents of some importance. On 18 June 1916, 2,000 people demonstrated outside the regional depot of the army medical service in protest against the behaviour of an officer towards two soldiers. It was not long before the crowd was 'booing the army'. It is significant that the prefect, though he noted the slack discipline of the soldiers, their lack of respect, even their rudeness towards their officers, thought it wise not to make too much of the incident. Limoges was a long way away from the front, and this demonstration may well have been no more than a sign of the perennial conflict between soldiers, supported by a population who set little value on things military, and their unpopular officers.

The second incident was probably more significant: in January 1917, some 400 women massed in the Place de la Mairie in Saint-Junien to hold a demonstration for peace. The head of the Sureté held an inquiry: what had given rise to the demonstration, to what social class did the women belong, had they been incited by meetings or by the distribution of papers and other publications, could something that happened in the commune have been the indirect cause of the demonstration? The answers he received to these questions are not available to us.

The case of Haute-Vienne therefore enables us to assess the importance of the rising wave of political opposition at the beginning of 1917. This department with a well-established socialist tradition witnessed a strong challenge to the majority view inside the party, hence to the government. Though that challenge was not taken up by the population, the mere fact that it could be made at all in wartime in however small a part of France and in however restrained a fashion, demonstrates the onset of a certain deep-seated shift in public opinion.

The Department of Gard

The department of Gard provides a good example of the slow rate at which trade-union activity gradually revived, even in a department with a progressive political tradition, with four socialist deputies out of a total of six in 1914, and a large concentration of workers, especially in the metal and mining industries, their ranks swollen by new recruits in the defence industries.

In the metal industry, there was little movement before the

autumn of 1916. Then, on 18 October 1916, the special commissioner in Alais mentioned that the metalworkers' union, dissolved at the outbreak of war, was to be revived. At that time it had 102 members in Tamaris, the headquarters of the Compagnie des Mines, Fonderies et Forges d'Alais, which then employed 2,463 workers.[2] At a meeting on 15 October 1916, attended by some sixty trade unionists, one speaker insisted that the workers in Tamaris were about to emerge from their apathy and torpor. The subsequent awakening was, however, slow — the number of union members remained very small and attendance at meetings sparse. Thus, on Sunday 5 November, there was an attendance of forty men only at a meeting of metalworkers convened at the *bourse du travail*, where the subject for discussion was wage claims based on the rise in prices. The next meeting, on 3 December, had a slightly bigger attendance of seventy-five, but officials complained that not only were the numbers of registered members small, but that they were also slow at paying their dues. On 18 December, the socialist deputy for Alais, Louis Mourier, addressed a meeting of fifty people.

Among the miners, whose number had increased by 35 per cent since the war — 17,340 as against 12,767 in 1912 — trade-union membership was still very small at the end of 1915: less than 3 per cent.[3] It was not until May 1917 that a trade union was set up in the most important coal mine of the region, that of La Grand-Combe.

The lack of industrial agitation was all the more remarkable in that the mining companies displayed so little understanding in their dealings with their employees. A report by the prefect did not scruple to speak of their 'absolute intransigence', and by the end of 1915 matters had reached a stage of acrimonious dispute. On the other hand, as Raymond Huard has noted, 'throughout 1916 and at the beginning of 1917, industrial calm continued to reign in the coal fields'. In Gard, therefore, it was not until 1917 that there was any trade-union activity to speak of.

At the end of May 1917, strikes broke out in the clothing industry in Nîmes, and in June they spread to the hosiery workers, shop assistants, printers, tram drivers and others. On the evenings of 1 and 2 June, processions of workers 400 to 500 strong marched through the boulevards of Nîmes. Their demands were concerned with wages only and the stoppages were generally brief, confined to

2. ANF 7 12985.
3. R. Huard, 'Les Mineurs du Gard pendant la guerre de 1914–1918', in *Economie et Société en Languedoc–Roussillon de 1789 à nos jours*, Montpellier, 1978.

one day, since the employers were fairly quick to give in under pressure from the authorities.[4]

The regional chief of police in Alais, who kept abreast of the situation in the small businesses of his town with the help of thirty informers (mostly older workers), claimed in June 1917 that morale was 'good'. He put this down to the 'judicious purge' he had carried out, coupled with strict discipline at work and the firmness of the military authorities. The larger metal shops and the mines, however, proved less submissive: on 12 June two meetings were attended by 225 metalworkers and 260 miners respectively. The mood was acrimonious. One speaker denounced the *Union sacrée* as 'a phrase as glorious as it is deceptive, whose sole object it is to keep the capitalists' coffers sacrosanct'. But again the discussion centred on wages, and there was no thought of calling a strike for the time being. The prefect of Gard could reassure the minister of the interior, to whom rumours of seditious movements in the department had percolated, that popular morale was 'fairly satisfactory', including that of the metalworkers (July 1917).

The temperature rose in August: during a meeting, one metalworker declared that it was not enough to sit by while the unions negotiated wages with the management and the ministry; the workers had to prepare for direct action. The prefect was worried: he feared the movement might spread to all metalworkers in the region unless wage negotiations were brought to a rapid and satisfactory conclusion, the director of the Tamaris works meanwhile proving to be most uncooperative.

In the end, the metalworkers declared a two-day strike — on 26 and 27 September 1917 — in Tamaris. However, some workers were not satisfied with such a rapid return to work and with the pusillanimity of the union (owing to fears that some of the large number of worker-reservists might be sent back to the front). The prefect was convinced that he had reason for continued anxiety.

Among miners, too, trade-union activity was stepped up in 1917, but no strike was called, thanks to negotiations between the unions and employers under the aegis of national representatives. Nevertheless, tension among miners, as among metalworkers, ran high in 1917, and a majority of miners in Gard passed a resolution endorsing the strike principle.

The year 1917 ended without major trouble in Gard. But it is worthy of note that the workers — even the reservists among them

4. R. Huard, 'Aspects du mouvement ouvrier gardois pendant la guerre de 1914–1918. Les grèves de 1917', *Annales du Midi*, 1968.

— had regained some of their peacetime militancy. The interminable war had become so much of a routine that people felt they were no longer obliged to ignore their class interests. For the time being, the political struggle still took second place to wage demands, but that situation might not last.

Haute-Vienne and Gard do not typify the whole of France. There were other departments in which political opposition was slower to emerge than in Haute-Vienne; there were other departments or towns where claims for higher wages were pressed more quickly than they were in Gard, and where, as we shall see, a much more explosive situation arose in 1917. But what we have tried to demonstrate by these two examples is the gradual change from blind acceptance of the *Union sacrée*, which anaesthetised political and social opposition, to a rejection of the *Union sacrée* resulting in much greater freedom of movement for everyone. For more than two years the defence of the country had taken precedence over everything else. The 'static war' brought the realisation that neither side was capable of winning an outright victory, and with it a quite spontaneous re-examination of attitudes to the conflict.

CHAPTER 14

The Strikes of the Spring of 1917

> In a town where five to six thousand women are
> employed in the military clothing industry, at a time when
> life is seeming more difficult by the day and wages are
> constantly under discussion, it is almost impossible to avoid
> conflicts between employers and employees. They have
> surfaced more than once at Vierzon, and although time and
> again a settlement has been reached quietly and amicably,
> the workers were at last persuaded that they could only
> obtain satisfaction by going on strike.[1]

Thus one reporter described industrial troubles at Vierzon in 1917.
May it then be taken that these troubles had no other causes? In an
attempt to reply to this question, we have again turned to two cases:
the strikes in the Paris region and the strikes in Toulouse.

The Strikes in the Paris Region in the Spring of 1917

Though there had been strikes before 1917, they had been neither
numerous nor very significant or widespread. In 1917, by contrast,
there were major stoppages, particularly in the Paris region. They
came in two waves — one in January, the other in the spring.[2]

The January strikes started in the clothing industry; the female
staff in two establishments — Agnès in rue Aubert and Bernard in
rue de l'Opéra — came out on 8 January. They were demanding
higher wages, and in the event a compromise was reached fairly
quickly.

1. AD Cher R 15 16, 'Histoire de Vierzon pendant la guerre'.
2. Cf. Christine Morel, *Le Mouvement socialiste et syndicaliste en 1917 dans la région parisienne*, DES, 1958.

At the same time, strikes also broke out in several factories doing war work: Panhard-Levassor, Vedorelli, Priestlez, Malicet and Blin. The longest strike was that at Panhard, which started in December and continued until 17 January. It could only be settled by the active intervention of the federal leaders of the CGT, of the leaders of the Metalworkers' Federation and of Albert Thomas, the socialist minister for armaments. A minimum wage scale was laid down for all munitions factories in the Seine department and in some regions of the department of Seine-et-Oise, and to make sure that there was no further trouble, a compulsory arbitration procedure was laid down: by the decree of 17 January a 'permanent conciliation and arbitration committee', on which workers and employers had equal representation, was set up in each department.

In a sense, compulsory arbitration meant challenging the workers' right to strike, and the leaders of the Socialist Party showed great reluctance in agreeing to this innovation (12 votes to 11 at the CAP). The leaders of the CGT, for their part, objected unanimously. However, in the munitions factories the workers themselves do not seem to have voiced any objections. In any event, strikes ceased in munitions factories in the Paris region.

However, other sectors in the Paris region were also in ferment, among them building workers, public officials and 'comparable public service employees' — by which was meant employees of the gas and electricity companies — as well as public transport workers.

All in all, Paris was fairly quiet during the first few months of 1917 but the fire was smouldering. Working-class discontent was acerbated by the rise in prices and the drop in purchasing power, which from the beginning of the war to the end of 1916 had fallen about 10.5 per cent. By now, even if wage rises momentarily satisfied the workers, these failed to keep pace with price increases, and as a result some members of the working class, and in particular women who had no previous experience of it, suddenly developed a taste for industrial action.

A veritable prices explosion took place in the spring of 1917, as shown by Table 10 and Fig. 4 on pages 207 and 194, taken from Christine Morel's work.

Quite apart from any other reason, this was enough to revive working-class militancy, the more so as the failure of the Chemin-des-Dames offensive had once again dispelled hopes that the war would soon be over.

May Day 1917 brought tensions to the surface. There had been no large demonstrations on May Day in 1915 or 1916; indeed, in 1915 the Préfecture had described the situation in Paris as follows:[3]

Table 10. *Price increases in 1917, compared to pre-war (%)*

Commodities	at 18 March	at end of May
Dried vegetables	110	200
Fresh vegetables	200	500
Coal	163	300
Rice	66	200
Fat	208	200
Soap	146	200
Wine	243	200
Meat	103	150
Sugar	125	125
Butter, eggs, cheese	136	100
Clothing	50	50

a very quiet day; a meeting of the union of *terrassiers* attended by 1,300 persons (including 900 wives of mobilised trade unionists and 400 'unemployed' — that is, men who had taken May Day off; a meeting of the stonemasons' union (about 200 persons); in the evening a 'private' meeting of the Seine Association of Trade Unions, with an attendance of about 2,000. There were also some 600 to 700 striking building workers.

May Day 1916 had also been fairly quiet: there had been a demonstration by 1,400 to 1,500 'unemployed' from the building trade. In the morning, Hubert, the secretary of the *terrassiers*, had addressed 1,200 people, but the stonemasons' union had only managed to attract 90 people, and the clothing workers' union just 100. A meeting in the evening called by the Inter-Union Committee of Metalworkers in the *bourse du travail* had been attended by just 120 people, who had, however, dispersed to cries of: 'Long live the Workers' International! Down with war!' Altogether, according to the Préfecture, the day had been 'very calm'.

Things were quite different in 1917. The building workers' unions called upon all workers to stay away from work on May Day, and their appeal was widely heeded: observers from the Préfecture had anticipated a crowd of 2,000 to 3,000 strikers in the clothing workers' building, and in the event there were 10,000.

The same observers had also anticipated an audience of 1,500 at a meeting called at the Maison des Syndicats by the Trade Union

3. ANF 7 13272.

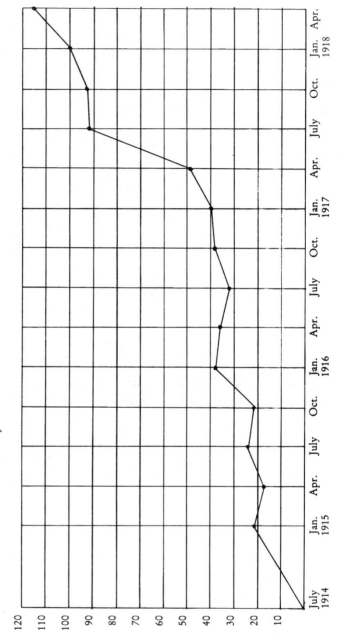

Fig. 5. *Price increases for thirteen food products in Paris, 1914–1918 (%).*
Based on a statistical survey in BOT 1917–18.

Defence Committee (the CDS), — that is to say by the minority anti-war group in the CGT. Again, many more attended. How many? The 'revolutionary' writer Henri Guilbeaux, although he was away in Switzerland at the time, and Maxe, a writer who specialised in denouncing the revolutionary danger, placed the figure at 10,000. It seems that both exaggerated. The Préfecture itself, after wavering at first, put the figure at what was still a very impressive 5,000. More important, however, than its precise number was the frame of mind the audience was in, especially at the end of the meeting. Here is an account taken from the Préfecture archives:

> As they left the hall, cries of: 'Long live peace! Down with war! Down with the Republic!' mingled with the chanting of the 'Internationale' and of 'Revolution', could be heard from all sides.
>
> In the passage that leads on to the rue Grange-aux-Belles, one-legged Méric, surrounded by members of the Trade Union Youth Movement and by Russians, invited passers-by to a demonstration on the place de la République and on the grand boulevards.
>
> At the end of the passage a crowd intoned revolutionary songs and moved towards the boulevard Magenta in great excitement. Once again there were cries of 'Down with war! Long live peace!' and even 'Long live Germany!'.

Outside No. 16 boulevard Magenta, the police intervened for the first time; there was a scuffle and the demonstrators were dispersed; but a great many managed to slip through the police cordon and reassembled in the place de la République under the statue and behind a pile of paving stones which they threatened to use against the police. The latter quickly gained the better of the demonstrators, who scattered in all directions.

> In general, these attempts to cause disorder and these anti-patriotic demonstrations have elicited a highly indignant reaction from the public. Foreigners, in particular, were taken to task by passers-by. Some were called Boches and even set upon.
>
> In the course of the demonstration, 10 arrests were made.[4]

Even though this demonstration was a fairly isolated incident, the mere fact that it took place at all was a significant new development. Moreover, it surprised the authorities, who had been told that the streets would remain 'as calm as they have ever been'.

The surprise of the authorities when their forecasts were proved

4. ANF 7 13272.

wrong was equalled by that of the organisers. The leaders of the Committee for the Resumption of International Relations (CRRI) — a group of anti-war socialists and trade unionists, minorities in their respective organisations — met in the evening of 3 May, and did not hide the fact that the meeting on 1 May and the demonstration that followed were considered unexpected successes, so many signs of a revival of syndicalist and revolutionary fervour. Members of the CRRI, among them Lariot and Louise Saumoneau, expressed the hope that their policies might prove victorious in the CGT and the Socialist Party in the near future.

May and June were, in fact, marked by a second wave of strikes in the Paris region, and these were much more fully supported than the earlier ones. The signal was once again given by the clothing workers: starting on 11 May in Maison Jenny on the Champs-Elysée, the movement had spread within about a week to the rest of the industry, involving 40 fashion houses and 10,000 strikers. The strikes were to continue until 23 May, and before they were over a strike would be declared by all unions incidentally related to the clothing industry — tailors, milliners, furriers, machinists, embroiderers, hatters, shoemakers.

Next, or at the same time, it was the turn of bank employees, assistant civil servants in some ministries, telegraph messengers and many other occupations of greater or smaller importance. These strikes started at the end of May and continued well into June.

Finally, at the end of May or the beginning of June, the wave of strikes spread to establishments making such defence equipment as helmets and gas masks, and to munitions factories proper, particularly in the aviation sector.

Altogether, 71 industries were affected and the number of strikers in the Paris region rose to 100,000. This figure may seem impressive. Several qualifications must, however, be recorded, not to minimise the movement, but to put it in perspective.

To begin with, the workers' demands were not political but strictly economic: cost-of-living allowances largely justified by the price rises and a five-and-a-half-day, or 'English', week. Everyone returned to work once these demands had been met wholly or even partly. This brings us to another important point: though the strikes continued through May and June, they were not the result of an orchestrated campaign to harass the employers or the authorities, but a spontaneous and uncoordinated reaction by workers in particular enterprises.

Nor is it without significance that 75 per cent of the strikers were women. As for the strikes in the munitions factories, they lasted no more than a few days at the most, and even then did not involve all the workers, since reservists, who made up a large part of the labour force, did not join in.

Still, the government did not ignore these social tremors, and Malvy, the minister of the interior, went out of his way to damp them down, not hesitating to exert very strong pressure on recalcitrant employers while keeping retaliatory measures against workers to a minimum. His intervention notwithstanding, there were some quite violent clashes between the police and, in particular, processions of *midinettes*.

As we have said, this wave of strikes was fuelled by economic, not revolutionary or anti-war motives. Wartime strikes may be said, in any case, to be little short of insurrection. Even so, high fashion in particular was not an indispensable adjunct of the war effort. Moreover, many of the women involved would have argued that they were fully justified in striking because the war did not prevent employers from making huge profits, even in factories concerned with national defence.

This does not alter the fact that many workers ignored the imperative that the least they could do while others were sacrificing their lives at the front was to work as hard as they could. In failing to do so, they demonstrated that other interests could prevail over the defence of their country, something that had not hitherto happened.

Even so, there was a wide gap between this new attitude and a revolutionary one. When Henri Guilbeaux declared that the strikes were the manifestation of the revolutionary spirit of an entire people tired of a war waged for imperialist motives, he mistook his own wishes for the reality. Again, when Maxe accused revolutionaries of fomenting the strikes, he was not basing his remarks on any real evidence. It goes without saying that a number of minority trade unionists tried to hitch economic dissatisfaction to the political wagon, that anti-war slogans were shouted, that pacifist tracts were distributed, but it was all very marginal, or with little influence. Thus when Hubert and Merrheim, the minority trade-union leaders, tried to enlist striking workers at a meeting at the *bourse du travail*, for an active peace campaign, the workers would hear nothing of it.

By and large we can therefore agree with Christine Morel: 'The strikes reflected the moral and physical fatigue of working men and working women; they did not reflect the birth of a revolutionary spirit.'

It should nevertheless be remembered that, if the circumstances are right, a revolutionary spirit can develop very rapidly indeed.

The Strikes in Toulouse in 1917

In his study of Toulouse during the war, Pierre Bouyoux[5] points out that the patriotism of the people of Toulouse was until 1917 beyond question, that all shared an 'absolute faith' in victory. But then, in 1917, the atmosphere changed dramatically, and there were widespread strikes. The history of this transformation cannot be reconstructed from newspapers, which were almost completely silenced by the censors, not so much for the sake of the public of Toulouse, which was obviously well informed, as for that of the rest of France. Fortunately, we have numerous reports from the prefect and police officers from which we can piece together what really happened.[6]

As Pierre Bouyoux remarks, 'the deterioration of the social atmosphere came as a surprise to the authorities, as it did to the trade-union leaders and militant socialists'. At the end of May 1917, the prefect had reported 'no evidence of ferment among the workers'. The trade unions had only just resumed their activities, and on a very small scale: it was not until 21 August 1916 that the departmental association of trade unions held its first meeting since the beginning of the war. On that occasion, as well as during subsequent meetings, the trade-union leaders had, moreover, been forced to admit that workers showed little interest in trade-union initiatives, especially of a political kind. There had been several alerts, some brief and partial strikes, and even some violent clashes: on 24 November 1916 in the cartridge works, on 17 January 1917 in the gunpowder factory, and on 14 April again in the cartridge works. These early strikes were spontaneous and did not enjoy the support of the union leadership: the leaders approved of the wage claims, but condemned the use of the strike weapon at a time when the country needed all the arms and ammunition it could produce. For the rest, the workers should bide their time and help build strong unions against the day when the social struggle could be resumed.

The unions, and the authorities who kept them under surveillance, had failed to spot the new mood. The workers may not have been very interested in traditional trade-union activities, but that

5. Pierre Bouyoux, L'Opinion publique à Toulouse pendant la première guerre mondiale, Toulouse, 1970.
6. AD Haute-Garonne 15 Z 520.

had not stopped them from growing increasingly restless. The price rises served as a catalyst: in May 1917, in Toulouse, prices of staple foods — bread, butter, eggs, meat and potatoes — had risen by between 50 and 300 per cent, while wages hardly changed, though there were considerable differences from one factory to the next. The best-paid workers were those employed in the cartridge factory.

This sharpening of social conflicts came before the failure of Nivelle's offensive, and certainly before the full scope of that disaster became known. Nevertheless, once the repercussions became clear, the effect of the news combined with resentment of the high cost of living. By May, pessimism was so widespread in Toulouse that defeatist views could be, and often were, voiced in public without eliciting the least protest. The prefect was aware of the situation and observed that these symptoms 'undoubtedly reflect a transitory decline of morale'.

All the same, May was a quiet month on the whole. The probable explanation is that, social tensions having led to greater interest in trade-union activity with a wave of new union recruits, Omer Bedel, the local secretary of the union of state employees (which included all workers in the arsenals), made a determined effort to ensure that resentment did not spill over into strikes. By the end of May, however, he felt that he might no longer be able to hold the workers back: 'General discontent, workers have had enough, demand for wage rises, stoppage of work probable, to avoid this intend going to Paris to see minister', he wired the national secretary of the union of state employees.

In the event, it was neither in the gunpowder works nor in the cartridge factory that the strike began. Unrest had spread to railway workers, shop assistants and to workers in the shoe industry. On Saturday, 1 June 1917, despite the opposition of their shop steward, women workers in the central clothing store voted to go on strike. They did not have time to implement this decision: on Monday, the store manager granted them an increase of 1 franc a day, backdated to 1 April. The same pattern was repeated during the next few days in the shoe industry, the Galeries Parisiennes and other department stores.

The authorities, in the person of the prefect, had made every effort to ensure that the employers showed a conciliatory attitude. Matters were different at the gunpowder and the cartridge works, where the wage rate was fixed by the government, so that negotiations had to be conducted through Paris. Tensions rose during this delay, and the women, in particular, grew more and more 'agitated', so much so that the prefect began to wonder whether they were not being incited by the men, many of whom were reservists, and as such had to hold back from taking an active role. As for the trade-union leaders who kept preaching moderation, it became more and more difficult for them to make themselves heard – they were booed at the almost daily meetings, while others who urged direct action were cheered.

In the face of growing unrest, emphasised in telegrams to Paris from the prefect and the regional commander, the government decided to call a joint commission meeting for 12 June. It was too late. That same evening, against the advice of his shop steward, an electrical worker successfully appealed for a strike.

How can we explain this haste even while serious negotiations were under way? For the prefect there were two answers: the first was that the workers lacked confidence in the government's promises; the second, that striking was 'a deliberate attempt to hasten the end of the war by any means'. Pierre Bouyoux, for his part, does not accept that the available information in any way corroborates the prefect's second conclusion; in the prevailing climate, however, it was only natural that the workers should have felt they could help the promised negotiations with a strike.

Whatever the truth of the matter, on 13 June 1917, 5,000 female workers in the gunpowder factory downed tools, the more determined having pulled the less resolute along with them. In the cartridge works, too, women workers began to come out on strike, but returned to work the next day, whereas the strike in the powder factory continued for a week. According to Pierre Boyoux:

> Toulouse witnessed three days of agitation and disorder. Processions, led by workers carrying red banners and singing the 'Internationale', moved through the streets in the direction of the railway stations of Saint-Agne and particularly of Matabiau, to protest against the departure of the trains carrying workers to the factories. On the 13th, there were violent clashes at 9.00 in the evening between 'a large and over-excited crowd' and the forces of law and order made up of gendarmes reinforced by 250 mounted artillerymen. The Matabiau railway station was finally cleared and numerous arrests were made (only those of three Spaniards and two Italians were publicised). During the night, the prefect decided to call in 80 gendarmes from neighbouring departments and 650 soldiers from Agen and Montauban. By the 14th, 1,500 men were guarding the munitions factories and the railway stations, especially Matabiau: all roads and bridges were closed to traffic — even to the trams — and the demonstrators were confined to the allée Lafayette and above all to the rue Bayard.

All this time negotiations were continuing in Paris, and during the night of 14/15 June, Bedel, the trade-union delegate, wired the prefect that an agreement had been reached and he was issuing orders for a return to work. However, a minority of the women workers at the gunpowder factory, supported by reservists, refused to comply. On the evening of 15 June, 2,000 people attended the biggest meeting of all. After heated discussion, and under pressure from reservists, the meeting decided to await the return of the trade-union delegation from Paris before resuming work. Another street demonstration then led to fresh clashes with the police.

On Sunday 17 June Bedel returned. He told a meeting that the government had made substantial concessions: wages in the gunpowder factory were to be brought in line with those paid to the cartridge factory workers, whose wages were then to be increased in turn: an increase of 50 per cent for the first group and of 30 per cent for the second.

On Monday 18 June the return to work was complete. The prefect, however, was not reassured. Convinced that it was no more than a lull, he asked for further police and army reinforcements.

More protests took place in Toulouse before the end of June 1917, affecting masons, bakery workers, railwaymen and munitions workers, but all were granted wage rises of 30 per cent without having recourse to strike action.

There were no further important protest movements in Toulouse until the end of the war, except for minor strikes in the shoe industry in October 1917 and in the central clothing store in January 1918. This is all the more surprising in that the substantial wage increases were rapidly whittled away by the continued price rises.

The course of the strike movement in Toulouse in the spring of 1917 suggests that conflict would probably have been avoided had wage claims been met earlier. Does this mean that the protest movement was based entirely on industrial claims? The strikers certainly deployed the trappings of revolutionary folklore — the 'Internationale', and red flags — but there was no reference to the Russian Revolution (which was admittedly still in its first phase), or to the projected socialist conference in Stockholm. However, as soon as they were told that their wage claims had been met, the workers, and above all the women workers who made up the bulk of the strikers, returned to work. The 'activists' may have been able to organise spectacular demonstrations, but they were clearly in a minority. Twenty thousand people were employed at the gunpowder works alone, yet the largest strike meeting was attended by a mere 2,000; street demonstrations were attended by, at most, 1,000 people, though there were scores of thousands of men and women workers in Toulouse.

However, the strike movement was initiated by the workers themselves and not by their trade-union leaders, who in most cases contented themselves with following or joining — when they were able to — the bandwagon. Bedel, for instance, a man who had been, before the war, a supporter of the syndicalist-revolutionary current, did his utmost to moderate the movement. Moreover, the strikes broke out in factories that had expanded considerably since the outbreak of war (from 200 to 20,000 women in the gunpowder factory), and hence employed a particularly heterogeneous work force. Those trade-union leaders who did not want to hamper the national defence effort were extremely irritated by the non-trade-union background of these new people, and their ungovernable impulses.

It would seem, too — even though it is very difficult to prove — that public opinion in Toulouse disapproved of strikes led by 'crazy women in the powder factory', as a veteran of the Franco-Prussian War put it! The socialists were deeply divided. Marcel Libert, one of the later founders of the Communist Party of Toulouse, supported the movement; others had grave reservations, not least the mayor, Jean Rieux, who told the town council on 14 June: 'Like the secretary of their union, we fervently wish to see the strikers return to the gunpowder factory tomorrow. . . . It is not material and moral concerns alone that demand the maintenance of order by the strikers, it is also, and above all, the national interest, their patriotic duty'.

There are several signs that other classes in Toulouse considered these strikes in factories working for the war effort to be clear evidence of a lack of patriotism, some going so far as to blame the entire working class.

The impression left in the end by the strikes in Toulouse in 1917 is very similar to that of those in Paris. Although the prefect thought otherwise for a while, Pierre Bouyoux contends that the strike movement was *in no way* inspired by revolutionary defeatism. It would nevertheless be rash to deny it a 'pacifist' dimension, a sign of war weariness. As in Paris, the strikers' objectives were not revolutionary, but it was significant that in the midst of war they did not hesitate to lay down their tools and clamour for an increase in wages. From that action to revolution is a long step, and one that needs the support of the rest of the population. In Toulouse, the workers seem to have been isolated from the rest of society. Did similar conditions prevail in the whole of France during the spring of 1917?

CHAPTER 15

The Crisis of Morale (Spring 1917)

The crisis that shook a section of the French army in the spring of 1917, from 20 May to 10 June precisely, is well documented. It has been studied in depth by Guy Pedroncini,[1] and summed up as follows by Pierre Renouvin:

> Two hundred and fifty cases of collective insubordination among combat troops, although never while in the line of fire; these acts of insubordination affected, on various dates, units in half the infantry divisions, the total of those affected probably reaching 40,000, although each act involved small groups of men only, often less than a hundred. In only one case did the movement reflect political ends: mutineers in one infantry division called for a march on Paris. A study of this crisis has revealed that its main cause was the failure of the major offensive of 16 April; the infantrymen had no wish to be called on to resume offensive operations that had been so badly handled by the high command, although they did declare that they were ready to resist any German attack. When the crisis was over, the morale of the army recovered quickly.[2]

The state of public opinion at the time is less well known. Yet there is no lack of documentation.

While it was still anticipated that the war would end soon, the morale of civilians and troops together had given little cause for concern, yet as it became clear that the war was becoming prolonged, this factor could no longer be safely ignored. In particular, the general staff came to realise more and more that civilian morale had inevitable repercussions on that of the army, and hence began increasingly to take notice of it. To assess the situation, they relied

1. Guy Pedroncini, *Les Mutineries de l'armée française*, 1968.
2. *La France et l'Italie pendant la première guerre mondiale*, Grenoble, 1973.

heavily on the postal censorship boards which had been set up in a number of towns for the express purpose of reading and analysing the mail that passed through their hands. For our example, we have chosen the Bordeaux military postal censorship board, which took a series of samples before it felt justified in preparing its monthly report. The first such report to give any real insight is dated March 1917, and provides a general overview of public opinion based on extracts from such letters as seemed typical to the inspectors.[3]

The report for March 1917 reflects a wave of general optimism: there was only one pessimistic letter for every ten expressing optimism, although that optimism was often tempered with numerous complaints against politicians ('the deputies are becoming more and more disliked as a whole by the nation'); with complaints from the soldiers about their food, their quarters, the cold, exploitation by war profiteers — all reflected in a lack of confidence when they came home on leave; and with general complaints about price rises, requisitioning and the taxes levied on peasants.

A not inconsiderable number of correspondents anticipated terrible calamities, famine or revolution, and the overall view that emerges is of 'a longing for an immediate peace'. Though some hoped for a 'victorious result', the great majority (of those who referred to the question 'wants peace and nothing but peace, with no argument about conditions'. 'Everybody wants peace,' the report concluded, 'and would greet it rapturously.' The optimism of March 1917 was therefore more in the nature of a façade, and patently vulnerable.

The reports of the postal censorship board over the next few months concentrated on three themes: the public attitude to the economic situation, to the strikes and to the signing of a peace.

Of the letters read by the board from 15 May to 12 June (147,996), from 12 June to 12 July (166,247), and subsequently, most were concerned with the economic situation. 'Few letters,' the May report stated, 'end without some complaint about transport difficulties, the high cost of living or the scarcity of coal and food supplies.'

These problems were often contrasted with the 'colossal' fortunes being made by army suppliers and food retailers. Complaints about the immediate situation were combined with fears for the winter: 'Everybody is thinking about the hard winter we are going to go through, and everything is getting very expensive. The bread is no longer edible. . . . Everybody has an upset stomach. . . . What a

3. Archives Militaires 7 N 985.

miserable winter it's going to be,' wrote a Parisian to a friend in Biarritz.

Some writers professed annoyance with the chorus of complaints, which they felt were unjustified in comparison to the sufferings of the soldiers and prisoners of war. But these 'sober-minded' people were few and far between. Indeed, the real hardships suffered by many were a cause for depression: 'Morale is no longer the same', wrote another Parisian. Economic difficulties exacerbated the differences between social groups:

> In the Midi [another correspondent alleges], the peasants I have seen have a really spineless attitude. Of course, they are against the war, but except for those who have been bereaved they have hardly suffered at all. These gallant tillers-of-the-soil reserve all their energies for protesting about the cost of living, and see nothing wrong in getting the most fantastic prices for their produce, which, when added to the rise in the separation allowances, lets them be as patient as you please.

The shortages had the curious effect of discrediting the press: many correspondents poured scorn on those journalists who, having joked so long about German shortages, now drew on their imagination to minimise those afflicting the French.

The most important consequence was that many people (more and more of them, we are told) began to feel — some in hope but the majority with trepidation — that the food shortages rather than the prolongation of the war might lead to a revolution.

The second important topic mentioned by very many correspondents, that of the strikes, did not in these circumstances reassure the censorship board.

The first brief reference to the subject is made in their report on the letters read between 15 May and 15 June 1917: 'Parisians are preoccupied with the strikes'. The correspondents' views about the cause, however, were confused, since at one and the same time they would mention both the hand of Germany and the justness of the strikers' cause. Thus one Parisian wrote: 'These troubles are justified, because while the people have to work themselves to death to scrape a living, the bosses and the big industrialists are growing fat in record time: it really is quite intolerable. And all we can do is grin and bear it'.

During the next month, however, the letters became increasingly uneasy: people were beginning to feel that revolution was in the air. A few extracts may convey some idea of the atmosphere (report on letters written from 15 June to 15 July):

Life is hard in Paris. And are all the strikes really over? The papers say so, but I don't believe them [letter from Bayonne to Paris].

There have been disturbances in my district, and for a time I was afraid the situation was getting worse. One morning a group of strikers marched into the factory yard shouting 'Up the strike!' and forced the factory to shut down. For work to start up again, they had to agree to the English week and twenty sous a day to cover the rise in the cost of living, and even then our workers, men and women, had to follow those from Maison Souchard about all afternoon in support of their claims. And they say that all these troubles are caused by those Boche who have been allowed to stay on in Paris. In fact, most of the go-betweens are Spaniards, who are pouring into Paris just now. Then there are the Greeks and the Turks. It all doesn't help matters much, and we must unfortunately face the fact that there won't be an end to it this year.

Mother has been upset by the strikes and by the soldiers shouting outside her house: 'Down with the war, long live the revolution.' All we can hope is that everyone will pull themselves together soon. It can only be the Boche behind all the latest tricks of persuading simple minds to join these wicked demonstrations.

Rumour has it that the strikers wanted to blow up the Renault munitions factory last night. We are living on a volcano and everyone is complaining. The example of the Russians bodes no good.

I shall not conceal from you that I am frightened, because I can see that the next winter will be a very hard one, perhaps even worse than the last. Add to the lack of coal the lack of food and that'll be all we need. I am afraid there will be unrest in Paris. The city is already in a state of agitation as it is, thanks to all the strikes, quite justified, I might add, since everything has gone up except wages. It worries me all the same when I hear all these people brawling. I just wish I didn't have to be in Paris during the cold weather.

The strikes are over, as far as our trade is concerned; I never told you how worried I was by the revolutionary movement we had here with the strikers marching into the shops, getting the staff to join them and then smashing the equipment. If the government does not stand firm, we shall witness some unfortunate scenes this winter.

Everybody is complaining, in Paris and elsewhere. People are on strike over the price rises and over the lack of fuel, and this winter the poor will have nothing to use for heating. Can't you just hear the rising strains of revolution! This winter, when the destitute are dying of cold or starving to death in their garrets because of the lack of foresight on the part of our ruling classes who do nothing to avert the danger, the mob will take to the streets, and will burn our furniture to keep warm, which will only be fair. But don't think for a moment that the deputies in parliament are likely to sacrifice their salaries to come to the aid of the poor.

Life in Paris is terrible; people are afraid of a workers' uprising. There has been quite a lot of noise in the streets recently, and I promise you that if it weren't for my son I should have left by now, because people think there will be trouble. We simply have to put an end to this war – the women with children are getting desperate, what with their husbands away at the front for three years. And food is far too expensive.

I am not working right now. The revolution is about to start, and everybody is on strike. You'll have read about it in the papers, but you really ought to see it for yourself. If only it will help bring the war to an end!. . . .

Life had become impossible, everything is indescribably nasty, including the bread, though right now we still have vegetables. What will happen in the winter? There is certainly going to be a revolution in Paris. Should your business shut down this winter, I urge you to close everything up and to come here to the country. It would be no fun finding oneself in the middle of a rioting mob, particularly since the revolution will be brought on by famine, and they are sure to loot your business.

The strikes are quite upsetting. Hordes of these bareheaded women with their hooligan brats are spreading revolution. We are heading straight for a patched-up peace, or worse. It's all very depressing.

The *nouveaux riches* were singled out for bitter attack:

The prices in Paris are all prohibitive. The rich are growing richer at the expense of those with small means and it is a shame and a disgrace to see these *nouveaux riches* flaunting their idle wealth in front of those poor devils. Some may envy them, but as far as I am concerned, I despise them, though I don't know where we'll finish up, what with all the grumbling and the complaints you keep hearing. Lots of things here have gone badly wrong, which must give comfort to the Boche. I just hope a stop will be put to this scandal.

A note of optimism had not, however, completely vanished:

I have been in Paris for a week and have seen some violent demonstrations. There is no doubt that prices are all high, but there are no real shortages yet and if we have enough strength to hold out another few months we shall be saved. It's a pity that some people refuse to make what sacrifices are demanded in the interests of us all.

The section concerning strikes and their effect on public opinion was dropped from the postal censorship board's report for the next month (15 July to 15 August). The wave of strikes of the spring had not entirely subsided; however, the Deuxième Bureau (the intelligence branch) of the army general staff, which prepared a daily bulletin of the latest events,[4] mentioned strikes in all parts of France. On 19 July, there was a strike of corn chandlers at Vire; on 21 July, 2,500 women at the national gunpowder factory in Port-de-Buis struck for two days; on 22 July, 500 women were reported on strike in the Audierne canning works; on the 23rd, 800 male and female textile workers were out in Vosges; on the 24th there was a strike in the gunpowder factory at Châteaulin in Finistère, and in the metal and naval construction works in Saint-Nazaire, and so on. How was it that public opinion had ceased being disturbed by these incidents? It is possible to think of at least two reasons: first of all, the strike wave had moved away from Paris, and Paris was in the public eye; and secondly, though some of these strikes might have involved a large number of workers, they were very brief and very scattered, so much so that, given the existing censorship, it was almost impossible for anyone other than the intelligence services to appreciate their extent.

The third subject to engage the attention of the Bordeaux postal inspectors in the spring of 1917, and to which they paid special attention, was that of peace. The conclusion for May is clear. 'The question of when the war will end intrigues the public, and there is near unanimity that it cannot be far away, that it will come before the winter of 1917. People are not very particular about the terms. Great weariness is reflected in almost all their letters. That is our main impression.'

In June, things were worse:

> The failure of the Champagne offensive has had a very depressing effect on soldiers at the front as well as on people in the rear. The morale of the troops is lower than we have found it to be for a long time. . . . The morale of the civilians is not much higher than that of the troops. Everybody has had enough. . . .

However, opinions were divided on exactly how the war would end. Some thought that it would come to a halt as a result of German exhaustion; others spoke of general exhaustion.

In July, the postal inspectors felt that the tone of the letters had become alarming: 'The prevailing mood is of dejection, a sort of weariness', and they quoted such extracts as: 'Anything is better

4. AM 16 N 1536 GQG. 2^e bureau.

than a war like this, and we are still nowhere near the end. . . . We shall doubtless get the better of them, but at what price? And think of the superhuman courage our soldiers have needed to keep holding out for such a long time'.

Attitudes to peace seemed important enough to the inspectors for embodiment in statistical tables. A combined graph (see Fig. 6) shows the development of the attitudes of four groups of correspondents from June to September 1917: one group expressing the wish for peace but without defining under what terms; a second group insisting on a victorious peace only; a third group contenting itself with a compromise peace; and a fourth group that could be called 'defeatist' because it would settle for peace at any price.

The graph cannot be, in fact, truly representative of public opinion since, although the inspectors who drew it did not specify the precise method they used, it seems clear that they relied exclusively on the relatively small number of letters in which the subject of peace was brought up. In August, we see that only 2,117 out of a total of 92,482 letters, or 2.28 per cent, mentioned the subject. A great many writers, of course, fought shy of political comment for obvious reasons, and their silence cannot be interpreted as lack of interest or opinion. The graph also ignored the fact that the total number of letters varied from month to month, so that the number of letters in each of the four groups must have varied as well.

It therefore seemed that a more reliable picture would emerge if the data were converted into percentages (Table 11).

Several points are raised by these figures:

(1) The advocates of peace at any price, who might have been called defeatists in as much as they considered the defeat of France to be a lesser evil than the continuation of the war, were in a small minority, and one, moreover, that continued to decline from June to September.

(2) The advocates of a compromise peace, one without victors or vanquished, though clearly more numerous, were also in a minority. Their number, highest after the failure of the April offensive, decreased during the summer, to rise again very markedly as winter approached.

If we add the advocates of peace at any price to the advocates of a compromise peace, in other words all those whose political views differed from official policy, we are still left with a minority, but one that approached 20 per cent in June and again in September, a far from negligible figure.

(3) The advocates of peace through victory were very numerous, but their number fluctuated: they accounted for more than a third

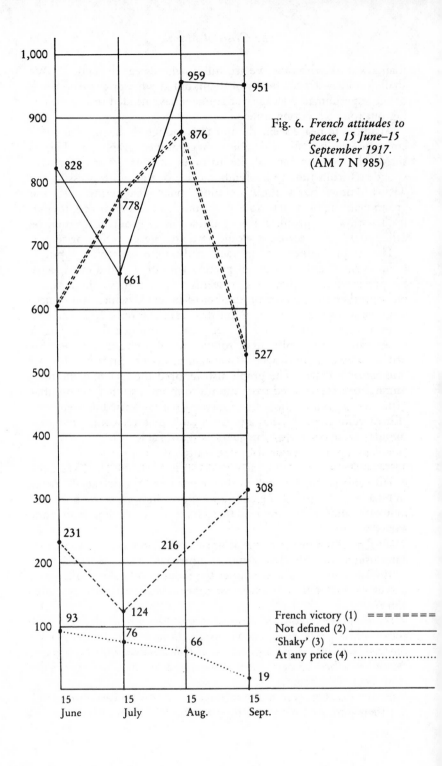

Fig. 6. *French attitudes to peace, 15 June–15 September 1917.* (AM 7 N 985)

French victory (1) ========
Not defined (2) ————
'Shaky' (3) -----------------
At any price (4) ....

Table 11. *French attitudes to peace, June–September 1917, revealed through postal inspection at Bordeaux (%). The number of letters cited are those that mentioned peace*

	June (1,758)	July (1,635)	August (2,117)	Sept. (1,805)
Desire for peace on undefined terms	47.09	40.42	45.29	52.68
Peace through victory	34.47	47.58	41.37	29.19
Peace through compromise	13.13	7.58	10.20	17.06
Peace at any price	5.29	4.40	3.11	1.05

of the letters in June, for nearly half in July, but in August the proportion began to drop and by September it had declined to less than 30 per cent.

(4) Finally, in June and August the proportion of writers evincing a desire for peace without specifying how it was to be attained was close to 50 per cent, and even higher in September. By and large, therefore, the number of advocates of peace on undefined terms increased as the number of advocates of a victorious peace decreased and that of advocates of a compromise peace increased. Would it then be wrong to suppose that a large number of those who called for an undefined peace really hoped for what the postal inspectors called a 'shaky' peace?

All we can say with some certainty is that in June, and again in September 1917, with a slight drop in August, most of the letters calling for peace that were read by the Bordeaux censorship board rejected one solution only, the defeat of France. Was that also the majority opinion in the rest of the country? Though there is no hard evidence, this can nevertheless be put it forward as a probable hypothesis.

The documents compiled by the various postal censorship boards show clearly that, at the end of the spring of 1917, a majority of Frenchmen and women, hard hit by price increases, perturbed by the waves of strikes, had come to long for the end of the war, if necessary without a victory. There had been a profound change in what had been, until then, a massively patriotic and confident attitude. Was this an indication that the French might refuse to continue the war? They they might slide from confidence to a mood of surrender? The civil and military authorities recognised that in order to begin to cope with the situation an assessment in depth of public opinion was necessary.

On 10 June 1917 the minister of the interior sent a telegram to all prefects asking them to report on morale and social unrest in their departments, and to specify what police and army reinforcements might be needed to maintain order. The replies, some of them very long, from eighty-three prefects, that is from nearly all of them,[5] provide a remarkable picture of France at the end of June 1917, and enabled the army to produce cartographic representations of French morale. Map 1 (p. 228) shows morale in France as a whole; Map 2 (p. 229), morale in the countryside; and Map 3 (p. 230), morale in the towns. The various departments were put into one of four categories, according to whether their morale was good, fairly good, indifferent or poor.[6]

There were only three departments in which morale was thought to be good throughout, in rural as well as in urban areas, namely Pas-de-Calais, Eure-et-Loire and Sarthe.

In Sarthe, as the prefect explained, 'morale is good throughout'. In his predominantly agricultural department, the efforts of all, he underlined, had ensured that agricultural activity and animal husbandry were kept at a satisfactory level and that, 'despite anxieties and bereavements, morale has been maintained'. As for the industrial sector, there were 'no signs of trouble or even of any restiveness'. The most important factories, the Chappée works employing nearly 2,000 workers, were immune to 'all forms of incitement', thanks to the social and economic inducements they offered. The employers of the other concerns — the Bollée, Carel, Loiseau and Maury factories — had agreed to wage increases and cost-of-living allowances, and there had been no difficulties. Moreover, as the prefect noticed, nearly all these factories worked on national defence contracts and were under the control of the military. Conclusion: 'The workers in Le Mans [75,000 inhabitants] have so far remained perfectly calm'. Though relatively small, the police force was adequate except, of course, in the event of social unrest.

Thirty departments — thirty-four if the countryside alone is taken into account, and thirty-one if towns alone are considered — received no better than 'fairly good' marks for morale.

According to the prefect of Cher, in the main towns of his department, 'the ruling classes, the big industrialists, professional

5. AM 16 N 1538 (1), GQG–EM–2ᵉ bureau, *service spécial 'Moral'*.
6. Departments annexed or occupied by the Germans — Bas-Rhin, Haut-Rhin, Moselle, Ardennes and Nord — could not, of course, be consulted.

people of all kinds, have, despite grievous losses, preserved their *sang-froid*. They want peace, but only as the outcome of total victory. . . . The attitude of the tradespeople is no less reassuring, although for less lofty reasons'. The explanation, apart from patriotism, was that 'business has never been so good'. Nevertheless, they quickly became dejected at bad news. Moreover, in the smaller towns which, unlike Bourges, had not had a vast influx of new people with an accompanying boost to business, 'local tradesmen are less staunch in the face of crises but have not given up. They still expect that our arms will triumph in the end, but consider the end a little too long in coming'.

The lower-middle classes and the skilled craftsmen, by contrast, felt ill at ease: *rentiers* whose income had decreased, small property owners whose rents were not being paid, the small shopkeeper who had to pay higher wages, were all hard hit by the war, and many of them wished that it would come to a speedy end, no matter what the price. Despite everything, however, they never aired their views in public. On the whole, the prefect added, 'the situation in the urban areas strikes me as being as satisfactory as it can be given the present circumstances of this country'.

He was, by contrast, less optimistic about the situation in the rural sector of his department. 'One cannot ignore the fact that morale has fallen considerably in the countryside, where the original fortitude and resolution are no longer evident.'

He attributed this decline mainly to the shortage of manpower. The call-up of the classes of 1917 and 1918, and of numerous classes previously exempt, had produced a serious and continuing crisis from November 1916. The agricultural community, unable to complete the sowing of winter crops, became deeply despondent. The proportion of unworked fields had increased from 15 per cent to 35 per cent between 1915 and 1916, and farm incomes had fallen considerably. A contributory factor was the demoralising influence of soldiers on leave as well as the antagonism caused by the presence of factory workers who were said to be 'shirkers'. However, the prefect believed that if the manpower problem could be solved through the return of the older classes, morale would quickly rise again.

Nor did the factories in Bourges give cause for great concern in June 1917, despite the massive influx of workers. The defence establishments (the foundry, explosives factory and arsenal) which had previously employed 9,000 workers now employed close on 30,000. The trade-union leadership was staunchly loyal: having embraced the *Union sacrée* without reservation, they encouraged

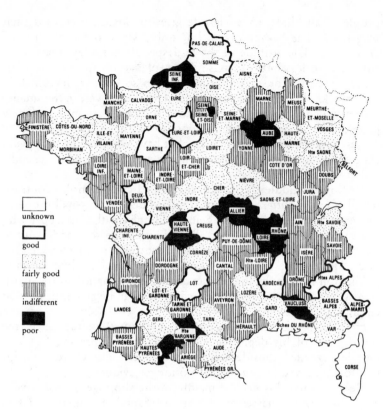

Map 1. French morale at the end of June 1917

their members to do the 'hard work the present circumstances demand'. However, the new workers included a number of 'particularly excitable elements', people who had 'not put their old doctrines behind them', and especially Van Gysel (from the department of Nord), Michel, Gaspiaud, Delhomme (mechanics from the department of Seine), Dalstein, Daguerre (electricians from the department of Seine), all of them 'Kienthal men' and all of them determined to oust Lucain, the general secretary of the trade union who represented the majority view. Their attacks had forced Lucain 'to adopt a more militant posture towards the military administration'. The prefect believed, however, that while continued vigilance was needed, there was no reason for taking drastic steps. The majority in the CGT was holding, the anti-war minority influenced a very small number of people only, most of them reservists who 'fear nothing so much as the possibility of being sent back to the

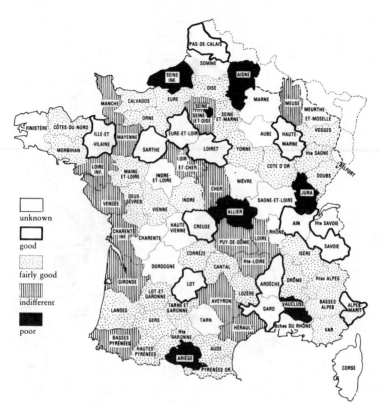

Map 2. Morale in the countryside at the end of June 1917

depots, and who therefore refrain from all actions or demonstrations that might bring this measure down on them'.

The prefect's confidence was not feigned, since although he had requested police reinforcements, these would merely serve to quell the growing crime wave following the sudden transformation of Bourges from a town with less than 50,000 inhabitants to one of 120,000. His present force consisted of twelve tired and elderly policemen, and the recruiting of auxiliaries was out of the question since the pay was so poor that factory work was preferred.

In twenty-nine departments, morale was considered to be 'indifferent'. A case in point was Gironde.

The prefect felt that the decline in morale after the 'relative' failure of the last offensive, the current low spirits, the weariness, the fact that the Socialist Party would wage an anti-war campaign without causing public indignation, and that soldiers on leave made

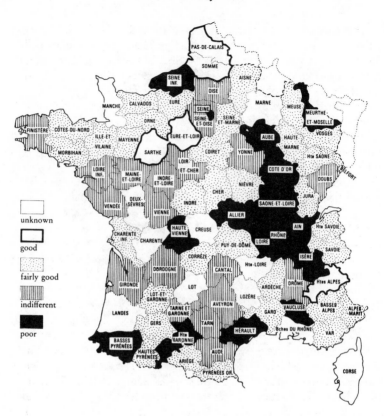

unknown

good

fairly good

indifferent

poor

Map 3. Morale in the towns at the end of June 1917

'scandalous' scenes which 'their superiors do not dare to or cannot prevent' – all needed to be explained in depth. At first, everyone had done his best for the war effort; then people had settled down to the war, the peasant farmers, shopkeepers and industrialists, although not the small *rentiers* and minor officials, benefiting considerably from the economic recovery. But everything had changed when the price rises, supply difficulties, and lower profits struck at all social classes in one way or another.

The prefect of Gironde did not believe that agitation had yet reached a dangerous level, but the signs were bad.

They could easily assume a revolutionary character. The word *revolution* is on everyone's lips, people of all classes speak of it as inevitable. The opposition parties are on the look-out, ready to take advantage should the case arise. The public mood is nervy, as if in a state of hyperaesthesia. It is hurt at the slightest touch, the smallest shock sets it quivering.

The prefect's views on maintaining law and order are revealing. In principle, there was no cause for alarm because he could call on 5,000 men of the class of 1918 encamped at Souges. But in practice he believed that 'if there were major street disturbances [these soldiers] would probably not obey orders'.

In eight departments (Allier, Aube, Haute-Garonne, Loire, Rhône, Seine-Inférieure, Vaucluse, Haute-Vienne), morale was considered 'poor', and that number rose to fifteen if towns alone were taken into consideration. By contrast, there were only six departments in which morale was poor in rural areas alone. In a total of fourteen departments, there had therefore been an appreciable, general or partial decline in morale.

By adding the departments in which morale was said to be 'indifferent' to those where it was judged to be 'poor', we arrive at the striking total of forty-four departments, or more than half.

These departments form an uninterrupted band of dissatisfaction running from Champagne to the Mediterranean on either side of the Rhône, the morale of the urban sector being particularly bad in a zone extending from Aube to Isère and from Allier to Ain. Socialists had been in strong positions in a fair number of these departments before the war, but the correlation was far from precise.

How did the prefects explain this state of affairs? According to the prefect of Allier, 'social problems' provided 'the leaven for the current fermentation'. Discontent was being stoked up and exploited by the 'proponents of the theory which the Russian Revolution has brought into vogue in this country, namely "land to the peasants"'.

In his view, the despondency of the rural population combined with the very intense agitation in such towns as Montluçon and particularly Commentry had created a situation whose gravity he did not wish to exaggerate but which needed to be watched with care.

The prefect of Ain did not fear popular subversion in his department as a whole, because the morale of the countryside had not been seriously affected. But conditions in Oyonnax were disturbing. The weariness and sullenness of the working class were plain to see. Clearly the effects had been limited so far, because there was no unemployment, wages were high and the 'main trade-union and political agitators' had been 'redirected' elsewhere by the last special reform commission (meaning they had been called up), but no one could be certain what the future held in store.

The prefect of Isère produced a lengthy analysis of the situation in his department:

Grenoble, 17 June 1917

The Prefect of the Department of
Isère to the Minister of the Interior
Office of the Sûreté Générale

I have the honour to reply herewith to the questions contained in your confidential telegram circulated on *10 June inst.*:

The inquiry I have myself conducted, or with the help of colleagues, to test the opinion of certain leading personages has shown that the morale of the people of Isère is far from satisfactory and that their exemplary spirit has suffered a general decline during the past two months. Today there is weariness bordering on dejection, a result less of the curtailment of the public diet and supply difficulties than of the disappointment caused by the failure of our armies in April, the feeling that military blunders have been made, that heavy losses have been sustained without any appreciable gains, that all further offensives will be both bloody and in vain. The inactivity of Russia, whose contribution now seems highly doubtful, has accentuated the decline in morale. The remarks of soldiers coming back from the front are the major cause of this decline: these remarks, made in the trains, in the railway stations, in the cafés on the way home, and then in the villages, convey a deplorable picture of the mentality of a great number of servicemen. Each one tells of and amplifies this or that unpleasant incident, this or that error committed by his commander, this or that useless battle, this or that act of insubordination presented as so many acts of courage and determination. These remarks, listened to with a ready ear by those who are already nervous or depressed enough as it is, are then peddled about and exaggerated with the result that discontent and anxiety are increased further. Each day, incidents in public places, particularly in the large railway stations and on the trains, reflect the most deplorable attitude in the minds of servicemen.

In the countryside, the restive mood is less obvious than it is in the towns; the peasants work, but they do not hide the fact that 'it's been going on too long'; they are tired of their continuous over-exertion in the fields, of the lack of hands and of the very heavy burden of the requisitions. They are growing more and more suspicious and indifferent to the idea of collective effort and mutual solidarity, and to patriotic appeals, and can think only of their immediate interests and their own safety.

Growers increasingly complain about price rises, even though they probably suffer less than others from the cost of living and even though their produce is sold at ever higher prices.

Nevertheless, it is among the rural population that one finds the greatest composure and resignation.

In the towns, and particularly in the industrial centres, the more impressionable and hence more excitable population — the workers, the ordinary people — are upset about the duration of the struggle, impatient with the increasing cost of living, irritated by the considerable profits being made out of the war by the big industrialists in their neighbourhood, and increasingly taken in by the propagandists of the united Socialist Party and their internationalist ideas. Under the influence of the Russian Revolution they already dream of workers' and soldiers' committees and of social revolution. These sentiments are aired frequently at workers' meetings, called ostensibly to discuss economic or union matters, and in their paper, *Le Droit du Peuple*, which is waging a very skilful anti-war and internationalist campaign.

This attitude, together with the constant rise in the cost of living, has fuelled a widespread demand for wage increases which the employers have quietly met to a large degree. Unfortunately, the calm following these increases has been momentary only. The cost of living keeps rising further and it is painful to watch each wage increase being followed directly by a corresponding increase in the price of food and the cost of board and lodging. Already those workers engaged on national defence contracts are finding that the new wage scales agreed less than two months ago for Grenoble and district have become inadequate; they are presently asking for a cost-of-living allowance of 2 francs a day and have made it quite clear that if their demand is not met there will be trouble in the streets; some of them have even gone so far as to declare that they know where to find the necessary arms, alluding to the shell and explosives factories in the suburbs of Grenoble. I know perfectly well that these remarks were presumably made in order to intimidate the citizens, but it is nevertheless symptomatic that they should have been made in the first place. When they lack the courage to speak out themselves, the factory propagandists use the women working beside them who, running smaller risks, are less restrained in their threats. The demands of the reservists in the munitions factories have been forwarded to the ministry of supply and a number of agitators have been sent away — not to the front, which would have been dangerous, but to other factories in various parts of the area. Calm has therefore been restored, but there are fears that the present lull may be temporary.

If working-class militancy were to make itself felt in the munitions factories in Grenoble and in the industrial centres of the department, it would be very difficult and extremely risky to try to control it by force: the local police force would prove inadequate, even if it were reinforced by gendarmes. It is clearly necessary to strengthen the police contingent, but this can only be done through the deferment of professional policemen serving in the territorial army or the reserve. The auxiliary policemen drawn from the ranks of the retired are admittedly men of goodwill, but they are physically and mentally worn out, and their contribution and energy are inadequate. The relocation, or rather the transfer, of some gendarmerie brigades would be very useful, but the consequent changes in domicile would involve cumbersome formalities. . . . It would not be unhelpful if an intelligent, serving special commissioner were put in charge, with particular emphasis on the surveillance of aliens who continue to move about freely in the department and can undermine the morale of our people even as these aliens go about the business of gathering information useful to the enemy.

In conclusion, I believe that the present situation, both in respect of morale and also of social stability, while not giving cause for alarm, is far from satisfactory and that it ought to be considered serious enough to call for precautionary measures, and if necessary for energetic intervention.

What is really needed to lift flagging courage and to restore confidence in the future is a military success by our armies, a major Russian offensive, or just a German retreat. . . .

In June 1917, such comments about workers dreaming of workers' and soldiers' committees, in imitation of the Soviets of the Russian Revolution, were rare indeed — only a small number of prefects made any reference to events in Russia. By contrast, there were many reports of more general revolutionary remarks: 'The word 'revolution' is on all workers' lips', noted the prefect of Haute-Vienne. And he went on to mention specific acts to support this claim: at Nedde, in the canton of Eymoutiers, people involved in the gold collection campaign had been greeted with stone-throwing and their vehicle damaged. The instigator of this action had been a soldier on leave. It was a soldier on leave, too, who told students from the teacher-training school in Limoges: 'Being a Boche is no worse than being a Frenchman', a remark, incidentally, that provoked their indignant reaction.

The Diagnosis?

Do the findings of the inquiry held by the prefects in June 1917 enable us to identify the real state of French morale? There had undoubtedly been a general decline, but did that decline threaten to bring France to her knees?

The evidence suggests, first of all, that nearly half the departments were in no such danger. Next, we find that the great majority of the peasants, though seriously troubled in some regions, was continuing to stand firm.

There remained the towns: the upper-middle classes, the shopkeepers, the liberal professions and the white-collar workers, might feel dissatisfied enough but they rarely gave voice to vehement protest. The workers, by contrast, did pose a problem. The authorities concerned with 'the state of morale' drew up a list of 'contaminated' towns, that is, of those towns in which working-class disturbances had occurred (see the list below). This list is the more impressive as, in the course of the war, some small towns became big industrial centres with, as we have seen, an original population immensely swollen by the influx of new, 'rootless', inhabitants.

'*Contaminated*' *towns (as listed by the military authorities* Oyonnax, Dijon, Nancy, Montluçon, Epinac (mines), Mauléon, Commentry, Périgeux, Le Boucau, Troyes, Montbéliard, Lyon, Romilly, Brest, Le Creusot, Narbonne, Toulouse, Montereau, Carcassonne, Bordeaux, Châlon, Aveyron, Montpellier, Saut-du-Tarn, Belfort, Grenoble, Castelsarrazin, Bourges, Saint-Étienne, Toulon, Bastia, Orleans, Châtellerault, Ajaccio, Angers, Limoges.

The word 'contaminated' was, moreover, imprecise and could cover various possible levels of unrest, so that it must be treated with some reserve. It was still a fact, however, that though many working-class areas remained completely peaceful, it was the view of the authorities that the working class had become the nation's weak link.

But was there a risk of a serious breakdown of law and order? The almost unanimous answer of the prefects was no. There was cause for anxiety, but no one anticipated a revolutionary uprising in the immediate future. Were all the prefects certain of their own prognosis? Perhaps not, for we find that some extremely anxious reports ended on a soothing note. The prefects realised that ministers have a tendency not to like prophets of doom, and it is therefore possible that they toned down some of their conclusions. Nevertheless their optimism was not unjustified. According to them, discontent was based mainly on economic grievances so that if the workers' wage claims were met, calm would be restored fairly quickly. The authorities did, in fact, prove particularly flexible in dealing with wage claims in the state sector, and for the rest did their utmost to persuade private employers to do likewise.

The prefects were equally convinced that since an appreciable number of the workers were reservists, the threat of sending them back to the depots and on to the front was likely to make them think twice before taxing the patience of the authorities. It was not until 1918 that this threat ceased to have its full effect, and even then only in certain regions.

A third reason for optimism was that, except in some cases where they were concentrated in particularly large numbers, workers lived among people who, though undoubtedly weary, were far from ready for subversion.

Subsequent developments were to prove the prefects right. It remains true, however, that at the end of the spring of 1917 the combination of masses of dissatisfied workers, over-excited soldiers on leave and a general decline in morale might have had grave consequences. Just one element was lacking for this to happen.

CHAPTER 16

Summer–Autumn 1917: Recovery or Relapse?

> The situation has improved appreciably and the nation's
> patriotism seems to have revived. Nevertheless there is need
> for continued vigilance.[1]

With these words the *Confidential Bulletin on Internal Morale*,
drawn up by the central intelligence section of the army general
staff, ended on 15 August 1917.

The crisis in the spring of 1917, apart from its gravity, had had at
least two other special features: first, it had been unforeseen, and
secondly, it had shown that neither the morale of the army nor that
of the nation at large was unassailable. The advantage for the
historian is that from then onwards the various military and civil
authorities never ceased sounding French public opinion lest they
once again be taken by surprise. As a result, a rich store of documentation has been handed down.

In addition to the reports by the regional commanders on which
the *Confidential Bulletins* were based, Jean Nicot and Philippe
Schillinger, curators of army records, were able to consult:

(1) The postal censorship boards in the country, especially at
Belfort, Bellegarde, Bordeaux, Bourg, Dieppe, Marseille and Pontarlier;

(2) The postal censorship boards at the front on which the
Reports on the State of Public Opinion were based;[2]

(3) These reports.

---

1. APP B/A 1639. The Préfecture received copy no. 10.
2. See Jean Nicot and Philippe Schillinger,'L'Opinion française face à la guerre:
   l'influence de la Révolution russe d'aprés les archives du contrôle postal'. (*Actes
   du 97ᵉ Congrès national des sociétés savantes.*)

All three reflect a significant upswing in morale, and it may be wondered in response to what. The explanations given, it must be said, are poorly reasoned: thus America's declaration of war is mentioned in the reports, when it actually took place before the crisis.

Most of the answers given were, in fact, more in the nature of observations than explanations: 'Calm has been restored. Morale in the depots and among soldiers on leave has improved. Reinforcements are leaving for the front today in orderly fashion. The young recruits of the 1918 class are generally in good spirits. . . . Confidence among civilians seems also to have returned'.

All the same, there was no bravado, for as the *Bulletin* for August remarked: 'Though public opinion is no longer subject to the wave of pessimism caused by the events of last April and by the enemy propaganda campaign, it nevertheless remains no less impressionable, disturbed, weary and subject to rapid reversals'. A relapse was therefore possible 'with the onset of the universally dreaded fourth winter of war'.

Did these general impressions vary from one region to the next? Did they reflect the overall or the average mood of the country?

The report of the second region (Rouen) stressed that the mood of dejection had quickly passed and that morale had greatly improved, especially in Le Havre. In the fourth region (Le Mans) morale was 'much better today than it was two months ago'; in the fifth region (Orléans) there had been 'a notable improvement in morale'; in the sixth region (Châlons-sur-Marne), after 'some dejection', morale among civilians had improved; at Besançon (seventh region) 'the mood is much more reassuring than it was last June'; at Bourges (eighth region) morale was satisfactory but soldiers on leave were displaying a frankly 'poor' state of mind. In the tenth region (Rennes) there had also been a very appreciable improvement. The low morale prevailing in Nantes at the beginning of July had disappeared, but 'the frame of mind of the population continues to give cause for anxiety'. In the twelfth region (Limoges) morale had been 'bad' in April, May and June but had improved in July. Clermont-Ferrand (thirteenth region) had been 'undeniably' perturbed between the beginning of May and the middle of July. In Lyon (fourteenth region), the morale of civilians and of the troops had been incontestably low in May and June. 'The morale of the population and of the troops was very bad two months ago, but is improving from day to day' (fifteenth region, Marseille). 'The morale, both of the civilian and also of the military element, has risen appreciably over the last month' (seventeenth region, Toulouse). Improvements in morale after July were also noted in the twentieth region (Troyes), where it had been remarkably low a month earlier. In the twenty-first region (Chaumont), morale had also declined.

Since the report about the Parisian region also mentioned a drop in morale, there was only one military region where it had never declined (the sixteenth region, which included Montpellier), if we disregard what went on in the trains and at the railway stations.

Nearly all of France had therefore witnessed a similar pattern of events: a decline in morale followed by a recovery. Yet the decline did not occur at the same time in all regions, but reached a maximum in some in May, and in others in June or even July, and the revival, too, started earlier here and later there. The overall impression is that, following the failure of General Nivelle's offensive, a wave of discouragement swept France before it gradually ebbed away. There is nothing to suggest that there ever was an orchestrated defeatist campaign, though the officer commanding the Marseille region did mention that soldiers on leave had distributed pamphlets originating in Paris and bearing the slogan: 'No more killings, we want peace!' He added that attendance by officers and soldiers at syndicalist meetings in Paris had fallen, an indication that it had been a frequent occurence. Such comments were, however, the exception.

On the other hand, the study of French attitudes region by region shows that the intensity of the revival should also not be exaggerated. Indeed, the reports were expressed with particular caution.

In the department of Nord there was pronounced 'weariness' caused by economic hardship and a desperate wish to see the end of the war; in Rouen, people 'are afraid of a winter campaign', even though they recognised the need for an Allied victory; there was 'profound weariness' in Besançon, where people complained about the 'length of the war' and there was 'some irritation which the slightest military reverse could, if played upon by ill-intentioned or disturbed people, transform into despondency'. There was 'weariness' in the army depots in Nantes; 'discontent' largely resulting from the high cost of living at Limoges; 'apprehension' about the new winter campaign in Toulouse; and so on.

The restoration of industrial peace deceived nobody. 'Nothing entitles us to declare that all danger has vanished', said the report dealing with the major industrial centres in the Lyon region. Even in Meurthe-et-Moselle, although close to the combat zone, metalworkers held frequent meetings to protest about their wages, and in several regions anarchist and anti-militarist slogans and insulting remarks about officers were scrawled on the walls of some buildings. The military authorities did not, however, seem to fear an imminent rising of the workers. What they were far more worried about was the attitude of the women. It was they who were calling for an end to the war, they who tended to listen to and spread alarmist rumours, and they who gave way to despair.

The military authorities also feared the collapse of the national consensus: different groups and classes tended increasingly to accuse one another of inequalities of sacrifice. Workers safely ensconced at home were resented by soldiers on leave, and, more generally, the country resented the towns. Thus the report from the 14th region (Lyon) expressed anxiety about the 'deep gulf' that had opened up between 'them [the country] and the towns'.

By August 1917, morale no longer gave the authorities cause for concern, though it was still far from good. Soldiers on leave, in particular, had not recovered their former spirits; some declared that they would stick it out, but that they would no longer obey orders to attack. In certain regions, such as that of Bordeaux, the trade-union movement was suspected of dark plots.

France was a moral convalescent, without a sure prognosis: would there be a continued improvement, a stabilisation of the condition, or a new crisis, a relapse which was, in the very nature of things, bound to be more serious than the one which went before?

As an over-simplification, we can say that the crisis in the spring of 1917 had been set off by a number of catalysts, including the failure of the April offensive and the actions of four groups: soldiers on leave who had demonstrated their anger, often with virulence; workers who had gone on strike, but whose objectives were almost exclusively economic; the urban middle classes; and the peasant masses, whose protests had on the whole been relatively mild.

If some new catalyst were now to appear, and if the different protagonists should react in unison, an even more sensational crisis could arise.

There was one threat which hung over the morale of the French like a sword of Damocles: the possible defection of Russia. No one needed to be a great strategist to realise how the balance of forces would be greatly changed to the disadvantage of France if, for any reason, the Russians stopped fighting the war.

The impact of events in Russia on French morale was, however, mitigated by the long delay between the first revolution in March 1917 and the signing of the treaty of Brest–Litovsk in March 1918.

The great majority of Frenchmen did not look at these events from either a Russian or a revolutionary point of view, but solely in terms of their possible effects on the course and outcome of the war, in other words, on the destiny of France. Nor is this very surprising: nations are apt to put their own interests first. And as we have already had occasion to point out, the French were so convinced of the justice of their cause that they judged world affairs in terms of the advantages and disadvantages these had for themselves.

Hence their reactions to the first Russian Revolution were quite favourable: it was seen as a national uprising against a regime incapable of pursuing the war, some of whose leaders were suspected of being pro-German.

Thus an analysis of the press in Franche-Comté[3] shows that three leading newspapers welcomed the latest development in Russia.

On 17 March, the day after the announcement of the Revolution, *Le Petit Comtois*, a radical–socialist paper, saluted it as a victory of democracy; *La Dépêche républicaine*, a moderate republican paper, wrote: 'The revolution that has just taken place in Petrograd and Moscow not only strikes at Russian Germanophiles, it strikes straight at the heart of Germany'; and *L' Eclair comtois*, the organ of the nationalist right, though it could not approve of revolutions on principle, nevertheless contended that there was reason for satisfaction with what was in effect a victory over the pro-German elements.

The press in Puy-de-Dôme reacted in similar fashion:

L'Avenir du Plateau central, a paper very much on the right, wrote: 'The Russian people have opted not for revolution but for evolution. They have changed their government in order to rid themselves of the German influence'. As for the radical *Moniteur du Puy-de-Dôme*, it welcomed the Russian Revolution with: 'The traitors are in prison and will be punished. From now on the patriots will be masters. A new nation has arisen in the radiance of its recaptured freedom'. The abdication of the Tsar, too, was

an act of patriotism and of faith in the destiny of Russia. But there is no longer any mystery, no longer even any secrecy, concerning the fatal role the Empress had played on the political stage both for the Empire and also for the Emperor.... Of German origin, and having remained a German in her heart, her relationships and her intrigues have made her a formidable public danger and threat.[4]

The views that the postal censorship boards came across were on

3. J. Annequin, *La Révolution soviétique et la presse bisontine de 1917 à 1920*, Besançon, 1965.
4. See Michelle Moret, *L'Opinion publique en 1917 dans le Puy-de-Dôme*, 1971.

this point almost at one with those of the papers. 'The dominant note is one of joy to see our ally freed from German influence and hence able to be wholly devoted to the war'.[5] The two socialist wings also approved, albeit for opposite reasons. Annie Kriegel[6] noted that the majority faction was very satisfied: the establishment of a democratic regime in Russia strengthened their thesis that the war was a struggle for national liberation. The anti-war minority was no less happy: it hoped that the Russian revolutionaries would put pressure on Allied governments to work for peace. In general, however, the majority was happier than the minority, who regarded the revolution as not having gone far enough.

In short, all shades of French public opinion felt they had cause for rejoicing. This attitude was to change rapidly. Extracts from the letters quoted by the Bordeaux postal censorship board[7] show that, by May, the main feeling had become one of uncertainty: for some correspondents, the new Russia had indeed prevented treachery by the old; for others, still a minority, Russia was moving towards a separate peace. All in all, public opinion wavered in the face of an event that it understood the less, the more it refused to see it from the Russian point of view.

Over the next few months, confidence in Russia continued to decline, in particular after the failure of General Brusilov's offensive. The majority still trusted the Russians, but the number of those who believed that they were about to 'leave us in the lurch' and the consequences would be disastrous kept rising. As one letter read in July–August 1917 put it: 'If the Boche can overrun that vast country, he must be unbeatable'. Others began to show their contempt for the 'Russian shambles', for 'this gross, brutish, spineless, indeed cowardly nation'.

As news of the worsening situation in Russia came in, French comments grew increasingly bitter. The Russians had ceased to be 'nice', and people mocked at a 'steam roller that couldn't crack a nut'. If, in August, they sometimes still thought there was a chance of some recovery, by September they had come to believe in it less and less. Certain correspondents thought General Kornilov would 'sweep out' all those who did the work of the Boche, but they were few and far between. Moreover, all Russians were lumped together:

5. Quoted by Nicot and Schillinger, 'L'Opinion française face à la guerre', whose study is particularly valuable.
6. 'L'Opinion publique française et la révolution russe' in *La Révolution d'octobre et le mouvement ouvrier européen*, Paris, 1967.
7. AM 7 N 985.

'From the Tsar down to the lowest muzhik, they are nothing but riff-raff who have landed us in a filthy mess', said one. 'The Russians are proving a cruel disappointment', wrote another. That disappointment could take the strangest forms. Thus the chief education officer in Doubs stated that, 'Russia's defection, soon after they [Russian lessons in some secondary schools] were inaugurated...has led to a temporary decline in attendance among the pupils, who at the beginning had been very keen'.

By the time news of the October Revolution arrived, the shock-effect was somewhat deadened, which does not mean that it was ignored, the less so as it had been preceded, a few days earlier, by the announcement of the rout of the Italians at Caporetto (24 October), while some people also had other than patriotic anxieties. Feelings ran high in Nancy where people were worried about the 'fate of French capital lent to Russia on such advantageous terms. . .'.

In the circumstances, it is not surprising that reports from the various military regions in December should have recorded a fresh drop in morale, and that the postal censorship boards discovered that the proportion of correspondents continuing to express hope in a victorious peace had fallen rapidly. As the report for the seventh region (Besançon) put it: 'The worsening of the Russian crisis and the Italian setback have made a very painful impression'. Nevertheless, though the 'Russian defection', as it was called, or 'anarchy', did worry and anger people, it was rarely their main preoccupation, certainly not in the Lyon region.

An investigation by the postal censorship board into the morale of civilians in the military zone at the end of 1917 ended with: 'Morale has suffered a further decline, even more marked than in June'. Was this true of the whole of France?

There was one important factor that differed considerably from one part of the country to the other, namely, the attitude of soldiers on leave. The *Confidential Bulletin on Internal Morale* constantly recorded an improvement in their behaviour:

15 October: Considerable improvement. Bearing more correct, improved discipline, less drunkenness. Incidents in trains and railway stations now very rare.

15 November: All signs of despondency have disappeared. Their bearing is better and there have been no more incidents in trains and railway stations. One small black spot only: soldiers often refuse 'to show outward marks of respect' (that is, to salute their officers).

15 December: The morale of soldiers on leave is *high* despite the approach of winter. Bearing still leaves much to be desired, but that is felt to be of little importance.

The first months of 1918 were to confirm this upward trend:
15 January: The morale of soldiers on leave is *very satisfactory indeed*. It is better than that of 'the civilian element'. Soldiers return to the front 'without hesitation, with the brave resignation of men fully aware of the significance of the coming clashes and firmly resolved not to let the enemy pass'. Even their bearing is improving!
15 February: 'The morale of combatants seems to have steadied of late, however great their desire for peace.'
Not only was their bearing and their behaviour on trains better and the number of cases of drunkenness stable, but soldiers on leave were again starting to salute their superiors!
15 March 1918: 'The morale of soldiers on leave is excellent.'
But what about the 'civilian elements'?
A valuable document enables us to examine the 'physiognomy' of Paris in December 1917. In that month the Préfecture began to publish a daily bulletin of about a dozen typewritten pages, an effort it kept up until the end of the war. The aim was to assess the view of Parisians from remarks overheard in markets, railway stations, cafés, at the Bourse and at the Palais de Justice.[8]
The first conclusion is that Paris does not seem to have been touched by the new wave of pessimism, if that wave ever existed.
A wounded non-commissioned officer sitting at a café table in the rue Royale on Sunday, 2 December, expressed his surprise at Parisian insouciance. According to him, 'we have reached the worst moment of the war' and in the circumstances 'it is strange to note the general lack of concern'. He believed that 'the press is trying to conceal the importance of the Russian defection'.
In fact, however, Parisians were by no means indifferent to what was happening in Russia. Almost every day, the Préfecture reports devoted a paragraph to the subject, under the heading 'Public Opinion and Russian Anarchy'. The two types of reaction already noted clearly predominated. First of all, there was a feeling of hostility towards everything Russian. Even Russian officers in France, who might have been thought to be no friends of the Russian Revolution, were not spared. There were numerous incidents.
At the corner of rue Gay-Lussac and rue Claude-Bernard, three 'fellows' shouted at a young Russian officer passing by: 'Look at him! He'd be better off without a uniform at all than turning up in that thing. Those Russians have no guts!' On the boulevard Saint-Michel, another Russian officer was greeted with a 'Hullo, here

8. APP B/A 1587.

comes the Russian steamroller'.

So high did anti-Russian feeling run that it soon seemed prudent to ask Russian officers not to wear uniform in public.

Not even Russians who protested their anti-Bolshevism escaped the hostility: they were accused of doing nothing but talk. After a large meeting organised by Russians in Paris to protest against the new regime, a police informer commented:

> All these fine words are all very well, but actions would speak much louder. Most of the men at the meeting seemed to be fully fit, and since all that was required of them was to listen to some speeches, lots of them turned up. But if there had been a recruiting office in that hall, there wouldn't have been a single volunteer out of all 2,000 of them.

Not one single remark favourable to the Bolshevik Revolution was reported by any informer, not even one used as a debating point. This does not, of course, mean that Parisians were unanimous in their hostility to the Russian Revolution; bitterness, however, was too widespread and too strong for anyone to express the contrary view with impunity.

A second type of reaction was to deplore the effects of the latest Russian events on the fortunes of France: people denounced 'the Russian treachery which has made it impossible for the war to end before the winter and has brought about the Italian disaster'. Some felt that 'the Russian defection places us in a very serious situation'; others, that the morale of French troops might be badly affected: 'They are already appalled at the prospect of having to spend a fourth winter in the trenches, all the more so when they expect to have to resist a furious assault by the Boche, reinforced by men and material brought back from the Russian front, and anxious to score a decisive victory before the American intervention'.

Parisians also dwelled on the ingratitude of the Russians, for whose sake France had entered the war, simply to honour her signature!

There was a fairly large section of opinion, however, which held that the last word about Russia had not yet been spoken: they clung to the hope that the Bolsheviks, or the 'maximalists', as they were called, were about to collapse under the weight of the German conditions. Some saw Russia resuming her place by the side of her old allies in the spring, and based their hopes on Generals Kaledin and Kornilov. This current was so strong that by the end of December the fears caused by the 'Russian defection' tended to be forgotten. The length of the Russo-German negotiations reassured people: they deluded themselves into thinking that the Germans were holding things up because they lacked confidence in the solidity of a government led by Lenin and Trotsky.

In keeping with a tendency mentioned earlier, hostility against the Russians — if that was something new — merged with the general xenophobic current, which was nothing new at all. All foreigners in Paris, whether or not they came from Allied countries, were its victims: 'Ill humour towards foreigners seems to increase among Parisians by the day'.

Here, too, it was not all that strange that people in the grip of so costly a war should have found it hard to tolerate the presence in their midst of 'tourists', men who should have been busy helping France to champion the right. It was therefore untrue that Parisians were not worried about Russian developments, or made no assessment of their consequences. But despite everything, confidence remained high. 'It is impossible that the Boche should win', people were reported as saying. There was no question of giving in: 'Russian treachery will mean greater sacrifices, but if our leaders are strong it will not mean a precipitate peace'.

On 8 December, an observer described the attitude of the inhabitants of the XVth arrondissement as follows: 'At this critical juncture of the war, public opinion is standing up well. . . . It is not keen on a sudden peace, but wants one that will ensure the triumph of right and justice'.

Nevertheless there were quite a few indications of a contrary trend. A section of the report of 7 December was headed 'The pessimistic wave', and mentioned a number of signs of the wavering of public opinion. The most significant was probably the lack of fervour shown in subscribing to the latest National Defence Loan, just launched. The reporters felt that the moment had been badly chosen, with the result that the relevant counters in several post offices in the XVth arrondissement were deserted. And yet the authorities had not been penny-pinching in their publicity: one counter had been set up in the gondola of an airship parked in the Invalides, and there had been an airdrop of leaflets over Paris enjoining the people to subscribe.

Rumour had it that, despite everything, the loan had been an 'unexpected success', inspired by the advent to power of Clemenceau on 16 November. But a few days later another rumour went round that the statements made by the minister of finance had been untrue and that the loan had not been fully subscribed.

Economic problems continued to arouse bitter resentment. All classes were worried above all about the question of fresh supplies, either because these were unreliable or because of high prices.

Potential coal shortages caused the greatest anxiety, especially among women: they were said not to be as patient as they had been during the previous winter; some 'cursed the length of this war' and hoped that it would 'end soon'. Incidents were only to be expected if economic problems became too severe. Some remarks were reported without comment: 'You might think the government was asking for a revolution'; 'Let them return our husbands, that's all we want'.

By contrast, and to some extent paradoxically, few Parisians — at least as far as we can determine from these reports — seemed to have much time for political alternatives. People stressed the need for a strong government that would keep an eye on those workers' centres 'where revolution is being fomented'. Others expressed their surprise that 'minority groups' at the CGT congress just held in Clermont-Ferrand should have been allowed to put forward pacifist ideas and that the 'majority groups' had to some extent concurred. If one were to believe the agents of the Préfecture, public opinion was in favour of firmness and supported the refusal of passports to socialists wishing to attend the Stockholm conference. 'These secret conclaves can only do harm to the morale of our soldiers'.

Perhaps the customer in a café in the rue de Rennes who recalled the case against the teacher Hélène Brion was unusual. He waxed indignant about the lack of firmness the government had shown towards this 'breed', was scandalised that the 'most ignoble ideas' could be advanced at public meetings, and felt that 'everyone who utters defeatist ideas in public should be arrested on the spot'. He may have been unusual, but no one apparently saw fit to contradict him. Defeatism encountered little sympathy anywhere. Joseph Caillaux was roundly abused, some even advocating the stripping of his parliamentary immunity, a relic from another age, and that he be taken into custody without further ado.

Was public opinion therefore unanimous in its patriotic fervour? We know from the postal censorship board that it was nothing of the kind. The observers from the Préfecture also realised that they needed to enter certain reservations, and that the opinions expressed aloud may have hidden others rather more discreet. According to the summary prepared at the beginning of December for the XVth arrondissement: 'The attitude of the workers is satisfactory on the whole'. There had been an improvement over the previous two months, thanks in particular to the appointment of shop stewards who had helped to convey the workers' demands more effectively. But though their behaviour was less blatant now, the reservists remained unreliable workers, expressed the 'worst opinions', and did not do their work properly. In fact, it was largely the massive relocation of these workers to army depots in the wake of the recent strikes in the aviation industry, and later in the rubber industry, that had persuaded them to tread more cautiously. Where adequate police forces were available, there had been no need to deploy them. The report nevertheless stressed the vigour with which the wage claims were being pressed, and the fact that many workers were intent on using force to make strikes stick. Whenever there had been recent stoppages, most strikers had been more circumspect. In particular, they did not take to the streets as they had done in May 1917.

Even so, their 'moderation' was 'unreliable', and 'would readily vanish if more extensive strikes were to coincide, be it by chance or as a result of enemy intrigue, with grave military or political setbacks, and particularly with supply shortages'.

What the report therefore, brought out, explicitly or otherwise, was that the apparent social equilibrium was no longer stable, but depended directly on the prosperity of the munitions factories, on their continued expansion, and on the high wages they could pay. Nor did this make everyone happy. Thus one report mentioned a conversation between two industrialists who had been ordered by the manpower commission to increase their staff. 'This is a new tax on profits', one of them sighed. 'It's all just to make sure those people in Paris don't give in, and to stop war-weariness from becoming obvious', said the other. 'The government always sides with the workers', observed a woman when bread ration cards were issued and workers were granted extra rations.

In December 1917, Paris was thus in a state of unstable equilibrium, teetering between the views of a majority that was still convinced that France, despite her serious, though not intolerable, economic problems, must not accept defeat, and those of a predominantly working-class minority, kept in check by fear of being sent back to the front as well as by the high wages they were being paid.

And all the while the war dragged on. 'There's no end in sight, and who would have said that in 1914?' was a remark quoted in the report for 6 December.

Was the attitude of Parisians at the end of 1917 typical of French opinion at large? The December *Confidential Bulletin* tried to answer this question by looking at each major social group in turn.

In the world of agriculture, the women on whom the management of the farms had fallen at the outbreak of war 'did not hide their fatigue, nor their wish for peace', but 'unexpected profits' had acted as 'a powerful comforter'. Moreover, the return of the older classes had somewhat eased the manpower problem. The farming community therefore showed little sign of weakening. The middle classes had been hit badly by economic problems. They bore them with 'the greatest dignity and courage', but the *Bulletin* did not disguise the fact that this backbone of the nation could be beginning to sag. However, the term 'middle classes' used by the *Bulletin* is not very precise. The report from the twelfth region (Limoges) tried to be more specific: 'In the towns, businessmen and industrialists are making large profits and the workers are paid large wages. As a result there are no complaints. It is among white-collar workers, petty officials and the lower-middle class that one more readily finds symptoms of anxiety'.

The report from the tenth region (Rennes) also underlined the worries of 'white-collar workers, small *rentiers*, and the liberal professions'.

After the rise in morale during the summer, it does not seem that the rest of 1917 witnessed another crisis comparable to that of the spring, or indeed any other real crisis. Despite events in Russia, the outlook seemed less bleak, perhaps because the French army had recovered some of its poise. This most recent mood, reflected by the behaviour of soldiers on leave, turned out to be a very important means of maintaining morale on the home front. The result was a new frame of mind that might perhaps be termed *patriotic gloom*, and this was to continue into the early months of 1918. It took the following expression: the continuation of the war is deplorable, but there is no way of putting an end to it, because a premature peace would be no less deplorable. Hence people refused to throw up their hands, though they found it increasingly difficult to tell how victory might be achieved. There seemed to be no way out of this quandary and hence there was little to arouse enthusiasm.

In these circumstances, economic factors were bound to play a considerable role. The *Bulletin* for 15 January 1918 made the point once again: 'All the reports by regional commanders agree that the supply of flour and bread is of paramount importance; domestic calm and tranquillity cannot be maintained if there are bread shortages'.

It was also essential to ensure that no important sector of the nation defected. There is no doubt, as we have already said, that working-class morale, under great strain, had grown frail. The way it evolved would therefore be a touchstone for other developments on the home front.

IV

1918

CHAPTER 17

The Workers in 1918

By the end of 1917, France had recovered from her deep crisis of
confidence in the spring; even so, morale had not returned to a
satisfactory level. For the authorities, the workers' attitude had
become a serious concern, particularly in the munitions factories.
As Max Gallo put it in a study of working-class attitudes at the
time:[1] 'Munitions factories are a crucial factor in the pursuit of war,
and the workers in these factories determine the fortunes of war no
less than the *poilus*.'[2]

The workers were aware of this, particularly since they had been
told it repeatedly, at times in the most flowery terms. Thus in 1916,
Albert Thomas, the socialist under-secretary of state for artillery
and munitions, climbed on a pile of shells in the big workshop at Le
Creusot and exclaimed: 'Up there, in the smoke that fills this valley,
victory soars above us. We count on you, comrades, to seize it.'[3]

Outside the Paris region, there were twenty-nine departments
that, in January 1917, employed more than 10,000 workers in
munitions factories. Far ahead of all the rest came Loire with
108,007, but Rhône (76,002), Bouches-du-Rhône and Gironde were
not very far behind. Most of these workers were members of the
metalworkers' union, whose secretary, Alphonse Merrheim, had
been one of the early leaders of the pacifist faction in the CGT. As a
result, the authorities were bound to keep a close watch on members of his union, and the records they compiled convey a fairly
accurate picture of their activities. We have chosen four examples
from different regions of varying importance, namely, Isère, Gard,

---

1. 'Quelques aspects de la mentalité et du comportement ouvrier dans le usines de
   guerre, 1914–1918' in *Le Mouvement social*, July–September 1966.
2. Ibid., p. 4.
3. Ibid.

Paris and its surroundings and especially Loire with the Saint-Etienne basin.

Isère

There were, several important industrial areas in the department of Isère where war work was undertaken, particularly Grenoble and Vienne. In 1914 the voters in this department had elected five socialist deputies out of a total of eight, among whom was the teacher Jean-Pierre Raffin-Duggens, one of the three socialist deputies to attend the pacifist conference in Kienthal in Switzerland in April 1916. Isère was therefore a likely centre of agitation against the war.

The dossier which the authorities compiled on trade-union activities in the department during the war[4] was opened at the end of 1916, the minister of the interior having advised the prefect of the arrival in his department of the secretary of the Metalworkers' Federation, Alphonse Merrheim, then head of the anti-war movement. Shadowed closely by policemen, the trade-union leader addressed a small meeting of eighty metalworkers at Grenoble on 11 November 1916, and then took the train back to Lyon. Nothing else of importance, or at least nothing that the prefectorial services either judged important or knew about, happened in that year, or indeed in 1917, which was another fairly quiet year in the department. Trade-union activity had clearly increased and wages had become the subject of keen discussion, but no strikes of any importance took place. Not that the pacifist movement completely bypassed Grenoble — an inquiry held on 2 September 1917,[5] very probably by the Renseignements Généraux, commented that the metalworkers' union had become the most important of all. Many of its militants were 'revolutionaries' from the department of Nord or from Belgium. They were waging a particularly active propaganda campaign in two large firms, each of which employed several thousand workers, Bouchayer and Viallet et Brenier. The report concluded: 'Public opinion [it is not clear whether this refers to working-class opinion only] is clearly against the war in the Grenoble region, where the three Kienthal deputies are being praised to the skies'.

This assessment notwithstanding, the workers in Grenoble were

4. AN F 7 12992.
5. AN F 7 12992, doc. P 11471.

apparently not yet ready for strike action. In December 1917, they showed themselves reluctant to follow the example of their fellow metalworkers in Saint-Etienne, no doubt because of the wage rises they had just been granted. The atmosphere changed in 1918, when the number of union meetings increased, audiences grew larger and many defeatist and revolutionary speeches were made.

The prefect did not hide his concern. Following a meeting held in Grenoble on 2 April 1918, he wrote to the minister of the interior:

> The proceedings at this meeting, as at the one held in Vienne, are symptomatic of the workers' attitude. . . . They have only one thought in mind: social revolution. They are preoccupied with it, and employ incessant propaganda in preparing for it: it is their *idée fixe*, and despite our country's difficult circumstances, they are ready to take to the streets at the first signal from their leaders.

It is a little strange that barely a month later the prefect, who had had fifty extra gendarmes assigned to him at Vienne, should have claimed that together with the extra fifty put at his disposal in Grenoble he had been sent too many men and that twenty-five additional gendarmes in each town were enough. It was at exactly this moment that a strike was declared: on 14 May 1918, the twenty-eight munitions factories in Grenoble came to a total or partial standstill. At Bouchayer's, for instance, more than 2,000 were on strike. Their militancy was not, however, absolute: threatened with the return to the front of all reservists, the movement collapsed in the afternoon. To prevent any further trouble the prefect made sure that the orders of recall already sent out were cancelled. At a big trade-union rally held on 18 May, the leaders called on all comrades to be ready for action, but wage increases took the wind out of their sails. As the prefect put it, the workers had demonstrated their 'prudence'.

Unrest was much more pronounced at Vienne. On 21 May a general strike was declared and all metal and textile factories joined the strike movement, which immediately adopted a 'revolutionary and pacifist' attitude. The prefect, so conciliatory at Grenoble, decided on rigorous measures: all meetings and processions were banned, all cafés closed, the sale of drink prohibited, and all the known union leaders — Miglioretti, secretary of the local Association of Trade Unions, Richetta, secretary of the textile workers' union, Herclet, his deputy, were 'all charged with inciting the troops to insubordination'. This show of strength had the desired effect: on 24 May all metalworkers returned to work and the textile workers decided to follow suit on Tuesday 28 May.

At Grenoble, whatever reservations some workers may have had, wage increases had settled the issue. At Vienne, things followed a different course. Here the strikes came immediately after a congress held by the pacifist minority in the CGT held at Saint-Etienne on 19 and 20 May. The strike order was given by two delegates, Miglioretti and Richetta. At 6.00 a.m. on 21 May, strike pickets were posted outside the gates of the factories. Richetta told a meeting that the strikes did not have economic objectives but were aimed at bringing the war to a halt. The government must define their war aims and agree to a general armistice with the Central Powers.

How did the mass of workers at Vienne react? According to the district police commissioner, the majority had not joined in the strike of their own free will, which did not, however, mean that they would be returning to work straight away. This remark was of singular importance. In some towns at least, the mass of workers were ready to follow, or have pressed upon them, instructions of a purely political nature, but were not convinced enough to persevere. This explains both the fairly ready build-up of the strike wave and, in the end, its fairly abrupt end: the workers were not prepared to wage a long struggle.

In June, a departmental congress of the CGT was held in Grenoble: it proposed a general strike for peace, but only on condition that foreign comrades would do likewise. And that was how it was left.

On 11 September, the prefect of Isère mentioned an 'upsurge' of trade-union agitation in the metal industry, but, he added: 'In view of the favourable military situation, the general attitude is fairly good; there are no visible signs of antimilitarism, and meetings are confined to economic discussions . . .'.

Gard

As we said earlier, the trade-union movement revived very gradually and the year 1917 ended without major industrial trouble. Matters were to change in 1918, and not only because of fresh wage claims. According to the authorities, the agitator-in-chief in Gard was Jean-Baptiste Lescalié, a former secretary of the Alais *bourse du travail*. Before a crowded meeting in the town hall of Bessèges, held on 17 February 1918 and attended by 400 people, Lescalié produced a report on the federal conference of the CGT which had been held in Clermont-Ferrand at the end of December: the war had to be stopped, he proclaimed, the bourgeoisie and the capitalists alone were responsible for it and also for its continuation, all workers were brothers, the Russians were right. He attacked the press for falsely alleging that the workers wanted to fight on 'to the bitter end' when all they really wanted was peace and the immediate cessation of hostilities. The order of the day at the conference in Clermont-Ferrand: 'Down with war, long live peace,' was received with 'unanimous and repeated' applause, and though some of the audience felt that the speaker had gone 'a little too far', a very large majority agreed with him.[6]

Alarmed by the tone of that meeting, the authorities made sure that, while not impeding trade-union business proper, a stop was put to anything that looked like defeatist propaganda. To that end, they did their utmost to prevent Lescalié from speaking at further meetings.

On 25 February, when a meeting of metalworkers was called at the Alais *bourse du travail*, the sub-prefect warned the secretary of the union that Lescalié had been banned from taking part. The union protested but complied, which did not, however, stop the members from discussing 'political' issues. One speaker declared that, at the next congress of the CGT, the agenda should not be confined to wages and priority should be given to the signing of 'a workers' peace'. The authorities quickly realised that the steps taken to prevent Lescalié from speaking had been ineffective: meetings at which he was billed to appear were announced just two hours in advance – too late for the authorities to ban them. On Sunday, 6 March, Lescalié addressed between 130 and 150 miners at Rochessadoule, in the afternoon; in the evening he spoke at Martinet-sur-Auzonet; on Monday, 7 March, he spoke at Saint-Jean-de-Valériscle. The Gard public prosecutor asked the *garde des sceaux*[7] for advice. Should Lescalié be prosecuted? He himself would prefer to bide his time while keeping a close eye on Lescalié's activities.

On 25 March 1918, a regional trade-union congress was held at Saint-Etienne: advised of it very late, the Alais metalworkers' union quickly appointed two delegates, Coche and Peroigot. On 31 March, Peroigot reported back to a meeting at the *bourse du travail* attended by eighty people. He told them that the congress itself had been attended by 375 delegates, and that the main item on the agenda had been peace and how to achieve it. Strike action had been agreed on in principle, but the date would have to be fixed by a

6. AN F 7 12985.
7. The head of the judiciary.

congress planned for 21 April. The Alais metalworkers decided to elect their delegates to this new congress by a secret vote.

In short, direct action against the war was beginning to be organised. At the more open meetings, speeches became increasingly virulent. Indeed, one of the delegates reported a resolution put at Saint-Etienne by some of those present: 'To take to the streets well armed, and to foment uprisings, so that the ruling class will recognise the firm intention of the proletariat to put an end to the carnage, which has gone on for far too long as it is'. Colliard, the secretary of the metalworkers' union, added that the majority in the CGT had 'lost touch with the feelings and aspirations of the working class', and called on all those present to join the Trade Union Defence Committee, that was, the pacifist minority in the CGT.

The public prosecutor, informed of these developments, considered it high time to ban what he described as 'all this pro-German and defeatist propaganda'.

On the evening of 21 May 1918, a strike was declared in the Tamaris ironworks: of 2,430 workers, 2,076 downed tools, among them 1,362 reservists. The miners, too, went on strike in Saint-Martin-de-Valgagues.

Oddly enough, the authorities, who had been keeping a careful watch on developments for some weeks, were taken by surprise: in telegrams they sent to the Sûreté next day, the departmental police claimed that the 'workers, whose action nothing had led us to expect', seemed to have heeded the anti-war directives of the congress of Saint-Etienne. There was reason to fear that miners at the important pit at Romabele would join in, since they were usually influenced by their neighbours in the metalworks, but the other mines in the Alais basin would probably not be affected. Moreover, not even the metalworkers seemed prepared to go to extremes since they had continued to keep the furnaces burning. On the whole, this was proving to be a peaceable strike: after stopping work, the workers had quietly gone home.

The next day, on 23 May, the movement spread to some of the ironworks in Bessèges, and more widely to the mines in that town. By contrast, no miners downed tools in Molières-sur-Cèze, Castillon-de-Gagnières, Saint-Jean-de-Valériscle or Le Martinet-sur-Auzonnet. More than 150 men returned to the Tamaris ironworks.

The prefect, who had been sent police reinforcements from Toulon and Marseille, summed up the situation as follows:

The strike movement is still wavering and its course depends primarily on the attitude of the miners at Rochebelle and Bessèges, and of the metalworkers at Alais and Bessèges. They will meet this evening and take a vote which will decide whether the strike is to spread or to stop. From various discussions I have had, I gather that the leaders of the miners' federation, even those loyal to the General Confederation of Labour, remain vigorously opposed to a general strike. There has been no trouble. The population is hostile to the strikers.

In the event, the miners of Rochebelle voted against the strike and, as an immediate consequence, 1,000 metalworkers in the Alais ironworks returned to work. However, the strikes spread even further to the pits at Bessèges.

Though most of the miners in the coalfield had stayed at work, the prefect did not know how long that situation would last. All he could claim on the evening of 24 May was that two days after the beginning of the strike, 'the action begun by the metalworkers has been checked. Order has been maintained everywhere and the freedom to go to work is assured.' Nevertheless, that same evening the miners held a congress at Rochessadoule and voted for an all-out strike. After some uncertainty, the movement seemed to be spreading and the prefect put in an urgent request for an additional thirty gendarmes.

At noon on 25 May, the situation was as follows: the strike wave seemed to be ebbing among the metalworkers — 1,134 had reported for work at Tamaris, 200 more than the night before; it had spread significantly among the miners, except for La Grand-Combe, where all 6,000 miners had reported for work.

Thus the strike movement was tailing off among the metalworkers who had instigated it, while at the same time spreading among the miners who had at first been reluctant to join. Perhaps it was to disguise these difficulties that the Alais sub-prefecture was informed that 6,000 strikers meeting at the *bourse du travail* had 'declared their support for the strike movement', adding that they would be 'prepared to return to work the moment it pleases the government to make its war aims known, as demanded unanimously by the congress of Clermont-Ferrand'. In fact, if we are to believe the prefect, no meeting had been held that day at the *bourse du travail* and the message had been drafted by a 'strike committee' made up of a group of about ten people.

In these circumstances, 26 May, which was a Sunday, was the day of decision. Both sides made great efforts either to persuade the miners at La Grand-Combe to join the movement on Monday, or to dissuade them from doing so. Posters calling for a forty-eight-hour strike in favour of peace were torn down by the authorities. A strike meeting called by the miners' union was attended by no more than a hundred people. The chief mining engineer posted up a warning reminding reservists that they were not entitled to strike, and Valette, the socialist deputy, let it be known that he would be visiting the coalfield the next day to exhort all miners to return to work.

Monday, in fact, was the crucial day: when the morning shift reported for work there were only 300 absentees out of a total of 1,600 workers at the Tamaris ironworks and 150 absentees out of a total work force of 550 at the Bessèges ironworks. Things were less clear-cut among the miners: the strike had not taken hold at La Grand-Combe, and in several pits the strike following had faltered, but at Rochebelle, Martinet and Rochessadoule the strike call was entirely, or almost entirely, successful. . . . However, during the day the leaders of the Gard Federation of Miners' Unions, meeting at Bessèges, decided to order a return to work on Tuesday, the next day. The prefect meanwhile increased pressure, combining appeals to patriotism with the threat of sanctions.

On 28 May the movement collapsed, among the metalworkers as well as among the miners. As a precaution, the gendarmes were retained for another two days to quell possible unrest following reprisals against ten metalworkers. There was no such unrest. On 31 May, Lescalié, the authorities' *bête noire*, was arrested on a charge of 'defeatist comments and anarchist intrigues'.

Thus the anti-war movement in Gard had lasted for a little less than one week. It had paradoxically combined resolution with vacillation, eagerness to stop work with a rush to return. How had this strange reaction come about, and what was its significance?

Its most obvious feature was the rift between the trade-union leaders: some had called urgently for action, others were more restrained, yet others thought only of putting a stop to the strikes. And no matter what the authorities said about it, not even Lescalié's attitude was unambiguous. An active militant, aged 51 at the time of these events, he had been successively secretary of the railway workers' union (for a time he had worked as a joiner in the workshops of the Paris-Lyon-Marseille railway), of the Alais and Nîmes *bourses du travail*, and of the Gard Departmental Association of Trade Unions. In that capacity, it was only natural that he should have been present at all strikes in the department. And in fact, on 26 May, he had gone to Nîmes, spending the whole day with the strike committee, and the next few days as well. But to do exactly what? At the preliminary hearing of his case, he was accused of making remarks calculated to 'mislead the troops and the population', of uttering 'seditious slogans', of 'inciting soldiers to insubordination'. The prefect, for his part, alleged that, under instructions from the CGT minority congress at Saint-Etienne, Lescalié had supervised and directed the spread of the strike movement. However, Lescalié put up a vigorous defence, declaring that he had in no way been involved in the outbreak of the conflict, and that, as soon as he had arrived at Alais, he had declared: 'Mr Secretary of the Departmental Association of Trade Unions in Gard, you would clearly understand that the movement in which you are engaged was started by you, acting without advice from our union, and that I am here at your request to ensure that your movement proceeds peacefully.'

In other words, Lescalié considered himself a moderating influence and not an agitator. Are we to believe him? Needless to say, he saw no reason to tell the judge-advocate the truth. Nevertheless the 'evidence' assembled against him was so tenuous that on 11 June he was released on bail. Moreover, the papers the authorities had seized included a letter dated 25 May 1918 from one of the leaders of the Bessèges strike committee, calling for Lescalié's help in bringing round those miners who had not yet decided to resume work at the end of forty-eight hours. This showed that Lescalié had indeed played a moderating role, no doubt because, though opposed to the war, he felt that the time was not yet ripe for a full-scale confrontation.

Those trade-union leaders who supported the majority in the CGT had made great efforts to confine and stop the strike movement, not without raising a storm of protest. The miners' leaders, Chabrolin, Jallet and Chapon, were rudely taken to task by striking metalworkers who called them hypocrites and double-dealers. Moreover, when the strike was over, these same leaders went on to the counter-offensive by, for example, expelling from the Miner's Federation the secretary of the miners' union at Saint-Martin-de-Valgagues, who had been associated with the minority group during the strike. Though they themselves had briefly supported the strike, it was only, as they explained, because they did not wish to turn their backs on their comrades and because they wanted to convince them that the metalworkers had misled them and thus to persuade their members to return to work. Moreover, the federal secretary had felt compelled to resign to mark his disapproval of the strikes.

As for the mass of workers, it has to be said that they did not need much persuasion to join the strike. This is the more significant in that the miners' leaders were cautious, to say the least. But then, neither did the workers need much persuasion to return to work. We may therefore take it that, at the outset, the strikes reflected a marked anti-war tendency, but that the strikers did not intend to make more than a brief protest. As a result the movement quickly crumbled. It was not supported by any large demonstrations, by any great propaganda campaign — the workers were probably afraid of reprisals, but then that is no sign of great firmness of purpose. Opposed to the continuation of the war without any doubt, they were not yet ready to go too far in demonstrating their antimilitaristic opinions. In any case, they did not give the impression of being filled with revolutionary fervour.

One further factor could have had a moderating influence: as the prefect declared on 23 May, the population was hostile to the strikers.

In short, in the spring of 1918 the most radical sector in Gard was undoubtedly in favour of peace but was not prepared to run any great risks for it. As the committee of the miners' union in Saint-Martin-de-Valgagues put it: 'Our strike movement has the sole objective of forcing our government to define their aims for war, and for peace, which is the wish of the working class, no matter what the bourgeois press may say'.

It is true that at a meeting in Alais, Louis Brujas, one of the ten workers who were punished and sent back to the army depot, proposed an immediate armistice and the opening of peace negotiations, and that his motion was carried unanimously by several hundreds of metalworkers and miners present, before the meeting disbanded to the strains of the 'Internationale'; but it also has to be recognised that this resolution was never translated into action. The workers in the department of Gard did not stir again until the end of the war.

The Paris Region

A major wave of strikes hit munitions factories in the Paris region in May 1918. Though enjoying mass support at the beginning, and openly aimed at putting a stop to the war, the strikes had fizzled out within four days.

In the late afternoon of Sunday, 12 May, a meeting of one hundred shop stewards from the Renault factory was held at the La Victoire restaurant in the place Nationale in Boulogne.[8] One of the

8. Archives Militaires 16 N 1543.

shop stewards, Bagot, explained that the meeting had been called to take decisions of the utmost importance. The delegates were invited to vote for the principle of a strike on the next day, Monday, 13 May. The strike would not be about wage claims alone, though these would serve as a pretext, but was intended to force the government to state its true war aims and hence to move one step nearer to peace.

Another speaker, Michelet, was even more specific: the strike would be in support of the resolutions passed at Clermont-Ferrand. Some delegates advised caution, but they were a small minority.

The attitude of even the most determined speakers was, however, more ambiguous than it looked at first sight. Thus Michelet declared that German workers were in a ferment and that he had hopes they would join the action of the French workers, but that 'if unfortunately they refused to listen to us, there is still time to wage total war and this time we shall put all we have into it'. In short: peace, yes; defeatism, no.

In the evening another, secret, meeting held in the Trade Union Hall, rue de la Grange-aux-Belles, was attended by 600 delegates from munitions factories in the Paris region. Michelet, who appeared to have taken on their leadership, declared: 'The time has come to stop the butchery and carnage. We shall go on strike tomorrow morning at nine o'clock. . .'. It was decided that the strike movement would start with the Renault factory, and that the other war factories in the department of Seine would follow suit.

Next morning, 13 May, the delegates passed the word to the Renault workers, and *all the workshops* shut down. During the day, the movement spread to the Gouin factory, in avenue de Clichy in Paris, with 614 strikers out of 1,000 workers. In the suburbs, in addition to Renault (22,000 strikers out of a work force of 22,000), the strike affected: Hotchkiss (Saint-Denis), 900 strikers out of 1,360 workers; Delaunay-Belleville (Saint-Denis), 9,600 out of 9,600; Salmson (Billancourt), 6,500 out of 6,500; and Blum-Latil (Suresnes), 687 out of 1,092. The total number of strikers on the first day was 40,301.

By the following day the movement had snowballed. At 6:00 p.m., 105,131 strikers out of a work force of 127,773 employed in the fifty-three munitions factories in the Paris region had downed tools. Moteurs Le Rhône, Panhard-Levassor, in the XIIIth arrondissement, Citroën (10,497 strikers) and Thomson in the XVth, De Dion and Unic at Suresnes, Clément-Bayard at Levallois-Perret, Chenard and Walker at Gennevilliers, Voisin at Issy-les-Moulineaux, were brought to a complete halt.

The movement quickly adopted an unequivocal stance. Bénabent, one of the speakers, told 450 strikers in the Moteurs Le Rhône factory that the aims of the strikes were to protest against the call-up of three classes of reservists working in the factories, to force the government to proclaim their war aims and to persuade them to sign a peace. Another speaker said that the movement intended to force the government and the bosses to explain why they insisted on continuing hostilities and massacring the unfortunate men at the front. Enough blood had been shed and the proletariat was resolved to force the government to make peace.

The same kind of language was used at a meeting of 1,500 strikers at Delage in Courbevoie: the present strike, it was said, had not been called in support of wage increases, but to hasten the end of the war 'because we believe that the massacre of Frenchmen has gone on long enough'.

Three thousand strikers from metalwork factories in the Saint-Denis area crowded into a meeting to which their leaders had invited them, and many more were left outside. Bestelle, the delegate from the Hotchkiss factory, defined the movement's position, even if in doing so he sometimes failed to avoid self-contradiction:

> From now on you ought to know why you have downed tools, so that you can tell our rulers and so that you can shoulder your responsibilities as we have shouldered ours.
>
> It is already being said that we want to hamper the call-up of the young classes. This is not so! We have no selfish motives and I am sure that you would not wish to lower yourselves to such actions.
>
> Tomorrow, they will accuse you of being defeatists and of wanting to lead our country into the situation Russia is in today. No! We are not defeatists and there are no defeatists in French munitions factories.
>
> What we do want is to be told first of all by the government what their war aims and conditions for peace are; we want to know why and for whom our people are fighting, because we feel that enough blood has been shed and that it is now time to try every possible means to bring the carnage to an end.
>
> We are not among those who call for peace at any price; even less do we want a peace of conquest and annexations, let alone a German peace that would put us into the situation that unhappy Russia is in today.
>
> What we do want is a people's peace, and on that I am sure all of you agree. (Loud shouts of: Yes! Yes!)

The Allies would have to take their fair share of the sacrifices, the speaker continued, and there was no need for foreigners and Americans in particular to replace French workers in the factories. Already, he said, two million Frenchmen had been killed; there was no need to draft a further 100,000 from the factories and send them to the slaughterhouse.

That evening, delegates from all the munitions factories would be drawing up a list of claims for presentation to the government, the speaker declared, and he concluded: 'If you are all united, the movement will be a short one and our success will be assured, because the strike now extends to all the factories in the Paris region and it is almost certain to be general by tomorrow'.

Did this anti-war movement, enjoying so much working-class support, constitute the irresistible political force which many people believed, or at least claimed, it to be? In the event, it succumbed to its many inherent weaknesses.

The first of these was that the strikers underestimated their adversary and overestimated their own strength. Referring to his negotiations with Colonel Weyl, director of war production in the ministry of supply, and to the colonel's warning of what would happen if work was not resumed, the Renault delegate, Michelet, declared that 'the strike movement has already spread so far afield that those who are in it are not in the least afraid of whatever measures might be taken against them . . .'. The government, for its part, was not slow to reply. It had originally intended to publish a denunciation of the aims of the strikers, but then realised that, though this might work at home, it could also have untoward consequences abroad. They accordingly took the opposite course and imposed a total press blackout, hoping that a movement of which no one had heard would die a natural death. At the same time, while realising that this operation might backfire, the government prepared to arrest the strike leaders and to have them dispatched to army depots.

The second weakness of the strikers was their complete failure to coordinate their actions with those of the CGT, something of which the strike leaders were actually proud: 'What constitutes the strength of this movement is that it was not thought up by the trade union bosses, but was called into being by the struggling masses who endure all the sufferings of war'.

It was, in fact, one of the unusual aspects of these strikes that, if they took the authorities by surprise, they surprised the trade-union movement even more.

The minutes of the meeting of the executive committee of the Seine Association of Trade Unions held on 13 May, the day the strikes began, bear eloquent witness to this fact. Jules Bled, the secretary of the association, proposed to deal with two questions of the utmost importance: namely, the Federal Congress and the general strike which had just broken out in the metal industry.

During the discussion, several metalworkers asked for information. They failed to understand why the shop stewards should have declared a general strike over the heads of the unions at an altogether unfavourable moment.

Bled asked what attitude the association should adopt to the strikes. He felt that the association ought not to give them any support unless the unions themselves asked for it. The association could not respond to the appeal of the shop stewards who had called a general strike without informing the unions concerned and the Federation of Metalworkers in particular.

He deeply regretted that the shop stewards should have taken a step that threatened to have grave consequences. Moreover, they had exceeded their mandate and were going over the head of the unions. Now the workers were involved in a general strike simply because some unknown persons had decided, without consulting the proper channels, that the government should not have called up three classes. The speaker did not believe that the meeting could declare its solidarity with a movement of that type and felt that the association should not accept responsibility for it. He then asked for Veber's advice.

Paul Veber, one of the leaders of the Metalworkers' Federation, replied that it would be wrong to deal with the strike leaders without first consulting the trade unions involved and particularly the Metalworkers' Federation. The association could not accept responsibility in the matter. For his part, he had only just learned that a general strike had been declared. He had attended a shop stewards' meeting and had seen strike notices posted up all over the hall: 'General strike against the war.' The movement seemed to be led by one Michelet, a shop steward from Renault, who had been in the union for less than a year and spoke of trade unionists as a general speaks of his troops. When he was asked why he had declared a strike, he had read out the Clermont resolution and said, 'That's why!'

Two other trade union leaders then intervened: Renaud, to ask if it would not be best to disown the movement; and Jacoud, who said he was afraid that this strike might lead to a military dictatorship which would declare a state of siege in Paris.

It was decided to await the advice of the Metalworkers' Federation before deciding what attitude to adopt to the strike movement.

Two days later, on 15 May, the Seine Association of Trade Unions called a general committee meeting. Opinions were at first divided. A number of trade-union officials sympathised with the strike movement, and said that the call-up of the young classes had been 'the last straw'. Others remarked that, all in all, the strikers were merely implementing the resolutions of the previous federal congress in Clermont-Ferrand, and that their movement deserved full support.

A crucial intervention then came from Bourderon, a spokesman of the anti-war minority and one of the two CGT leaders (the other was Merrheim) to have attended the Zimmerwald Conference in 1915. He refused to support a movement that he described as being doomed to failure, a trap.

Jules Bled finally summed up the feeling of the meeting. Neither the majority nor the minority had wanted the strike and neither had done anything to encourage it. The Association of Trade Unions ought not to issue instructions in support of the current conflict: 'First, because the time is not right, and secondly, because anyone intending to put up effective resistance to the war must be prepared to take power. It must be recognised that for the moment the working class lacks the strength for that particular task'.

There was thus a clear split between the strikers and the trade unions, and this constituted the strike movement's second great weakness. The third and most fundamental weakness of the strikers was that they were not part of any mass movement.

The numbers for people out on strike were misleading: many enterprises preferred to close rather than continue production with a reduced or unreliable work force. Hence some of the strikers had in effect been locked out. Moreover, many workers had blindly followed the instructions of their shop stewards, a new-fangled office whose functions they did not always fully understand. Thus one observer noted that 'working-class circles were very surprised by the strikes and a number of strikers had no idea why they had been called out'.

What is certain is that the strikers were quickly being pulled in two directions: in some factories the strike was still spreading at a time when it had already started to crumble in others.

On 14 May, that was, *on the second day* of the strike, 7,000 of the 22,000 workers at Renault went back to work; at Delaunay-Belleville in Saint-Denis, 2,400 workers (out of a total work force of 9,600) signed a petition calling for a return to work. The authorities quickly realised that the strike was about to collapse at a number of companies unless militant workers managed to prevent a return to work by violent means. It had originally been the strikes at Renault which effectively forced the workers at Salmson to come out.

By 16 May, nearly 10,000 Renault workers, or almost 50 per cent of the work force, had returned. Most factories in Courbevoie, Suresnes, Puteaux and Levallois were working with 30 to 60 per cent of their full complement. By contrast, the strike showed little sign of abating elsewhere, for instance at Citroën, where the number of men returning to work was small.

On 17 May, the strike also started to fall apart at Issy-les-

Moulineaux and at Boulogne-Billancourt. At Renault, 15,000 were
now back at work. On 18 May, shop stewards representing the
180,000 workers in the munitions factories saw reason and voted to
end the strike. Work was back to normal everywhere on 21 May,
after the Whitsun holidays. General Dubail, military governor of
Paris, wrote to the commander-in-chief: 'In the area of the Paris
military government, the strikes in the national defence industry are
over'.

In fact, the shop stewards did not keep control of the movement
to the end but, quickly realising that they had taken on more than
they could handle, abdicated to the Metalworkers' Federation. Its
secretary, Alphonse Merrheim, then entered into active negotiations
with the authorities to prepare for a return to work. All in all, the
strike wave had collapsed within five days, and when the dejected
strikers returned to work after their pointless demonstration, they
were roundly abused by the non-strikers in a number of factories —
the very opposite to what usually happens.

The strike waves during the spring of 1918 in Paris, in Isère and in
Gard respectively had very similar characteristics. There is no doubt
that they reflected the anti-war feelings of a fairly large section of
the working class, but the course they took also reflected the
uncertainty of men who wanted peace but did not know how to
achieve it. This contradiction very quickly led to the strangulation
of the movement. The workers had come up against harsh reality: in
a country at war one cannot be a pacifist, at least if one does not
wish to confine oneself to mere words, without being a revolutionary as well and without being ready to face the ultimate consequence: the possibility of the defeat of one's own country if the
enemy is not also bent on peace. It would, in fact, seem that the
great majority of French workers were anything but defeatist.

Loire

This study of the attitude of French workers in 1918 would be
incomplete if we did not pay special attention to Loire, a department that witnessed some of the most important protest actions. At
the time, the Saint-Etienne coal basin was to some extent the centre,
the mainspring and the very model of the French labour and
anti-war movement.

The war had helped to turn the coal basin into a strategic region
of prime importance. According to General Gouze 'the fate of
France depended. . .on the output of the factories on the banks of

the Ondaine, the Furens and the Gier'.[9]

As Gérard Raffaelli[10] has shown, the population of the Loire department had doubled between 1911 and 1917 thanks to the huge influx of workers employed in the local defence establishments. In the Saint-Etienne arrondissement alone (see Table 12), 108,007 of these workers were employed in 825 factories, forty of which each employed more than 300 workers.

The very large number of companies must not, however, mislead us: most of the workers were employed in a few establishments only. Thus in Chambon-Feugerolles, 1,864 workers were employed at Claudinon; in Firminy, almost 10,000 in the iron and steel works; in Unieux, 3,833 at Holtzer; in Rive-de-Gien, although the concentration of workers was smallest, three factories employed more than 3,000 workers (Arbel-Brunon, Valette, Marrel); in Saint-Chamond more than 17,000 people worked in the naval iron and steel works. In Saint-Etienne, which had a tradition of small or fairly small firms, six factories employed more than 26,000 workers, Manufrance, the national munitions factory, accounting for 12,043, the Marais steelworks for 3,514 and Leflaive for 2,484.

To understand what follows, it is important to recall that the largest concentrations of workers were found at Firminy-Unieux and Saint-Chamond, where one or two firms employed almost the entire local work force.

The rather belated outbreak of unrest in the Saint-Etienne basin came on 27 November 1917. That Tuesday morning, Clovis Andrieu, a reservist working at the Holtzer metalworks in Unieux, was given orders by the local manpower control commission to rejoin his unit, the 86th Infantry Regiment in Puy (Haute-Loire).

Andrieu, who was forty at the time, a native of Picardy and a constructional ironworker by trade, had been a leading trade-union activist before the war, as secretary of the Federation of Iron Construction Workers in the Seine department, and a member moreover of the revolutionary wing of the trade-union movement renowned for the strength of its antimilitarist sentiments. He had been one of the first to be sentenced at the trial of the eighteen leaders of the CGT charged with illegal membership of the Sou de Soldat, a charity considered to be an antimilitaristic organisation.[11]

---

9. *Revue historique de l'armée*, 1963.
10. 'Les mouvements pacifistes dans les usines d'armement de la région de Saint-Etienne' in *Actes du 98ᵉ congrès national des sociétés savantes*, Saint-Etienne, 1973.
11. J. -J. Becker, *Le Carnet B*, Chapter I.

Table 12. *Workers and factories engaged on war work in the Saint-Etienne basin. (From G. Raffaelli: 'Les mouvements pacifistes dans les usines d'armements de la région de Saint-Etienne'.)*

Communes	No. of workers						No. of factories
	Reservists	*Civilians*	*Women*	*Children*	*Foreigners*	*Total*	
Chambon	2,887	1,184	1,127	293	36	5,527	64
Firminy	5,033	2,551	2,001	622	1,328	11,535	35
Caloire	1	—	—	2	—	3	1
Fraisse	18	9	—	3	—	30	1
Unieux	2,359	689	184	2	627	3,861	5
Rive-de-Gier	3,906	1,775	588	43	818	7,130	68
Grand-Croix	118	60	—	—	—	178	6
Lorette	219	96	11	—	6	332	6
Saint-Martin-La-P.	101	60	44	—	3	208	10
Saint-Paul-en-J.	15	68	118	—	—	201	4
Saint-Chamond	11,524	3,963	6,127	21	1,010	22,645	70
Doizieux	7	1	—	—	—	9	1
L'Horme	1,165	439	267	—	160	2,031	10
Izieux	82	52	3	—	—	137	5
Saint-Julien	363	149	153	—	3	670	19
Saint Martin-en-Coailleux	5	—	—	—	—	5	1
La Terrasse	2	4	20	—	—	26	1
La Valla	1					1	1
Saint-Etienne	17,953	13,681	15,898	1,682	2,664	51,978	491
L'Etrat	5	31	23	5	—	66	3
Prélussin	2	6	—	—	—	8	1
Planfoy	5	16	—	—	—	21	1
La Ricamarie	75	68	38	53	3	237	2
Roche-la-Mollière	6	4	2	—	—	12	1
Rochetaillée	13	12	25	3	—	53	2
Saint-Genest-Lerpt	12	5	7	4	—	28	1
Saint-Priest	1	4	3	—	—	8	1
La Talaudière	1	4	18	3	—	27	1
Terrenoire	270	356	303	50	—	979	11
Villars	11	26	13	11	—	61	2
Total	46,163	25,313	27,074	2,797	6,660	108,007	825

Condemned on 26 March 1914 to eight months' imprisonment and a fine of 100 francs, his appeal had not yet been heard when war was declared. He was called up to serve in the forces, but in 1915 he was redirected to a factory in the department of Loire where as a matter of course he became secretary of the metalworkers' union.[12] His redeployment, incidentally, makes it clear that, in their selection of essential workers, the military authorities completely ignored pre-war trade-union or political activities. On the other hand, Andrieu's activities in Loire quickly attracted the attention of the civil and military authorities in that department. Thus General Dantant recalled on 22 November 1917 how, on 11 June of the same year, he had asked that Andrieu be sent back to his army unit, because he was a 'trouble-maker' and his punishment would set 'a good example'. The general considered that Andrieu's speeches were revolutionary, pacifist and even defeatist: thus, at a meeting, Andrieu had called upon his audience to fight 'the real war', the 'war against the Bosses'! 'The workers', he had added, 'must not exhaust their strength for the benefit of those scoundrels who use their brothers in the trenches as cannon and machine-gun fodder. . . .'

The general was not, however, in favour of Andrieu's arrest and prosecution, because he feared that this would merely be inviting sympathetic action from 'working-class circles'.

In the event, the authorities preferred to move gingerly, though the future was to show they had not been cautious enough.

For some time past, tension had been rising in Loire[13] following wage demands and delays in applying a new wage scale. On 3 August, workers in the Laflaive factory protested against their employers' bad faith; on 5 August, 500 workers in the Roanne arsenal demanded the same wage scales as had been agreed in Paris; on 10 August, 220 skilled tradesmen at the Holtzer factory in Unieux, harangued by Andrieu, threatened to go on strike if they were not granted a wage rise; on 13 August, workers at Saint-Chamond set upon the manpower officer and demanded his replacement; at the end of August, there was a clash at Firminy when the management of the Verdié works proposed dismissing a worker called Noir, a member of the local metalworkers' union and a close associate of Andrieu. In the event, the military authorities reversed this decision since it seemed wholly unwarranted and also risked adding fuel to the flames.

In September and October there were many more skirmishes between employers and workers. The impression given is of a sort of guerrilla warfare while both sides took stock of each other, the military authorities only intervening when things threatened to get out of hand.

According to Emile Montoux, a former secretary of the elec-

---

12. Ibid., *1914. Comment les Français sont entrés dans la guerre*, p. 415.
13. This account of events in Loire is based on AN F 7 12994, 14607.

tricians' union and at the time secretary of the reservist workers' club in Firminy, a member of the majority faction and also one of Jouhaux's friends, the *marked discontent* in Firminy was not the result of 'extreme antipatriotism' but solely of industrial dissatisfaction. It was the direct result, he told Malvy, the minister of the interior, in July 1917, of the reluctance of the large metallurgical firms to apply the agreed wage scale, combined with the high cost of living, the appalling living conditions — because of the vast influx of workers, many of whom had been forced to move into lodging houses of the worst kind — and long delays by the authorities in remedying these complaints.

But was that really the whole story? On 12 August 1917, a congress of the Association of Trade Unions in Loire was held at Chambon-Feugerolles, in the presence of the leaders of the CGT minority faction — Merrheim and Dumoulin, the latter a reservist miner in Roche-le-Molière. That congress took the majority faction to task for its adherence to the *Union sacrée*, and hence for its betrayal of the working class. The congress also voted for peace negotiations as proposed by Soviet Russia.

Speeches at a number of meetings tended to show that wages were not the sole preoccupation and that pacifist ideas played at least some part in the unrest, though it is difficult to make an accurate assessment of their relative importance. In any case, the fact that the workers rallied to the defence of Andrieu, who had made no secret of his anti-militaristic sympathies, proved that such views were by no means exceptional.

Then, early on 27 November, Andrieu was ordered to rejoin his unit in Puy. The workers' immediate response was to call a mass meeting at 2.00 p.m. in the Firminy *bourse du travail*. The local police commissioner did not have enough men to stop them; indeed, he even had to wait for the result of a vote before being allowed to enter the building. The hall was packed, and Andrieu took his place on the platform among the other trade-union leaders. Speaker after speaker denounced the victimisation of Andrieu, the meeting then voting to prevent his departure. Thus, when Andrieu went to the railway station, his comrades carried him back to the *bourse du travail* in triumph. Even while he was still addressing the crowd to thank them, a strike committee was being organised. From the Holtzer factory in Unieux, where 4,000 workers – among them 3,000 reservists – downed tools, the movement spread to factories in Firminy and Chambon-Feugerolles that same day, even the town hall staff in Firminy deciding to join the strike.

On 28 November, at 6.30 in the morning, the strikers marched on the largest concern in Firminy, the Aciéries et Forges (the Verdié steel and iron works). The works manager, an unpopular man even according to the Firminy police commissioner, did nothing to reduce the tension. He merely protested to the local authorities and asked for protection. He also sent a telegram to the prime minister:

> I have the honour to inform you most respectfully that our factories employing seven to eight thousand workers have been besieged for the past twenty-four hours by anarchist and defeatist gangs with the declared intention of bringing the factories to a halt in order to force a peace.
>
> Our employees are being molested and assaulted. Three of our engineers have been badly hurt. More severe incidents feared. Loire prefecture kept informed hourly but takes no action. Compelled to shut down our factories and blast furnace. All ringleaders reservists from our area.

On the morning of 28 November, after 1,000 people had once again escorted Andrieu (who had decided to report to Puy) to the railway station, a meeting held in the *bourse du travail* agreed to demand a 50 per cent wage increase. Then a column of 5,000 strikers marched on Chambon-Feugerolles, before returning to Firminy at about noon, where they converged on the Verdié works. The Holtzer factory had been closed, but according to the police commissioner the Verdié management insisted on standing up to the strikers. As the day shift came off work at 6.15 in the evening there were serious incidents: some non-striking workers were attacked with sticks and stones. The police presence was too small to intervene.

On 29 November, the strike was almost complete in Chambon-Feugerolles, Unieux and Firminy — in other words, in the entire Ondaine valley. In response, the manager of Verdié threatened to close the works canteens, which fed more than 900 workers, a threat he had to revoke under pressure from Ernest Lafon, the socialist deputy and mayor of the town.

On Friday, 30 November, the strike spread to the metalworks in Saint-Etienne and in the Gier Valley (Saint-Chamond, Rive-de-Gier). In the Saint Etienne *bourse du travail*, 5,000 workers met and demanded Andrieu's reinstatement; another 3,000 to 4,000 working men and women from Saint-Chamond, L'Horme and Saint-Julien-en-Charrez responded to the appeal of the strike committee and assembled on the place de la Liberté at Saint-Chamond, where their leaders explained the objectives of the strike: the reinstatement of Andrieu, an immediate 50 per cent increase to offset the rising cost of living and the general introduction of fixed wage scales. According to estimates, some 25,000 workers had by then downed tools in and around Saint-Chamond. Four thousand people attended a large meeting on the place de la Mairie in Chambon-Feugerolles, and another 2,000 assembled on the Place du Breuil in Firminy.

There is no doubt that the movement had, by 30 November, taken on considerable proportions: the entire industrial region of Saint Etienne was affected, but apart from the serious incidents in Firminy, which the trade-union leaders condemned, peace more or less reigned. The Andrieu case, moreover, took second place as wage claims assumed greater importance.

Everything now seemed to hinge on the miners' support. On 30 November, Brioude, the president of the local miners' union in Firminy, asked his members not to interfere in what was happening, but the next day, 1 December, he received orders from the Miners' Federation to call a strike on Tuesday, 4 December, unless Andrieu had been brought back before that date.

Things were fairly quiet on 1 December: the strike had by now spread to most of Rive-de-Gier. In Saint-Etienne, the strikers concentrated their attention on the munitions factory, which was still working. At the same time, a delegation from the strike committee left for Roanne to persuade the workers in the munitions factory there to join the movement. In Saint-Chamond and Saint-Etienne thousands of people turned up to listen to Flageollet, the secretary of the departmental Association of Trade Unions.

The authorities also took stock of their forces: 130 gendarmes had arrived as reinforcements, 110 more were expected. Most of the soldiers at their command were men of the 1918 class still in training. As a precaution, the prefect asked that no soldiers be sent home on leave.

Though the government watched developments very closely, it acted with the utmost caution, no doubt believing that the situation would not become explosive if the authorities avoided an unnecessary confrontation. Moreover, when the general commanding the 13th Region proposed to 'protect the right to work' – that was, to take vigorous action so as to ensure that all who wanted to work (and he believed there were many) could do so without let or hindrance – Pams, the new minister of the interior, telegraphed 'with extreme urgency' that army reinforcements would reach Saint-Etienne that night, but that 'any steps which might tend to over-excite the people' and 'all surprise measures' should be avoided, and that the 'mood' of the soldiers who might be used to protect the right to work must be tested very carefully. 'It is essential,' the minister concluded, 'to impress on everyone the need for the utmost caution and for extreme moderation. [At] the present hour, all our efforts must be directed at the preservation of national unity.' In other words, the government did not wish to let it come to a test of strength at a time when the loyalty of their troops was not altogether assured.

The next day, 2 December, was a Sunday. The authorities tried to persuade the strikers to return to work: notices were posted up but immediately torn down, at least in Firminy, where the prefect also noted that they had no effect whatsoever. Strike meetings, by contrast, continued to draw large crowds. In Saint-Chamond, an audience of 2,000 heard Clemenceau being denounced as 'an enemy of the working class', and applauded a resolution defining the objectives of the strike movement: 'Comrades meeting on 2 December. . .agreed not to return to work unless Comrade Andrieu, assigned to the 86th Infantry Regiment, and falsely accused of defeatism, is reinstated in the factory where he belongs, and until the wage rises they have been demanding are met in full'.

At Saint-Etienne, 4,000 workers met at the *bourse du travail* and again resolved to close down the munitions factory. At 1.00 p.m. they had to admit failure: a large number of male workers in particular reported for work, more than the women, and absentees amounted to only 30 per cent. As a result, the end of the day shift was particularly rowdy, the strikers loudly booing the workers as they left.

Even so, Monday did not bring the general return to work for which the authorities had been hoping, the appeal by Loucheur, minister of labour, having fallen on deaf ears. If anything, the strike movement had hardened and spread. The presence of cavalry and gendarmes with orders to protect all those wishing to return to work had had 'negligible results', as the prefect noted. At the Aciéries et Forges in Firminy, the socialist deputy and mayor (whom the authorities suspected of supporting the strikers) was present to see 'just a few workers' pass through the factory gates. The munitions factory in Saint-Etienne, by contrast, kept working, the absentees on Monday morning accounting for only 10 per cent of the work force. A meeting in the *bourse du travail* that afternoon, attended by 7,000 strikers, decided to put an end to this 'scandal'. 'Violently over-excited', they moved in a body towards the factory from which, on orders from Paris, the workers who had ignored the strike order were quickly sent home to avoid trouble. The night shift, too, was later cancelled. Between 6.00 and 7.00 p.m. the situation at the approaches to the factory was extremely tense, and the crowds were tumultuous. 'Had the troops been sent in, there would surely have been a disaster,' the prefect's office told the minister of the interior by telephone.

The general commanding the region felt that the situation was fast deteriorating. The authorities no less than the strikers anticipated that, within the next few days, the strike wave would have spread to the miners at Creusot and Roanne. There was even talk of involving Lyon.

In the event, intensively active negotiations, of which few details are known, were being conducted between trade-union leaders and representatives of the ministry of supply. A new prefect, respected by trade unionists, was sent to Saint-Etienne. As for Andrieu, he was no longer at Puy but 'on leave' in Paris. Marius Blanchard, a secretary of the Metalworkers' Federation, was rushed to Saint-Etienne with proposals for a settlement. According to him, if the government really believed that Andrieu had committed an offence, they ought to have taken him to the joint commission set up to deal with cases of this type. That was clearly a considerable climb-down from the earlier unqualified demand for Andrieu's reinstatement. Similarly, the call for a 50 per cent wage increase was replaced with one for an increase of 50 centimes an hour, which came to a little less.

On 4 December the movement still appeared to be spreading, some of the workers in the Roanne arsenal joining the strike — not for very long, however, since the next day the strikers, threatened with being posted back to their army units, thought better of it and returned to work. The miners, too, had promised to join the movement, but as 4 December, St Barbara's Day, was traditionally a miners' holiday, they could not come out before the 5th.

By 5 December, as it happened, a compromise had almost been reached: as proposed, Andrieu was to appear before a commission set up by the minister of supply. If the charges were found to be false, he would be reinstated; as for the general wage claims, they would be raised by an amount to be negotiated as soon as work was resumed.

How was this compromise, which largely satisfied the workers' demands, received?

In different ways. At Saint-Chamond it was with something akin to a sense of triumph. To commemorate their brilliant victory, the strikers marched in procession through the streets of the town; they also declared a boycott of all shopkeepers who had opposed the strike and of the two Saint-Etienne dailies, *La Tribune* and *La Loire*, which were accused of having had 'not a single good word for the working class' during the six days of the strike. They finally decided to return to work *en bloc* on 6 December. And at that

precise moment, a procession of 8,000 day-shift workers entered the
naval steelworks led by delegates of an inter-union committee. At
the explosives factory, 1,500 workers did likewise.

At Saint-Etienne and Firminy, reactions were mixed. At Firminy,
in particular, some strikers continued to demand the unconditional
reinstatement of Andrieu. Work in the munitions factory was
resumed all the same, on the evening of 5 December. In other
enterprises work was resumed at 6.00 in the morning.

Thus the strike which had begun on 27 November was over by 6
December: it had lasted ten days, and a few days later the strikers'
success was complete when Andrieu, cleared of all charges, resumed
his place in the Holtzer factory and as leader of the militant workers
in the Saint-Etienne region.

A working-class victory, then, but an ambiguous one, or that was
how some people saw it. For almost immediately after the settlement the prefecture heard rumours that the strike was about to be
resumed because the mass of the workers was dissatisfied with a
compromise they believed had been foisted on the union leadership.
Had they therefore been pressing wage claims as a front for more
revolutionary ambitions?

According to *L'Humanité* of 9 December 1917, the workers had
only gone on strike because their trade-union rights had been
attacked, and they had done so 'despite qualms about deserting the
cause of national defence for even one moment'. This was also the
view of the socialist deputy, Pierre Laval, who on 8 March 1918
inveighed bitterly in a column in the very short-lived paper, *Oui*,
against those who thought they could teach the workers of Loire a
lesson in patriotism. All the workers had done was to protest
against 'an arbitrary and completely unjustified measure'. This
claim calls for several comments.

To begin with, the strike movement had enjoyed massive and
resolute support from the metalworkers, whose meetings had attracted vast crowds. The strikers had clearly been determined to
make their strike effective. Thus, when gendarmes and policemen
tried to post the appeal of Minister Loucheur at Firminy, they were
relieved of their gluepots and the commissioner had to order them
to beat a retreat to the jeers of thousands of workers. If, in the end,
there had been no really serious incidents, it was more thanks to the
conciliatory attitude and skill of the government (not of the employers, some of whom were clearly spoiling for a fight) than to the
apparent calm of the workers.

Secondly, the strike leaders had great difficulty in winning over
other unions, the miners only joining late in the day, and then

somewhat grudgingly.

Finally, the strike leaders had carefully avoided revolutionary appeals, if only for tactical reasons. It is true that the police commissioner of Firminy, in a general report published after the end of the strike, contended that 'speeches at meetings gave off a large whiff of sedition inspired by the Russian Revolution'. One speaker had exclaimed: 'If only we had a Lenin!' At Roanne, on 6 December, a delegate from Saint-Etienne regretted that the unions in general had not made common cause with the movement, because, he said, it could have been turned into a general strike, and that would have meant the end of the war. Berthet, the secretary of the steelworkers' union, after expressing his regret that the workers had not used their strength to stop the dreadful nightmare, had gone on to say that 'a new era is about to arise from the war: the working-class revolution will pave the way for the social revolution'. However — and this was the opinion of most observers on the spot — the mass of workers did not seem to follow their leaders: in spite of what *L'Humanité* said, they were ready to stand up in defence of their rights and interests without bothering too much about the effects on the national defence effort, but that was as far as they were willing to go. This was probably why their, doubtless more radical, leaders did not try to convert the strike movement into a revolutionary one and accepted a compromise. However, the authorities, who had no illusions about, for instance, Andrieu's true attitude, gained no particular reassurance from this climb-down: they knew that they were on shaky ground and realised that, unless they used the most extreme prudence, yet more fuel would be added to the flame.

Would this subtle game between the authorities, the revolutionary workers' leaders and the wavering masses be continued into the next year?

By the beginning of 1918, the atmosphere in the department had changed radically. Until then, the labour movement had been hesitant in pressing political demands, at least in public, but now they were afraid no longer. The strength of the movement in November 1917, the re-instatement of Clovis Andrieu and the conciliatory, or at least circumspect, response of the authorities had given a great boost to the anti-war current.

Two bodies shared its leadership: first, the executive committee of the Association of Trade Unions in Loire, which was in the hands of the minority of the CGT with Charles-Eugène Flageollet, a thirty-five-year-old papermaker of anarchist views at its head; and second, the Loire Inter-Union Committee, which included twelve metal and building unions, represented approximately 20,000 members, and considered itself the main instigator of the 1917 strikes. Its secretary, Jules Spriet, was a reservist metalworker employed at the Leflaive works in Saint-Etienne.

The Firminy *bourse du travail* seems to have been the linchpin of the whole movement and Andrieu played a leading role in it. It was on his initiative that the Association of Trade Unions and the Inter-Union Committee had been invited to suggest ways of putting an end to the war. To begin with, on 13 January they each elected three delegates with instructions to go to Paris and to contact the Trade Union Defence Committee, the Metalworkers' Federation and the Building Workers' Federation in Paris for the express purpose of launching an anti-war movement. The revolutionaries in Loire were, in fact, convinced that though they could initiate the movement, it would fail unless it could be extended to other parts of the country.

At the local level, they organised a large number of protest meetings and initiatives aimed at preventing the departure of soldiers of the most recent classes or of men recalled from the factories. Such measures had little success in Saint-Chamond, but they led to serious incidents in Saint-Etienne. On 28 January, when a detachment of conscripts was due to leave the barracks for the railway station, a large crowd of demonstrators, mostly women and young girls, gathered in front of the barracks shouting, 'Down with the war, long live peace!' Cajoled by them, if indeed they needed cajoling, a number of soldiers abandoned the march to the station and, singing the 'Internationale', repaired to the *bourse du travail* instead. And while seventy-one men boarded the train, the rest listened to the 'harangues' of the workers' leaders, including Andrieu. Once the demonstration was over, most of these soldiers returned to barracks and in fact entrained several days later. However, in all the stations through which their train passed, they sang the 'Internationale', shouted seditious slogans, and were noted for their 'unruliness' and their 'scandalous' behaviour, as the prefect's report put it.

Countless meetings were held, and though a speaking tour by Merrheim in Loire from 19 to 21 January caused some anxiety, the prefect had to concede that 'his language was not of a revolutionary or pacifist nature' — which was hardly surprising, since the leader of the metal-workers was about to break with the Trade Union Defence Committee. Violent language was confined to local militants. 'All now work in the open', the prefect stated in a report of 4 February. In contrast to what had been taking place a few weeks earlier, the movement's leaders were no longer ahead of their troops, or at least only of some of them: during a general meeting of the metalworkers' union attended by 1,000 people at the Saint-Etienne *bourse du travail*, a speaker wanting to discuss wages was shouted down amid protests that the true crux of the matter was to stop the war at the earliest possible moment.

On 25 January, Flageollet, haranguing strikers in Saint-Julien-Molin-Molette, told them that a general strike would be declared in the near future. He went on to call for revolution as the only means of stopping the war; the French workers had to act like the Russians and 'slaughter half the millionaires'.

On the same day in Firminy, before 2,000 or 6,000 people, depending on sources, a meeting of metalworkers, ostensibly called to discuss trade-union business, turned into an anti-war, indeed virtually a defeatist, rally:

> Comrades, the question of wages is of little importance; it is the war which matters most.
> All that is needed to stop it is for the *poilus* at the front to make common cause with you. To that end they need do only one thing: throw down their arms and quit the front.
> Comrades, I tell you, enough blood has been shed, enough people killed. I end with the cry: 'Long live Peace, down with War'.

When the meeting ended, a procession was formed that marched, singing the 'Internationale', through the streets of Firminy.

From that time on, at least one or two meetings were held almost every day in various towns in the coal basin. A (probably incomplete) calendar reads as follows:

27 January: meeting in Rive-de-Gier called by the metalworkers' union. The audience of 400 left the hall to shouts of 'Long live syndicalism, long live peace!'

29 January: meeting in Saint-Etienne of the executive committee of the Association of Trade Unions. A full programme of meetings and demonstrations is drawn up, and links with other unions and unions in neighbouring departments are discussed.

31 January: meeting in Firminy at the *bourse du travail* attended by 5,000 people. Chambon-Feugerolles: 1,200 metalworkers pass a resolution castigating 'the pointlessness of wage increases which merely serve to prolong the scourge of war' and send a message to congratulate Russia on her fine example, and to Lenin and Trotsky for having made the Russian people realise that the time had come 'to get rid of the reactionaries'.

1 February: Andrieu addresses 1,500 people in Firminy. 'In Austria-Hungary, the people have risen and called for peace. In Germany, the workers have followed their example. It is our turn, comrades, the hour has come for us to copy the German and Austrian workers', the speaker declared.

2 February: meeting in the Saint-Etienne *bourse du travail* attended by 7,000 workers, according to the Inter-Union Committee, and by 3,000 to 3,500, according to the prefecture. At the end of the meeting a procession marches on to the prefecture, singing the 'Internationale'.

3 February: inter-union meeting at Saint-Chamond attended by 750 people. Redzon, a trade-union leader from the naval steelworks, praises the attempts made to prevent young soldiers from leaving for the front, 'a libertarian action that has struck fear into the civil and military authorities'. Flageollet advises his comrades to 'prepare to take to the streets in the very near future'.

11 February: meeting of the Inter-Union Committee in Saint-Etienne attended by 5,000 to 6,000 people (main speaker: Merrheim).

15 February: meeting in Firminy of the metalworkers' union addressed by Andrieu with 5,000 persons present.

Meanwhile attention had shifted to Roanne, where there had been a number of serious incidents. On 4 February, Andrieu had gone to Roanne to challenge Albert Thomas at a public meeting. That same day, 250 young metalworkers, drafted into the army as part of the call-up of the latest classes, had left Roanne singing the 'Internationale' and shouting, 'Long live the Revolution!' A day later, on 5 February, things threatened to get out of hand following demonstrations protesting about the temporary bread shortage. At 3.00 p.m. workers in the Raffin cloth mill downed tools, other factories followed suit and a crowd of 3,000 persons quickly gathered, shouting, 'We want bread, down with the war!' The demonstrators moved first to the town hall, then to the sub-prefecture, and finally to the *bourse du travail*. Swollen by workers from the arsenal, the demonstration became increasingly violent. Shouting 'Down with the war, we want bread, give us our men or give us bread', singing 'La Carmagnole' and the 'Internationale', they smashed the windows of trams and of a café, then suddenly converged on the home of a leading Roanne cotton-goods manufacturer, Monsieur Brechard. They broke down his front door, ransacked his house and then set it on fire. By the time the gendarmes arrived, the place had been gutted.

Next morning, groups of 300 or 400 people rushed through the streets, singing the 'Internationale' and looting shops. The police and infantrymen managed to keep them out of the arsenal.

Following negotiations between Dugelay, secretary of the textile workers' union, and the mayor of Roanne, a series of steps was taken to ensure regular bread supplies and the gendarmerie patrols were withdrawn.

Trade-union delegates met in the afternoon at the *bourse du travail*. Apparently taken aback by the violence of the movement, they decided to call off the strike, but when they communicated their decision to a meeting held soon afterwards, not even the fact that Flageollet endorsed it stopped part of the audience from rounding on them with shouts of: 'What about the war?' Work was resumed all the same, though disturbances continued into the next morning.

The sub-prefect, reviewing events, blamed the mayor for failing to ensure the regular provisioning of the town, and especially of the workers' cooperative, on which most of the workers relied for supplies. He thought nevertheless that the shortages had merely served as a pretext: 'What the factory workers really wanted was to demonstrate against the war'; and he thought that without an adequate police force the town hall or the sub-prefecture would be the next to go up in flames.

The wave of unrest had obviously spread from the Saint-Etienne coal basin to all other industrial centres in Loire. Nor did its leaders intend to confine their action to that department. On 8 February, two leading militants, Dardet and Bonnefond, addressed a meeting at Alais, in Gard; that same day, Andrieu spoke at Bourges and two other activists at Lyon.

Despite the transport problems they must have faced, these leaders seem to have been ubiquitous. This raises a puzzling question: how was it possible that Andrieu, for example, a worker employed at the Holtzer works, and moreover a reservist, should have been able to travel so often and so far afield? That question was indeed raised in high places — on 22 February the prime minister asked the prefect to let him know the exact number of hours worked by the 'above-named' Andrieu since 1 January and why and by whom each of his absences from work had been authorised. The regional commissioner in Saint-Etienne was forced to reply lamely that, as far as he knew, 'the reservist Andrieu has worked just one full day since 1 February'.

The answer shows clearly that the departmental authorities were out of their depth and unable to cope with a movement they had decided not to ban in December 1917. Numerous reports reflected their great anxiety. Here is what the special commissioner for Saint-Etienne wrote on 4 February:

> At this moment a strike movement, or more precisely a revolutionary movement, is being launched in our region, and particularly in the Ondaine Valley, . . . The leaders cannot keep abreast of developments and are no longer in control of their men. . . . According to the labour organisations, the movement is likely to involve a million workers, especially in Loire, Haute-Loire, Rhône, Montluçon, Bourges, Dijon and Paris. Its chief supporters are metalworkers, textile workers and glass workers.
>
> No date has yet been set, but the least incident can put a spark to the powder keg. . . .
>
> At the moment the trade-union leaders are travelling from one place to the next for the sole purpose of rallying waverers and cementing the unity of workers' organisations.
>
> It is generally believed that as soon as this strike wave starts, demonstrators will sabotage telegraph and telephone communications and attempt a march on the prefecture. . . .

That same day, the regional police commissioner reported that a general strike was being prepared quite openly: it was due to begin in Saint-Etienne on the orders of the Trade Union Defence Committee, possibly following 'the call-up of new classes of conscripts '. 'I believe that the situation is extremely serious, and that precautionary steps should be taken immediately.'

In a report running to more than ten pages, the prefect put forward his own views in greater detail: though he did not think that the working masses in his department had really been won over to the anti-war camp, the 'pacifists' might, by 'launching a conflict ostensibly based on industrial claims', succeed in 'infecting almost the entire working class'. He admitted that the December strikes 'called in defence of trade-union freedom' had been run in all factories with 'an impressive show of discipline'. He feared that the majority of the *more timid* workers would be dragged in by the active minority. However, the revolutionaries had been unable to weaken the patriotic resolve of the miners, which gave 'some comfort to the authorities'.

Another important factor was the Russian Revolution, which had 'over-excited the hopes' of local revolutionaries 'who had been filled with admiration for the exploits of the Bolsheviks'. One of their Firminy groups even proposed calling itself a 'soviet'. All in all, the prefect anticipated a 'serious crisis' in the near future. And he added:

In these circumstances, there are two alternatives: to be as conciliatory as possible and to close one's eyes within reasonable limits to the excesses of language, the provocations and the appeals, in short, to give the movement its head and so avoid any clashes until the end of the war, while, of course, ensuring the maintenance of public order and of personal liberty; or else to repress, if necessary by force, the outrages committed every day by antipatriots, at the risk of provoking, if not an uprising, at least a general strike, with all the turmoil that would entail. I have so far shown the greatest moderation, believing that I am acting in accordance with your wishes, but it is clear that there may come a time when further tolerance would mean the abdication of all authority.

The prefect went on to appeal for police and army reinforcements: 'At present, I have a total of 350 gendarmes and 3 cavalry squadrons garrisoned at Saint-Etienne. Should disturbances break out simultaneously in Saint-Etienne and Roanne, I should find myself unable to contain them, even to the most limited extent'.

Next day, he sent a new, even more alarmist, report: he had reason to believe that the mob was aware of his weak position, and that the moderate element in the trade-union movement was increasingly being outflanked and cowed by the extremists. He accordingly asked for the urgent dispatch of another 2,000 cavalrymen to protect public buildings, and for political countermeasures: the strike movement must be defused by a government declaration of war aims and by giving workers' organisations permission to attend an international conference.

On 12 February, the general commanding the region revealed that he had 'hard information' that an insurrectional movement was about to break out. At this point, abruptly, the tone of the reports changed: a *détente* had been reached; the danger of revolution was receding.

How can we explain this complete about-turn? One answer may be that there had never been a real threat, that the authorities, for reasons best known to themselves, had merely played at being alarmed. However, even though an exaggerated alarmist note was struck by some — policemen set on repression often tend to exaggerate dangers as a means of exerting greater pressure on the political authorities — this explanation does not hold water. It is undeniable that revolutionary workers, though reservists, delivered very many 'subversive' speeches before large crowds; that noisy processions had marched through the streets singing the 'Internationale'; that a 'pre-revolutionary' climate had prevailed in a number of working-class areas in Loire and that there had been 'massive support' for possible revolutionary action.

An alternative explanation is that the arrival of troops in great numbers had helped to dampen revolutionary ardour. This explanation, too, is not very satisfactory. The revolutionaries had good reason to think that they would not be opposed by a show of force, and in any case, far from beating a hasty retreat, they would have tried to win over the troops, the more so as their 'reliability' was open to doubt.

The real explanation, it would seem, must be sought within the workers' movement itself: the leaders were forced to restrain the rank and file even while urging them on, for fear that the masses might rise up before the time was ripe. It is clear that Andrieu, for instance, was forced to play for time on several occasions, to the point where some of his keenest supporters sometimes misunderstood him. Thus at Firminy on 31 January he was called 'turncoat, traitor, coward', and he needed all his wits to prevent a strike planned for the next day. This 'state of nerves' was, indeed, diagnosed by Merrheim, who, during his last visit to the region, exclaimed in surprise: 'You people really have got worked up!'

But the workers' leaders in Loire knew perfectly well that even if they were ready, other departments were not, and that it was therefore essential to lie low for another one or two months. In particular, they felt that the movement was making headway in the Paris region. This belief was probably wrong: an enquiry made at that moment in Parisian working-class circles showed that, though there was an undeniable desire for peace, only a small fraction was ready to hasten it by insurrection.

Again, it was not clear whether or for what the masses were ready, even in Loire. Tension was, of course, high among the metalworkers, but, as we know, the miners did not follow their lead. The same reluctance was shown by the building workers, whose union secretary, Lorduron, an active pacifist, deplored his members' lack of eagerness to come out.

Moreover, even the unity of the metalworkers was less solid than appeared. Their leaders were divided, some advising revolutionary and insurrectional actions, while others did no more than indulge in revolutionary speeches. The crisis came into the open on 26 February 1918, when the secretary of the metalworkers' union, Jean-Baptiste Barlet, resigned following attacks by Flageollet and Bonnefond: he had refused to go beyond industrial action. As early as December he had voiced strong objections to the idea of turning the strike movement into a revolutionary one, and he had called for a return to work. 'When young metalworkers were due to join the forces, some people tried to incite the workers to rise up in arms. I did not want that,' he declared, and added: 'Had any of you decided to take to the streets, I should have stopped the workers from following you'.

Even the attitude of the leading extremists had not been entirely unequivocal. Thus Andrieu had denied being a defeatist, and had violently refuted the accusation that he was in the 'pay of the Boche'. Even the words he had used were revealing, for he explained that when he called for peace he did not mean 'that the Germans should retain Belgium, the north of France, Serbia, Montenegro and Rumania'. It was a point which summed up the workers' dilemma in a nutshell: how was it possible to call for immediate peace without accepting that the Germans would hold on to conquests that they had never shown the least intention of relinquishing? At that very moment, Lenin had been forced to cede to the Germans all the vast territories to which they had laid claim.

Would the *détente* reached at the end of February 1918 continue, or would there be a fresh wave of revolutionary activity? According to police informers, the workers in Saint-Etienne had had 'second thoughts' and no longer rounded on those of their leaders who preferred talk about wages to calls for peace. The informers mentioned two causes: indignation with the Bolsheviks for being prepared to accept a 'German' instead of insisting on a 'people's' peace, and an espionage affair that had just been uncovered in Saint-Etienne, or that the authorities had just made public, dropping hints that the culprits had been the very men who instigated the strike wave in November–December 1917.

The workers' leaders in Saint-Etienne did, indeed, have to go to great lengths to clear themselves of the charge that they were more or less in the pay of Germany, and to reiterate that they were 'pacifists', not 'defeatists'. In order to quash all such ugly rumours, the Departmental Association of Trade Unions and the Inter-Union Committee put up large posters advertising public meetings, which were, in the event, very poorly attended, so poorly, in fact, that Andrieu complained about 'speaking to empty seats'. The working-class base of the anti-war movement seemed to have collapsed. The prefect, who had formerly been so deeply perturbed, was able to express his great relief.

The calm was, however, of short duration: the militants had little difficulty in refuting the charges against them — they had, in fact, had no connection with the alleged spies. In March they prepared to recapture lost territory and to regain control over their troops: they

made preparations for a departmental congress of trade unions in
Loire; for an interdepartmental congress one day later; and for a
propaganda tour of Lyon, Clermont-Ferrand, Vienne, Dijon,
Montluçon, Bourges, Valence and Nîmes. Once again the general
commanding the region displayed his anxiety, even though the
indefatigable leader of the radicals seemed this time to be no longer
Andrieu, but Charles Flageollet. It was rumoured that Andrieu was
sick or that he preferred to lie low for tactical reasons — in view of
the arrival of army reinforcements, it might have been preferable for
him to keep out of the limelight and to re-emerge promptly when
required.

In fact, however, the new revolutionary impetus was blunted
from the outset. Many workers' organisations wanted no truck with
pacifism, as, for instance, the Roanne section of the railway workers' union demonstrated when they refused to attend the interdepartmental congress called in Saint-Etienne for 25 March 1918. Nor
was there unanimity among the eighty delegates from eleven departments who agreed to attend: from Loire, of course, but also Rhône,
Saône-et-Loire, Gard, Bouches-du-Rhône, Isère, Drôme, Cher,
Puy-de-Dôme, Nièvre, and Gironde. The national leaders of the
anti-war wing were present, among them Merrheim, now a moderating influence, and Hubert, the ebullient secretary of the Paris
union of *terrassiers*, deputising for Péricat, who had stayed in Paris.
Two currents made themselves felt at the meeting: while some
called for strikes as an overture to full revolution, others were far
more temperate in their demands. Merrheim was the spokesman for
the second group. According to the police in Saint-Etienne, who
managed to get detailed reports of these meetings, his attitude
reflected the conviction that the working class, and Paris metalworkers in particular, had changed their minds following the bombardment of Paris by long-range German artillery. As a result, the
movement could no longer count on support from more than
30,000 metalworkers out of a total of 300,000 in the Paris region.

This division was highlighted by two conflicting motions before
the congress. At first sight, the main bone of contention seemed to
be the date on which the next wave of strikes was to begin.
Merrheim proposed to hold the CGT congress on May Day, a day
on which all workers would be asked to down tools. His adversaries, led by Andrieu, wanted the congress of the CGT to meet on
21 April at the latest and insisted that if the CGT refused to call it,
the Trade Union Defence Committee should organise the meeting
instead and that, on May Day, all leaders should return to their
departments to take personal charge of the strike. What was the

difference? If Merrheim had his way, the strikers would be downing tools for just one day, while their leaders met in congress; if Andrieu's view prevailed and if circumstances were favourable, May Day would see the beginning of a widespread revolutionary movement. In the end, Andrieu's motion was carried, but only by 35 votes to 19, many of the delegates having left by the time the vote was taken. Thus even in the department that had rallied behind Andrieu, the movement lacked a cutting edge. Hubert stayed on to address a meeting at Saint-Chamond which was attended by only 550 people.

Flageollet, secretary of the Loire Association of Trade Unions, was nevertheless sure that if only Loire set the example, the rest of France was bound to follow. As it turned out, revolutionaries in his department became increasingly isolated.

Thus when Merrheim, as instructed, asked the federal bureau of the CGT to endorse Andrieu's motion, Léon Jouhaux countered that it was inopportune to call a congress at a time when decisive battles were being fought on the Somme. It may be recalled that the Germans had launched a major offensive in Picardy on 26 March, that the British line had collapsed and that, in order to repair an extremely grave situation, the higher coordination of the Anglo-French forces was entrusted to Foch at just about the time that the federal bureau of the CGT met.

In these circumstances, even Péricat was in favour of playing for time, and of simply asking the Trade Union Defence Committee to hold a congress at Saint-Etienne on 19 and 20 May. In a letter addressed to Flageollet, he insisted that the peace demonstrations on May Day must in no circumstance extend beyond twenty-four hours. This view infuriated Flageollet, who objected to the timidity of the Defence Committee. It also elicited a strong protest from Andrieu, who could not understand why the Defence Committee should bother about 'frontier fluctuations', a euphemism for the latest German offensives. In the circumstances, the workers in Loire would have no alternative but to launch out on their own, he concluded. 'Morale excellent, the troops are fresh.' However, even in Loire, there was some wavering: at a meeting of the general committee of the Departmental Association of Trade Unions held on 15 April, supporters and opponents of a May Day demonstration clashed and the final decision had to be postponed for lack of participants at the meeting.

The prefect was worried all the same. He was particularly afraid that 'pressure' by Flageollet and Andrieu would strengthen the 'defeatist' wing, and he thought that the police and other reinforcements which had stayed on after the last alert were inadequate. His renewed request for reinforcements bears the word 'Approved' pencilled in the margin, clear evidence that the ministry of the interior shared his anxiety.

In the event, the revolutionaries in Loire were forced to fall in with the wishes of the Defence Committee. At a meeting, Andrieu enjoined his audience to further patience, adding that 'Loire will do its duty and press the government to start peace negotiations', even if the CGT or the Defence Committee did not go along with this policy. On May Day there would be just 'one day's stoppage of work', supported by meetings held the day before and the publication of a special issue of the *Syndicalist*. Worse still for the more radical wing, the *bourse du travail* in Saint-Etienne proved very cool towards the 'activism' of the departmental association, its secretary, a teacher by the name of Reynard, expressing strong opposition to any strike whatever on May Day and certainly to any street demonstrations. Even so the minority faction was able to register a resounding success on the eve of May Day: it managed to seize control of the union branch in the Roanne arsenal, until then in the hands of the moderates. An active member of the metalworkers' union in Firminy, Héro, who had been sent to Roanne for that very purpose, was appointed secretary of the union branch.

May Day, when it finally came, did not have the effect which some had hoped for and the authorities had feared. The response was uneven. At Saint-Etienne, it was impressive: 30,000 strikers, large attendances at all meetings, a street demonstration followed by a clash with the police, a charge by dragoons and the arrest of four demonstrators whom the prefect subsequently thought it best to release. There was also a strong response in Firminy and Chambon-Feugerolles, and though there was general calm in Roanne, the entire textile industry, all dyers, some building workers, and some 250 workers from the arsenal — a total of 5,000 workers — went on strike. By contrast, the movement was not very successful in Saint-Chamond and Rive-de-Gier. Summing it all up, Henri Raidzon, a revolutionary activist from Saint-Chamond, had this to say about May Day in Loire: 'I cannot tell what will happen tomorrow, but we have seen that there is a healthy and vigorous hardcore of activists . . .'.

May Day had thus failed to give the revolutionary signal some had expected, though it was to bring a marked rise in tension in Loire. Following an accident during the 'stoppage' on May Day, the management of the Aciéries et Forges in Firminy decided to suspend eleven workers, which meant that some of them were being sent back to their units, a measure taken against the advice of the military authorities who feared that the workers might retaliate in much the same way as they had at the end of 1917. Nor was the response slow in coming: Andrieu threatened a general strike in Loire if the suspended workers were sent to the front, and gave the authorities eight days to have them reinstated. The protest movement spread quickly in the Saint-Etienne region, accelerated by the fact that other reasons for popular anger existed: the call-up of metalworkers of the classes of 1910, 1911 and 1912, and a number of industrial claims, which the special commissioner for Saint-Etienne admitted demanded urgent attention if the movement were to be defused.

The revolutionary leaders, feeling that the time was appropriate, pressed home their advantage. The Inter-Union Committee planned to meet on 15 May and to declare a general strike the next day.

The authorities, for their part, prepared for confrontation: Commissioner Oudaille was specially sent from Paris to Saint-Etienne to take charge of the forces of law and order: according to him, though the trade unionists were wavering, the authorities must, if necessary, intervene 'with the utmost vigour'. Reinforcements had been sent to the department, and especially to Firminy: 210 gendarmes, six squadrons of cavalry drafted in from a long way away, and three infantry battalions.

Trade unionists in Saint-Etienne had held back in order to coordinate their action with that in other regions. The prefect therefore felt that nothing would happen before the meeting of the Trade Union Defence Committee due to be held in Saint-Etienne on 19 and 20 May, and certainly not before the return of a delegate who had gone to Paris on 17 May to consult Péricat. He was quickly proved wrong: in the course of the night of 17-18 May, the first strike notices were posted on the walls of Chambon. During the morning about 800 workers in two firms downed tools. At Firminy, where, it seems, the posters had not arrived in time, work nevertheless stopped on Andrieu's direct orders. By contrast, there were no stoppages in Saint-Etienne, Saint-Chamond or Rive-de-Gier.

Once again, Firminy and Le Chambon had given the signal, had precipitated the action. Why? The most likely explanation is that Andrieu and his comrades wanted to force the hand of the congress due to meet in Saint-Etienne: Péricat's recent reservations gave them grounds for fearing that the congress would show little enthusiasm for a general strike. Moreover, as strikes had already broken out in the Paris metal industry, they felt there was no need to wait.

Whether or not this explanation is correct, the Trade Union Defence Committee gave orders for a strike, and after some delay the rest of Loire followed Firminy's lead.

On 21 May the situation was as follows. Nearly complete stoppages in Firminy, Unieux, Le Chambon, La Ricamarie; part stoppages only in Saint-Etienne — 5,000 workers out of 45,000 had come out and only the steelworks were really involved. In Rive-de-Gier 60 per cent of the labour force reported for work, in Saint-Chamond the strike had not yet started. In Roanne, 6,000 workers ultimately downed tools in the textile mills and the arsenal, the strike movement also spreading during the day to all engineering and metallurgical factories.

The strikers were peaceful on the whole, except at Firminy, where they violently set about some of the office staff in the Verdié factories: one disabled ex-serviceman was hurt. A troop of cavalry summoned to the rescue was assaulted by the strikers, and the troopers, all of them young recruits, were scarcely able to mount their horses! The lieutenant-colonel in charge of the sector was manhandled. The authorities thought it best not to protect the 'freedom to work' at Firminy, the more so as there seemed to be hardly anybody with any real desire to use that freedom. For all that, the forces of law and order were more in evidence and more active than they had been in December: at Saint-Chamond, particularly, the streets were scoured by patrolling gendarmes and dragoons before any trouble started, and all the cafés were shut.

As the strike spread, so the number of meetings redoubled, all attended by large crowds. The strikers' objectives were embodied in a number of resolutions. At Chambon-Feugerolles, 3,000 workers, meeting at the Maison du Peuple, declared that they were resolved more than ever not to return to work until the government decided to sign a truce. A meeting at Saint-Etienne resolved that 'a return to work will only take place on condition that the government agrees to sign an immediate truce, to publish its peace conditions and to start peace negotiations'. Greetings were sent to the Russian revolutionaries and to imprisoned militants.

Many similar resolutions were passed throughout the department. The objectives of the movement were thus perfectly clear: *this was to be a strike for peace*, to last until it was achieved. The movement, moreover, was running before the wind. On 22 May, the general commanding the region wrote a pessimistic report:

The situation is far from showing any improvement at Firminy, Unieux and Chambon-Feugerolles, where work is at a complete standstill and

Andrieu has proclaimed himself top dog; the strike seems to be becoming general in Rive-de-Gier, and to be spreading to Saint-Chamond and Saint-Etienne, where an active propaganda campaign is being waged by strikers going around the factories, large and small . . .'.

At strike meetings, the speakers used revolutionary phrases and even called openly for insurrection, a call that was not, however, translated into immediate direct action. It was understandable, in the circumstances, that the arrival in Saint-Etienne on 22 May of Marius Blanchard, a delegate from the CGT, was not welcomed by the revolutionaries. He was the secretary of the Metalworkers' Federation and he had come for the express purpose of persuading the strikers to accept a compromise solution before things got out of hand. For two hours, from seven to nine o'clock in the evening, he was prevented from leaving the *bourse du travail* by a jeering crowd of 2,000, his eventual exit proving lively, despite the escort provided by a number of militants.

For Andrieu and his comrades there could be no compromise: the spread of the strike to the whole of France was essential; meanwhile 'vigilance committees' were set up to ensure that everyone kept away from the factories. There was one snag: some strikers had already returned to work in the Paris region. Andrieu, however, brushed this aside; the strikers would soon change their minds, he declared with conviction. It was announced to an enthusiastic crowd meeting in Roanne on 21 May that troops had been fraternising with strikers.

The crucial day was probably to be 23 May, when the workers recalled to the army were due to leave. What happened at that point was likely to be of some importance.

Early that morning, a crowd of demonstrators marched on the station, where the classes of 1911, 1912 and 1913 were preparing to leave for Valence. Groups of women among the demonstrators were particularly militant, attempting to grab the recruits' haversacks, kitbags and call-up papers, and it was only because of the presence of two cavalry squadrons that the men were eventually able to leave. The demonstrators, reinforced by contingents of strikers, then made for those factories where the workers had not yet come out. At about 11.00 a.m. marchers clashed fiercely with the police and troops and a serious incident took place: a senior police officer received two knife wounds and demonstrators with revolvers opened fire.

Hitherto the authorities had acted with reserve, trying to avoid bloodshed, but on 24 May they decided that a show of strength was badly needed. Théophile Barnier, Georges Clemenceau's deputy principal private secretary, arrived to take charge of operations. In Paris, the importance of what was happening in Loire was fully appreciated, the more so as a number of increasingly serious acts of sabotage involving railway signals and telephone lines had been reported.

On 24 May, the movement had reached a critical point. The government let it be known that it would no longer tolerate the excesses of people whose aims were so blatantly political. In particular, it could not stand by while the manufacture of war equipment was brought to a halt in so important an industrial centre as Loire and at so critical a juncture in the war. Last but not least, it could not continue to deploy troops to maintain law and order in the rear when they were needed to help stem the formidable German offensive about to be launched on the Chemin-des-Dames (27 May).

The trade unionists, for their part, could not allow their action to peter out: they had either to move it on a stage further, or call it off, particularly since for the moment it was gaining no ground.

On the morning of 24 May, the prefect had the feeling that the strikers were growing weary: though attendance at meetings was still large, there was a marked tendency to avoid confrontation. But, by the afternoon, tempers had risen again. Several speakers called for direct action against all those who were still working. As the munitions factory night shift was due to report for work that evening, there were virulent clashes between soldiers and strikers, and the cavalry had to make several charges to clear the factory gates.

The leaders of the CGT meanwhile redoubled their efforts to bring the strikes to an end — among them not only the majority faction but also such men as Merrheim who had come to consider the position of former allies in the Trade Union Defence Committee as absurd.

> For it to succeed [he wrote], the strike would have to continue for many more weeks and then to have been imbued with revolutionary vigour from the outset. Since that is not the case, the strike leaders in the departments of Loire and Seine must realise that bargaining with the government is the only way, if not to reach an agreement, then at least to gain time.

And he asked Blanchard to stay on in Saint-Etienne, despite his difficult position, not to break up the strike movement, but to bide his time until he could take charge of it. The call for an armistice was pointless, in any case, since the French government could not end the war unilaterally.

All of these developments persuaded the authorities that it was time to move. On 25 May, Commissioner Oudaille, who had largely confined his activities to Firminy, and who had at first been constrained to adopt an extremely accommodating pose, calling on Andrieu at the *bourse du travail* and attending meetings he had tried hard to prevent, decided to take strong measures against a crowd determined to break into the Verdié factory. He not only insisted on protecting the 'freedom to work', but also on maintaining the 'freedom of the streets', and at the head of a contingent of gendarmes, some on foot and some mounted, he took a personal hand in driving the demonstrators back. In the process, the socialist deputy-cum-mayor was peremptorily arrested, the gendarmes having apparently failed to recognise him.

The more the strike movement seemed to weaken, the more firmness the authorities showed. And the strike was clearly collapsing in Saint-Etienne, Saint-Chamond, Rive-de-Gier and Roanne. In the Roanne arsenal there were only 630 strikers on the morning of 25 May and 522 in the evening, as against 1,390 the morning before.

Flageollet left for Nîmes and Marseille and another militant left for Valence, but they were by now seeking support for a campaign that was running out of steam.

Moreover, Barnier, Clemenceau's representative, had the impression that public opinion was growing increasingly hostile to the strikers, not only among the other classes of society but also among 'the mass of honest workers'. In these circumstances, he thought, the time had come to deal with the ringleaders. During the night of 25/6 May, forty-three trade-union officials in the Saint-Etienne basin, including Andrieu, were arrested and immediately transferred to Clermont-Ferrand. Another seventy-three workers were put at the disposal of the military authorities. Charles Flageollet was arrested in Marseille and locked up in Fort Saint-Nicolas. All meetings in the Saint-Etienne *bourse du travail* were banned.

At Roanne, events took a slightly different course. By Monday, 26 May, nearly 40 per cent of the work force were back in their factories. At a meeting held in the *bourse du travail*, the strike leaders were forced to admit that their movement had not caught on: in Lyon, there had been no strikes at all and the position in Paris had not yet been assessed. They went on to propose, without great conviction, that the strikes be continued for another forty-eight hours. By the afternoon it appeared that this extension was too long and that the whole strike movement was in danger of imminent collapse. Héro, the leading revolutionary figure in Roanne, accordingly proposed a return to work next morning, Tuesday, 28 May. That night he and three other trade-union leaders were arrested. In parenthesis it might be mentioned that the head of the government mission told the prime minister indignantly that 'some of the men who had been singled out for the intemperance of their comments and their aggressive attitude during the last few days were found in bed with the wives of front-line soldiers'. Certainly an inconsistent attitude: they ought not to have been so impatient for the husbands to return!

What happened in Roanne raises the question of whether these arrests were really necessary. It would seem that the answer was no, that the strike would have collapsed in any case. This was what Andrieu maintained, a little mockingly, when Police Commissioner Oudaille came to arrest him: 'You're twenty-four hours too early, we're due to resume work on Monday.' At best, the government could claim that their vigorous measures had forestalled a possible recrudescence of revolutionary activity in Loire.

In any case, the police operation had been carefully planned. On 20 May, Commissioner Oudaille sent a telegram to the Sûreté Générale:

> Events in Loire caused by agitators encouraged by apparent impunity, adulation of their comrades and belief that government is either afraid or powerless. Situation deplored by sound section of population and a vast majority of serious workers amounting to 90 per cent in Basin. These last unanimous they joined strike for reasons of solidarity and particularly for fear of reprisals, but welcome with pleasure the suppression of what they denounce as anti-French.
>
> Unaware of whatever imperative considerations may be dictating government policy, we are astonished to find two laws applying, and that what is vigorously suppressed in Paris is tolerated here. . . .
>
> Should not stringent measures against ringleaders be employed to restore calm and ensure return to work?

On 25 May, Commissioner Oudaille sent Paris a list of 'ringleaders'.

In following the suggestions of its representatives on the spot, and arresting trade-union leaders, the government ran the risk of reviving the strike movement and of unleashing a solidarity campaign. In the event, these fears proved largely groundless, except perhaps in Firminy: on the morning of 26 May, those local leaders who had not been rounded up seemed to be in a 'stupor', but in the afternoon, they recovered their equilibrium, and with the support of the deputy-cum-mayor, Lafont, called an open-air protest meeting despite the government ban. Troops and a violent rainstorm helped to disperse the demonstrators. Tension persisted at a fairly high level in Firminy for some time, but in Rive-de-Gier and Saint-Chamond the factories were working normally, and in Saint-Etienne they were almost back to normal by 27 May. In Chambon, 60 per cent of the work force continued to strike and in Firminy the strike was almost total.

By 28 May, however, most workers in the coal basin were back at work, and even in Firminy the strikers accounted for no more than 20 per cent by the time the workers clocked off.

By 11.15 p.m. on 28 May, Théophile Barnier could put his name to a victory telegram: 'I consider that industrial life has resumed its normal course in this department.'

Thus the strikes which had started on 18 May 1918, and which were intended to continue until peace was declared, had been snuffed out within ten days, without the workers even having made any serious stand on behalf of their arrested leaders. How are we to explain this failure amounting to a fiasco?

The answer is of paramount importance. Having followed thus far our long re-construction of events in the department of Loire from the autumn of 1917 to the spring of 1918, the reader will realize that if there was ever a time when revolutionary action against the war had the slightest chance of success in France then it must indeed have been at this moment. There are probably a great many reasons for its failure, but two main causes clearly predominate: the narrowness of the movement's social base and the contradictions in its ideological foundations.

The strike movement in Loire seems, in practice, to have been confined to the working class. A report stated that in Roanne, for instance, not only the Socialist Party was hostile to it but also the majority of the population. Similar remarks were recorded in many other towns, and even those who do not feel that much credence need be given to police reports will agree that, generally pessimistic as these reports were, they would hardly have failed to voice any suspicion of other social classes becoming involved. Again, at no time did the workers' leaders make any reference to support coming from other social groups, except perhaps from soldiers, although they were invariably identified as workers too.

The observations of the postal censorship boards tend to confirm this impression. 'There is clear disapproval by the general public of the ringleaders, often mixed with hatred.'[14] However, Table 13 gives us a more subtly shaded view of public opinion.

14. Jean Nicot and Philippe Schillinger, *L'Opinion publique et les grèves de la Loire*.

Table 13. *Attitudes to the strikes in Loire, according to the postal censorship board*

	% of letters sent to soldiers from			
	Roanne (27 May)	Vienne (28 May)	Unieux/Firminy/ Chambon (29 May)	St-Etienne
Containing no reference	51	20	38	57
Neutrally expressed reference	30	71	50	35
In favour, *or* for the quest for peace through strike action	9	3	2	1
Against	10	6	8	7

The proportion of letters disapproving of the strike movement was evidently much greater than that of letters of approval, except in Roanne. For the rest, one is forcefully struck by the large number of letters that did not mention the strikes at all or else passed no judgement on them. It seems, nevertheless, fair to say that the strikers were isolated from the rest of the population.

Not only did the movement remain confined to the working class, but even in Loire it had the additional weakness of not enjoying the unanimous support of the unions. Thus while some textile workers joined the movement, for instance in Thizy and Roanne, the miners, who were the largest group after the metalworkers, did not. It was true to say that they did not stand completely aloof: on 26 May the Federal Committee of Mineworkers in Loire decided to make a show of solidarity with the metalworkers by declaring a twenty-four-hour strike on 29 May. Nevertheless, this belated initiative apparently left the authorities untroubled, for they licensed a meeting in the *bourse du travail* despite its occupation by the military. The miners then passed a motion of protest against the ransacking of the *bourse du travail*, against the recent wave of arrests and against the deployment of military strength. It was probably the least they could do, and they left it at that.

As for the one-day strike, agreed in principle after long discussions, it had a rather uneven, but on the whole good response, with approximately 75 per cent of all miners in the department taking part. Even so, no one could have claimed that the miners had stood solidly behind the metalworkers.

This raises the question of the metalworkers themselves. The great majority unquestionably followed the strike call (with some reservations in the arsenals). Does it therefore follow that it was only fear of their comrades which made them do so, as many writers have suggested? It is beyond doubt, there being a great deal of evidence to support it, that militant strikers had no intention of respecting their fellows' 'freedom to work' and that they were fully determined to use every means possible to make the strike stick. However, a small minority can rarely impose its will on an immense and hostile majority: hence, at the very least, the majority of workers must have *accepted* the strike in principle. On the other hand, it seems that the majority of strikers did not display a great deal of zeal. They admittedly attended the twice-daily meetings but not in the numbers recorded in November and December 1917. The speakers, moreover, voiced many complaints about the indifference of their comrades; in Roanne, Héro deplored the lack of fervour shown by workers in the arsenal. Another speaker violently denounced comrades who spent their time fishing, and in Firminy, Andrieu remarked on 24 May that there were too many comrades who would rather visit the countryside than attend meetings. And surely, the lack of protests against the arrests of the militants reflected a marked lack of conviction on the part of many strikers.

In any case, the strength of the strike movement in Loire should not be exaggerated: the workers in this department were not united, did not always act with the necessary resolve, and, above all, were unable to extend their action into a general strike. To keep up the fervour of their followers, the leaders often referred to strikes in other parts of the country, but these strikes were either mythical, or took place at times different from those in Loire, or were of limited scope. At no time during the war was there a serious threat of a general strike throughout France.

The leaders of the CGT played a significant role in curbing the strike movement. The federal committee, meeting on 25 May, felt there was only one solution: to end what they called 'this act of folly' at the very earliest opportunity. According to Lenoir, one of the secretaries of the Federation of Metalworkers, 'the leaders in Saint-Etienne have behaved criminally towards the working class'. The CGT feared that the army might be brought in to repress the strikes and that there would be a 'massacre'. Nor had they forgotten how the workers in Saint-Etienne had treated Blanchard.

In sum, the prime cause of the failure of the strike movement was its lack of a broader base. But this is more of a diagnosis than an explanation. We should also try to grasp why this was so, why the movement was incapable of spreading among the working class as a whole and beyond. It seems that the explanation lies in the strike movement's inner contradictions. Its methods and objectives were overtly *revolutionary*. In a discussion with Commissioner Oudaille, Andrieu explained that the campaign he was leading must inevitably culminate in revolution:

> We have had enough of the war, we want peace, and we have only one way to achieve it, by winning all workers over to our cause. Work in all munitions factories will then be halted, thus paralysing the production of the tools that have for the past four years enabled us to kill each other. We shall use all possible means to achieve our ends. Within a few days the movement will have spread to the entire basin and the strike will have become general. . . . We want to parley with the Germans. We want to meet workers' delegations from enemy countries and have discussions with them. . . . If the government refuses to let us, we shall have to use force to persuade them.

Other speakers called openly for revolution, among them Marius Vernay, who said in Chambon on 23 May: 'Remember that in 1789 the Revolution started in a small village in the Dauphiné; today it is in Firminy that the revolution for peace has begun'.

At Roanne, a textile worker by the name of Ducharme called for a general uprising. But what ends did all these revolutionary calls hope to attain? Peace, to be sure, or more precisely an armistice, the announcement of the French war aims, and discussions with German workers, but on what basis? In other words, were the French workers ready to accept any German conditions? Officially, no one dared to say so, no one dared to admit to defeatism.

Andrieu did not cease to deny that the strikes were of a defeatist nature. He recalled the interview with Clemenceau that he had had in December. He had told the prime minister then that he had been 'a pacifist before the war and that he would always be a pacifist, but never a defeatist'. He said the same thing to Commissioner Oudaille: if the talks with the Germans did not produce positive results, 'we shall again face the enemy in defence of our country'.

The position of the Loire revolutionaries was thus inherently contradictory: at a point in the war when Germany felt that victory was within her grasp, it was unreasonable to expect that she would suddenly opt for peace or that German workers would rise in rebellion. To strike for peace was absurd if one refused the enemy's conditions. This is not a contradiction to which attention is only now being drawn: Merrheim and the leadership of the CGT were quick at the time to give it prominence.

There is no means of telling whether the workers in Loire fully realised the contradiction inherent in the course they were called upon to follow, but it is likely that they had at least some vague inkling, and this would explain their lack of enthusiasm and their failure to extend the influence of their movement.

It is also quite probable that, despite their protests, Andrieu and some of his comrades *were* defeatists, but the mere fact that they did not dare to say so shows that the masses, at any rate, were resolutely opposed to defeatism. In short, however virulent their language, however sick they were of the war, even the most revolutionary among the French workers were not prepared to sacrifice their country for the sake of the revolution.

The Barrier of National Sentiment

Had the French working class become so unreliable a component of the community of the nation that it endangered the national defence effort and threatened to force France to call off the war? In other words, was there a danger in 1918 that France might find herself in the same position as Russia in 1917? The answer is complex.

Working-class agitation had been intense in the spring of 1917, but it had essentially been concerned with higher wages. It had come as a surprise in a country where, for two years, social unrest had been strictly limited, but it had hardly assumed revolutionary dimensions. In 1918, the situation was radically different. Strikes for higher wages alone were fairly rare, so that in that respect 'a relaxed social climate prevailed'.[15] Not that the economic condition of the working class had improved dramatically, but the authorities, having learnt from experience, pressed, or tried to press, reluctant employers to meet the workers' claims. In any case, by 1918 the agitation had undoubtedly shifted into the political arena, and its objectives, often avowed, were to force the government to make peace. However, the strike movement of 1918 did not coincide with that of 1917, either geographically or industrially. Thus the workers in the Paris clothing industry and in the Toulouse munitions works who had been in the forefront in 1917 took no action in 1918; by contrast, the metalworkers in Loire who had not made their presence felt until the very end of 1917 were at the head of the struggle in 1918. Simplifying a little, it may be said that two distinct elements

15. Annie Kriegel, 'L'Opinion publique française et la Révolution russe', p. 102.

of the French working class took the stage on each separate occasion. For the rest, the strikes of 1918 had a following comparable to, or even slightly higher than, those of 1917.[16]

On the other hand, although the strikes of 1917 took place simultaneously in different parts of the country, they were not – contrary to what has often been said – the result of a coherent nationwide strategy. In 1918, by contrast, determined attempts were made to coordinate the strike campaign, which explains, to a certain extent, the curiously fitful course of developments. Pressure started to build up in November 1917. According to the *Confidential Bulletins*, a very strict watch had to be kept on the metalworkers, many of whom seemed to be forgetting that they were reservists. In January 1918, the temperature rose by another degree. Trade unions were founded or organised with 'future events' in mind. Political aims became increasingly clearly discernible amid the wage claims. 'Tempers are over-excited,' the official observers reported. Despite the outward calm, many people began to suspect that preparations were being made for a general strike intended to paralyse the entire country.

There was a fresh escalation in February 1918: speakers at workers' meetings had begun to call for revolution, and anti-war feeling rose appreciably, even though it still seemed to be confined to certain regions. Complacent reports speaking of calm and the 'sound attitude' of the workers became increasingly rare. Perhaps more disconcerting still for the observers was the fact that working-class opinion was often so unpredictable: within the space of a few minutes, on 31 January, 2,000 railway workers in Sotteville-lès-Rouen applauded a patriotic speech by Albert Thomas, then voted by a majority of fifty to cease contributing to 'charities associated with the national defence effort' until the defects of the capitalist system had been made good.

In the Orléans military region, the anti-war movement was gaining ground. In Oyonnax, in Dole and in Montbéliard, at least part of the working class had been won over to, or showed sympathy for, 'maximalist' theories. Pamphlets appeared in increasing numbers in the Bourges region, where the trade unions seemed to be running a purely political campaign 'to hasten the end of the war'. At the arms factory in Tulle, the workers elected as shop stewards two men who had been sent to prison for inciting soldiers to insubordination.

16. Jean-Louis Robert, 'Les Luttes ouvriéres pendant la Première Guerre mondiale', in *Cahiers d'histoire de l'institut Maurice-Thorez, 1977*.

Thus, at the start of 1918, conditions looked ripe for an explosion. Suddenly, at the end of February, there was a *détente*. Then agitation resumed in April and there was an actual flare-up in May, which we have described in some detail, in Gard, in Isère, in the Paris region and above all in Loire, marked also by strikes or fierce agitation in Seine-Inférieure, in Nièvre, at Bourges, Lyon and elsewhere.

This development in stages could be seen as the reflection of successive and spontaneous waves of anti-war sentiment, but the course of events does not appear to have been as orderly as that implies. Hence, just when tension was running at its highest, in January and February 1918, nothing or very little happened; in May, however, when the psychological climate was much less propitious following the German offensives of 21 March and 9 April, strikes, in theory coordinated but in practice fairly disorganised, broke out in several regions. What are we to make of this phenomenon? The loss of momentum suffered by the strike movement could not have been the result of the German offensives, as some reports would have us believe: the decline began in February, and therefore preceded these events. Subsequently, it is true, the fortunes of the anti-war movement did reflect the precariousness of the military situation, but the basic explanation of the strange course of developments must be sought elsewhere. It lies, clearly, in the doubts of the leaders of the anti-war movement, in their lack of confidence. Uncertain of their ability to carry the working masses with them as they needed to — the anti-war movement being strong in certain regions only — they preferred to defuse what seemed to be turning into an explosive confrontation. The main question, therefore, concerns what the working masses themselves wanted.

In some regions at least, and often in those that were vital industrially, they were, it would seem, imbued to a large extent with anti-war ideas. The proof is the docility with which they followed orders to strike or to demonstrate. But they were not prepared to run great risks to see these ideas triumph, as is witnessed by the relative speed with which they returned to work after what was intended to be a strike until peace. But then, as Max Gallo has recently shown by way of a striking example, the number of political activists in Bergerac and Bourges, two anti-war strongholds, probably did not exceed 1 or 2 per cent of the total work force.[17]

17. Max Gallo, 'Quelques aspects de la mentalité et du comportement ouvrier dans les usines de guerre (1914–1918)'.

There was thus a revolutionary nucleus, but at the beginning of 1918 the revolutionary potential among the working masses at large was, in fact, still far from being fulfilled, as the course of events in May 1918 shows. Launched by revolutionary militants who wanted a show of strength come what may, the strike wave ended in the discomfiture of the anti-war movement, so much so that no serious revolutionary movement reappeared before the end of the war.

Prudent yet effective government counter-measures also played their part, but it remains self-evident that a revolutionary movement that could be left rudderless by the arrest of a few dozen militants and by the call-up of a somewhat larger number, could not be said to have as yet much momentum or force.

During the first half of 1918, because a section of the working class was clamouring for peace, France experienced a shock-wave of an intensity that was probably greater than that of 1917. But because the majority of the workers, no less than of the nation, continued to believe that it was not in their interest to lose the war, France remained a long way from following the path Russia had taken the year before. In the face of the latest German onslaughts, France — despite some anxieties — was in no danger of internal collapse, at least not from her workers.

Despite all the speeches, and indeed the bluster of some of its leaders, the anti-war movement never managed to break down the invisible and apparently insurmountable barrier of national sentiment.

CHAPTER 18

French Morale in 1918

In 1918 the attitude of the workers, and especially of workers in munitions factories, was crucial, but was clearly influenced by that of the rest of the population. Thus the strikes of 16 and 17 May 1918 in Seine-Inférieure failed to spread 'because of the hostility of the public',[1] and the fairly large number of strikes in Lyon came to an end having failed to gain 'the public's encouragement and sympathy'. What then was the general attitude of the French in this, the last year of the war, a fact of which they were, of course, unaware, the end of it being an event for which they would scarcely have dared to hope? We have chosen three examples: the departments of Puy-de-Dôme and of Deux-Sèvres, and Paris.

Puy-de-Dôme in 1918

We can gauge the mood of the public in Puy-de-Dôme not only from the usual sources but also from the collection of documents of all kinds assembled by Georges Desdevises du Dézert, a lecturer in the local arts faculty. He was not merely an observer, but had a part to play in events as he travelled up and down the department, lecturing almost everywhere, either in order to invite his audience to contribute to various war charities or to subscribe to various loans, or else simply attempting to boost morale. The discrepancy between what he said in his patriotic addresses and the notes he took for himself on the true state of public opinion is often startling.

During the first few months of 1918,[2] public opinion was in-

1. Archives de la Préfecture de Police B/A 1639.
2. G. Lang, 'L'Opinion publique dans le département du Puy-de-Dôme et la Guerre de 1914–1918'.

fluenced by a series of recent events: the defeat of the Italians, the defection of Russia and several scandals and cases of treason. These events did not give rise to a marked decline in confidence: on the contrary, various authorities noted that morale had improved, and that the renewed vigour of the government under Clemenceau had made a good impression. The population was nevertheless continuing to suffer from the consequences of the war – its attitude might be described as one of *resigned weariness*, which in some cases came very close to despondency; and this was precisely what Desdevises du Dézert found in two towns he visited, especially Issoire: 'There is a defeatist clique on which it is hard to have any influence. Serious-minded people are finding it is all taking too long. One of the town councillors present had lost a son, many women were in tears. The will is still there, but there is much sorrow. People are weary . . .'.

During the first three months of 1918, unlike the spring of 1917, conditions were therefore calming down, but the calm was 'equivocal' to the extent that it was difficult to tell what lay beneath it. By contrast, economic problems concerned people a great deal. As Ambert, the sub-prefect, reported on 28 January 1918: 'The economic difficulties, the restrictions and the daily rise in food prices are causing much disquiet . . .'. However, even here hardships were generally borne passively — generally, but not always, and especially not when it came to bread. Indeed, the shortage of bread and the poor quality of flour caused a riot at Thiers on 30 July 1918. The mob invaded and looted the sub-prefecture, and order was not restored until the urgent dispatch of edible flour together with a large contingent of gendarmes and infantry. This riot, the most serious disturbance in Puy-de-Dôme during the course of the war, was the consequence of a series of administrative errors and it would be quite wrong to consider it a revolutionary ferment. It nevertheless bore witness to the potential threat of supply difficulties.

The department of Puy-de-Dôme comprised extensive working-class areas set in the midst of a predominantly rural population.

The workers in Clermont do not seem to have given the authorities cause for great concern: their wage claims were moderate, their trade-union leaders level-headed, their mood conciliatory and rarely swayed by political demands. There may have been some slight tension at the time of the Loire strikes: the metalworkers considered coming out in sympathy, but in the event did not do so. The only threat to the authorities was thought to come from 'the new militants, mostly strangers to the region'. By and large, the mass of workers in Clermont continued to support the national defence effort, even though the appearance of a trade-union paper, *Le Travailleur*, foreshadowed an intensification of working-class agitation.

The reports of the departmental authorities tended not to dwell on the peasants. They did not conceive of them as a possible threat to public order, even though the peasants were deeply resentful of taxes and requisitions. As Desdevises du Dézert noted: 'Having offered up his children, the peasant expects to sell his produce at whatever price he can get, and not to have to pay any taxes . . .'.

What effects did the German offensives have? It would have been odd had they not caused anxiety, indeed anguish, particularly when the shells started to fall on Paris, clear evidence of the enemy's advance. But there was no reaction comparable to that of 1917. Public opinion 'held'; the French seemed unable to believe in the possibility of defeat. 'Since May, I have been unable to detect any signs of unease, the recent military events notwithstanding,' commented the prefect on 29 June 1918. 'The results of the last enemy offensive and the threat to Paris have been noted with anxiety, but not for a single moment have they affected the morale of the population . . .'

This was not the whole truth, of course: morale had suffered and the prefect and sub-prefect did not hesitate to say so after the event: 'The morale of the population has improved with the advance of our armies . . .'; 'The morale of the population, which had declined at the time of the last German advances, improved very rapidly with the fortunes of the Allied armies', were the respective conclusions of the sub-prefect in Thiers and the prefect of the department in August 1918.

Nevertheless, although people had largely retained their confidence even during the worst moments in the spring of 1918, in the summer 'the certainty of victory seemed slow to dawn' (G. Lang). It was not until September or October that this certainty became widespread, by which time Spanish influenza had become a major preoccupation.

The department of Puy-de-Dôme, as far as we can tell from the available documents, never experienced a consistently defeatist or even anti-war current. Its example is all the more illuminating when we try to assess the importance of that current on the national scale. While Puy-de-Dôme did not exude enthusiasm during the first half of 1918, after the alarms of 1917 a kind of indifference had set in, and the people seemed resigned to whatever hardships still lay in store for them.

Deux-Sèvres in 1918

Though the department of Deux-Sèvres was predominantly rural, it was shaken by the spring crisis of 1917 much like the rest of France, the sub-prefect of Melle noting in August of that year that morale had improved and that despondency had made way for hope. The prefect, too, expressed satisfaction about the significant rise in morale among civilians.

But what was the morale of the inhabitants of the department in 1918? We can answer that question from official records kept in Niort, Melle, Bressuire and Saint-Maixent on which the prefect based his monthly reports to the minister of the interior.[3] Morale was said to be good, very good, or even excellent in the first quarter of 1918, supply problems and other restrictions being the only causes for complaint.

During the German offensives, the reports were less optimistic: morale was no more than fairly good at Bressuire at the end of April, the population having been badly frightened although apparently rallying. At the end of May, the sub-prefect of Bressuire wrote: 'The situation is as good as it can be, and even the most optimistic of us could not have wished for better after the events of the last few months'.

At Saint-Maixent, in June, morale was only fairly good, although all the reports agree in acknowledging that the soldiers in the depots – that is, those on the point of leaving for the front – together with the soldiers on leave, had shown complete confidence at all times. And then, from the end of July, morale improved greatly to become excellent once more.

All the reports mention anti-war intrigues that never came to anything. This may not have been entirely true, as the police commissioner in Niort noted at the end of July that 'the brilliant counter-offensive' had 'helped to restore the morale of those who have a tendency to be swayed by pacifist opinions'.

What conclusion can be drawn from these reports? Even allowing for the fact that the observations are meagre, with little qualifying detail, they do tend to tally with our impression of the attitude of the inhabitants of Puy-de-Dôme: despite the gravity of the military situation at any one point, there were no great fluctuations in the state of morale. Whether this was because of government intervention – the firmness of which, we are told repeatedly, made a favourable impression on the population of Deux-Sèvres – or for

3. AD Deux-Sèvres 4 M 6/29.

more complex reasons, there was no repetition in 1918 of what had happened in 1917. The determination to 'hold out' did not seem to have been seriously called into question in this department.

Paris

We can reconstruct the attitude of Parisians during the final period of the war fairly accurately, thanks to a large dossier based on the daily observations of the Préfecture and entitled *Physionomie de Paris*.[4]

New Year's Day 1918 was bound to be a painful reminder that the fourth year of the war had begun, and the good wishes people exchanged on 1 January could be summed up in just one hope: 'May there be a speedy end to the war'.

But this unanimous hope covered a host of speculations on how the war could be brought to a close. In a cinema in the XVth arrondissement at a performance of *Le Père la Victoire* ('Father Victory'), a woman in the audience was heard to remark: 'Better that Father Victory brought us peace', and in a café on the place de la République some customers agreed that the war was bound to fizzle out', that it would end in a 'compromise'. Despite reports to the contrary, it became clear that Germany was no more 'worn out' than France, that 'her economic situation is not much more critical than ours' and that it would 'improve following the resumption of relations with Russia'. The French leaders, it was said, had come to realise that Germany could not be beaten by force of arms.

But when would it all end? Tip-offs and 'inside information' abounded. The rumour of peace in about June and July was attributed to the Military Academy. The soldiers would revolt if the war continued, some people claimed. 'The economic crisis is hitting everybody and everybody is going short. A settlement must be reached quickly.' The wives of front-line soldiers retailed comments in letters from their husbands showing that morale was at a low ebb: 'Morale very low, which has never happened before,' one of the soldiers wrote home. 'The soldiers have had more than enough', he continued.

Others believed that the war would not end that year. What was important was to maintain French morale, and to that end the government restrictions 'were to the point'. 'Thanks to them, we shall hold out until the end without weakening.' It would be better

4. APP B/A 1587.

to postpone victory for another year, by which time American support would have been 'brought to bear to its full extent'.

As the uncertainties mounted, so a myth that had been circulating throughout the war gained even greater credence: that of Japanese intervention. Some accused the Entente of having prolonged the war unnecessarily by failing to seek Japanese aid. The Japanese ought to have been handed Indo-China as an inducement, in which case Russia would not have defected, and Turkey and Bulgaria would have been stopped from joining the Central Powers. The war would have been cut short and France could have been compensated with the German colonies in Africa. Now it was too late, which did not stop the risk to Indo-China from Japan.

In February 1918, there were rumours that Japan was about to replace the faltering Russian ally. Japanese troops were already massing on the Eastern Front. Speculation on the subject could be heard almost daily, coupled with the hope of a collapse of German morale. And then, quite abruptly, it became clear that the whole story had been a fantasy.

In different forms – fostered, moreover, by official comments and wishful thinking – the Japanese 'mirage' had thus haunted French public opinion throughout the war, as part of a more general delusion that the entire world was on France's side. Paradoxically, that delusion went hand in hand with the belief that her allies were not playing their full part in the struggle for right and justice. As always, strangers on French soil were the butt of popular resentment: they were 'having it easy', they should have been sent off to the front before now. It was 'bizarre' that after three years of war 'no such arrangement' had been made; it was 'high time to plug that particular gap'.

People spoke less about the Russians at the beginning of the year, if only because the Russians seemed to be marking time in their negotiations with Germany. When Russia was mentioned, the comment was invariably unfriendly. You could no longer count on the Russian people, they had 'gone to seed', and were too weak to get rid of Lenin and Trotsky, men who were 'handing their country over to Germany on a platter'.

By February, there was no longer any doubt that the Russians were pulling out of the war. The headings in the Préfecture report on the French reaction are revealing: 'Maximalist capitulation'; 'Russian treachery'. Once again the revolutionary dimension of the Bolshevik movement was completely ignored; people simply felt betrayed: 'We shall never forget their cowardice. They dragged us into the war in 1914 and now they're leaving us in the lurch'.

To judge by remarks overheard in the street, the only people not to share the general desire to see the end of the war at the earliest possible moment were women workers employed in munitions factories who had become used to earning big wages: 'They seemed quite willing to do without their husbands and as soon as the war is over, there will be a spate of divorces and disasters. The woman who has stood in for her husband and done her job well will no longer put up with his complaints and demands'.

Though this remark was, with its touch of misogyny, not without a grain of truth, it was also, of course, far too sweeping. In any case, at the beginning of 1918 the mood in munitions factories was anything but euphoric. In particular, feelings were running high in the XVth arrondissement because of the call-up of the classes of 1913 and 1914. The walls of the electrical factory in the rue Lecourbe bore the inscriptions: 'Long live Caillaux, man of peace!' and 'Down with Clemenceau and his war!' Discontent and disquiet were heightened by a rumour attributed to some engineers: the call-up of workers of the classes of 1909 to 1912 was about to follow. In the Belleville district, the workers reacted with anger: these classes were thought to have an essential part to play in the manufacture of arms. There were plenty of shirkers about and, anyway, the Allies were not matching France's effort, least of all the Italians, who even expected assistance.

Public opinion was aware of a certain seething unrest among the working population: 'It's obvious that the workers are tired of the war,' it was said in the XIIth arrondissement in February, but many nevertheless objected to the fact that 'fanatics [sic] like Renaudel, Longuet, Brizon, etc. should be allowed to take advantage of the sacrifices made by the workers to work for the victory of policies which have, in Russia, shown what they will eventually lead to'. Some admitted regretfully that the anti-war movement enjoyed some support: 'Opinion is divided in my workshop', said one café customer, 'but it has to be said that the idea of peace has taken hold in some minds, particularly the women's'. Another customer added: 'Unfortunately the working class is allowing itself to be taken in by fine words and is blindly following a handful of traitors and double-dealers'.

The arrest of Hélène Brion nevertheless astonished people: why her, when so many deputies were saying the same things with impunity? Petitions were passed round and signed in many factories, especially in the suburbs of Paris, where a large number of female workers were employed.

One police informer warned against an imminent wave of strikes, and there were many rumours about which unions would be among the first to act. There were also rumours about serious disturbances in Saint-Etienne, where large numbers of workers were said to have been sent back to the front.

Mixing truth with falsehood — unsurprisingly in view of the censorship in force — and confusing the real with the possible, the public had the impression that the anti-war and indeed the defeatist campaign was gaining momentum despite the arrests. 'They are more active than ever,' it was being said.

The hunt for traitors and the arrest of Joseph Caillaux, whose parliamentary immunity had been lifted on 22 December 1917, were the main subjects of conversation during the early months of 1918. Had the government wished to encourage speculation, it could not have done better.

At first, the public seemed to welcome Caillaux's arrest almost unanimously, many expressing surprise that the authorities had not done it sooner or, alternatively, that they should actually have dared to seize a person of such influence. Moreover, the arrest of a former prime minister opened the way for the most preposterous fabrications. It was said that Caillaux had wanted to seize power with the help of two Corsican regiments recruited by the former radical deputy Thalamas, then deputy director of education in Corsica. The imminent arrest of many very different personalities was predicted: General Sarrail, the radical deputy and friend of Caillaux, Ceccaldi, and even the President of the Republic! But it is also possible to detect from the reports that, behind the hostile torrent let loose against Caillaux, there ran an appreciable current of sympathy. Thus one man from Sarthe declared that the people of that department had retained their faith in Caillaux; another described him as the man of peace. A hostile witness deplored the fact that so many French people — and workers in particular — should be doubting his guilt and siding with him. Yet another commentator declared that the workers in Ivry were behind Caillaux and that Clemenceau had manufactured the evidence against him. Some expected the Caillaux affair to lead to a workers' uprising: Clemenceau would be overthrown and Caillaux acquitted and restored to office and he would then quickly make peace.

It is difficult to gauge how representative these opinions were, when so many of those whose views were recorded wished only to see Caillaux shot out of hand. Yet it is significant that a pro-Caillaux current should have surfaced at all when every newspaper was violently against the former prime minister. Had opinion polls been invented at the time, they would probably have shown that Caillaux's was far from being a voice crying in the wilderness. Indeed, some claimed that he would have won a peace plebiscite, the workers and peasants wanting nothing so much as peace since they bore the entire weight of the capitalist war.

By contrast, when the Bolo affair came to the fore a month later, Bolo's sentence was greeted with general satisfaction as the start of the 'clean-up of the home front'.

Though it is difficult to determine what Parisians really felt during the first weeks of 1918, the often-contradictory remarks we have quoted seem to reflect the divided state of public opinion. On the one hand, there was an apparently growing tide of anti-war feeling; on the other, the mass of the population did not question the need for a continued war effort, albeit through habit, resignation or else on logical grounds. That Parisians were weary, and sometimes deeply troubled by the duration of the war, is certain. Their morale nevertheless remained sound, thanks to the widespread belief that that of the army, which had 'not been all that good for the past few months', was about to become 'as sound as in 1914' once more.

Their response to the 'military tribulations' that Parisians suffered make a good starting-point for examining the variations in their morale. The French capital sustained a major raid by Gotha bombers during the night of 30/31 January 1918, and observers thought that 'in general the attitude of Parisians was excellent'. Their fury was directed above all at French airmen who were accused of not having done their duty and of having allowed themselves to be outclassed by the enemy; they were said to be 'thinking of nothing but riotous living and of sitting the war out in comfort'. Set beside the positive attitude of the Parisians as a whole, there were also some lapses, or at least cases of exaggerated caution. Thus factories in the XIth and XIXth arrondissements were unable to open on 31 January because the employees had refused to report for work, and there were large queues of people anxious to leave Paris by train. At the Gare de Lyon, on that day, the ticket offices were 'beseiged'. The frequency of German air raids in February and March greatly affected Parisians, even though there was no real panic. People argued about the best way to make the Germans stop: the most widely held opinion was that the French air force should hit back at German cities, which would force the 'Boche' to abandon this kind of unconventional warfare. However, there were also those who felt that in the circumstances it would be best to give up completely. One man was heard to say: 'If the Boche came back and bombed us another ten times or so all the faint hearts would go over to the pacifists and start clamouring for peace'. For the rest, few exaggerated the military significance of the raids: their sole purpose, they said, was to throw Parisians into a panic, the Germans knowing 'that the French in general, and Parisians in particular, were beginning to get a bit tired of the war'.

Were the Germans succeeding? The railway stations were the place to find out.

On 10 March 1918, there were many more departures than usual from the Gare de Lyon.

On 11 March, there were still very many more departures than usual. 'There were endless queues at the ticket counters, especially for the third class.'

On 12 March, 'trains left the Montparnasse and Austerlitz stations, as well as the Gare Saint-Lazare, jam-packed with passengers'.

On 13 March, so many people tried to leave from the Gare de Lyon that the staff could not cope with carrying and registering all the luggage.

On 25 March, staff at the Gare d'Orsay declared: 'You have to go back to August 1914 to find an exodus like it'.

On the whole, the exodus took place in an orderly fashion, but there were exceptions. At the Gare d'Orsay, for instance, the pressure of the crowd was such that plate-glass and shop windows were smashed and the ticket offices stormed. On 26 March at about 8.00 a.m., 2,000 people were waiting in front of the ticket offices, resulting in 'indescribable crowding and jostling'. There was a 'throng' in the hall at the Gare Saint-Lazare.

Unquestionably, people left Paris in March *en masse*. During the last week of March, the Gare de Lyon alone issued up to 20,000 tickets a day (more than double the usual number). Some train services had to be quadrupled. At Montparnasse there were 58,000 departures during the period 18–25 March, and 123,518 during 26 March–6 April.

Though there was no general alarm, the term 'panic' was used to describe the scene at the Gare d'Orsay, with the added comment: 'This is bound to be even more demoralising to the provinces, which, alas, could do without it'.

There was another revealing event: 'At the Crédit Lyonnais, on the boulevard des Italiens, the staff in charge of the safe deposit boxes had to open extra counter positions to cope with the crush. There was a queue of 200 to 300 people'.

What significance should we attribute to these departures? They were certainly acts of prudence, but probably no more than that. For there were at the same time numerous favourable comments on Clemenceau's energy, said to be rebuilding confidence, while Poincaré's star continued to wane, many people even blaming him for the war. The informer from the Préfecture thought this view was 'stupid', but he recorded it all the same. He also mentioned that Poincaré was particularly unpopular with the soldiers, so much so that he no longer dared to visit them.

The first three months of 1918 were, despite everything, months of waiting. People knew that with the spring the war would enter a new phase, that the moment of truth was near.

Unquestionably, at the beginning of April 1918, after the successes of the first German thrust, morale was not very high in Paris. Business was 'stagnant', those theatres that were still open were playing at a loss, the neighbourhood cinemas had lost many of their regulars, and though there were no longer crowds of people at the railway stations, departing trains continued to be full. Unfortunately, we know less about the 'physiognomy of Paris' during this period than we do about the period just before, because the daily reports were reduced by half. The conscripts who boarded the trains at various stations showed no signs of weakening. They were as often as not in high spirits, sometimes perhaps too much so, many having taken a glass too many.

From the middle of May, the police dossiers give some indication of how Parisians reacted to the wave of strikes. Since the papers were silent, the news had to spread along other channels. One place that was well informed was the Bourse, so much so that one of our observers marvelled how it got its news despite the censorship. Thus, as soon as the metalworkers' strike started, the Bourse was humming with the event. The reaction was significant: there was no panic or even much agitation; instead there was confidence in Clemenceau's firmness and in Lucheur's diplomacy, and developments were quickly to justify this optimism. For the rest, stockbrokers did not hide their exasperation – which, it was said, was rife in all bourgeois circles – with the behaviour of the workers. That the 'bourgeoisie' should not have been particularly sympathetic to the strike wave is not surprising; what is significant, however, is that their reaction should have been not defensive but vigorously offensive. This is borne out by the following entry:

> In the Métro people talk a great deal. . .about the strikes and particularly about the complete silence of the papers. The strikers are getting no sympathy at all; they are much criticised and many people say quite openly that the recently 'mobilised' workers were afraid of fighting for their country. The soldiers who join in the conversation say they are quite ready to intervene [against the strikers] just as soon as they are asked.

Similar reactions were recorded during the next few days when news filtered through of the strikes in Loire: 'People rounded on the workers both for being unpatriotic and also for being insatiable in their wage demands'. Oddly enough, the clerks in the Bourse, with salaries a good deal lower than wages in the munitions factories, were all the more vociferous in their denunciation of the strikers.

This frame of mind should be put in context. Despite their optimistic front, people lived in expectation of a major and decisive German offensive; its time and place were topics of daily speculation. It was not a propitious climate for the calm consideration of working-class unrest, whether based on unsatisfied wage claims or on anti-war sentiments.

And in fact, a new 'German onslaught', as *Le Matin* called it in a headline the next morning, came on 27 May 1918. This attack was the more ominous in that, as had happened four years earlier, it posed a direct threat to Paris. What was the Parisians' response? At the Palais de Justice, for example, 'anxiety was stamped on all faces' but there were no 'signs of agitation', 'let alone of panic' in the streets. The reports written on 2 June spoke of 'absolute confidence' 'in the skill of the High Command' and 'the courage of our soldiers'. By 4 June tension had died down. According to the official communiqué, there had been 'a revival of interest' in the war; it was again as keen 'as it had been in 1914'. 'Maps of the front were seen once more in the shops.'

In this connection, we may also quote a comment by a reporter from Vierzon: 'Every morning, as in the tragic days of 1914, a pious pilgrimage sets off to read the official communiqués displayed outside the post office; and each evening people rush to the station to meet the train from Bourges which carries the latest news in the form of the *Dépêche du Berry* . . .'.

As for the workers – whether as a result of the recent strikes or because of national solidarity in the face of danger – their attitude had become a source of general satisfaction. The official report for 31 May contained a long passage about the munitions factories:

> Information received this morning from Citroën in Paris, and from Renault and Salmson in Billancourt, shows that in the factories on the Quai de Javel the morale of the workers is excellent. Production is above average and even the workers in the lorry and explosives shops have been doing overtime during the past few days.
>
> At the Renault works the departure of Bagot, Michelet and Le Bihan has done much to calm tempers. True, some militants have not dropped attempts to cause trouble, but their example is not being followed. On the contrary, in some shops the workers, men and women, who bitterly regret having lost a week during the last strikes, are determined to use force against anyone trying to start a new one.
>
> Moreover, application of the Mourier law has dampened the ardour of the hotheads, who now fear they may be redeployed.

At Renault, as at Samson, 'no stoppages need be feared for the moment'. That impression was corroborated by an inquiry held the next morning, on 1 June, in all munitions factories. 'Work is continuing normally.' 'No need to fear strikes.'

The inquiry also showed that in Paris, and particularly in the industrial plants in the XIIIth and XVth arrondissements, the great majority of working men and women were convinced that the latest battle would end in France's favour.

In Boulogne the German advance caused some 'anxiety', but the general attitude was 'good'. At Neuilly, the recent events did not particularly interest the workers, but 'when they spoke of them' it was to express confidence that the Germans would be stopped. The same attitude prevailed at Suresnes-Puteaux: 'general anxiety' but confidence in the outcome. 'In the factories at Saint-Ouen, Saint-Denis, Ivry and Issy-les-Moulineaux, people conceded that the military situation was serious, but felt confident about the outcome of the battle.'

A few days later still, on 12 June, the section of the report covering the munitions factories ended with: 'Morale is excellent and output up to, if not greater than, normal'.

There was no doubt that, for the immediate present at least, the risk of a social upheaval in the munitions factories was minimal. As during the first weeks of the war, the closeness of the German threat overshadowed all other preoccupations.

The reports moreover stressed the Parisians' steadfastness in face of imminent danger, and expressed pleasure at the fact that the railway stations had ceased to be the scene of 'the kind of panic we saw last March'. Of course, it could simply be argued that all who had wanted to leave had already done so. The reality, however, seems to have been somewhat different, since some spoke of another exodus comparable to that of 1914. Whom are we to believe? It is true that, in contrast to what happened in September 1914, travellers no longer queued up day and night for train tickets, but the list of departures shows that throughout June the trains continued to be more crowded than usual: at the Gare de Lyon alone the increase in the number of departures was between 5,000 and 7,000 a day. Instead of mass flight, Paris was witnessing a new phenomenon, the slow haemorrhaging of her population. Those who left planned their departure carefully and carried a great deal of luggage, so much so that rather than the passenger services it was those dealing with luggage which were overstretched, especially at the Gare de Lyon. The stations were therefore bustling, and some evenings were described as 'eventful'. The continuing departures can be explained by fears of a new German thrust, but also by the repeated air raids, together with shelling from the 'super-cannons', as they were known. One cannot help thinking that, despite their general stead-fastness, the confidence of Parisians had been dented. Indeed, the banks, which had sent the securities in their keeping to safety in the provinces, followed up this precaution by sending off their safe deposit boxes as well.

'Bitter' remarks were heard in the queues at the railway stations about the need to make peace in order to avoid worse. Many shops selling luxury goods closed down; the big stores had an 'insignificant' turnover, and the gendarmes began to stop young civilians who looked as if they were 'of military age' to see if their papers were in order.

It would have been very surprising if the German successes in the spring of 1918 had not been reflected in some lowering of Parisian morale, but there is no solid evidence for this being tantamount to a defeatist spirit. As soon as the German offensives stopped at the end of June, the railway stations returned to normal. A report dated 21 June even spoke of 'excellent' morale. The decision to include Paris in the zone of operations did not seem to worry anyone. 'Calm has returned', it was said.

Significantly enough, the July reports no longer mentioned morale, an indication that one Allied success had been enough to restore complete confidence. And that had taken place when, on 16 July, the German offensive was halted prior to what became known as the Second Battle of the Marne. The movement away from Paris went into immediate reverse, as the observers noted on 22 July. Within a few days, that is by 5 August, the stations were again thronged, this time with people flocking back to the capital. Public opinion quickly agreed that this was the end of 'German supremacy'. An oft-repeated phrase: 'We've come a long way', was typical of the new attitude, one of 'great confidence in the future'. Even house-wives, it was said, had stopped complaining about prices. Army recruiting boards could again meet in a calm atmosphere; there was no longer any question of 'anti-militarist and defeatist' tracts being distributed and the morale of the recruits was 'excellent' (14 September). Political disputes seemed forgotten and any demonstration by a group that did not join in the new chorus of national unity was considered to be 'in bad taste'.

This undoubtedly euphoric atmosphere contained an odd ingre-dient: the end of the war was not mentioned. Victory, it is true, was no longer doubted, but German strength had been so impressive that no one seemed able to envisage the enemy's imminent collapse. It was not until 3 October that the first speculation appeared, not about the end of the war, but about when the German army would be thrown out of French territory. So widespread was the view that this would happen before winter that, when rumours about a German request for an armistice began to circulate on 6 October, surprise quickly made way for the generally held opinion that an armistice should not under any circumstances be accepted. The report in the *Physionomie de Paris*, dated 6 October, merits being quoted almost in its entirety.

THE FACE OF PARIS

Sunday, 6 October

The Armistice Proposal and Public Opinion

The announcement of the armistice proposal by Germany and her allies was a cause for general surprise. A demonstration of the desire for peace by the Central Powers had not, at least, been expected so early or in this particular form.

Coming as it did on a public holiday, the news was bound to be the main topic of discussion and in fact many promenaders crowding the boulevards and cafés, and many spectators at theatres and music halls talked about little else.

Observations made yesterday in various circles and more particularly in the centre of Paris, always busy on a Sunday, revealed keen satisfaction that our enemies should have called for a truce: regardless of what they felt our response ought to be, one and all saw this proposal as a sure sign of a growing weakness of the German army and of a worsening situation inside the [German] Empire.

As for the French response, there was near unanimity that negotiations should not be started and no armistice agreed until 'the Boche has been completely beaten' and driven from all the invaded territories.

Great confidence was also expressed that the statesmen of the Entente, and especially Wilson and Clemenceau, would know what reply to make to the enemy in order to foil any Machiavellian manoeuvres on his part.

The conversations reported below fairly reflect this attitude:

At the Café Napolitain: 'It's all happened a little too fast, we have to be on our guard'.

Café des Princes: 'We've got to be careful, we've got to watch out. Germany isn't as weak as people think — it won't work like that'.

Café de Madrid: 'Maybe the Germans have set a trap for us?'

'Well, if they have, Clemenceau will know how to get the Entente out of it again.'

Café Louis XVI: 'It's been a surprise for everybody. Who would have thought it two months ago?'

Théâtre Cadet Rousselle: 'Wilson will probably give the reply on behalf of the Entente and he's sure to keep to the conditions he mentioned in his speech'.

'The Boche won't accept, and they'll fight on to the end.'

'You have to be firm when you negotiate with people like that.'

Café de la Paix: 'This time we've got them and we'll finish them off before long'.

At the Restaurant Au Régent, 200 rue St-Lazare:

'This isn't the right time for any deal.'

'Peace should be signed on their soil.'

'We must go on to the end and not give them any chance to dig in.'

People in groups, in various public places (streets, buses, trams, the Métro):

'No parleys before the Boche are completely smashed, and certainly not before they've been cleared out of France and Belgium.'

'Their move is a sign of impotence — but we mustn't fool ourselves, the war can go on for a long time yet.'

'As victory is certain, let's have it to the full.'

'Above all we mustn't be taken in by their offer of a premature peace — we must go on with the war until German militarism is destroyed and we have been given full satisfaction.'

'There can be no middle way, it's either peace or war.'

'Isn't this just another Boche ruse, this armistice, so that they can establish another line of defence further back?'

'Everybody wants peace, but it still has to be our kind of peace.'

'We trust Clemenceau, Lloyd George and Wilson, who are not the men to compromise.'

'Before the Germans declare themselves even half beaten, the Austrians must first follow the Bulgarians.'

At L'Olympia, a group talking between two performances commented favourably on a declaration by Josephus Daniels, Secretary of the US Navy: 'The Americans will finish the war with a march down the Unter den Linden in Berlin'. Another considered his declaration 'proof that the

Americans will not be fobbed off with excuses, and that they are determined to go on to the end'.

Late one night, there was a slight scuffle at the Concorde Métro station between passengers who were anxious to get home and were afraid of missing the last train. Someone shouted: 'Now that the war is over, don't let's squabble among ourselves'. His words were greeted with cheers.

Mention should be made, however, of reports of contrary views, even though these were small in number.

At the Café des Princes, among a group of customers including two soldiers, the following remark was overheard: 'Let's have peace, that'll stop any more futile slaughter'.

At Alfortville, where a hundred or so people were queuing outside a butcher's shop, a discussion of the armistice led a female factory worker to say: 'Let's have peace right now, and then we can have our men back.' 'The quicker the better', said another woman, 'we're sick of having to queue like this.'

However, the great majority of those present favoured continuing the war.

Throughout October 1918, Parisians seemed to waver between a desire to display firmness against Germany and disappointment when the end of the war seemed to be receding once again. While cold logic led them to reject an armistice that would not seal the fate of German militarism, their hearts made them long for it all to be over as soon as possible.

On 7 October, firmness had the upper hand: the armistice terms proposed by Germany were regarded as cynical in that the German Chancellor was believed to have no intention of doing more than grant autonomy to Alsace-Lorraine.

Firmness still prevailed on 8 October, not only at the Bourse and the Palais de Justice but also in the markets. The conditions of a possible armistice were not, it is true, the main topic of conversation among housewives, but those who mentioned the subject declared that the war should go on 'until our enemies beg for mercy'.

On 9 October, speculation was rife as to whether the Germans were about to give in, or, on the contrary, would resist to the end. Lawyers were divided. While the young advocate, César Campinchi, a future minister, contended that Germany would accept the Allies' conditions within a month, his learned friend, Maître Dominique, believed the war would go on for another year.

During the next few days, the belief spread that the war would be over in the very near future. And remembering the situation a few weeks earlier, with Paris under the threat and bombardment of German guns, people exclaimed with relief and astonishment: 'What a long way we've come since July!'

And then there was another switch in opinion: 'The public is a little too excited at the prospect of an impending peace.' Some wanted the government to bring matters to a head and put a stop to slanted news (14 October). 'People realise that things are going to take longer than they had hoped.' On 17 October, the reports again mention that public opinion was against signing an armistice before the Germans had been driven out, and that soldiers on leave declared a preference for the war to last a little longer so that they could march on German soil. The observers stressed that this was the view of the 'large majority'.

By 21 October, there was again belief and hope in a speedy end: a huge map called 'Panorama of the Battle of Liberation' posted up by *Le Matin* in the boulevard Poissonnière drew large crowds. 'We are coming to the end', people said in the Bourse on 22 October. But next day, the impression gained ground that German resistance was hardening and public opinion once more swung about. 'It's sure to take longer than we thought.'

In the course of October, while public opinion kept vacillating, other preoccupations returned to the fore, especially the cost of living and the Spanish influenza epidemic. During this period of 'national triumph', as it was called, the ravages of that disease provided a counterpoint. It began to dominate conversation: statistics showing that mortality had doubled in Paris caused great apprehension. It was contended that 'this scourge, in the number of its victims, is more dreadful than the war, and certainly than "Big Bertha" and the "Gothas"'. Even the lawyers in the Palais de Justice spoke more about influenza than they did about the war. Rumour had it that the epidemic was even worse in the provinces, particularly in Lyon, where the dead were buried at night so as not to alarm the population.

On the whole, however, national solidarity prevailed, as we know from a long report dated 16 October and entitled: 'On the morale of Parisian workers in the light of current developments'.

The Socialist Party and the CGT, having endorsed the proposals of Woodrow Wilson, were now beginning to turn their attention to the post-war social struggle. Merrheim argued this point forcibly at a meeting in the *bourse du travail* held on 13 October: 'For us the real war will start only the day after peace has been signed. That will be when we shall rise up against our exploiters, and we must not allow ourselves to be beaten as we were beaten in 1914'.

Trade-union meetings were, on the whole, poorly attended. Does that mean that revolutionary or just anti-war sentiment had evaporated? Though the Committee for the Resumption of International

Relations was barely heard of, and though the Alliance Committee
of Syndicalist Youth had 'ceased to exist except in name', revolutionary groups did continue their agitation among the working class, but
not with any great effect. The Trade Union Defence Committee,
though weakened by the secession of the *terrassiers*, kept up its
pressure. Even so, a well-organised meeting of protest against the
imprisonment of trade-union militants attracted no more than 1,200
people, when some of the organisers had hoped 'to spill into the
streets' if the hall proved too small.

The anti-war movement had suffered a severe blow when Merrheim, who had total control of the metalworkers' union, had
removed the latter from the influence of the Trade Union Defence
Committee. As a result, the document went on to declare, no
trouble need be feared in the munitions factories. Protests against
government reprisals had been feeble.

Of the workers' journals, only *La Vague*, run by Brizon and
Marcelle Capy, struck a 'discordant' note, but its circulation was
strictly limited. According to the observers at the Préfecture, the
workers, like all other classes, greeted what they believed to be the
imminent approach of victory with enthusiasm.

At the end of October, the general view was that peace was very
near indeed, and by November people had come to expect the
armistice any day, and — revealing their deeply held feelings — no
longer expressed any desire to continue the war or to invade
Germany. On 8 November there was widespread belief that at last it
was all over; the day before there had been scenes of delirious joy
on the grand boulevards following the — premature — announcement that an armistice had been signed. Disillusion followed: 'One
had gone to bed on the soft pillow of peace with such confidence
that the awakening was a little hard to bear'.

Nevertheless, it could only be a matter of hours now, people
thought. On Sunday, 10 November 1918, a fine day, the streets
were particularly crowded. 'People kept straining their ears all the
time, thinking they had just heard the report of the "gun of
liberation"'; that is, of the gun that would herald the signing of the
armistice.

They had to wait one more day before the great news was
published. Then Paris erupted: 'All faces [are] drunk with joy',
stated the report for 12 November. Traffic rapidly came to an
almost complete standstill on the grand boulevards and countless
flags flew ('all the buildings are gay with bunting'). The stockbrokers' administrative committee, which had wanted to keep the
Bourse open, had to think better of it.

On 12 November, enthusiasm was greater even than on the day before. 'Extraordinary excitement' reigned in the streets: people danced round the statue on the place de la République, and many processions were formed. Young people perched on statues, brandishing flags. 'At 2.30 p.m., the band of the Republican Guard lined up on the steps of the Opéra and when, at 3.00 p.m., it struck up all the Allied national anthems, an extraordinary wave of enthusiasm seized the crowd, who shouted and sang. Many bystanders were seen to burst into tears.'

At 2.00 p.m. the place de la Concorde was 'black with people'. Processions of students and grammar-school pupils marched in unbroken line past the Strasbourg statue.

These expressions of joy were, of course, helped along by strong drink, and the Préfecture report noted that drunkenness began to claim victims 'not only among our own soldiers but also among the Americans and the British'. No wonder, for the Americans were being fêted above all others.

It was not until 13 November that the festive mood began to subside. Gradually people returned to work, and as they did so the first postwar problems began to appear: what would happen to all the workers, and the women workers in particular, employed in the munitions factories? But these were problems of peace and so are no longer part of this story.

To judge from all the available sources, there was unqualified enthusiasm in Paris, the reservations of those who would have liked to continue the war a little longer being swept aside by the force of events: 'Everyone seems satisfied' with the clauses of the armistice agreement. As crowning evidence of that joy, people rushed in droves to subscribe to the latest loan. Predictions at the Bourse were that it would prove an 'enormous' success.

It does not seem that Paris, as had so often been the case in the past, expressed the feelings of the rest of France in any exaggerated form. At Clermont-Ferrand, a journalist described local reaction as follows: 'The enthusiasm surpassed all imagination. . . . At Jaude, the square was swarming with people, long clusters of them hanging on to the walls of the theatre, sweeping up the steps, clambering on to the statues of Desaix and Vercingétorix . . .'.

Much the same happened, scaled down in proportion, in the villages, as at Chavannes in the Cher (260 inhabitants): 'The moment [the armistice was announced] the local authority hastened to proclaim the good news by ringing the church bells. Flags flutter from public buildings and private houses. The great Victory has come. Everywhere people are filled with joy and a great sense of relief'. And at Chapelle-Saint-Ursin in the same department: 'The shopkeepers lit up their windows, and flags were brought out. Many of the old people wept. There was real elation in this small, quiet, country hamlet . . .'.

Conclusion

The dust jacket of this book carries Forain's famous cartoon: 'Let's hope they hold out!' 'Who?' 'The civilians!' On 11 November 1918, the response could have been: they did hold out! But why did they?

Strangely enough, this is a question which historians have left unasked for a very long time. Perhaps they considered it iconoclastic, something that should not be raised, that would call into question the whole epic of a Great War acclaimed from the very first days of mobilisation so fervently by a nation eager for revenge and the recovery of Alsace-Lorraine. Yet, as we have shown, the great majority of French people did not want that war. They accepted it, but only because they thought it would be of short duration. Why then did they hold out for four years?

Gilberte Lang concludes her study of public opinion in Puy-de-Dôme during the First World War with: 'It was by degrees, as year followed year and fresh hope followed upon fresh disappointment, that they "held out" until the end. But there were moments when public acquiescence defied all reason and every attempt to explain it.'[1]

Can we accept that we are incapable of fully understanding what happened? For a long time historians have thought that they could explain everything: all they had to do was to marshal the material facts with the utmost care, whereupon the analysis of their logical connection would quite naturally reveal why things occurred as they did. Modern historians have come, or are coming, to realise that it is not events, but people who make history, and that what happens to the alchemy of people's unconscious is often an essential element of any explanation. However, though this element is the most difficult of all to assess, the historian stands on more solid

1. G. Lang, 'L' Opinion publique', p. 244.

ground, on his own ground as it were, when he has to examine the factors that might have acted upon the unconscious, moulding it or the 'attitude of mind' of a people, of a region or of a social group, provided, of course, that he does not rely exclusively on the immediate data but also considers the influence of the past.

It has often been said that the 'magic potion' of the French people during the First World War was the *Union sacrée*. It allegedly solved every problem. The ancient Gallic people whose divisions had led to their defeat almost 2,000 years before had been miraculously united. The reader may perhaps have wondered why we have made so few references to the *Union sacrée* in these pages. The answer is that it was a somewhat nebulous concept. The *Union sacrée* as it has so often been defined — the ideological union of all French people based on patriotic feeling — has never been a reality. Even while proclaiming adherence to the *Union sacrée*, each one of the ideological groups (socialists, radicals, Catholics, nationalists and so on) had their own views on the nature of the war and on why it was being waged. The French were never really agreed except on one thing: France had been the target of foreign aggression and had therefore to be defended. The *Union sacrée* was nothing except a temporary and exceptional alliance for the *practical* purposes of national defence. At the grass roots, there was an undeniable climate of unity, and no doubt many a man in the street asked himself why it could not always be like that. But there were also not a few blots on the landscape, and if clericalist-anti-clerical antagonism, one of the main sources of division in the Third Republic, had lessened, it nevertheless remained appreciable during the war. Still, even though the political or religious groups did nothing more than tone down their disagreements, waiting to resume battle once peace had been declared, a climate of national harmony undoubtedly reigned at the beginning of the war. Without feeling the need to evoke the *Union sacrée* time and again, the French basked in its ambience until just before the end of 1916. At that time, oddly enough, the French had not yet come to terms with the idea of a long war and still clung to the belief that it would all be over in two or three months. In 1917, and above all after the disastrous April offensive, however, hopes for a quick outcome evaporated and people began to long for peace, without being able to say how it could be achieved. According to Pierre Renouvin, that was the year in which the national consensus 'broke'. Even the façade of the *Union sacrée* was shattered, and political and social conflict came virulently into the open once again. If people still spoke of the *Union sacrée* they were invariably of the Right, people who condemn all political and social challenges as so many threats to the established order.

However, and this is the essential fact, one element of the national consensus survived among all but a tiny minority; namely, the idea that peace must not be bought at the price of defeat. There was never more than a very brief moment — in the spring of 1917 — when French morale dropped to a dangerously low level following the sudden crumbling of hopes in a speedy victory. However, once that crisis was over, morale rose and remained adequate even during the worst moments of 1918.

How can we explain this? When we analyse the behaviour of the French people, we find that material problems — mainly those concerned with incomes and provisions — played a major role throughout the war. The questions of incomes bore differently on different social groups. As soon as prices began to rise appreciably, peasants and farmers looked forward to, and in fact made, substantial profits. For the workers, full employment was assured: in addition to the soldiers recalled from the front, it had been necessary to rely heavily on female labour, and to make increasing use of colonial and foreign workers. By contrast, what wage increases there were, particularly in the munitions industry, were won only after bitter social strife, and even then they lagged behind the price rises. The fate of the middle classes varied: while the big industrialists and merchants took considerable advantage of the situation, the lower middle class, the minor officials, clerks and *rentiers* had to bear the full brunt of the price rises on fixed incomes. Moreover, in view of their way of life, separation allowances, so important a factor in the life of workers and peasants, made no appreciable difference to these families. Hence it was probably the lower middle class which suffered the greatest material hardship during the war.

Supplies posed no serious problem, certainly not in comparison with what happened during the Second World War, and on the whole there were no real shortages. But France during the Great War cannot be compared to what happened to the French and their children twenty-five years later, and early and often from 1915 people began to worry about serious stoppages in supply — of, for example, coal. There was also extreme nervousness about the shortage of bread or the risk of having to go without it — public attitudes had clearly not changed since the French Revolution! A lack of flour was enough to drive many a French town to the verge of riot, and, indeed, quite often beyond the verge in 1918.

On the whole, the material circumstances of the French were not too unpleasant during the war. Not that people did not grumble, occasionally react violently or feel an almost permanent sense of anxiety: the farmers complained about the lack of labour, and many workers were housed in lamentable conditions, especially in industrial centres with their vast influx of new inhabitants.

Nevertheless, national and local authorities — some with greater skill and efficiency than others — tried to ensure that material conditions did not deteriorate to the point of threatening serious breakdown.

The importance of these conditions should not, however, be exaggerated. Thus, as we have seen, the middle classes in particular stood firm even when their pockets were badly hit; the workers, by contrast, showed signs of giving way twice, first in 1917 and much more obviously in 1918, and this despite the fact that their wages were good and that large numbers of them had been spared from the mass slaughter at the front. They had to work hard, it was true, and often in arduous conditions, but most of them had evaded immediate danger. And in looking for an explanation for what we must call their irresolution, we should bear in mind that they were aware, when pressing their demands, of how untenable their position was when compared to that of the men at the front.

What, then, was the real explanation of French steadfastness? Without doubt, it lay in the intellectual, spiritual and political leadership of the people; a near consensus, whether among teachers — except for a very small minority — or clergymen, or writers, existed when it came to the need to defend their country, and even though some writers felt an aversion to heroic and chauvinistic presentations of the war, and described its horrors with great realism, they never questioned the need for French participation.

Political and trade-union leaders took much the same view. Thus the Socialist Party and the CGT, who were undoubtedly placed in a dilemma by the continuation of the war, stood their ground against the anti-war minority for a long time, and it is certain that the attitude of the majority acted as a powerful brake on those who posed a serious threat to national unity. The lack of determined revolutionary organisations and leaders was another important factor, but then that lack was not just a matter of chance but was dictated by the realities of the French situation.

And then there was the press, the real influence of which is hard to assess. Some sources claim that it was a mainstay of French patriotism, others argue that its sometimes ludicrous presentation of the facts destroyed its credibility. In fact, the press, then as always, could not have played a crucial role in moulding public opinion because newspaper readers generally read into their papers what they want to read. That does not alter the fact that however small the influence of the French press may have been, it helped to cement French morale.

Reasonable material conditions, sound moral and psychological direction — are these sufficient explanation of why the French held out for four years? Yes, but only to a certain extent. The fact is that the authorities, the political groups, the press, the writers, the teachers, the clergy, could have achieved nothing, and would probably not have wanted to try, had they not found a receptive audience. We have seen this often enough in the past.

We cannot be sure that the French would have accepted the war if they had known from the outset how long and how cruel an ordeal it would prove to be, but in the end the very length of the war unquestionably nurtured their resolve, or their resignation: how could one admit defeat after so much effort, so much sacrifice, so many dead?

In the final analysis, despite the weariness, the grumbles and even the anger, the national fabric was too firm and had been knotted together for too long to tear apart. Even those who looked for revolution stopped short, as if before sacrilege, at the idea of doing something that could call the integrity of their country into question; at the very least they realised that the masses would not follow them — or not for the time being.

We can only repeat what we have said about what inspired the attitude of the French people in 1914: they accepted the war because they were part of one nation and they tolerated it for the same reason. Whether they said so or not; indeed, even if they expressed the opposite view at moments of difficulty or despondency, the sense of nationhood ran too deep in the great majority for it to have been otherwise. France was one of the oldest nations in Europe, gradually and securely built up over the centuries. That is why France, a part of her territory occupied or devastated, her youth cut down just at a time when her birthrate was falling, more cruelly tried than the United Kingdom, less rich in resources and men than Germany, despite everything, never gave in.

But the strength of national feeling is a peculiar thing, and the somewhat vague sense of resignation in the last year of the war was a portent that the sentiment reached a peak in the First World War, and that it might never again prevail.

The unbowed France of 1918 heralded the humbled France of 1940.

Appendix

War Losses

These tables are taken from Alfred Sauvy, *Histoire économique de la France entre les deux guerres*, vol. I, Fayard.

Table A. *French military losses*

Categories	Dead	Missing	Totals
Europeans	1,010,200	235,300	1,245,500
North African troops	28,200	7,700	35,900
Colonial troops	28,700	6,500	35,200
Foreigners (Foreign Legion)	3,700	900	4,000
Total number of men	1,070,800	250,400	1,321,200
Officers	34,100	2,500	36,600
Total number of soldiers	1,104,900	252,900	1,357,800
Sailors	6,000	4,900	10,900
Naval officers	300	200	500
Navy	6,300	5,100	11,400
Total for all French forces	1,111,200	258,000	1,369,200

Died between				
11 November 1914	Officers	600		600
and 1 June 1919	Men	28,000		
	Total	28,600		28,600
	Grand total	1,139,800		1,397,800

This table, published in Michel Huber, *La Population de la France pendant la guerre* (p. 414), is based on the following public records:
— for the army, Chamber of Deputies 1920, doc. 633, *Bilan des pertes en morts et blessés.*
— for the navy, Chamber of Deputies 1920, doc. 634, *Bilan des pertes faites sur mer*, p. 10.
(As at 24 October 1919)

Table B. *Proportion of losses among servicemen*

	Mobilised	Dead	Missing	Totals	Dead and missing %
Officers —combatants	157,500	32,000	2,600	34,800	22
—non-combatants	37,000	1,400	—	1,400	4
—total	195,000	33,000	2,600	36,200	19
Men —combatants	6,830,000	981,000	240,000	1,221,000	18
(French)—non-combatants	910,000	23,200	1,600	24,000	3
—total	7,740,000	1,004,000	241,000	1,245,800	16
Men —N. African	294,000	28,000	7,700	35,900	12
—colonial	275,000	28,700	6,500	35,200	13
—total	569,000	56,700	14,200	71,100	12
Final figures (army)	8,504,000	1,094,700	258,400	1,353,100	16
Naval officers	4,000	300	200	500	12
Seamen	152,000	6,000	4,900	10,900	7
Final figures (navy)	156,000	6,300	5,100	11,400	7

This table, first published in Huber, ibid., p. 416, is based on docs.
633 (pp. 27–9) quoted above. The numbers of dead and missing
differ slightly.

Table C. *Dead, missing and wounded (by occupation)*

	Male working population in 1913	Dead			Dead per 1,000	Wounded
		Killed	Missing	Total		
Agriculture	5,400,000	397,500	140,500	538,000	996	161,200
Industry	4,730,000	306,900	108,500	415,400	887	123,300
Transport	4,730,000	35,100	12,400	47,500	810	13,400
Commerce	1,300,000	90,900	32,100	123,000	940	37,000
Liberal professions	310,000	24,500	8,700	33,200	1,070	10,000
Servants	160,000	12,100	14,300	16,400	1,025	5,100
Civil servants	520,000	40,500	14,300	54,800	1,055	15,900
Regular army	100,000					
Various		50,000	16,800	66,800		22,900
Final figures	13,100,000	957,700	337,600	1,295,100	990	388,800

This table, prepared by Edmond Michel, p. 21 (after corrections of the main errors), should not be taken at face value.

(a) The proportion of men killed listed by profession should have been determined by different criteria. The working population was computed from the approximate distribution of conscripts, and hence differs slightly from the figures given elsewhere.

(b) It would have been better to consider the distribution of the working population by age. The result would have been an increase in the proportion of agricultural workers killed and a decrease in the proportion.

The most significant difference is that between agriculture on the one hand and industry and transport on the other. This reflects the fact that some workers in the last two sectors were recruited locally.

Table D. *Dead and missing by region (officers not included)*

Military regions	Servicemen	Killed and missing	Killed and missing (%)	Prisoners of war
1st Lille	625,000	89,300	14.2	61,600
2nd Amiens	310,000	42,600	13.8	26,300
3rd Rouen	298,000	50,600	17.0	18,700
4th Le Mans	236,000	47,200	20.0	20,800
5th Orléans	235,000	47,600	20.2	18,900
6th Châlons-sur-Marne	273,000	37,500	13.4	14,100
7th Besançon	234,000	40,600	17.4	14,800
8th Bourges	288,000	55,400	19.3	17,300
9th Tours	333,000	59,100	17.7	18,000
10th Rennes	318,000	62,100	19.5	22,000
11th Nantes	470,000	87,600	18.6	35,700
12th Limoges	309,000	59,800	19.6	19,700
13th Clermont-Ferrand	385,900	68,000	17.6	19,600
14th Lyon	279,000	48,900	17.6	17,100
15th Marseille	577,000	68,600	11.9	24,400
16th Montpellier	337,000	57,000	16.9	20,900
17th Toulouse	261,000	45,800	17.5	18,300
18th Bordeaux	406,000	63,000	15.5	19,900
19th Alger	137,000	24,800	18.1	6,000
20th Nancy	174,000	29,400	16.9	10,400
21st Epinal	112,000	16,500	14.7	6,500
Mil. govt. (Paris)	1,083,000	114,200	10.5	43,400
Mil. govt. (Lyon)	163,000	20,100	12.3	7,900
Various		27,300		48,200
Final figures	7,843,900	1,263,000	16.1	531,300

This interesting table, published by the *Impartial français* on
15 March 1924, was reproduced 'with reservations' by Huber, ibid.,
p. 426. Rural areas account for the largest percentages.
   We might add (by way of example) that those killed in the war
included:
   — 883 former students of the Ecole Polytechnique;
   — 230 students or former students of the Ecole Normale
Supérieure (41 per cent of active students);
   — half the number of art teachers called up;
   — a host of writers, including Péguy, Psichari, Alain-Fournier,
Pergaud. . . .

Sources and Select Bibliography

The Great War has been the subject of a multitude of studies, most of which have, however, been devoted to its military or diplomatic aspects. By contrast, studies devoted to the attitude of the French people and especially those at home have been few and far between.

The most important general works are:

Pierre Renouvin, *La Crise européenne et la Grande Guerre* (1904–1918) (Coll. Peuples et Civilisations, vol. XIX), Paris, PUF, 1962, 779 pp.

Jean-Baptiste Duroselle, *La France et les Français* (1914–1920), Paris, 1972, 395 pp.

Marc Ferro, *La Grande Guerre 1914–1918*, Gallimard, 1969, 384 pp.

Pierre Miguel, *La Grande Guerre*, Fayard, 1983, 667 pp.

Gabriel Perreux, *La vie quotidienne des civils en France pendant la Grande Guerre*, Paris, Hachette, 1966, 348 pp.

Below are listed those sources and books only on which the present book has drawn.

I Autumn 1914

Public records

National Archives (AN) F 7 13074 (socialist party), 13571 (CGT), 13572 (CGT), 13194 and 13195 (Action Française), 12911, 13372 and 13375 (pacifism).

Departmental Archives (AD)

Records, by teachers, of public opinion in their communes: Hautes-Alpes (200 R 82), Charente (J 76 to J 95), Côtes-du-Nord (série R), Gard (8 R 1), Isère (13 R·54), Puy-de-Dôme (R O 1342).

Records by clergymen: Haute-Savoie (1 T 218). Cf. Yves Lequin: '1914–18 L'opinion publique en Haute-Savoie devant la guerre', in *Revue savoisienne*, 1967.

Other records: Cher (R 15 16) 'Histoire de Vierzon pendant la guerre'; Nord (R 145) Union Départementale des Syndicats Ouvriers; Saône-et-Loire (51 M) Police Générale (1914–17).

Archives du Service Historique de l'Armée (AM) 5 N 230, 7 N 569: losses in numbers, 5 N 334, 335, 372, 374: press and censorship problems.

Censorship Archives in the Bibliothèque Internationale de Documentation Contemporaine (492, 493, 558, 559).

Other archives: reports of various industrial and financial enterprises, Bulletin of the Paris Chamber of Commerce, Minutes of meetings of the Presidents of Chambers of Commerce.

The Press

In addition to numerous papers in Paris and the provinces, the following collections of articles by journalists and writers:

Maurice Barrès, *Chronique de la Grande Guerre*, 13 vols., Plon.

Gustave Hervé, *La Patrie en danger* (Collection of articles published in *La Guerre Sociale* from 1 July to 1 November 1914).
Après la Marne (Collection of articles in the same paper from 1 November 1914 to 31 January 1915), Paris, 1915.

Romain Rolland, *Au-dessus de la mêlée*, Paris–Neuchâtel–Ollendorf–Attingen, October 1915, 163 pp.

Or analyses by historians:

Michel Baumont, 'Gustave Hervé et *La Guerre Sociale* pendant l'été 1914' (1 July to 1 November 1914), in *Information Historique*, 1968, No. 4.
'Un témoignage sur la guerre de 1914–1918: *Chronique de la Grande Guerre* de Maurice Barrès', in *Information historique*, January–February 1973.

Alain Lévy, 'Un quotidien régional, *Le Midi socialiste* (1908–1920)', thesis, Toulouse, n.d., 215 pp., Ms.

Eye-Witness Accounts

Letters

Alain, *Correspondence avec Florence et Elie Halévy*, Paris, Gallimard, 1958, 467 pp.

Henri Barbusse, *Lettres à sa femme (1914–1917)*, Paris, Flammarion, 1937, 261 pp.

Jean-Richard Bloch, 'Lettres 1914–1918', in *Europe*, 1957, Nos. 135–43.

(Emile Guillaumin) Roger Mathé, *Cent dix neuf lettres d'Emile Guillaumin*, Paris, Klincksieck, 1969.
— Jean Gaulmier, 'Le pacifisme d'Emile Guillaumin', in *Le Bourbonnais rural*, 9 November 1973.

Eugène–E. Lemercier, *Notes (1905–1914)*, followed by *Lettres inédites*, Paris, Berger–Levrault, 1924, 108 pp. (Killed in 1915, the author was a painter and composer.)

Memoirs and reminiscences
Of prefects
Gabriel Letainturier, *Deux années d'efforts de l'Yonne pendant la guerre* (August 1914–August 1916), Auxerre, 1916, XXXII, 452 pp.
Of writers and academics
Alain, *Souvenirs de guerre*, Paris, 1952, 246 pp.
Maurice Barrès, *Mes Cahiers*, vol. 10 (January 1913–June 1914), Paris, 1936, VIII, 475 pp.; vol. II June 1914–December 1918), Paris, 1938, XXII, 443 pp.
Léon Daudet, *L'Hécatombe — Récits et souvenirs politiques — 1914–1918*, Paris, 1923, 308 pp.
Gyp, *Le Journal d'un cochon de pessimiste*, Paris, Calman-Lévy, 1918, 358 pp.
Romain Rolland, *Journal des années de guerre (1914–1919)*, Paris, Albin Michel, 1952, 1910 pp.
Charles Tillon, *La Révolte vient de loin*, Paris, 10/18, 1972, 446 pp.
Of various columnists and reporters
Marius Beaup, 'La guerre de 1914 à Lalley et dans le Trieves'. Notes and impressions published in *Dauphiné* (small Isère weekly) from 11 October 1914.
Fernand Berrette, *Une commune rurale du Lot-et-Garonne: Fieux* (2 August 1914–2 August 1915), Agen, 1915, 46 pp. (The author was mayor of Fieux).
Raphaël Dufresne, *Journal pendant la Grande Guerre d'un Beauvaisin non mobilisé*, Beauvais, n.d., 42 sheets of 6 recto columns. Published in instalments in the *République de l'Oise*, during the war. Covers the period 1 August 1914–10 April 1915.
Arthur Lévy, *1914, août, septembre, octobre à Paris*, Paris, Plon, 1917.
André Lottier, *La guerre de 1914–1918 vue du village*, Auxerre, 1965, 15 pp. (Extract from the *Bulletin des sciences historiques et naturelles de l'Yonne*, vol. 100, 1963–1964.
Jules Momeja, "Journal de guerre 1914–1918", 12 manuscript books (Archives of Tarn-et-Garonne).
Joseph Pascal, *Mémoires d'un instituteur*, Paris, La Pensée Universelle, Paris, 1974, 160 pp.
P. Perrier, 'La guerre vue du Creusot', Manuscript (Archives of Saône-et-Loire, Liasse Vie locale).

Other documents
On wages
Statistique générale de la France. Ministère du Travail et de la Prévoyance (Wages and cost of living at various periods). Imprimerie Nationale, 1911, 527 pp.
Annuaire statistique publié par le Ministère du Travail et de la Prévoyance sociale, vol. 33, 1913 (Paris, 1914).
Statistique de l'industrie minérale en France et en Algérie, (Annual publication of the Ministry of Works).
On socialism and syndicalism
Jean Maitron and Collette Chambelland, *Syndicalisme révolutionnaire et*

Communisme, Les Archives de P. Monatte, Paris, Maspéro, 1968, 462 pp.

Le Parti socialiste, la Guerre et la Paix (All resolutions and documents by the Socialist Party from July 1914 to the end of 1917), Paris, Librairie de *L'Humanité*, 1918, 224 pp.

Confédération générale du Travail, XIIIth Congress, July 1918, *Compte-rendu des travaux*, Paris, Imprimerie Nouvelle, 1919, 306 pp.

Works covering this period

The year 1914

Jean-Jacques Becker, 1914, *Comment les Français sont entrés dans la guerre*, Presses de la Fondation National des Sciences Politiques, 1977, 638 pp.

Henry Contamine, *La Victoire de la Marne* (Coll. Trente journées qui ont fait la France), Paris, Gallimard, 1970, 460 pp., and *La Revanche* (1871–1914), Paris, Berger–Levrault, 1957, 280 pp.

The labour movement and the war

Trade unions

Robert Brécy, *Le Mouvement syndical en France*, bibliographical essay, Paris–The Hague, Mouton, 1963, 219 pp.

Edouard Dolléans, *Histoire du mouvement ouvrier*, preface by L. Febvre, vol. II (1871–1920), Paris, A. Colin, 1953.

Georges Lefranc, *Histoire du mouvement syndical français*, Paris, Librairie syndicale, 1937, IV, 472 pp.

V. M. Daline, 'The C.G.T. at the beginning of the First World War', in *Annuaire d'Etudes français*, Moscow, 1964, pp. 219–53 (in Russian, but with a French summary).

Edouard Dollé, *Alphonse Merrheim*, Paris, Librairie syndicale, 1939, 47 pp.

Bernard Georges and Denise Tintant, *Léon Jouhaux, cinquante ans de syndicalisme*, vol. I (up to 1921), Paris, PUF, 1962, 551 pp.

On the socialist movement

Francis Conte, 'Christian Rakovski (1873–1941): Attempt at a political biography', Ph. D. thesis, Bordeaux, 1973, 3 vols., 898 pp. (duplicated).

Jacques Droz (ed.) *Histoire générale du socialisme*, vol. II, *From 1875 to 1918*, Paris, PUF, 1974, 674 pp.

Annie Kriegel, *Aux origines du Communisme français (1914–1920)*, contribution à l'histoire du mouvement ouvrier français, thesis, Paris, Mouton, 1964, 2 vols., 995 pp.

Shaul Ginsburg, 'La jeunesse de Raymond Lefebvre: un itinéraire (1891–1914)', in *Mouvement social*, January–March 1973.

Alfred Rosmer, *Le Mouvement ouvrier pendant la guerre*, vol. I, *De l'Union sacrée à Zimmerwald*, Paris, Librairie du Travail, 1936, 590 pp. (Passionately partisan but useful.)

On unionised teachers

François Bernard, Louis Bouët, Maurice Dommanget, Gilbert Serret, *Le Syndicalisme dans l'enseignement* (history of the Teachers' Federation from its origins to the unification in 1935), edited by Pierre Broué, vol. I, 264 pp.; vol. II, 301 pp. (duplicated), Grenoble, Coll. Documents de l'IEP, 1966.

Max Ferré, *Histoire du mouvement syndical révolutionaire chez les Institu-teurs, Des origines à 1922*, thesis, Paris, 1955, Sudel, 335 pp.

Jacques Alègre, 'Les Instituteurs', in *Europe*, 1964.

Two polemical works which, as such, must be mentioned separately:

Charles Favral, *Histoire de l'Arrière*, Paris Jidéher, n.d. (probably 1930, to judge by the contents), 318 pp.

J. Rocher, *Lénine et le mouvement Zimmerwaldien en France*, Paris, Bureau d'Editions, 1934, 83 pp. (On the beginnings of war opposition. Full of errors or inventions but is still quoted in modern publications.)

II The Banality of War

It goes without saying that many of the documents and works used for this part have been mentioned in the previous section of this bibliography. The list is therefore confined to whatever new titles are relevant to the chapters concerned.

The duration of the war

Louis Debidour, *Lettres* (August 1914–September 1915), 2 vols., 387 pp., typescript.

André Kahn, *Journal de guerre d'un Juif patriote* (1914–1918), Paris, 1978, 331 pp.

Jean-Noël Jeanneney, *François de Wendel en République*, Seuil, 1976, 660 pp.

Paris in 1915

AN F 7 12936. Reports by departmental prefects to the minister of the interior and by special commissioners to the director of the Sûreté Générale on the mood of the public.

Teachers and the war

Yves Racine, 'Les instituteurs et l'ecole publique dans le département du Doubs pendant la guerre 1914–1918', thesis, Besançon, 1977.

Noël Tronquoy, 'Le combat pacifiste des instituteurs pendant la guerre (1914–1918)', thesis, Paris, 1977.

Writers and the war

Jean Vic, *La Littérature de guerre*, methodical and critical review of French language publications (2 August–11 November 1918), Paris, 1923, 5 vols.

Maurice d'Hartoy, *La Génération du feu*, bibliography of fighting French writers of 1914–18, Paris, 1923, 225 pp.

André de Chambure, *Quelques guides de l'opinion en France pendant la Grande Guerre (1914–1918)*, 1918, 223 pp.

André Billy, *Histoire de la vie littéraire, l'époque contemporaine*, Paris, 1956.

Pierre-Henry Simon, *Histoire de la littérature française au XIXème Siècle*, Paris, 1967.

Frank Field, *Three French Writers and the Great War* (Barbusse, Drieu La Rochelle, Bernanos), Cambridge, 1975, 212 pp.

On Guillaume Apollinaire

Claude Debon-Tournadre, *G. Apollinaire de 1914 à 1918*, Doctoral thesis, Paris, 1978.

On Maurice Barrès

Michel Baumont, 'Maurice Barrès et les morts de la guerre de 1914–1918', in *Information Historique*, January–February 1969, no. 1.

Jean-Marie Domenach, *Barrès par lui-même*, Seuil, Paris, 1954, 192 pp.

Jacques Madaule, *Le nationalisme de M. Barrès*, Sagittaire, Marseille, 1943, 272 pp.

Jean Touchard, *Le Nationalisme de Barrès. Maurice Barrès*, proceedings of symposium organised by the Faculty of Letters and Human Sciences of the University of Nancy, 1963.

Zeev Sternhell, *Maurice Barrès et le Nationalisme français*, Paris, A. Colin, 1972, 396 pp.

On Romain Rolland

Henri Massis, *Romain Rolland contre la France*, Paris, 1915, 40 pp.

Charles Albert, *Au-dessous de la mêlée. R. Rolland et ses disciples*, Paris, 1916, 47 pp.

Henri Guilbeaux, *Pour Romain Rolland*, Geneva, 1916, 64 pp.

———, *Du Kremlin au Cherche-Midi*, Paris, 1933, 271 pp.

Jean-Bertrand Barrère, *Romain Rolland par lui-même*, Paris, 1955, 192 pp.

René Cheval, *Romain Rolland, l'Allemagne et la guerre*, Paris, PUF, 1963, 769 pp. (thesis).

Marcelle Kempf, *Romain Rolland et l'Allemagne*, Paris, 1962, 298 pp.

Sven Stelling-Michaud, 'La choix de R. Rolland en 1914', in *La Pensée*, 1967, no. 132.

Articles on Rolland in the special edition of *Europe* 1914 (May–June 1964):
'Romain Rolland et la guerre', by René Cheval.
'Sur Romain Rolland et la guerre', by Robert Ricatte.
Romain Rolland, 'Lettres à sa mère'.

On Henri Barbusse

Alain des Lys, *A propos d'un livre, 'Le Feu' d'Henri Barbusse, par un sergent de tirailleurs marocains*, Angoulême, 1917.

Annette Vidal, *Henri Barbusse, soldat de la paix*, Paris, 1953.

———, 'Henri Barbusse et le Feu', in *Europe* (November–December 1955).

Churches and the war

Documents
AN F 7 13213, F 7 12881. Notes sur l'activité des catholiques.
La Grande Revue (April 1915–August 1917): 'Enquête sur la renaissance religieuse en France'.
Comité catholique de propagande à l'étranger (Catholic Foreign Propaganda Committee), 'La Vie catholique dans la France contemporaine', 1918, 527pp.
_____, 'La Guerre allemande et le Catholicisme', 1915.
Vicomte Maurice de Lestrange, *La Question religieuse en France pendant la guerre de 1914*, 1915.
Antoine Spire, *Les Juifs et la guerre*, Payot, 1917, 281 pp.

Publications
Joseph Brugerette, *Le Prêtre français et la Société contemporaine*, Vol. III (1909-1936), Paris, Lethielleux, 1938, 793 pp.
Jacques Fontana, 'Attitude et sentiments du clergé et des catholiques français devant et durant la guerre de 1914–1918', thesis, Lille, 1973, 779 pp., duplicated.
Jean-Marie Mayeur, 'Le Catholicisme français et la première guerre mondiale', in *Francia*, 1974, vol. II.
_____, 'Monseigneur Duchesne et la politique religieuse de la France pendant la première guerre mondiale', in *Mélanges de l'Ecole française de Rome*, vol. 88, 1976, 1.
Pierre Renouvin, 'Le Gouvernement français devant l'offre de paix du Saint-Siège', in *Mélanges André Latreille*
_____, 'L'Episcopat français devant l'offre de paix du Saint-Siège', in *Mélanges G. Jacquemyns*, Brussels.
Daniel Robert, 'Les Protestants français et la guerre de 1914–1918', in *Francia*, 1974, vol. II.

III The Crisis of 1917

Archives

National Archives (AN) F 7 13023, Rapports sur la situation en Haute-Vienne (1915–26); F 7 12985, Rapports sur la situation du département du Gard (1916–19); F 7 13272, Les 1er Mai 1915, 1916, 1917, 1918.
Archives de la Préfecture de Police (APP) B/A 1639, Bulletins confidentiels mensuels sur l'état d'esprit.
Archives Départementales (AD) Deux-Seèvres 4 M 6/29, Haute-Garonne 15 Z 520.
Archives militaires (AM) 7 N 985 Rapports sur l'état moral en France et à l'étranger (March 1917–May 1918): commission de contrôle postal de

Bordeaux; 16 N 1536 Etat moral à l'intérieur; 16 N 1538 (1) Rapports des préfets (1917).

Publications

Pierre Bouyoux, *L'Opinion publique à Toulouse pendant la première guerre mondiale*, Toulouse, 1970 (microfilm), Hachette, 528 pp.

Raymond Huard, 'Les Mineurs du Gard pendant la guerre de 1914–1918', in *Economie et Société en Languedoc–Roussillon de 1789 à nos jours*, Montpellier, 1978.

Jacques Lacombe, 'Le Moral des Français en juin 1917', thesis, 1984, Nanterre.

Christiane Morel, 'Le Mouvement socialiste et syndicaliste en 1917 dans la région parisienne', Diplome d'études supérieures, 1958.

Guy Pedroncini, *Les Mutineries de 1917*, Presses Universitaires de France, 1967, 328 pp.

Pierre Renouvin, Rapport introductif (L'opinion en France en 1917). Colloque *La France et l'Italie pendant la première guerre mondiale*, Presses Universitaires de Grenoble, 1973, 619 pp.

Public Opinion and the Russian Revolution

J. Annequin, 'La Révolution soviétique et la presse bisontine de 1917 à 1920', thesis, Besançon, 1965.

Jean Nicot and Philippe Schillinger, *L'Opinion française face à la guerre: l'influence de la Révolution russe d'après les archives du contrôle postal*, (Proceedings of the 97th National Congress of Learned Societies).

Annie Kriegel, 'L'Opinion publique française et la révolution russe', in *La Révolution d'octobre et le mouvement ouvrier européen*, Paris, 1967.

IV 1918

Archives

AN F 7 12992 Rapports sur la situation dans l'Isère (1916–19); F 7 12994 Rapports sur la situation dans la Loire (1917–18); F 7 14607 Les grèves de la Loire en 1917. APP B/A 1587 *Physionomie de Paris* (1917–18).

Publications

Max Gallo, 'Quelques aspects de la mentalité et du comportement ouvrier dans les usines de guerre (1914–1918)', in *Le Mouvement social* (July–September 1966).

Jean Nicot and Philippe Schillinger, *L'Opinion publique et les grèves de la Loire* (Proceedings of the 98th National Congress of Learned Societies, Saint-Etienne, 1973).

Gilberte Lang, 'L'Opinion publique dans le département du Puy-de-Dôme et la guerre de 1914–1918', thesis, Clermont-Ferrand, 1979.

Gérard et Michèle Raffaelli, 'Le mouvement ouvrier contre la guerre'. (Bibliographical, methodological and biographical introduction to the study of the economic and social development of the Saint-Etienne region, 1914–20.) Thesis, 1969.

Gérard Raffaelli, *Les Mouvements pacifistes dans les usines d'armement de la région de Saint-Etienne*. (Proceedings of the 98th National Congress of Learned Societies, Saint-Etienne, 1973.)

Jean-Louis Robert, *Les Luttes ouvrières pendant la première guerre mondiale (Cahiers d'Histoire de l'Institut Maurice Thorez*, 1977).

Marie-Joëlle Vandrand, 'Les Campagnes du Puy-de-Dôme pendant la premiere guerre mondiale', thesis, Clermont-Ferrand, 1984.